# Door of HOPE

## A Devotional Study of the Minor Prophets

# WARREN HENDERSON

*Door of Hope – A Devotional Study of the Minor Prophets*

By Warren Henderson
Copyright © 2018

Cover Design by Benjamin Bredeweg

Published by Warren A. Henderson
3769 Indiana Road
Pomona, KS 66076

Editing/Proofreading:
    Marilyn MacMullen, Dan Macy,
    Gary McBride, and David Lindstrom

Perfect Bound ISBN 978-1-939770-45-5
eBook ISBN 978-1-939770-46-2

Available through many online retailers.

# Other Books by the Author

Afterlife – What Will It Be Like?
Answer the Call – Finding Life's Purpose
Be Holy and Come Near– A Devotional Study of Leviticus
Behold the Saviour
Be Angry and Sin Not
Conquest and the Life of Rest – A Devotional Study of Joshua
Exploring the Pauline Epistles
Forsaken, Forgotten, and Forgiven – A Devotional Study of Jeremiah
Glories Seen & Unseen
Hallowed Be Thy Name – Revering Christ in a Casual World
Hiding God – The Ambition of World Religion
In Search of God – A Quest for Truth
Infidelity and Loyalty – A Devotional Study of Ezekiel and Daniel
Knowing the All-Knowing
Managing Anger God's Way
Mind Frames – Where Life's Battle Is Won or Lost
Out of Egypt – A Devotional Study of Exodus
Overcoming Your Bully
Passing the Torch – Mentoring the Next Generation For Christ
Relativity and Redemption – A Devotional Study of Judges and Ruth
Revive Us Again – A Devotional Study of Ezra and Nehemiah
Seeds of Destiny – A Devotional Study of Genesis
Sorrow and Comfort – A Devotional Study of Isaiah
The Beginning of Wisdom – A Devotional Study of Job, Psalms, Proverbs,
    Ecclesiastes, and Song of Solomon
The Bible: Myth or Divine Truth?
The Evil Nexus – Are You Aiding the Enemy?
The Fruitful Bough – Affirming Biblical Manhood
The Fruitful Vine – Celebrating Biblical Womanhood
The Hope of Glory – A Preview of Things to Come
The Olive Plants – Raising Spiritual Children
Your Home the Birthing Place of Heaven

# Table of Contents

# Preface

Priests represent man to God, and prophets speak for God to man. God chose ordinary men of consecration, compassion, and conviction to deliver His messages. They received revelation from Him through dreams, visions, and audible words. Some prophets spoke to kings, but most were sent to plead with common people. Their ministries were often accompanied by personal hardship, suffering, and loss.

The twelve Minor Prophets beginning with Joel and Obadiah in the ninth century B.C. and ending with Malachi in the fifth century B.C. spoke to various people groups. Three prophets delivered oracles to foreign audiences: Obadiah addressed Edom; Jonah and Nahum preached to Israel's enemy Nineveh. The remaining prophets spoke to their Jewish countrymen – Amos and Hosea were sent to warn Israel (the Northern Kingdom) and Micah, Habakkuk, and Zephaniah sounded the alarm in Judah (the Southern Kingdom). Joel issued a general indictment against Israel and then revealed God's prophetic plan to restore the Jewish nation, to judge the wicked, and to establish Messiah's kingdom in the future.

The post-exile prophets Haggai and Zechariah were commissioned to motivate a disheartened Jewish remnant to rebuild the temple; however, both prophets also spoke of the coming Kingdom Age. Malachi, in about 420 B.C., closes out the ministry of the Minor Prophets with a final rebuke against Jewish defiance. His messages were followed by four centuries of divine silence until God spoke to Israel again through the incarnate Word – His own Son (John 1:1, 14; Heb. 1:1-3).

One of the striking features of the prophecies for Israel is how expressions of divine grace and affection are frequently embedded within scathing denunciations of the people's stubborn waywardness. The prophets are severe in rebuking Jewish unfaithfulness and warning them of stern consequences for their sin, yet their appeals for repentance also convey God's enduring love for His people. The tenderness of God for them and His desire to restore and to bless them is often expressed in the sermons of the Minor Prophets. Consequently, the Jewish nation has had, and always will have, a *door of hope* before them.

> *I will give her vineyards from there, and the Valley of Achor as **a door of hope**; she shall sing there, as in the days of her youth, as in the day when she came up from the land of Egypt* (Hos. 2:15).

> *Return to the stronghold, **you prisoners of hope**. Even today I declare that I will restore double to you* (Zech. 9:12).

In a future day a refined remnant of the Jewish nation will pass through that door of repentance and will enter the stronghold of God. There they will bask in God's love, being lavished with all His goodness. God has not abandoned His covenant people of old.

Through the literal interpretation of Scripture we understand that God's future plan for glorifying the Church is quite different than His agenda for restoring the nation of Israel to a position of honor and blessing. Hosea refers to this latter event as *"a door of hope"* for Israel. Not only do such prophetic promises bestow hope on the Jewish nation, but these should also excite every Christian to love *"the blessed hope,"* the appearing of the Lord Jesus Christ (2 Tim. 4:8)! Consequently, both the nation of Israel and the Church have all their hopes in Christ!

*Door of Hope* is a "commentary style" devotional which upholds the glories of Christ while exploring the twelve books of the Minor Prophets within the context of the whole of Scripture. I have endeavored to include in this book some principal gleanings from other writers. The short devotional format allows the reader to use the book either as a daily devotional or as a reference for deeper study.

— Warren Henderson

# Hosea

# Overview of Hosea

## The Author

Hosea was the son of Beeri (1:1). The meaning of Hosea's name, "salvation" or "deliverance," amplifies his main message to Israel: "Only Jehovah can deliver you – turn to Him!" Nothing else is known about Hosea or his family.

## Date

Hosea's prophetic ministry to the Northern Kingdom occurred *"in the days of Uzziah, Jotham, Ahaz, and Hezekiah, kings of Judah, and in the days of Jeroboam the son of Joash, king of Israel"* (1:1). At the same time Isaiah was addressing the Southern Kingdom (i.e., the mid-eighth century B.C.). Hosea was also a contemporary of Amos. Both prophets were sent to the Northern Kingdom and began their ministries a few years before Isaiah. Since King Jeroboam II ruled over Israel from 793-753 B.C. and Hezekiah sat on Judah's throne from 715-686 B.C., Hosea's ministry would have lasted a minimum of 39 years and more likely in the sixty-year range. Some commentators, like E. B. Pusey, believe Hosea prophesied for roughly eighty years.[1]

## Theme

Hosea, and then later Jeremiah and Ezekiel, liken Israel's departure from their covenant with Jehovah into moral filthiness and idolatry to a virgin bride who, after marriage, became lascivious – a harlot. The Lord, foreknowing that Hosea's wife would also be unfaithful to him, incorporates Hosea's painful marital experience into the narrative to dramatically express His own heartache over the spiritual infidelity of His people. To this end, Hosea 13:4 vividly expresses the theme of the entire book: *"Yet I am the Lord your God ever since the land of Egypt, and you shall know no God but Me; for there is no savior besides Me."*

The book of Hosea exemplifies the longsuffering nature of God and His unfailing love. Gomer, Hosea's adulterous wife, was abused, abandoned, and then redeemed and restored by Hosea to her proper marital relationship. Likewise, in a future day, God will cleanse the long-chastened Jewish nation of their infidelity, redeem them, and restore them to their proper covenant relationship with Himself. Afterwards, the Jewish nation will remain pure and faithfully devoted to Jehovah forever.

## Outline
Hosea's Tragic Personal Experience (1:1-3:5)
Israel Indicted for Unfaithfulness (4:1-8:14)
God's Retribution on Israel (9:1-10:15)
God's Unfailing Love for Israel (11:1-13:8)
Israel Restored Forever (13:9-14:9)

# Devotions in Hosea

# The Blood and the Day of Jezreel
## Hosea 1

Hosea's messages were delivered *"in the days of Uzziah, Jotham, Ahaz, and Hezekiah, kings of Judah, and in the days of Jeroboam the son of Joash, king of Israel"* (1:1). Although other kings of Israel ruled during this era, Hosea does not name them, for they were wicked and God took no pleasure in them. Jeroboam, though wicked, did accomplish much good for the Northern Kingdom during his reign, such as recovering much of Israel's land that had been previously lost.

Hosea's prophetic ministry to the Northern Kingdom roughly parallels Isaiah's ministry to the Southern Kingdom, although Hosea likely preceded Isaiah's service by about twenty years. Since Jeroboam II ruled Israel from 782 to 753 B.C. and Hezekiah began his reign over Judah in 716 B.C., Hosea's prophetic ministry likely centered between 760 B.C. and 710 B.C.

Hosea's marital crisis and restoration, recorded in the first three chapters, forms the thematic framework for the entire book. The unfaithfulness of Gomer, Hosea's wife, projects into the text the Lord's own heartache over Israel's idolatry. Such blatant infidelity resulted in harsh consequences for Israel and also, as we will see, for Gomer. But eventually redeeming love triumphs to restore Gomer to Hosea, just as it will in a future time to reestablish the Jewish nation with the Lord. Throughout the book, this theme is reinforced with two intertwining ideas: judgment for rebellion is inescapable and abounding mercy is available for deliverance.

From a human perspective, the Lord's opening command is troublesome: *"Go, take yourself a wife of harlotry and children of harlotry, for the land has committed great harlotry by departing from the Lord"* (v. 2). Did the Lord really command Hosea to marry a prostitute or a lascivious woman? Commentators do not agree on this point. Unfortunately, some interpret the narrative as a parable, which undermines the literal aspects of the question altogether. Others, like William Kelly, believe that the Lord did ask Hosea to marry a woman of ill repute:

> The prophet is commanded to do that which was necessarily most painful in itself, and suggestive of what he as a man of God must have felt to be humbled as well as repulsed. But such was the attitude of Israel to their God, and Jehovah would make the prophet and those who heeded the prophecy to understand in measure what He must feel as to His people. ... At the very least we can say that the expression intimated to the prophet what Gomer was going to be. But it must be allowed that the phrase naturally conveys the impression that she had already been guilty of an impure life too common where idolatry reigned.[2]

Likewise, E. B. Pusey suggests that Gomer "must then, amid the manifold corruption of Israel, have been repeatedly guilty of that sin [whoredom], perhaps as an idolatress, thinking of it to be in honor of their foul gods."[3] H. A. Ironside also believes Hosea married a whore:

> As in the case of Isaiah, he and his were to be for signs in Israel; so he is told to unite himself in marriage to a woman devoid of character – a harlot; thus signifying the wretched condition of unfaithful Israel, who nevertheless remained the object of Jehovah's love, despite their iniquity, and the filthiness that was in them.[4]

While this certainly may have been the situation, there is also good reason to believe that the Lord's statements were either predictive concerning the character of Hosea's wife or that He was referring to the land of harlotry from which Gomer had come. Some argue that since the Lord ties the wife of harlotry with her offspring, He is anticipating what she will prove to be in time – a disloyal wife; He is not speaking of her sexual impurity at the time of marriage. R. B. Chisholm Jr. suggests that this interpretation of the Hebrew language is in keeping with numerous other examples in the Old Testament:

> Both the language of Hosea 1:2 and the following context support this interpretation. The expression is similar to others in Hebrew that describes a married woman's character (e.g., "wife of one's youth," "a quarrelsome wife," "a wife of noble character"). ... The Hebrew

word *zanuwn* translated "adulterous" [or "harlotry" in v. 2, NKJV] refers elsewhere in Hosea to the activity of Israel under the figure of a married woman (e.g., 2:2, 4, 4:12, 5:5).[5]

This conclusion also aligns with the allegory posed in Ezekiel 16 where Israel is presented as the pure virgin bride of Jehovah, who later became adulterous (i.e., idolatrous) and was rejected and chastened by the Lord. The expression *"for the land has committed great harlotry"* emphasizes the widespread nature of Israel's idolatry, which would have adversely influenced Gomer's thinking.

Given this understanding, it seems preferable to view verse 2 as not speaking of Gomer's premarital sexual purity, but rather prophetically what she would become. This conclusion is confirmed when Hosea takes abandoned Gomer back to himself after previously rejecting her for her adulterous behavior (3:1-3). It seems doubtful therefore that he would have married her initially (i.e., that the Lord would have commanded him to) if she were actively fornicating with other married men, an offense punished by death under the Law.

In summary, Gomer may have been a lascivious woman before marriage, or she may have only participated in pagan sexual rites before marriage, or she may have been a virgin who being adversely influenced by a pagan society became adulterous after marriage. Regardless, Hosea did not question God's will, nor did he delay in doing what the Lord commanded; *"so he went"* reflects the faithful attitude servants of God should have in fulfilling their callings. Hosea married Gomer, the daughter of Diblaim, even though he foreknew that she would be unfaithful to him and would bear children of unfaithfulness (v. 3). J. M. Flanigan notes that there is a consensus among commentators as to implications of Gomer and Diblaim's names: "The name *Gomer* means 'completeness' or 'ripeness,' and *Diblaim* means 'cakes' or 'layers of figs.' It is thought that these names signify that in the land from which Gomer came there was a fullness of sensuality and corrupt pleasures."[6]

However, commentators do not agree as to whether some of the children born to Hosea were fathered by other men (vv. 3-9), or whether they were born to Hosea by his promiscuous wife. Verse 4 seems to indicate that their first child was Hosea's son; however, there is no masculine pronoun in the text to confirm that he fathered the next two children. If he did father his daughter and second son, then perhaps

9

the children are not associated with Hosea, because the adulterous character of their mother had been stamped upon them. That is, as children of harlotry, the Lord would have no regard for them, other than to appropriately name them to convey His stern message to Israel (2:4).

This is a good reminder that God is not seeking just children from the union of a husband and wife; Malachi reminds us that God desires a "godly seed" that will live for Him (Mal. 2:15). In principle, God is more interested in quality than quantity of children. In other words, parents should not be having babies for the sake of obtaining a large family, but rather for the added capacity of serving the Lord and bringing honor to His name. To have more children than what parents can spiritually, emotionally, educationally, and economically care for is not wise. As the prophet Ezekiel informed the parents of his day, children are born unto the Lord – they are for Him (Ezek. 16:20). The psalmist declares that *"children are a heritage from the Lord"* (Ps. 127:3), and then explains:

> *As arrows are in the hand of a mighty man, so are children of one's youth. Happy is the man who hath his quiver full of them; they shall not be ashamed, but they shall speak with the enemies in the gate* (Ps. 127:4-5).

The psalmist reminds us that parents are mere stewards, and not owners, of the children God graciously entrusts to our care. If reared in the ways of the Lord, these skillfully sharpened and straight arrows become a rich blessing to all. Children must be trained up for the Lord. Untrained children, not surprisingly, remain foolish (Prov. 22:15) and predictably absorb outside influences that fill their void of understanding. Children are natural sponges – they are compelled to learn and to develop an understanding of the world in which they live. Unfortunately for Hosea's family, the lascivious and perhaps pagan lifestyle of Gomer ruined the children – they were not being nurtured for the Lord.

The Lord, through Hosea, will name all of Gomer's children as each one reveals different aspects of the broken relationship between Himself and His covenant people and the judgment that they will suffer. What name did the Lord choose for their first child? *"Call his name Jezreel, for in a little while I will avenge the bloodshed of Jezreel on the house of Jehu, and bring an end to the kingdom of the house of Israel"* (v. 4). The significance of Jezreel here is not in the meaning of the name, but rather it relates to a previous incident where blood was wrongly shed. Righteous Naboth, the Jezreelite, was murdered by Ahab through the wicked plotting of his evil wife Jezebel to obtain a vineyard that Ahab wanted to own (1 Kgs. 21). Ironically, a century later, the bloody massacres of the house of Ahab and of the house of David commenced by Jehu on this very property of Naboth (2 Kgs. 9-10).

Joram, the king of Israel, and Ahaziah, the king of Judah, along with many others were slain by Jehu. While the judgment against the house of wicked Ahab had been predicted by Elijah (1 Kgs. 21:21-24), commanded by Elisha (2 Kgs. 9:1-10), and approved by the Lord (2 Kgs. 10:30), Jehu's massacre of Ahaziah and his relatives was not. Jehu's slaughter of Baal worshippers in Israel was appropriate (2 Kgs. 10:18-28), but his brutal slaughter of David's wayward descendants was not sanctioned by God and would be punished. Jehu was not motivated for the glory of God, but rather by pride and selfish ambition. Because Jehu acted on his own behalf, God would judge his house for the unsanctioned bloodshed at Jezreel.

This prophecy was fulfilled in 752 B.C. when Shallum killed Zechariah and ended Jehu's dynasty in the fourth generation (2 Kgs. 15:10). The Lord informed Hosea that the fulfillment of this prophecy would signal the complete collapse of the Northern Kingdom, as symbolized by Israel's defeat in the valley of Jezreel (v. 5). This occurred in 733 B.C. when Tiglath-Pileser III of Assyria overtook the Jezreel plain, which led to the fall of Samaria in 722 B.C. Israel then became a province of Assyria and many of her surviving inhabitants were exiled.

The second child born to Gomer was a daughter, whom the Lord named Lo-Ruhamah, which means "she is not loved" or "she has not obtained mercy" (v. 6). This would be a difficult name for a child, especially a daughter, to bear, but it was necessary to convey both the Lord's heartache over Israel's apostasy and that He would be withdrawing His goodness towards them. The Lord never stopped loving Israel, but He could not commune with her in covenantal bliss while she was entrenched in idolatry and under His chastening hand. Similarly, Hosea could not engage in marital intimacy with his wife while she was in the arms of other men.

In contrast, the Southern Kingdom, which was not yet in full rebellion, would continue to experience God's grace for a season. Judah would not be conquered by the powerful Assyrians; God would supernaturally defend them (v. 7). This is one of the main messages repeated throughout the book of Isaiah. Indeed, the Lord did intervene in response to King Hezekiah's faith. In one night He wiped out 185,000 Assyrian soldiers that were threatening Jerusalem (Isa. 37:36).

Notice the language of verse 8: *"Now when she had weaned Lo-Ruhamah, she conceived and bore a son."* Jewish women commonly nursed their children for two to three years (2 Macc. 7:27). As there was no reference to the weaning of the previous children, the time between the second and third child is distinct and likely refers to the specific time of Israel's chastening before restoration.

Lo-Ammi was the name given to Gomer's third child, a son (v. 8). His name means "not my people" and signified that God was no longer among His covenant-breaking people (speaking of the Northern Kingdom). Israel did not want Jehovah as their God and He therefore ceased to identify with them from a covenantal standpoint. In summary, the names of Gomer's three children prophetically indicate that Jehovah would: scatter Israel, have no pity for Israel, and disown Israel.

Unfortunately, this estranged relationship would also extend to Judah in the next century. The Lord withdrew from unrepentant Judah and permitted the Babylonians to conquer them shortly afterwards. Ezekiel vividly describes the Lord's glory leaving the temple and Jerusalem, and then explains that God's glory would not return from heaven for a very long time (Ezek. 10).

During Old Testament times, Jehovah dwelt in a tabernacle or temple among His covenant people. Hence, His visible glory is identified with His favor and blessing towards His people. Because of national idolatry, God's glory and blessing departed from Judah just prior to the Babylonian invasion. His people were immoral, idolatrous, and wicked; He could no longer reside among them. Hence, in the post-exile books Jehovah is often referred to as "the God of heaven." This estrangement continues to this day, but as W. J. Hocking explains, this is a temporary reality:

Now the ancient people of God are in the "Lo-Ammi" condition (1:9), and for their sins are regarded as a Gentile people, but eventually they will no longer be outcasts, for, in accordance with prophecy, Jehovah will say to Israel, *"Thou art My people"* (2:23).[7]

It is with this shift toward hope that the chapter concludes. In the Hebrew Bible, chapter 1 closes with verse 9, which better punctuates the thematic transition. In a future day, God will extend mercy to His people, both restoring and blessing them again. In the meanwhile, they will not be affirmed as God's people until the time that Hosea says they will be *"sons of the living God"* (v. 10). The Jews will then greatly multiply under God's care and become *"as the sand of the sea."* Additionally, Hosea prophesied:

> Then the children of Judah and the children of Israel shall be gathered together, and appoint for themselves one head; and they shall come up out of the land, for great will be the day of Jezreel! (v. 11).

Hosea informs us that when the Jews are restored to Jehovah, they will be one nation again with one king, not two separate kingdoms. Their king will be Messiah, a descendant of David, a fulfillment of God's vow to David centuries earlier (2 Sam. 7:11-16). Ezekiel also prophesied that Judah (the Southern Kingdom) and Israel (the Northern Kingdom) would no longer be two nations when they come into their inheritance in Christ's Kingdom (Ezek. 36:16-21). Ezekiel symbolized this truth by taking two sticks and making them one, the result of which he called "Israel" (Ezek. 36:28). This was the name God gave to Jacob, the father of the nation (Gen. 32:28). Jeremiah foretold the same event (Jer. 3:18), but only Ezekiel foretells what this united nation would be called – "Israel."

Ezekiel also foretold that by the end of the Tribulation Period, every Jew remaining among the nations will be physically brought back to dwell in the land of Israel (Ezek. 39:28-29). Jezreel means "God sows." So the great *day of Jezreel* will occur when God draws His people "up out of the land" (speaking of their various hiding places in the world) and plant them again in Israel, their promised inheritance (v. 11).

At Christ's second advent, He will end Gentile oppression and restore the Jewish nation to Himself. Israel will then receive the full benefits of the New Covenant. Until then, the Lord Jesus Christ is building His Church, which, although including both Jews and

Gentiles, is chiefly composed of Gentiles. For this reason, Paul reapplies the phrase *"you are not My people"* in verse 10 to affirm that Gentiles could also become *"sons of the living God"* (Rom. 9:24-26). Paul then reveals that God is blessing Gentile believers to provoke the Jews to jealousy; this will ultimately result in their return to Him (Rom. 11:11-15).

The Jews stumbled over Christ at His First Advent, and the blessing He offered them instead fell into the laps of the Gentiles, who were not expecting it (Luke 20:9-16; Rom. 9:32). This permitted God to righteously call a people that were not His covenant people to be His children also. Through Christ, God brings Gentiles into the good of the New Covenant and all the rich blessings associated with it. Praise the Lord!

Having overviewed Israel's sorrowful spiritual state through willful neglect, we close this chapter with a sobering challenge for the Church from C. A. Coates:

> In Israel there was such unfaithfulness that Jehovah had to completely disown them. Such a state will soon be found in the Christian profession that it will be spued out of Christ's mouth as nauseous to Him. But there is still a remnant marked by faithfulness in the affections, those who keep Christ's word and do not deny His name. That there should be such a remnant is the fruit of sovereign love that has wrought from the divine side for the satisfaction of divine Persons. After all Israel's unfaithfulness, and their being disowned by Jehovah, He will yet bring about that *"it shall be said unto them, Sons of the living God"* (v. 11). They will be secured in family relation, with a nature capable of response to God in holy affections. There will not then be any breakdown in the marriage relation. At the present time there are those who love our Lord Jesus Christ in incorruption. The privilege is open to us of being found amongst them.[8]

## Meditation

O Christ, He is the fountain, the deep, sweet well of love:
The streams on earth I've tasted more deep I'll drink above.
And to an ocean fullness, His mercy doth expand;
And glory – glory dwelleth in Immanuel's land.

O I am my Beloved's, and my Beloved's mine;
He brings a poor, vile sinner into His house of wine!
I stand upon His merit; I know no other stand,
Not even where glory dwelleth in Immanuel's land.

— Anne Ross Cousin

# The Door of Hope
Hosea 2

Verse 1 concludes the thought of Israel's restoration raised in the final two verses of the last chapter and confirms that an opposite meaning of the children's names will exist: *"Say to your brethren, 'My people,'* [Ammi] *and to your sisters, 'Mercy is shown'* [Ruhamah]." When Israel is reestablished to God in the Kingdom Age, the "Lo" [not] will be removed. Then, the Jews will express to each other in child-like terms their delight in being God's children again – "Ammi" and "Ruhamah."

The tenor and focus of the narrative again abruptly changes in verse 2 from future bliss with God to the present dismal reality of not having Him. In hopes that a future generation will be led to self-judgment and repudiation of sin, the prophet carefully outlines Israel's grievous covenant-breaking behavior which led her away from the Lord. After indicting Israel, Hosea will call her to repentance, threaten her with chastening, and then ultimately pronounce judgment on her for infidelity.

Ezekiel explicitly describes Israel's treachery against Jehovah, as allegorically displayed in this narrative by Gomer's marital betrayal. Ezekiel likens Israel to a newborn girl who had been abandoned and left to die in an open field. But Jehovah, being moved by pity, labored sacrificially on her behalf; He washed her, anointed her with oil, clothed her in fine linen, adorned her with ornaments and jewels and cared for her (Ezek. 16:1-13). As a result of His special care and gifts, Israel became a spectacle of beauty among the nations, a declaration of God's own splendor (Ezek. 16:14).

Unfortunately, Israel developed an ever-deepening lust for secular thrills and sensual pleasures and the gods associated with such things. In time, she forsook the Lord and embraced these false gods, even giving to them in worship the abundance that God in His love had provided her (Ezek. 16:15-19). This wicked behavior caused God to summon Israel to appear before witnesses to publicly accuse her:

16

*"Bring charges against your mother, bring charges; for she is not My wife, nor am I her Husband"* (v. 2)! The children (individuals of Israel) need not be identified, as the expression is for rhetorical effect to add realism into the unfolding official drama. The point was that Israel, as the children's mother, was no longer united to Jehovah by faith and love, nor did He any longer identify with her in a marital relationship. Hence, her orphaned children who had lost the protection of their Father were to earnestly plead with their mother in respect to her sinful disposition.

This public decree is followed by a passionate call to repentance: *"Let her put away her harlotries from her sight, and her adulteries from between her breasts"* (v. 2). *"Between her breasts"* is not a sexual statement, but rather an expression associated with profound marital communion, which Gomer had perverted through disorderly passion. For example, when the bride in Song of Solomon speaks of her beloved resting all night between her breasts (or upon her bosom), she is speaking poetically of her longing for sweet, uninterrupted communion with her husband (Song 1:13).

Unfortunately, Israel's yearning for false gods and the wickedness they promoted demonstrated that she no longer valued her purity – a requirement if unhindered companionship with Jehovah is to be enjoyed. Israel is charged with pervasive idolatrous infidelity by Jeremiah: *"Lift up your eyes to the desolate heights and see: Where have you not lain with men?"* (Jer. 3:2). What faithful husband would not weep when speaking of such lascivious conduct by the one he loves? The prophets labor to convey to us both God's profound pain over His people's abandonment and His yearning heart to have them back.

The Lord's plea in verse 2 for Israel to repent of her harlotries affirms that He has not yet taken Israel to divorce court, but is trying to repair the relationship. This is a good reminder that adultery does not demand divorce, which God hates, but divorce is permissible for continued marital infidelity (Mal. 2:16; Matt. 19:8-9). God is most honored when the marital relation can be repaired and His design for marriage is submitted to (1 Cor. 7:10-11).

Jehovah's fervent appeal is immediately followed with the threat of punitive measures if Israel did not repent and return to Him: *"Lest I strip her naked and expose her, as in the day she was born, and make her like a wilderness, and set her like a dry land, and slay her with*

17

*thirst"* (v. 3). Ezekiel refers to the judicial custom of stripping an adulteress naked before her public execution to add to her shame and to reinforce the necessity of faithfulness among the populace (Ezek. 16:38-40). Because an adulteress secretly exposed her nakedness to her lovers, she would be publicly stripped naked for all to see; this was a punishment suitable for such criminal disloyalty. This meant that God would utterly humiliate Israel among the nations, if she continued embracing false gods. He also promised to smite Israel with drought, meaning there would be no agricultural reproduction in the land, again a fitting punishment for illicit sexual behavior – no procreation (v. 3).

Continuing the allegory of the public execution of a guilty adulteress, the Lord additionally promised to show no mercy to her illegitimate children after her death (v. 4). As witnessed throughout the Old Testament, God visits the sins of the parents upon the children, until the decreed curse is removed in mercy through repentance (Num. 14:18). As stated previously, there is no need to identify the children. The statement is meant to add distress to the guilty party – mothers are naturally concerned for the wellbeing of their children. So God promised to disown Israel's children born of harlotry (idolatry); they would become destitute orphans. This harsh language was for shock effect, so to speak. Hosea was trying to awaken Israel to the severe punishment ahead if they did not repent of their idolatry, yet God was not threatening to permanently sever His covenant relationship with them.

To heighten Israel's awareness of God's own heartache over her betrayal, the prophet Hosea is permitted to suffer an additional hurt by his lascivious wife Gomer:

> *For their mother has played the harlot; she who conceived them has behaved shamefully. For she said, "I will go after my lovers, who give me my bread and my water, my wool and my linen, my oil and my drink"* (v. 5).

Hosea watched Gomer bless her lovers for the very provisions (bread, wool, linen, oil, etc.) that he had sent to her to sustain her. Everything that Gomer (picturing Israel) could make shameful, she did – her behavior, her children, and herself. Not only had Israel failed to acknowledge the Lord as the source of her wealth and provisions, she even used the gold and silver that He provided to manufacture images of Baal, which Israel then praised for her abundance (v. 8). E. B. Pusey describes the magnitude of Israel's elicit passion:

> The Hebrew word "Meahabim" denotes intense passionate love; the plural form implies that they were sinful loves. Every word aggravates the shamelessness. Amid God's chastisements, she encourages herself, "Come, let me go," as people harden and embolden, and, as it were, lash themselves into further sin, lest they should shrink back, or stop short in it. "Let me go after." She waits not, as it were, to be enticed, allured, seduced. She herself, uninvited, unbidden, unsought, contrary to the accustomed and natural feeling of woman, follows after those by whom she is not drawn, and refuses to follow God who would draw her (Ezek. 16:31-34). The "lovers" are whatever a man loves and courts out of God.[9]

Israel's treachery at this time was so profound that she built high places and shrines to honor pagan deities, and even offered the children, which the Lord had given her, as burnt sacrifices to them (Ezek. 16:20-21, 24-26). To be abandoned was hurtful to God, but then for Israel to praise false gods for what He had provided them in mercy was an even worse insult. God's goodness had been used to fuel their rebellion; therefore He was withdrawing His blessing from them. Israel would learn the hard way who really controlled all goodness and wanted the best for her.

But even with this injury, the Lord still vowed not to give up on His people. He would even block Israel's way with thorns and stone walls when she sought to find her lovers (i.e., to venture to pagan shrines; vv. 6-7). This intervention would cause her to lose the path so that she could not find her way. Without the influence of her lovers and without provisions hopefully commonsense would cause Israel to examine the consequences of leaving Jehovah and return to Him: *"I will go and return to my first husband, for then it was better for me than now"* (v. 7). Given the retribution Moses promised his countrymen for idolatry, and what we know of Israel's history, these divine hedging efforts to redirect Israel would be pestilence, famine, invasion, and exile (Lev. 26:14-22). True, "better for me then, than now" is not the same as "better to follow the Lord now," but their loss of blessing would be the impetus that would cause Israel to reconsider her sorrowful position without Jehovah. Seeing her shift in perspective, the Lord will then woo her with tender words of love back into His arms (v. 14).

In a practical sense, Paul says something quite similar to believers in Galatia who were leaving their simplicity and joy in Christ for the cold, humanized legalism:

> *But now after you have known God, or rather are known by God, how is it that you turn again to the weak and beggarly elements, to which you desire again to be in bondage?* (Gal. 4:9).

> *What then was the blessing you enjoyed?* (Gal. 4:15).

Were they happier now that they were pursuing the mutable tenets of human tradition than they had been in intimately knowing and following Christ? The answer is obvious. If in our Christian experience we are less content, less fruitful, or less joyful, it is not God's fault. We have moved away from Him, that is, from His Word, and His mind. God is most honored and glorified when we are satisfied with Him alone. Hence, the words of Hosea to wayward Israel sound true for all generations of believers: *"Come, and let us return to the Lord"* (6:1) and may we do so at once! C. A. Coates summarizes this important realization for us:

> All that constitutes true happiness for the intelligent creature is to be found in God Himself. But the result of sin having come in is that the natural heart prefers anything to God. Any foolish propensity, or momentary gratification, any form of self-confidence or self-righteousness, or self- pleasing in a religious way, may be a Baal to seduce us from faithfulness to the only true God and Jesus Christ His sent One.[10]

Since Israel had strayed from Him and now praised Baal for the benefits He had provided to sustain her in the land, God's solution was straightforward: *"Therefore I will return and take away"* (v. 9). The Lord would cause the loss of wool, linen, wine, grain, etc. in Israel. He would not be privy to His people's idolatry, so He would take back what He had freely bestowed in grace.

When Israel was thus deprived, her lovers would mock and desert her; she would be left destitute and naked (v. 10). Because Baal worship had corrupted Israel's feasts, annual celebrations, New Moon sacrifices, and Sabbath observances, the Lord was going to remove them all (v. 11) This outcome further suggests that invasion and exile would be involved in Israel's chastening. Verse 12 reiterates God's plan to limit the fruitfulness of Israel's vines and fruit trees, which she viewed as rewards from the pagan fertility deities she worshiped. As an unfaithful wife, Israel had forgotten her God; she burned incense and adorned herself with rings and jewelry as seductive ploys to attract her lovers (v. 13).

Hosea has been conveying God's jealous anger over Israel's idolatry and His righteous judgments to purify her spiritual harlotries; however, for a second time in the book, the prophet transitions (v. 14) to a message of assurance. As previously mentioned, the Lord will speak tender words and with wooing gestures will allure His wife back to Him: *"Therefore, behold, I will allure her, will bring her into the wilderness, and speak comfort to her"* (v. 14). Jehovah will bring Israel into a place of isolation to ensure no one else can compete for her affection and devotion. There, the Lord will cause Israel to taste His love and provide her a glimpse into the joy and blessing that will thrill her soul and cause her to follow after Him forever.

Once restored to Him, God will lead Israel through *"the Valley of Achor,"* and into the land of Israel which will flourish with agricultural prosperity (v. 15). In the days of Joshua, the Valley of Achor (which means "trouble") was where Achan, his family, all his belongings, his animals and what he had stolen in Jericho were burnt and buried under a pile of stones (Josh. 7:24-26). This event represented the first departure from walking with God after crossing into the Promised Land, and therefore was immediately and severely judged. The ramifications of not having God's presence with them in battle would be devastating (as shown by the defeat at Ai).

The huge heap covering the bodies of the defectors remained for generations as a public testimony to the consequence of sin in the camp. In the future, however, Israel's journey through Achor with the Lord would not be troublesome, but rather it would be *"a door of hope"* into better things to come. Once back in the land, the Lord will supply all Israel's needs forever and she will joyfully sing of her Beloved. This event is reminiscent of Israel's beginning days when Jehovah drew the Jewish nation out of bondage in Egypt to be alone with Himself in the Sinai wilderness and then forty years later He led them into the Promised Land (v. 15).

After Israel's restoration in the Kingdom Age, she will call Jehovah her "Husband" (*'iysh)* and the expression of "Master" (*Ba`ali*) will be purged from their vocabulary (v. 16). Although these two Hebrew words referring to husband are similar in meaning and were sometimes used synonymously (2 Sam. 11:26), the use of the latter term *Ba`ali* would be a reminder of Israel's former worship of Baal; therefore, its use will be prohibited (v. 17). Hosea confirms that during the Kingdom Age there will be complete peace between Israel and the beasts of the field and all Gentile nations (v. 18). Isaiah describes in much more detail what the earth will be like when the original curses for sin are removed from nature and Christ rules the nations with justice and righteousness (Isa. 11, 65, 66). Hosea says that God will ensure that the Promised Land will burst forth with oil, wine and grain (vv. 21-22). Then, Israel will be restored to her proper covenant relationship with God and the Lord will also assure her of His enduring love:

> *I will betroth you to Me forever; yes, I will betroth you to Me in righteousness and justice, in loving kindness and mercy; I will betroth you to Me in faithfulness, and you shall know the Lord* (vv. 19-20).

The Lord conveys a similar expression of devotion and complete restoration through the prophet Jeremiah:

> *"For I am with you," says the Lord, "to save you; though I make a full end of all nations where I have scattered you, yet I will not make a complete end of you. But I will correct you in justice, and will not let you go altogether unpunished"* (Jer. 30:11).

> *You shall be My people, and I will be your God* (Jer. 30:22).

Ezekiel, likewise, concludes his marital allegory previously discussed with the same assurance:

> *"Nevertheless I will remember My covenant with you in the days of your youth, and I will establish an everlasting covenant with you. Then you will remember your ways and be ashamed ... I will establish My covenant with you. Then you shall know that I am the Lord, that you may remember and be ashamed, and never open your mouth anymore because of your shame, when I provide you an atonement for all you have done," says the Lord God* (Ezek. 16:60-63).

Despite Israel's unfaithfulness to Jehovah, the Lord will be moved with compassion and mercy to restore her to a place of special intimacy. God has not abandoned His adulterous wife, His covenant people of old; He has an agenda for restoring the nation of Israel to a position of honor and blessing. Isaiah records the feats that God's Servant-Messiah would accomplish: First, He would *"bring Jacob back to Him, so that Israel is gathered to Him"* (Isa. 49:5). Second, He would also be *"a light to the Gentiles, that You should be My salvation to the ends of the earth"* (Isa. 49:6). Hosea confirms that same twofold plan in verse 23:

> *Then I will sow her for Myself in the earth, and I will have mercy on her who had not obtained mercy; then I will say to those who were not My people, "You are My people!" And they shall say, "You are my God!"* (v. 23).

Paul explains in the Epistle to the Romans how God would accomplish restoring Israel to Himself and also show mercy to the Gentiles, who were not His people by covenant:

> *That He might make known the riches of His glory on the vessels of mercy, which He had prepared beforehand for glory, even us whom He called, not of the Jews only, but also of the Gentiles? As He says also in Hosea: "I will call them My people, who were not My people, and her beloved, who was not beloved." "And it shall come to pass in the place where it was said to them, 'You are not My people,' there they shall be called sons of the living God"* (Rom. 9:23-26).

Paul quotes Isaiah once and Hosea twice in this passage to further explain that it was always God's intention to offer salvation to both Jews and Gentiles. In fact, God would use believing and blessed Gentiles to provoke Israel to jealousy and draw them back to Himself (Rom. 11:11). So, Jehovah would call a people His children that were not His people (v. 23), and then He would rebuild the Jewish nation to become a beacon of divine truth among the nations (Amos 9:11-12). This is why Paul was so zealous to share the gospel with his fellow countrymen: *"Brethren, my heart's desire and prayer to God for Israel is that they may be saved"* (Rom. 10:1). He knew Israel's future, but it was not to be in his lifetime.

Presently, God is calling to Himself a people (Gentiles) that had no hope and no God (Eph. 2:11). When the Church is complete, the Lord Jesus shall descend to the clouds and with a trump and a shout He will gather all who are His from the earth. This will happen in the twinkling of an eye (1 Thess. 4:13-18; 1 Cor. 15:51-52). Then He shall begin to spiritually refine and awaken the Jewish nation and, after their conversion, establish the throne of David forever (Rom. 11:25). While the Church is vertically raptured to meet Christ in the clouds prior to the Tribulation (1 Thess. 4:13-18), all Jews worldwide will be gathered horizontally back to the land of Israel to worship Him there at the end of the Tribulation Period (Ezek. 39:28-29).

Jehovah is not finished with the Jewish nation, for He decreed an everlasting covenant with Abraham's descendants through Jacob. Jehovah is a covenant-keeping God and He has established irrevocable promises that He must fulfill.

## Meditation

Christ is coming! Let creation from its groans and labor cease;
Let the glorious proclamation hope restore and faith increase:
Christ is coming! Christ is coming! Come, O blessed Prince of peace.

With that blessed hope before us, flutes are tuned and harps are strung;
Let the mighty advent chorus onward roll from tongue to tongue:
Christ is coming! Christ is coming! Let each heart repeat the song.

Long your exiles have been pining for your promised rest and home,
But in heavenly glory shining, soon the risen Christ shall come.
Christ is coming! Christ is coming! Joyful, shout the victory psalm.

— John R. MacDuff

# The Unworthy Is Redeemed
## Hosea 3

The prophet continues to overview Israel's past, present, and future relationship to God, in respect of His care to her and her wavering devotion for Him. This chapter opens with one of the most astounding commands in all of Scripture – God instructing a righteous man to again love his wife who had deserted him to be in arms of other men:

> *Then the Lord said to me, "Go again, love a woman who is loved by a lover and is committing adultery, just like the love of the Lord for the children of Israel, who look to other gods and love the raisin cakes of the pagans" (v. 1).*

Israel was baking raisin cakes to honor false gods. Jeremiah condemns the same practice a century later in Judah: Jewish families throughout Judah were uniting for a festive celebration in honor of the goddess Ishtar, the so-called "Queen of Heaven." The event included preparing special cakes that bore her image and were offered to her in a sacrificial rite (Jer. 7:18). The Jews did not seem to care who they honored through these casual social traditions; apparently they did not consider these celebrations idolatrous, but just an opportunity for families to enjoy doing something together (i.e. children gathered the wood, fathers kindled the fires, and women kneaded the bread). Sadly, much of Christendom today also robs devotion from the Lord by honoring fictitious entities through various cultural practices and traditions.

Israel's false gods were not a threat to Jehovah; human imaginations cannot hurt Him or diminish His glory. However, God's anger was provoked by the confusion of truth among His people. They no longer had clear distinctions between what was right and what was wrong, between what was holy and what was unholy. Yet, there was no reason for them to have "confused faces" (Jer. 7:19); the Lord had

25

expressly revealed the way of righteousness to them, and had also commanded them to walk in it.

The same confusion of face is common today among those who associate themselves with the name of Jesus Christ. It is caused by a blurring of what is righteous and what is not. For example, many families gather to commemorate various "Christian" holidays which have pagan origins (e.g. Christmas, Easter, Halloween, etc.). Over time, various traditions have developed around these celebrations, which sound very similar to the practices of the Jews in Jeremiah's day. In these supposed Christian holidays, cookies, cakes, breads, chocolate figurines, etc. are often shaped after ancient pagan images. Fictitious personalities are honored through various traditions and gift-giving practices. May the Church learn from the Lord's revulsion against Israel for such practices and seek to only honor Him in all that we do.

The prophet Hosea was allowed to experience the unfaithfulness of his wife Gomer to illustrate not only the Lord's heartbreak over Israel's idolatry, but also His resolve to again be reconciled to her. Even after Hosea had observed Gomer thanking her lovers for the provisions he had secretly provided for her, God commanded Hosea to redeem his now abandoned wife and take her back. It is significant that the Lord does not call Gomer, "Hosea's wife," but rather He refers to her as "a woman" – an adulteress – and thereby she had no claim on Hosea in respect to covenantal privileges. The command to "go again love" signified that there had been no excuse for Gomer's infidelity; she had been previously and appropriately loved by Hosea.

Of course, all these facets wonderfully reflect God's interaction with idolatrous Israel, His wife. That God could continue loving a people and still desire to bless them again after extreme unfaithfulness to Himself displays the amazing wonder of God's immutable, eternal love. God does not change, nor does His love for His people, even in their rebellion (Isa. 41:11). Why would anyone drinking from the pure fountain of sacrificial goodness ever labor to hew out of rock cisterns which cannot hold water? As Jeremiah informs us, doing so is offensive to God: *"For My people have committed two evils: they have forsaken Me, the fountain of living waters, and hewn themselves cisterns – broken cisterns that can hold no water"* (Jer. 2:13). Love which has its fountainhead in the heart of God cannot be fully understood, but it can be wholly appreciated for its thirst-quenching, soul-satisfying virtue.

In contrast to God's sacrificial love, Gomer's lovers exploited her, consumed her resources, and then forsook her. Though destitute, she would also experience the further humiliation of being stripped bare and sold as property to the highest bidder at a slave auction. Hosea was there and purchased his own adulterous wife for fifteen pieces of silver and a homer and a half of barley (v. 2).

Fifteen pieces of silver was half the common evaluation for a female slave between twenty and sixty years of age (Lev. 27:3-4). Her low sale price depicts her insignificant value to others in her loathsome state. As worthless as she was, she still could not purchase herself from bondage; she had to be bought by someone who wanted her. Fortunately for her, there was one present who still valued her in the sense of what she could become when his. Despite her past treachery, Hosea redeemed his Gomer. This wonderfully portrays Isaiah's prophecies foretelling Israel's future redemption and restoration: *"You have sold yourselves for nothing, and you shall be redeemed without money"* (Isa. 52:3). *"Return to Me, for I have redeemed you"* (Isa. 44:22).

The homer and half-homer of barley (about forty-five bushels) was approximately the annual allowance of food for a slave among the Romans (four bushels a month). E. B. Pusey emphasizes that barley was the offering of one accused of adultery, and, being the food of animals, prefigures that she was like horse and mule which have no understanding. The barley may have been a part of the ransom price (in addition to the silver) or it may have been the food allowance for Gomer while dwelling in a solitary place as to prove her faithfulness to Hosea. In other words, Hosea bought Gomer back from her evil, not to live with him as his wife initially, but to be adequately cared for until it was fitting for her to be completely restored to him after a period of moral purification.[11]

As here, both silver and barley are used to symbolize redemption throughout Scripture (Ex. 30:12-16; Lev. 23:9-14, 25:9; Ruth 3:15). The Lord Jesus was betrayed for thirty pieces of silver, which was later referred to by the Pharisees as "blood money" and indeed it was (Matt. 26:15, 27:3-9). Additionally, the Lord most likely broke unleavened barley bread at the Passover Feast the night before His crucifixion (Luke 22:14-20). Both these symbols of redemption in Scripture are associated with the Lord's redemptive work at Calvary. However, the payment, the pain, and the shame Hosea suffered to redeem Gomer is incomparable to what the Lord Jesus suffered on our behalf. H. A. Ironside writes:

> Hosea had to bear the shame of having espoused one of so wretched a character, but he did not have to die for her. It was far otherwise with our blessed Lord Jesus. He not only came where we were in our sin and shame, but on Calvary's cross He was made sin for us that we might become God's righteousness in Him. There He purchased us with His own precious blood, *"that He might redeem us from all iniquity and purify unto Himself a peculiar people, zealous of good works"* (Titus 2:14).[12]

Having purchased Gomer at the slave market, Hosea turned to her and said: *"You shall stay with me many days; you shall not play the harlot, nor shall you have a man – so, too, will I be toward you"* (v. 3). Though plucked from the mire of filth she was immersed in, it would be many days before Gomer would be restored to full marital status and normal marital relations would occur (e.g. Deut. 21:13). During this period she would refrain from sin and have no conjugal privileges. Hosea would be her guardian, but as yet, nothing more. Allegorically speaking, this verse prophetically declares how much the Lord desires to be with His people, the ransom He paid at Calvary to redeem them, and that it will be many days before His people will be with Him in a full covenant relationship.

Hosea did not want his Jewish audience to miss the connection. Gomer's lengthy separation from himself and the resolution of his marital crisis pictured Israel's long estrangement from God and her future restoration:

> *For the children of Israel shall abide many days without king or prince, without sacrifice or sacred pillar, without ephod or teraphim. Afterward the children of Israel shall return and seek the Lord their God and David their king. They shall fear the Lord and His goodness in the latter days* (Hos. 3:4-5).

Gomer's restoration to full marital status was subsequent to her adulterous behavior, her redemption, followed by a lengthy period. This later period has already been nearly two thousand years to date and the Jewish nation is still not experiencing the full covenant love and communion that God longs to have with them. They were purified from their adulterous infatuation with idols after the Babylonian exile, and were redeemed five centuries later at Calvary. The first two chapters did not allude to this prolonged period between Israel's deliverance from her idolatry and her ransom being paid before her full restoration to God in the Kingdom Age. During this long interim, "the time of the Gentiles," Israel will miserably learn that there is no substitution for the love of God: no king, no sacrifice, no ephod, nor teraphim can take His place. Nothing but Christ can satisfy the human soul!

I tried the broken cisterns, but ah the waters failed;
Even as I stooped to drink they fled, and mocked me as I wailed.

Now none but Christ can satisfy, none other name for me!
There's love and life and lasting joy, Christ Jesus, found in Thee.

The pleasures lost I sadly mourned, but never wept for Thee,
Till grace the sightless eyes received, Thy loveliness to see.

— Frances Bevan

For centuries now the Jews have been abiding *"without king or prince, without sacrifice, or sacred pillar, without ephod or teraphim"* (3:4). The Jewish nation today reveres Jehovah, but she is unfortunately estranged from Him and ignorant of His ways. As an example, orthodox Jews have a longstanding practice of not saying *Yahweh* (Jehovah) because of their fear of God and reverence for His name, yet they reject the Lord Jesus Christ – their only hope of salvation. Divine authority without a proper relationship prompts fear. The Jewish nation is out of touch with God; their spiritual state precludes them from knowing God intimately and experiencing His goodness.

Thankfully, love and not fear is to rule the believer's disposition towards God, though love does not displace proper awe and reverence for God. The Lord knows that love is a stronger motive for willful service, submitting to His commandments, and pursuing holy living than fear is. If one loves the Lord, yielding to His Word will be a delight. Love for the Lord is a stronger reason for obedience than is the fear of consequences: *"There is no fear in love; but perfect love casts out fear, because fear involves torment. But he who fears has not been made perfect in love"* (1 Jn. 4:18). Because of Christ's finished work at

Calvary, the judicial penalty for the believer's sin has been satisfied. This means that God is no longer angry with those He has forgiven. As a result, believers are liberated to experience and share God's love: *"But if anyone loves God, this one is known by Him"* (1 Cor. 8:3). *"We love Him, because He first loved us"* (1 Jn. 4:19). This means that we are no longer to be ruled by the fear we suffered from before becoming a child of God.

Gomer learned much from her horrible experience and she did not forsake Hosea again. Likewise, God's covenant people, having suffered centuries of affliction for their wayward affections, will never leave the Lord again once fully restored to Him in the Kingdom Age. The Mosaic Law did not contain a provision of forgiveness for adultery – offenders, like Gomer, were to be put to death. But Hosea's dealings with his unfaithful wife demonstrate that God could afford a provision for grace which the Law could not extend. Only through a new and everlasting covenant can God fully forgive Israel's sin and ours too (Jer. 31:31-34; Ezek. 16:60-63; Heb. 8:8). There is a day coming in which God will claim what He has redeemed and Israel will never depart from His side again.

## Summary and Application

The story of Hosea and Gomer conveys a vivid picture to us of how God feels when we direct our praise and devotion, which He deserves, to others. The prophet Hosea was an honorable man, but his wife Gomer was lascivious and possibly conceived children that were not Hosea's. In time, Gomer abandoned Hosea to pursue a fast-life with her various lovers. It wasn't long before Gomer found herself poor and desperate. Hosea demonstrated sacrificial love for Gomer and sent supplies to her. From a distance Hosea watched his wife Gomer praise her lovers for the very provisions he had sent to assist her. God allowed Hosea to feel this hurt and shame and to write of the incident that we might better understand how God feels when we rob Him of the praise that He deserves, when we value worldly pleasures more than our communion with Him. Gomer was abandoned by her lovers and sold into slavery. The redeeming love of God is exemplified when Hosea bought back his own adulterous wife during a slave auction. After experiencing the magnitude of Hosea's love, she never departed from him again.

Paul reminds believers in the Church Age that they are the espoused bride of the Lord Jesus (Eph. 5:22-25; 2 Cor. 11:2). If believers could understand Christ's redeeming love in even a small measure, they would not commit adultery by fraternizing with the world. In the face of such love, how could a person break the heart of God? The ideologies of the world oppose God and God opposes them. Gomer's lovers did not care for Gomer nor about the pain they were causing Hosea; they used and abused Gomer until the thrill of the moment was gone. This was what the prodigal son learned in Luke 15. The world does not offer anything of lasting value; it only takes what is valuable to God.

Worldliness is any sphere from which the Lord Jesus is excluded. James likens worldliness to the sin of spiritual adultery: *"Adulterers and adulteresses! Do you not know that friendship with the world is enmity with God? Whoever therefore wants to be a friend of the world makes himself an enemy of God"* (Jas. 4:4). Worldliness is the love of passing things, and things have no eternal value, except as they are used to please God. Worldliness opposes God, and God hates it. May the Church learn from Israel's idolatrous past, as pictured in Gomer's harlotry and not invoke the chastening hand of God. Consistent gratitude is a guard against depression and regression. Satisfaction in the Lord alone honors Him!

## Meditation

> Redeemed, how I love to proclaim it!
> Redeemed by the blood of the Lamb;
> Redeemed through His infinite mercy,
> His child and forever I am.
>
> Redeemed, and so happy in Jesus,
> No language my rapture can tell;
> I know that the light of His presence
> With me doth continually dwell.

> — Fanny Crosby

# Israel Indicted
Hosea 4

Having illustrated through his own marriage crisis the enduring, redeeming, restoring love of Jehovah for wayward Israel, the prophet now addresses the nation's present pathetic situation. The next five chapters form a lengthy indictment by the Lord against His people's wickedness and idolatrous ways. The majority of this chapter is accusatory in tone, with brief pronouncements of forthcoming judgment interspersed throughout the oracle.

Historically speaking, God revealed Himself and His Law to the Jewish nation after loosening their bonds and leading them out of Egypt to Mount Sinai. Moses verbally reviewed God's Law with the people and acknowledged their verbal acceptance of it (Ex. 21). A few days later, God would formally ratify the covenant with them and document the matter in writing in order to have a permanent record (Ex. 24). Moses built an altar at the foot of Mount Sinai according to the instruction provided in Exodus 21; this altar was for all the people since it had twelve pillars (stones), one for each tribe.

Moses then reviewed the Law (which he had now written again) with the people. Oxen were prepared and offered upon this altar as burnt offerings. Half of the blood of the oxen was sprinkled on the altar to sanctify it and the remainder was sprinkled upon the people to sanctify them:

> *And Moses took half the blood and put it in basins, and half the blood he sprinkled on the altar. Then he took the Book of the Covenant and read in the hearing of the people. And they said, "All that the Lord has said we will do, and be obedient." And Moses took the blood, sprinkled it on the people, and said, "This is the blood of the covenant which the Lord has made with you according to all these words"* (Ex. 24:6-8).

By sprinkling the people with blood, Moses was acknowledging the basis of the established covenant – shed blood. Hosea begins this chapter by charging *"the children of Israel"* (the entire nation) with a breach of this covenant: *"There is no truth or mercy or knowledge of God in the land"* (v. 1). As witnessed in Hosea and Gomer's marital crisis, covenantal failure meant there could be no nearness in the relationship. Likewise, God could not be nigh to His wayward people. E. B. Pusey concisely summarizes the offense:

> The union of right knowledge and wrong practice is hideous in itself; and it must be especially offensive to Almighty God, that His creatures should know whom they offend, how they offend Him, and yet, amid and against their knowledge, choose that which displeases Him.[13]

Their wicked behavior demonstrated that they had no regard for Him or His Law, hence a contrary separation persisted. As an example of Israel's covenantal failure, the prophet cites five of the Ten Commandments that Israel had blatantly violated (v. 2): By falsely or frivolously swearing they had invoked God's name in a disrespectful way – this violated the third commandment. Shedding innocent blood (e.g., offering their children in pagan sacrifice) was murder and broke the sixth commandment. Their widespread adultery in pagan practices affronted the seventh commandment, stealing violated the eighth, and lying, the ninth.

"Knowledge," "acknowledge," or "know" are key words found seventeen times in Hosea. "Knowledge" is found three times in chapter 4; the only Old Testament chapter with more occurrences is Proverbs 1 with four. The Hebrew word for "knowledge" is *da`ath* which means "discernment or understanding." The Jews knew Jehovah's name, but had no understanding of Him or discernment as to what He expected of them. Psalm 111:9-10 exactly identifies why the Northern Kingdom was in such a poor spiritual condition:

> *He has sent redemption to His people; He has commanded His covenant forever: Holy and awesome is His name. The fear of the Lord is the beginning of wisdom; a good understanding have all those who do His commandments* (Ps. 111:9-10).

Because the Lord had displayed His holy character in all His gracious actions to Israel, He should be feared and His name revered: *"Holy and awesome is His name."* The psalmist then stated the foundational principle for understanding human existence and obtaining spiritual awareness: *"The fear of the Lord is the beginning of wisdom."* This implies that those who have a proper disposition towards the Lord will have the wisdom to do His commandments and praise His name! Israel did not have such a temperament, even though they insincerely cried out to God, *"We know You"* (8:2). It was evident that they neither knew nor feared God because they were blatant covenant violators who suffered from divided affections (10:2).

Accordingly, the Lord says: *"My people are destroyed for lack of knowledge"* (v. 6) and *"people who do not understand will be trampled"* (v. 14). In the next chapter the Lord also reveals His solution for Israel's problem: *"I will return again to My place till they acknowledge their offense. Then they will seek My face; in their affliction they will earnestly seek Me"* (5:15). Only chastening would awaken God's covenant people to who He is and what He expects of them. Thankfully, the restored Jewish nation will possess such knowledge in the Kingdom Age: *"I will betroth you to Me in faithfulness, and you shall know the Lord"* (2:20). C. A. Coates notes that whenever God has a controversy with His people, it always centers in their deficient knowledge of Himself:

God's people were destroyed in Hosea's time "for lack of knowledge," or, more literally, "the knowledge;" that is, the specific knowledge referred to in verse 1. So how the knowledge of God is acquired becomes the most important matter for our consideration. It is evident that we cannot get it by pursuing idolatry; it was said, *"Their doings do not allow them to return unto their God"* (v. 4). We can understand this, but it is said also, *"They shall go with their flocks and with their herds to seek Jehovah; but they shall not find Him: He hath withdrawn Himself from them"* (v. 6). He is not to be found on that line. People would often be prepared to make great sacrifices if they could thereby obtain the favor of God. But this prophet and, indeed, the whole of Scripture make plain that He can be found only through affliction, and through learning that there is no help anywhere else. The deepest affliction anyone can pass through is to be convicted of sin, and to learn that death is upon one. It is by the cutting off of all hope from any other quarter that men are brought to turn to God.[14]

However, in Hosea's day Israel was without the knowledge of God, their hope was misplaced, which meant they were destined to perish. Hosea promised that God would afflict them with severe drought which would cause human life to *"waste away"* and fish, beasts, birds, and fish to be *"taken away"* (v. 3). Wasting away and taken away well describe the parched soul that is estranged from the knowledge of God.

## The Guilty Prophets and Priests

Before addressing the guilt of the overall populace, Hosea first charges Israel's religious leaders with moral and spiritual negligence (vv. 4-10). As the entire Jewish population was guilty of rebellion and violating God's law, there was no one innocent who could object to God's charges (v. 4). In the Northern Kingdom, prophets and priests were detached from proper worship at the temple in Jerusalem as the Law demanded. These leaders were immersed in paganism, and controlled by the wicked courts in which they served (1 Kgs. 22:6-8). Sadly, Israel's prophets used their esteemed position to deceive others, and to pursue personal gain and self-gratification. Because they had morally stumbled, they would experience a punitive downfall (v. 5).

God would hold Israel's leaders responsible for the deplorable spiritual condition of the people, whose *"lack of knowledge"* was because their leaders had *"rejected knowledge."* Isaiah said that it was this refusal of knowledge that would lead the people into captivity (Isa. 6:13). While praying to His Father, the Lord Jesus affirmed that true knowledge of God gives abundant life to one's soul: *"And this is eternal life, that they may know You, the only true God, and Jesus Christ whom You have sent"* (John 17:3).

In God's economy, love, light and life cannot be separated from each other. So the Lord was particularly angry with the priests for obscuring the light of His truth from His people. Since the priests had *"forgotten His Law,"* He promised to reject them and cut off their descendants from priestly ministry. This threat was executed when the Assyrians conquered the Northern Kingdom in 722 B.C. and slaughtered or exiled Israel's priesthood.

The prophet Ezekiel confirms God's judicial decree concerning Israel's deviant priests. During the Kingdom Age, only priests from the lineage of Zadok will be able to enter God's sanctuary and to offer sacrifices to Him on behalf of the Jewish nation (Ezek. 44:6, 15-16). Zadok was a faithful priest and loyal to both King David and then to

King Solomon (1 Chron. 29:33). Zadok was the first high priest to oversee Solomon's temple and now his descendants would have an honored position of authority within God's Millennial Temple. The Lord indeed rewards faithfulness.

One might think that having more priests in Israel would prompt spiritual and moral growth, but instead it resulted in only greater sin (v. 7), for in their greed the priests encouraged the people to sin, and to offer more sacrifices to God because of their sin. Since the priests received portions of these sacrifices and may have even charged fees for the expiation of sins, the priests benefitted financially from Israel's sin. It is no surprise then that Isaiah's opening message revealed God's hatred of Israel's sacrifices and feasts because they were vain religious practices without devotion. Hence, Hosea says that the priests *"eat up the sin of My people"* (v. 8). The prosperity that God had lavished on His people had not turned their hearts to Him, but rather had fueled their greed and selfishness; therefore, He had to completely withdraw from them.

God promised to severely punish the priests for exchanging the glory associated with their esteemed office for shame; those who followed after their indignity would also be judged (v. 9). Because of the priests' selfish motives to gain more food, they would suffer hunger during the forthcoming penal droughts. Additionally, their efforts to promote fertility in Israel through cultic prostitution would fail (v. 10, 2:13). The priests had wrongly presumed that more people meant more sacrifices, which meant more food for them.

The priests would experience God's indignation because they had abandoned His Word for the worst possible substitute – idolatry. Besides engaging in sexual practices with pagan prostitutes, which was expressly forbidden by God's Law, the priests had become enslaved to gross sin themselves: *"Harlotry, wine, and new wine enslave the heart"* (v. 11). The mastering influence of wine and the insanity of sin are pictured as blending in one intoxicating drink to deprive man of his proper affections and sound reasoning and to render him a brutish beast. H. A. Ironside notes that the same foolishness rules in the hearts of men today:

> It has often been noticed that when people get away from God, they can be most punctilious about self-imposed rites and superstitious observances, while counting it a hardship to obey the voice of the

Lord. The same is true as to credulity and faith. He who finds it difficult to trust the simplest of the Holy Scriptures can accept with amazing ease the most remarkable hypotheses and notions of unbelieving theorists. So was it with Israel at this time.[15]

## The Guilty People

Corrupt leaders cannot produce in the people they oversee anything better than what they themselves are. Because Israel's leaders had forsaken God's Word and had sought counsel from lifeless wooden gods, the entire nation was engulfed in immoral and pagan practices (vv. 12-14). Many young men and women in Israel were engaging in pagan sexual rites with "ritual harlots" to gain favor with so-called fertility deities. The Hebrew word *qedeshah* is translated *"ritual harlot"* in verse 14. The Hebrew word *qedeshah* means "devoted one" and is used three times in Genesis 38:21-22 to describe what Judah and his Adullamite friend believed Tamar to be – a temple prostitute. The general populace was showing their devotion to Baal and Asherah (Astarte) through sexual perversion. So widespread was Israel's ignorance of the consecrated life that God concludes their unavoidable ruin: *"Therefore people who do not understand will be trampled"* (v. 14).

This somber announcement is combined with an even more startling decree: *"I will not punish your daughters when they commit harlotry."* Though errant, every child of God who values his or her relationship with the Lord will welcome His correction: *"O Lord, correct me, but with justice; not in Your anger, lest You bring me to nothing"* (Jer. 10:24). God's people understand that divine chastening is proof of God's abiding presence and love: *"But if you are without chastening, of which all have become partakers, then you are illegitimate and not sons"* (Heb. 12:8). However, when God says He will no longer correct His people for their willful sin, it means that He has ceased dealing with them as His children and will rather treat them as an enemy (Isa. 1:24). Hosea's statement meant that God had disowned Israel and would permit her to experience the full destruction of her own depravity (e.g., Rom. 1:24).

## Judah Warned – Israel Rebuked

Hosea now warns the Southern Kingdom to avoid the gross sin of her northern sister, Israel: *"Though you, Israel, play the harlot, let not*

*Judah offend. Do not come up to Gilgal, nor go up to Beth Aven, nor swear an oath, saying, 'As the Lord lives'"* (v. 15). The threefold warning "do not come up," "nor go up," "nor swear" is a rhetorical device to accentuate the grossness of Israel's sin in such a way as to rebuke Israel, while also warning Judah. The Southern Kingdom should not follow the corruption of Israel who made Bethel, meaning "the house of God" (this site was named by Jacob after making a vow to God; Gen. 28:19, 31:13), to become Beth Aven, meaning "the house of wickedness." Bethel was where Jeroboam erected a pagan altar and the image of a gold calf to be worshipped (10:5; 1 Kgs. 12:25-30).

Interestingly, the prophet then likens Israel to what she was worshipping – a stubborn calf (v. 16). Since she would not listen to the Lord, He had decided to let her go her own way, like a wandering lamb looking for the best forage, but without God's protection and care. Ephraim had chosen to join herself to idols and God therefore could not be joined with her, but rather He must give her over to the inevitable outcome of pursuing her selfish passions – shame and destruction (v. 17). William Kelly explains the principle governing God's dealings with Israel here:

> "Ephraim is joined to idols [lit. toils]: let him alone." God chastises as long as there is the smallest feeling, but when He ceases to deal with the guilty, all is over, morally speaking. When to Ephraim or any other He gives such rest as this, it is because hope is abandoned, and the evil is allowed to run its course unchecked. "Their drink is turned; her rulers greatly love infamy": that is, they give themselves to nothing else than that which is and brings inevitable shame. "The wind hath bound her up in its wings, and they shall be ashamed of their sacrifice." They refused to learn of God in peace and righteousness, and must be given up to the winds, dispersed afar off by their enemies, and there be humbled, seeing they refused it in their own land.[16]

When man ventures away from God and His goodness, it does not take long for man's inherent badness to become evident (Rom. 1:20-32). Having abandoned God for pagan forage, Israel had digressed into an idolatrous, immoral, dishonorable, and rebellious nation (v. 18). She was now so far lost that no amount of prophetic pleading or rebuke could guide her back to God. Consequently, God, having exhausted all possible avenues of bringing the stubborn wanderer home, is content to let her go her own way and suffer utter ruin. He would wrap Israel up in the wind and sweep her out of the land; and then, too late, she would realize the sheer stupidity and shamefulness of her idolatry (v. 19).

The Lord's response here is similar to what a local church is commanded to do with one in their fellowship who is unrepentantly engaging in sin. Such a person was to be put out of the local assembly and be allowed to pursue the inevitable destruction of his or her unchecked lusting: *"to deliver such a one to Satan for the destruction of the flesh, that his spirit may be saved in the day of the Lord Jesus"* (1 Cor. 5:5). Hopefully, the erring believer would be brought to a state of brokenness and would return to the Lord before the buffeting by Satan resulted in his or her death.

In verse 15, Hosea issued a brief warning to Judah to stay clear of Israel's pagan appetites. Similarly, Paul warns the assembly in Corinth to not fellowship with someone identifying with Christ, but was clearly not in fellowship with the Lord because of his or her stubborn sin: *"Do you not know that a little leaven leavens the whole lump? Therefore purge out the old leaven, that you may be a new lump, since you truly are unleavened"* (1 Cor. 5:6-7). If sin in the Church is not dealt a deadly blow by God's people it will thoroughly corrupt all who do not esteem holiness as necessary for maintaining Christ's fellowship in the Church. Sadly, Judah did not heed this warning – the Southern Kingdom was influenced by the idolatrous leaven of the Northern Kingdom.

About a century into the future, Jeremiah will indict Judah for ignoring this warning and will call her to repentance just as Hosea is doing here with Israel. Jeremiah uses the analogy of two sisters, Israel and Judah, to present his message to Judah. Both sisters had pledged their loyalty to Jehovah through a marriage covenant. Israel was the first of the sisters to commit fornication. She embraced false gods and worshipped their idols in various high places throughout the northern kingdom. The cover of every green tree became the canopy over her bed of adultery (Jer. 3:6). God called Israel to repentance, but she would not forsake her idols and return to Him. God responded by writing her a bill of divorcement and sending her away to Assyria in 722 B.C. (Jer. 3:8).

Even though the other sister, Judah, had witnessed firsthand God's harsh judgment of Israel, she also committed spiritual fornication by worshipping images of stone and wood (Jer. 3:7-9). But as Jeremiah explains, God was more angry with Judah than He had been with Israel:

> *"So it came to pass, through her* [Israel's] *casual harlotry, that she defiled the land and committed adultery with stones and trees. And yet for all this her treacherous sister Judah has not turned to Me with her whole heart, but in pretense," says the Lord. Then the Lord said to me, "Backsliding Israel has shown herself more righteous than treacherous Judah"* (Jer. 3:9-11).

Judah would experience greater judgment than Israel did, for two reasons. First, Judah, having seen the harsh consequences of the sin of adultery, deliberately chose to be unfaithful despite this understanding. Second, Israel was blatantly idolatrous, but two-faced Judah embraced other lovers while still sweet-talking the Lord with vain pleasantries. The people of Judah acted religious, but their hearts were not with God. They pretended to be devout but embraced pagan gods whenever they thought they could get away with it. Israel did not try to hide her adultery, but Judah disguised her treachery in order to appear righteous; thus, she deserved greater judgment.

Both Israel and then Judah would learn through severe chastening that a covenant-keeping God never backs out of His unconditional promises to love and bless. Whether God's love is affirmed through blessing or chastening, it is always consistent and effectual, and therefore should be appreciated by those He deems worthy of receiving it.

## Meditation

With one consent we meekly bow beneath Thy chastening hand,
And, pouring forth confession meet, mourn with our mourning land;
With pitying eye behold our need, as thus we lift our prayer;
Correct us with Thy judgments, Lord, then let Thy mercy spare.

— John Hampden Gurney

# The Lord Withdraws
## Hosea 5

Thus far, Hosea has acknowledged Israel's sin, called her to repentance, and threatened divine chastening if she did not turn back to the Lord. Although Judah was briefly warned in the last chapter not to follow Israel's idolatrous ways, Israel remains Hosea's chief prophetic focus. In this chapter, the prophet continues asserting guilt (vv. 1-5) and then declares that widespread judgments were coming to Israel and would affect Judah also.

While Hosea's rebuke is to the entire house of Israel, he especially singles out Israel's priests and kings in his opening indictment. These leaders had *"been a snare to Mizpah and a net spread on Tabor,"* resulting in the slaughter of the people (vv. 1-2). There are at least two possible understandings of what Hosea's statement refers to. First, E. B. Pusey notes that there was an ancient Jewish tradition suggesting that Israel's leaders organized and covertly placed ambushers on the passes around Mizpah and Tabor "to intercept and murder those Israelites who would go up to worship at Jerusalem."[17] The next verse gives further credence to this prospect.

The second possible explanation of Hosea's statement is that he is alluding to the spiritual slaughter of the people and not their physical demise. By encouraging the people to worship false gods at pagan sites such as Mizpah and Tabor, the rebel priests were entrapping the people in a deadly snare. These priests were reminded that an omniscient God knew all about their defiling ways, even what was done in secret (v. 3). Israel had become so overpowered by cultic prostitution that the entire nation was locked in a corrupt state of mind which prevented them from turning to the Lord (v. 4). God did not need to call witnesses against Israel; her own arrogant pride was sufficient to affirm her guilt (v. 5). Unfortunately, the working of sin spreads like the influence of leaven in a lump of dough, and Israel's perverse behavior was plunging Judah into moral ruin also (vv. 4-5).

As often observed in Scripture, there is an insanity to sin, the ultimate expression being that somehow a man or an angel can overcome their Creator and rule in His place, or put someone else in His place. This was Lucifer's sin, which caused his ruin, and it is the same mindset that his children, the sons of disobedience, continue propagating today through various world religions. Rejecting God and going our own way, or desiring to be on His throne, never ends well, but humbling ourselves before Him always will.

## Judgment Pronounced

The Lord would chasten His covenant people in two ways. First, He would withdraw His presence from them, which meant His blessings also (v. 6). The time of repentance had passed. There was no love for the Lord; rather, the hearts of His people had turned away from Him. In response, He would permit sin to run its destructive course; fear and calamity would awaken Israel to their deepest need, for true satisfaction is found in Jehovah alone. Even if they sought Him through the sacrifices of their flocks and herds, He would not answer, because they were still engaging in adulterous behavior that produced illegitimate children through pagan sexual activities (v. 7).

Second, the Lord would punish them through invasion; the sound of battle trumpets would be heard throughout Israel's borders, even as far south as Beth Aven at Judah's border (vv. 8-9). Hosea is foretelling that the Assyrian invaders who conquer Ephraim in southern Israel would then advance on Benjamin in northern Judah to seize their land. Why would Judah be punished with Israel? Because their leaders also had no regard for God's covenant-Law, they were like those who moved boundary markers to secretly steal land from a neighbor (v. 10).

Ephraim's desolation was sure because they were entrenched in the vanity of humanized religion (v. 11). Israel was not aware that God was secretly leading her down the pathway to destruction. To Israel, the Lord was like a silent moth eating away her garment, and to Judah, He was like hidden bone decay in her body that would go unnoticed until a sudden snap occurred (v. 12).

Although Israel and Judah could not discern God's dealings against them, they did notice their deteriorating political condition: *"When Ephraim saw his sickness, and Judah saw his wound, then Ephraim went to Assyria"* (v. 13). Though both kingdoms had sought alliances with Assyria (King Tiglath-Pileser) to remedy their ailments (2 Kgs.

16:7-8, 17:3), Hosea foretold they would not be healed. When God afflicts, or wounds, there can be no cure apart from Him – Assyria would be no help. Rather, God would use them to afflict both Israel and Judah.

The Lord was against His people and there was a day coming in which His subtle doings, like a moth, would be transformed into the merciless attack of a raging lion. He would be like an adult lion in its full strength against Israel, and like a young lion against Judah (i.e., He would inflict judgment to a lesser degree; v. 14). Both prophecies were fulfilled by the Assyrian invasion which resulted in the complete collapse of Israel and much devastation in Judah until God miraculously delivered the Southern Kingdom through righteous Hezekiah's faith. The latter portion of verse 14 predicts the exile of both kingdoms: *"I, even I, will tear them and go away; I will take them away, and no one shall rescue."* This prophecy was fulfilled in 722 B.C. when Assyria deported captives from the Northern Kingdom and in 605-586 B.C. when Babylon exiled captives from Judah.

The ultimate goal of disciplinary action is to correct inappropriate conduct and to restore proper behavior. While His covenant people were being chastened and purified of their idolatry, the Lord would be like a lion returning to his lair after conquering his prey: *"I will return again to My place till they acknowledge their offense. Then they will seek My face; in their affliction they will earnestly seek Me"* (v. 15). E. B. Pusey elaborates on the meaning of the latter phrase of this verse:

> God does not only leave them hope, that He would show forth His presence, when they sought Him, but He promises that they shall seek Him (i.e., He would give them His grace whereby alone they could seek Him, and that grace should be effectual). Of itself affliction drives to despair and more obdurate rebellion and final impenitence. Through the grace of God, *"evil brings forth good; fear, love; chastisement, repentance."* *"They shall seek Me early,"* originally, *"in the morning"* (i.e., with all diligence and earnestness, as a man rises early to do what he is very much set upon).[18]

The Lord would remain apart from His people until His grace had accomplished its intended work: Israel willingly admitting her guilt and seeking Him through genuine repentance, in lieu of vain ritual sacrifices or merely seeking escape from their punitive hardship (v. 6). True repentance will be evident when God's people genuinely urge each other: *"Come, and let us return to the Lord"* (6:1). Then the Lord would again reside with His people and they would enjoy His providential care and blessed fellowship.

> True repentance has a double aspect; it looks upon things past with a weeping eye, and upon the future with a watchful eye.

> — Robert Smith

God's dealings with His errant people in this chapter serve as a good reminder for believers in the Church Age not to blame others to avoid taking responsibility for their own failures and sinfulness. The believer's sole purpose in life is to live for the praise of His glory (Eph. 1:12-14). Denying personal responsibility for our offenses hinders our spiritual growth. As witnessed in this chapter, restoration to God requires true repentance (v. 15; 1 Jn. 1:9). Genuine repentance acknowledges what was offensive to God, accepts personal responsibility for the damage, grieves over the crime, and turns from the wrong behavior to seek God's forgiveness on His terms. When this occurs, God is pleased, for *"there is joy in the presence of the angels of God over one sinner who repents"* (Luke 15:10).

## Meditation

> Come to the Savior now! He gently calls thee;
> In true repentance bow, before Him bend the knee.
> He waits to bestow salvation, peace, and love,
> True joy on earth below, a home in heaven above.

> — John M. Wigner

# What Shall I Do With You?
## Hosea 6

The difficulty in properly interpreting verses 1-3 is to discern who is speaking. Are we listening to the insincere voice of Israel, or of a faithful, future remnant, or is the agonizing prophet appealing to his countrymen in response to God's withdrawal (5:15)? Isaiah often permitted the voice of the future Jewish remnant (who was seeking the Lord) to be heard in his oracles; perhaps Hosea is employing that same literary style here. Some commentators believe these opening statements are from the shallow and disingenuous Jewish nation, which obviously did not result in a spiritual revival.

While this scenario does characterize much of Israel's history, the referenced yearning for swift restoration with God and the desire to be in His presence seem to better indicate the aspirations of the prophet or of a future righteous generation on behalf of the nation. These believers had learned through chastening what grieved the heart of God, and they had turned from their stubborn waywardness to seek the Lord. This two-parallel-stanza song then, when sung, would encourage the remnant to continue to seek the Lord and to do His will.

To that end, verses 1 and 3 commence with the exhortations: *"Come, and let us return," "let us know,"* and *"let us pursue."* These subjunctive pleas are then followed by the motive for pursuing the Lord: to avoid chastening, to experience healing, to be revived, and to be raised up to enjoy God's presence and blessing. This is symbolized by the abundance of rain – a sign of God's favor (Deut. 11:13-15). An awakening in Israel had occurred to some degree and at least a remnant realized why their nation had suffered so much and for so long – Israel lacked knowledge of the Lord (v. 3).

The faithful remnant did not want to repeat the sins of the past; they wanted their God and knew that they would, after two days of separation, be revived on the third day and be completely restored to Jehovah. It is likely that the reference to the third day (after two days) is a Jewish idiom which infers a quick response. That would mean that the two days relates to the long interim between Israel being redeemed but still separated from Jehovah (as pictured in the restoration process of Hosea and Gomer in 3:4-5). With the dawning of the third day that estrangement will swiftly end. Peter reminds us not to forget *"that with the Lord one day is as a thousand years, and a thousand years as one day"* (2 Pet. 3:8). Perhaps Israel's long wait of two days commencing at Calvary is nearly over, and the third day, speaking of the thousand-year Millennial Kingdom, is about to commence!

Of course, the reference to faithful Israel being revived on the third day is a lovely foreshadow of Christ's own pattern of life, death, and resurrection as the One who became true Israel. He came down from Heaven in grace to fully identify with a nation fallen from grace, to suffer Gentile oppression, to be called out of Egypt, and to experienced their separation from God for their sin, and to be resurrected from the dead on the third day to again commune with God. These similarities are prophetically profound and illustrate God's own awareness of where His people were, what it will take to awaken them to their own depraved condition, and then the cost of saving and reviving them.

## Lamenting Israel's Sin

The glimmer of light and hope afforded in verses 1-3 fades quickly as Hosea launches into a lengthy section to identify and lament the poor behavior of God's people (6:4-11:11). This prolonged indictment initially charges Israel with gross sin which necessitates severe punishment (6:4-8:14), before reiterating and further explaining arguments to substantiate her guilt (9:1-11:11).

The Lord begins this section by sharing His frustration and anguish over His unresponsive wayward people: *"O Ephraim, what shall I do to you? O Judah, what shall I do to you"* (v. 4). Reviewing the history of the Jewish nation, their devotion towards Him was fickle and inconsistent at best; their expressions of love were as brief as a passing morning shower. They had not genuinely responded to His gracious appeals and kindnesses; therefore He sent waves of prophets to denounce their behavior, to threaten them with corrective agencies, and to call them to repentance.

Despite the prophets' extreme measures of hewing off dead wood and unfruitful branches in Israel (symbolizing their stern messages and judicial pronouncements), the nation remained rebellious and spiritually vain (v. 5). The Lord did not want His people's ceremonies void of truth and devotion; rather He says: *"For I desire mercy and not sacrifice, and the knowledge of God more than burnt offerings"* (v. 6). The "for" describes the ministry to which the prophets were called: the Lord wanted His people to approach Him in the knowledge of revealed truth, not humanized religiosity. Interestingly, the Lord Jesus at His first advent quoted Hosea 6:6 (on two different occasions) to declare a similar message to hypocritical and ceremony-oriented Israel (Matt. 9:13, 12:7).

Verse 6 reveals one of seven things mentioned in the Bible that God values more than burnt offerings – the knowledge of God (v. 6). The other six are: obedience to His word (1 Sam. 15:22), a broken heart (Ps. 51:17), genuine praise and thanksgiving (Ps. 69:30-31), walking humbly with God in justice, love and mercy (Micah 6:8), loving God with your whole heart (Mark 12:33), and doing the will of God (Heb. 10:9-10). These are the things that please the Lord and cause His face to shine on His people in any dispensation, including the Church Age.

To demonstrate that the Lord's case left Israel defenseless, Hosea, like Isaiah, mentions Adam's transgression in Eden against God's original covenant with humanity (v. 7; Isa. 43:27). The NKJV translates the Hebrew *adam* as "like men" in verse 7 to highlight the wider reality that all humanity fell in Eden; the NASV renders *adam* literally: *"But like Adam they have transgressed the covenant."* The point is that Israel's propensity to rebel is inherent in their fallen nature which was passed down from the first dissident Adam. William Kelly further expounds this point:

> As the head of the race, his position was well defined and peculiar. Adam had a relationship with God, but the fall broke up the state of innocence, and God "drove out the man," instead of keeping him in the earthly garden of His delights. The position of man since is that of an outcast from paradise. But Israel was called externally to a place of favor, separate to Jehovah from all the rest of mankind. There was a new trial of man, though of man fallen. Indeed this forms the proper scene of man's probation: either when in Eden, and there Adam comes before us; or out of Eden, and in due time the Jew manifests his course and issue.[19]

Indeed, Paul confirms that all of us suffer from the same corrupt nature and the consequences caused by that original transgression: *"Therefore, just as through one man sin entered into the world, and death through sin, and so death spread to all men, because all sinned"* (Rom. 5:12). There is only one solution to sin and death – Christ! This is the truth that the restored Jewish remnant will realize in a future day (Isa. 53:1).

Hosea then points to Israel's inclination towards wrongdoing, physical violence, murder, and vile sexual sins under the guise of religion (vv. 8-9). For example, Gilead, a priestly city, should have been a standard for upholding God's holiness in the region, but rather was *"a city of evildoers and defiled with blood"* (v. 8). If the priestly cities were corrupt, then the general populace of the Northern Kingdom would also be debased. Indeed, the people had relentlessly and repeatedly breached God's covenant, which Hosea says was a "horrible thing" to do (v. 10).

The last verse of the chapter speaks of a harvest appointed in Judah: *"Also, O Judah, a harvest is appointed for you, when I return the captives of My people"* (v. 11). Is Hosea's harvest alluding to imminent judgment (e.g., Jer. 51:33; Rev. 14:15) or to a future joyful and fruitful era after her chastening (Isa. 27:6)? Commentators disagree. The reference might be to the forthcoming Babylonian invasion and exile, or to the joyful restoration of Judah to the Promised Land afterwards. While the judgment of Israel was final (they would be captured and dispersed), the Lord here seems to be extending hope to Judah after their chastening as the projected harvest is connected with the return of Jewish captives.

Hence, verse 11 introduces the theme of the next section: God longed to restore Israel and to bless His people, but He was hindered from doing so because of continuing outbreaks of sin. Judah's blessed restoration after chastening pictures the Jewish nation's final reinstatement in the Kingdom Age. In a future day Israel will be purified and in communion with God. Then they will enjoy all the rich provisions that God has been withholding from His rebellious people.

## Meditation

Let it be your business every day, in the secrecy of the inner chamber, to meet the holy God. You will be repaid for the trouble it may cost you. The reward will be sure and rich.

— Andrew Murray

Cast not away your confidence because God defers His performances. That which does not come in your time will be hastened in His time, which is always the more convenient season. God will work when He pleases, how He pleases, and by what means He pleases. He is not bound to keep our time, but He will perform His word, honor our faith, and reward them that diligently seek Him.

— Matthew Henry

# A Cake Not Turned
Hosea 7

The last verse of the previous chapter introduces the somber refrain of this chapter: *"When I would have healed Israel, then the iniquity of Ephraim was uncovered, and the wickedness of Samaria"* (v. 1). Israel usually speaks of the entire Jewish nation in Scripture, but after Solomon's death, the nation divided into two kingdoms. So during the period of 930 to 722 B.C., Israel more specifically spoke of the defecting ten northern tribes. Of them, the tribe of Ephraim obtained a large portion of inheritance in the southern region of the Northern Kingdom; Samaria was the capital of Ephraim. Although the Lord desired to restore and heal His people in Israel, He was unable to do so because of their ongoing covenant-breaking behavior; theft and fraud are given as examples.

Despite His patient mercy and endearing appeals from His prophets, His people only waded deeper into sin. This meant that with each expression of God's goodness, His people's wickedness became more and more exposed. Their abhorrent condition was further compounded by a do-not-care attitude. The Jews were unconcerned that the omniscient God observed all their evil doings, or that the holy God would be offended by their sin, or that the just God might even invoke retribution (v. 2).

The Jews were so engulfed in shameless sinning that their consciences had become numb to guilt and to the fear of chastening. To willfully break a covenant with the One who has shown Himself to be the one true God is alarming, but to not even care how He feels about it or how He might respond reveals the innermost depravity of the human heart. The leaders, who were to set a good example, did not. Rather they endorsed carnal living and as a result the general population was locked into a godless mindset (v. 3).

The indictment *"they are all adulterers"* in verse 4 is not explained. Was physical adultery rampant among the Jews, or was Hosea speaking of their spiritual desertion of Jehovah for idols? Jewish history has shown that both transgressions usually go hand-in-hand, so perhaps that is why Hosea did not clarify the sin, but rather chose to describe Israel's disposition through a metaphor: They were like a baker, who does not stir the coals in his oven so as to maintain a low temperature that permits the leaven to permeate the dough and cause it to rise. When the leavening process was complete, then the oven would be fully heated and the bread would be baked.

Israel had an underlying and unquenchable passion that was always ready to spread sinfulness throughout the society: *"having eyes full of adultery and that cannot cease from sin"* (2 Pet. 2:14). The leavening process should have been constrained by contemplating and honoring their covenant with Jehovah, but was not. Consequently, these adulterers rested from their lustful cravings only long enough to refuel themselves to engage in further debauchery. Adultery commences when one's lusts for what is outside of God's will and unchecked passion lead to unconstrained behavior. The Northern Kingdom was thoroughly under the influence of this type of leaven-philosophy.

God's passion for holy living is the same in all dispensations. In the New Testament, believers are commanded to abstain from fornication, which is any sexual relationship outside the bounds of marriage: *"For this is the will of God, even your sanctification, that ye should abstain from fornication"* (1 Thess. 4:3, KJV). If married, a man is to have only his wife and the wife only her husband; there is to be no sexual lusting after, or "touching," of another person for sensual reasons (1 Cor. 7:1). God's judgment falls not only on fornicators, but also upon those who *"approve of those who practice"* fornication (Rom. 1:32). Believers are not to even look on those committing fornication with any sense of approval. It is this *looking* upon sexual perversions to achieve pleasure that has become a scourge to our society and has led to many broken marriages and splintered families.

Having the same root word, pornography and *porneia* ("fornication") are closely associated in meaning. *Porneia* is used in the New Testament to address all forms of sexual impurity and wanton behavior. The word initially meant "to act the harlot" but later evolved to mean "to indulge in unlawful lust." *Porneia* (and its root word) specifically describes various types of sins: premarital sex (1 Cor. 7:1-2), physical adultery (Matt. 19:9), any form of unchaste conduct (1 Cor. 6:13, 18), prostitution or harlotry (Rev. 2:20-21), homosexuality (Jude 7), and spiritual adultery (Rev. 14:8, 17:4). Interestingly, when sins are listed in the New Testament, fornication normally tops the list (1 Cor. 5:11; Col. 3:5). Besides hurting others, fornication is a grievous sin which afflicts one's own body (1 Cor. 6:18).

In Proverbs 7, Solomon instructed his son to avoid the strange woman while journeying through the city streets, for death would result from her traps. With today's technology, a man no longer has to venture out of his home to meet the strange woman – techno-filth is readily available for private viewing anytime and anywhere. The word pornography is directly derived from the Greek word *pornographous* which meant "to write about prostitutes" (from the root words: *porne,* "harlot," and *graphos,* "writing"). Thus, pornography is a virtual form of fornication!

The ultimate goal of pornography is to promote fornication: the former stirs up unlawful lusting; the latter satisfies those lusts through immoral sexual acts. If we are to abstain from fornication, we must put up a mental defense that will maintain a pure thought life. We cannot lust in our members and expect to be holy in conduct. Indeed, the Lord Jesus taught that if a man looks on a woman with lust, he has already committed sexual immorality with her in his heart (Matt. 5:28).

Physically we are what we eat, but spiritually we are what we think: *"For as he thinks in his heart, so is he"* (Prov. 23:7). By properly controlling our thought life, we control our behavior! When we choose not to stimulate our flesh through suggestive media, we will find it easier to maintain a Christ-honoring thought life. Unchecked lusting leads to sin and separation from God (Jas. 1:14); He cannot have fellowship with us while we are in sin (1 Jn. 1:5-7). An individual cannot change our current social situation, but, on a personal level, he or she can determine to remain pure and to pursue precautionary measures to maintain that commitment. Sadly, the general populace of the Northern Kingdom had no desire to turn away from doing what was breaking God's heart.

R. B. Chisholm Jr. suggests that verses 5-7 pertain to the period between 752-732 B.C. when four of Israel's kings were assassinated (2 Kgs. 15).[20] Hosea was backing up his previous heart evaluation of the people by citing examples of how unchecked carnal impulses had led to deliberate hideous behavior. For example, the princes carousing with the unsuspecting king at merrymaking feasts were plotting how to murder him (v. 5). Hosea returns to the low-temperature oven metaphor to show how this premeditated crime was indicative of Israel's real problem: the secret burning of unchecked passions in the heart which must eventually lead to a blazing oven when the baker returns in the morning to bake the bread that has fully raised (v. 6). Because the Law no longer stayed their lusting, they "made ready in their hearts" mischief; it was, in effect, always stored up within, says E. B. Pusey:

> Their heart was ever brought near to sin, even while the occasion was removed at a distance from it. "The oven" is their heart; the fuel, their corrupt affections and inclinations and evil concupiscence, with which it is filled; "their baker," their own evil will and imagination, which stirs up whatever is evil in them. The prophet then pictures how, while they seem for a while to rest from sin, it is but "while they lie in wait;" still, all the while, they made and kept their hearts ready, full of fire for sin and passion; any breathing-time from actual sin was no real rest; the heart was still all on fire; "in the morning," right early, as soon as the occasion came, it burst forth.[21]

The importance of this statement is valid for today. A child of God should never harbor smoldering bitterness or fuming lusts within his or her heart, for then, when proper conditions exist, evil will blaze up and incinerate what God appreciates. The prophet then provides an example – their murderous plots against His prophets: *"They are all hot, like an oven, and have devoured their judges; all their kings have fallen. None among them calls upon Me"* (v. 7). Hidden sin within the believer's heart inevitably becomes sinful behavior which then must afflict its originator through the overruling providence of God. This means that God's correction and justice will eventually ensure that illicit human passion, malice, evil, and misplaced devotion for God will all be collected and masterfully delivered into the offender's lap.

Continuing the baking analogy, the prophet says that besides murderous plots, Israel was also guilty of intermingling with foreigners. This may suggest that intermarriages forbidden by the Law were prevalent, or that Israel sought security through foreign alliances. Such unlawful mingling is likened to the baker mixing ingredients for a cake. However, these associations would prove to be destructive for Israel – the outcome would be like an unturned cake that burns on one side and remains unbaked on the other, hence not fit for use (v. 8).

Hosea then explains how foreign alliances had been detrimental to Israel's political autonomy, and their national wealth was waning (v. 9). Their economic attrition resulted from paying tribute to foreign nations to obtain the security that only God could afford them. However, Israel was like an elderly man who did not recognize the slow diminishing effects of aging (i.e., his loss of strength and hair, etc.). Yet, even in this weakened state, Israel refused to acknowledge their covenant with God and repent of their evil doings – this was self-incriminating behavior (v. 10).

From 743 to 722 B.C., Israel agreed to be subservient to Assyria, but then repeatedly rebelled, even seeking an alliance with Egypt before succumbing to a full Assyrian invasion (2 Kgs. 15, 17). The prophet likens their restless, wavering, senseless behavior to that of a silly dove whose flight patterns are unpredictable (v. 11). However, Hosea promised that because Israel had no contemplations of God in their naïve dove-like behavior, He would come to them like a wise and well-equipped fowler and would catch them in His net (v. 12).

This promise of entrapment is associated with the "woe" in verse 13 that announces imminent judgment. Although He had redeemed His people, had brought them out of Egypt, and had entered a covenant with them, they had rebelled against Him and strayed away from Him. He counted them as liars deserving retribution. When they had crop failures, they did not seek Jehovah, but rather wailed to Baal and cut themselves to try to gain his favor (v. 14). The Septuagint translates *"they assemble together"* as the act of cutting themselves, which is brought out in the ESV rendering *"they gash themselves."* This understanding does better fit known pagan rituals at this time (1 Kgs. 18:28; Jer. 47:5), which the Law forbade the Jews to take part in (Deut. 41:1).

Despite the Lord having previously strengthened and trained His people so they could protect themselves in thwarting invaders, they now treated Him as an enemy (v. 15). The Lord bemoans their cold-hearted disposition towards Him – "they devise evil against Me." To illustrate Israel's unnatural and spiteful response to receiving divine grace, Hosea likens the Northern Kingdom to a faulty bow which was unreliable when most needed (v. 16). Just as a defective bow fails to respond the way the archer anticipates, God's people had failed to respond as He desired. They had proudly rejected His ways and His assistance; they were missing the mark, so to speak. As a result, Israel and her leaders would falter in battle, and, ironically, Israel would become an object of scorn in Egypt, whose aid they had previously sought to stave off the Assyrian invasion (v. 11; Isa. 30:2).

In this chapter Ephraim, representing Israel, was likened to the unusable "cake not turned" (v. 8), a senseless "silly dove" lacking convictions and direction in life, and a powerless "deceitful bow" (v. 16). This chapter shows us that complacency in what matters to God naturally permits secular corruption to control our thinking, which then leads us far away from the Lord and into utter chaos.

## Meditation

I believe that one reason why the church of God at this present moment has so little influence over the world is because the world has so much influence over the church.

— Charles Spurgeon

The stiff and wooden quality about our religious lives is a result of our lack of holy desire. Complacency is a deadly foe of all spiritual growth. Acute desire must be present or there will be no manifestation of Christ to His people.

— A. W. Tozer

# Reaping the Whirlwind
## Hosea 8

This chapter concludes the metaphor-saturated section that began in chapter 6 which describes Israel's sin and rebellion. Hosea's descriptive language conveying just how destitute, worthless, and miserable God's backsliding people really were has been extensive. He has likened Israel to an adulterous wife, a staggering drunkard, a stubborn calf, a band of robbers, a leavened lump, a cake not turned, a silly dove, and a treacherous bow. In this chapter the Northern Kingdom is compared to a wild donkey, a cheap harlot, and *"a vessel in which is no pleasure"* which will soon be discarded among the nations.

Because of Israel's continued rebellion, God instructed Hosea, *"set the trumpet to your mouth"* (v. 1). The prophet was to blow the *shofar* (the ram's horn) to signal Assyria to swoop down on Israel (God's house). This alarm announcing Israel's impending doom was designed to startle and awaken the Jews from their spiritual slumber. Later, the Lord instructed Isaiah to sound a similar warning: *"Cry aloud, spare not; lift up your voice like a trumpet. Tell My people their transgression, and the house of Jacob their sins"* (58:1). Moses warned the Israelites in the wilderness that if they forsook the Lord, He would chasten them by foreign invaders (Deut. 28:45). When this calamity unfolded, Israel would cry to God, *"My God, we know You"* (v. 2)! But God promised not to be moved by theatrical insincerity; in rejecting what was good, they had fully abandoned Him (v. 3).

Hosea then cites two examples to prove that Israel's devotion was a farce (vv. 4-6). First, Israel had anointed kings without consulting Jehovah; in fact, none of Israel's kings had been appointed or properly anointed by the Lord. Consequently, several revolts occurred against Israel's kings after Jeroboam II, which resulted in assassinations and the quick successions of rulers. Second, Israel crafted idols to worship (v. 4). The golden calf image that Jeroboam I erected in Samaria (Bethel) after the Jewish nation split into two kingdoms is used to symbolize the long-standing idolatrous spirit of the Northern Kingdom (v. 5).

After enduring their stubborn idolatry for more than two hundred years, an angered Jehovah rhetorically inquires: *"How long until they attain to innocence?"* (v. 5). It is ludicrous to think that something fashioned with human hands could ever be a god! The Lord had a solution to prove this point. He would show that the golden calf was nothing more than a religious prop by breaking the image in pieces (v. 6).

The expression, *"they sow the wind, and reap the whirlwind"* in verse 7 speaks of Israel's disposition for worshipping idols (vv. 4-6), seeking foreign alliances (vv. 8-10), and the unavoidable outcome for doing so – divine wrath. Israel's futile practice of sowing vanity would reap tornadic destruction in the land when Assyria invaded. H. A. Ironside points out that there is an aspect of sowing to the wind (pursuing our carnal whims) which we often ignore until we are reaping the whirlwind:

> Yet how slow we are to learn! *Theoretically*, all saints know that there can be no real blessing apart from walking with God, but *experimentally,* how easily most of us are lured aside, and led after other gods, when some opportunity seems to present itself for profit or advantage! But at last all have to realize that the only result of such sowing will be disappointment and sorrow. *"The bud shall yield no meal; if so be it yield, the strangers shall swallow it up"* (v. 7). Apply this to every department of life, and it will be found to be a rule to which there are no exceptions. Apparent success may seem to follow upon disobedience, but "the end is not yet." We may fancy God and His Word can be disregarded, but we shall prove in bitterness of soul that it is an evil thing indeed to choose our own path.[22]

Indeed, Israel was about to learn that there are always consequences for ignoring God's Word and engaging in corruption. Paul explains that what *"a man sows, that he will also reap; for he who sows to his flesh will of the flesh reap corruption"* (Gal. 6:7-8). The Jews were quite aware of the "sowing and reaping" principles of the harvest, but needed to learn that these applied to their sin also. The three laws of the harvest are as follows. First, you reap what you sow. Second, you reap more than you sow. Third, you reap later than you sow. All the suffering Israel was about to reap under the Assyrians would be the result of sowing idolatry in the land for two centuries. As a result, the Gentiles with whom Israel had sought security would despise the Jews as a discarded vessel: *"Israel is swallowed up; now they are among the Gentiles like a vessel in which is no pleasure"* (v. 8). J. M. Flanigan writes:

> Israel would be despised by the Gentiles who carried them into captivity. They would be treated as a vessel in which men had no pleasure. Some think that this is an allusion to a rotted and corrupted skin bottle, no longer fit to contain drinking water. More probably it might refer to a crude and cheap earthenware vessel, of no value, perhaps even cracked or broken and hardly worth keeping. How unbelievably sad is this, that the nation which Jehovah had chosen for Himself to be His own peculiar treasure should be counted as worthless by the *goyim*, the Gentile heathen nations who had swallowed them up.[23]

Assyria was already swallowing up Israel's wealth through tribute payments, but in the coming days would conquer her, despoil her, and then toss her away like a worthless vessel, speaking of her exile.

Hosea then employs two metaphors to describe Israel's wandering and self-destructive ways (v. 9): She was like a wandering wild donkey which would not yield to any master, and she was like a confused harlot who chose to hire lovers who did not care about her well-being. Being a harlot for profit is one thing, but the prophet Ezekiel explains how absurd Israel's harlotry with foreign nations and their gods was:

> *You are an adulterous wife, who takes strangers instead of her husband. Men make payment to all harlots, but you made your payments to all your lovers, and hired them to come to you from all around for your harlotry. You are the opposite of other women in your harlotry, because no one solicited you to be a harlot. In that you gave payment but no payment was given you, therefore you are the opposite* (Ezek. 16:32-34).

Because of Israel's unabashed lewd and wicked conduct, Jehovah was forced to take action against His unfaithful wife. He would use Assyria, one of the Israel's chief hired lovers, to punish her and to end her wild wanderings and lascivious behavior among the nations (v. 10).

Of particular offense to God were all the altars Israel had erected to promote artificial rituals and sinful behavior contrary to His Law (vv.

11-12). They were even offering blood sacrifices to Him for religious show, in order to eat the meat of the animal sacrificed in merry making revelry. What audacity! All this was so offensive to God that He promised to deliver them into exile and slavery (as symbolized by Egypt – their former place of bondage) to teach them to respect His Law (v. 13).

Hosea has been primarily speaking to Israel, but he concludes this three-chapter indictment with a final charge against both Judah and Israel – both kingdoms were self-sufficient and high on their own achievements (v. 14). Israel, especially, had forgotten the Lord and had built many temples to worship Him and false gods. Both actions were contrary to His Law. Judah was fortifying herself against the Assyrian threat, instead of turning to Jehovah to ensure their security. This mindset is one of the main focuses of God's rebuke in the book of Isaiah. Thankfully, King Hezekiah heeded Isaiah's warning and Assyria's assault was stayed.

Though the Jews had forgotten their God and His Law, the Lord had not forgotten them nor His judicial promises against them for rebellion. He was bound by His Word to severely chasten them through invasion for their willful disobedience (Deut. 28:47-57). In just a few years Assyria's army would destroy Israel and conquer dozens of Judah's strongholds, before God would intervene. God is a covenant-keeping God, meaning that His actions, for better or for worse, always have the good of His people in mind.

## Meditation

One great power of sin is that it blinds men so that they do not recognize its true character.

— Andrew Murray

The inward area is the first place of loss of true Christian life, of true spirituality, and the outward sinful act is the result.

— Francis Schaeffer

# God's Retribution
Hosea 9

The previous chapter concluded a lengthy lament over Israel's behavior and the Lord's promised chastening in response (6:4-8:14). This chapter begins a new three-chapter section, in which Hosea reiterates and further explains Israel's guilt and deserved punishment (9:1-11:11). Lawyer Hosea will clearly show God's watertight case against the guilty defendant, Israel.

Israel had prostituted herself at every threshing floor by giving praise to Baal for their agricultural prosperity (v. 1). Hosea warned that her rejoicing would be short-lived, for God was withdrawing His blessing from the land (v. 2). An unregenerate person can be relatively happy in life, as compared to a child of God who is estranged from his or her heavenly Father because of sin. This is why Hosea says, *"Do not rejoice, O Israel, with joy like other peoples"* (v. 1). Their situation, having been in a covenant with the one true God and then deserting Him, was vastly different than a heathen thanking his dumb idol for a good harvest.

Furthermore, Israel had defiled the Lord's land by her idolatry; therefore, He was going to deliver the nation back into slavery (as symbolized by Egypt) and exile her to pagan Assyria (v. 3). In Assyria the privilege of appropriately worshiping Jehovah would not be possible. In that foreign land they would be considered unclean, like a mourner who had touched a dead body. This meant that none of their sacrifices or offerings would be accepted by God until they had experienced cleansing and had returned to Israel (v. 4).

The rhetorical question of verse 5 further highlights that fact; in Assyria the Jews would not be able to celebrate religious feasts or special days. Many would not survive the Assyrian invasion and those who did would live as though dead in Egypt (i.e., in bondage). This mention of Memphis, a famous Egyptian burial place south of Cairo, further suggests this understanding. All their possessions in Israel would be lost, and thorns and briers would grow up in the ruins of their homes (v. 6).

In addition to their idolatry, Hosea states that another reason for their stern, coming punishment was their animosity towards God's prophets (v. 7). Israel ridiculed and despised them as insane fools. The irony of the matter was that Israel had sought to entrap God's prophets whom He had placed as watchmen over His house (Israel) to warn His people of being entrapped by sin and its consequences (v. 8). Because Israel had rejected the messages of God's prophets, the nation had sunk into a depraved condition that rivaled the gross carnality of the men of Gibeah during the era of the Judges (v. 9). The bisexual men of Gibeah first wanted a visiting Levite for their pleasure, but had to settle for gang raping his concubine which resulted in her death (Judg. 19).

From God's perspective this entire scenario was reminiscent of the nation's regression soon after being delivered out of Egypt. God's initial exhilaration for His people at Sinai is likened to the elation of a famished traveler unexpectantly finding succulent wild grapes while journeying through a wilderness, or the delightful surprise of a husbandman to find the first ripened fruit on a fig tree in summer (v. 10). God enjoyed wonderful communion with His people until many Israelites deserted Him at Baal Peor to bow down to the idols of the Midianites. In doing so Israel committed a shameful abomination!

"Ephraim" is mentioned six times in this chapter. The only other chapter in the Bible with more occurrences is Hosea 5, with nine. The book of Hosea refers to "Ephraim" thirty-seven times, which is more than any other book in the Bible. The meaning of Ephraim, "double fruit" (implying fruitfulness), is applied in Hosea's prophecy in a negative way: Because Ephraim had engaged in Baal fertility rituals (v. 10), God's people would suffer infertility (v. 11). The population growth that Israel sought through paganism would disappear as swiftly as a bird takes flight and vanishes from sight. Many Jewish women would be barren (either through the loss of husbands in battle, sterility, or miscarriages), and the fortunate few who did deliver children would watch many of them die in the coming Assyrian annexation (vv. 12-14). Israel, likened to the booming seaport city of Tyre, had previously enjoyed economic prosperity, but soon she would be removed from their prosperous environment.

The Lord's love had been spurned by a rebellious people, who sought fertility blessings from the gods of the region (the pagan rituals practiced at Gilgal is given as an example): *"All their wickedness is in Gilgal, for there I hated them"* (v. 15). In holy indignation, the Lord further says, *"I will love them no more."* During the days of Joshua, Gilgal is where God began anew with His people. Great mercy was shown to the Israelites by "rolling away" (the meaning of Gilgal) their shame and reproaches. But now the very place that God had displayed tokens of His love had become an idolatrous bed of wicked passions. For the Father of mercies to be provoked to such displeasure as to say *"I hated them"* and *"I will love them no more"* could only mean that the coming judgments on Israel would be equally severe!

God has an enduring love for His people which is unchangeable, but the context indicates that the good favor of that love had been lost, and now God would be demonstrating His love in a different way than by grace. True love abounds in knowledge (Phil. 1:9), meaning it seeks what is best for others. God's love for Ephraim was not motivated by feelings of pity for the consequences that they will suffer for self-imposed sin, but rather for what would ultimately benefit them. Likewise, we should not seek to assist another unless the overall good of that individual is served. If we are motivated by pity and not by love, we may undermine God's dealings with an individual in sin. God chastens those He loves in order to bring the erring child of God back into fellowship with Himself (Heb. 12:6).

As a result of Ephraim's stubborn waywardness, Jehovah was promising to drive them from His land to wander among the nations (v. 17). Furthermore, they would suffer widespread sterility and high infant mortality rates. Instead of being "double fruitful," they would be as fruitless as an uprooted plant and discarded plant left to wither (v. 16). God did not delight in invoking such measures of "tough love," but He knew that it was the only way to purify His people of their idols and draw them back to Himself. As a holy God who loved His people, Jehovah had no other option but to honor His part of the covenant (which Ephraim had broken) and judge His people.

## Meditation

God is interested in developing your character. At times He lets you proceed, but He will never let you go too far without discipline to bring you back. In your relationship with God, He may let you make a wrong decision. Then the Spirit of God causes you to recognize that it is not God's will. He guides you back to the right path.

— Henry Blackaby

The battle of prayer is against two things in the earthlies: wandering thoughts and lack of intimacy with God's character as revealed in His word. Neither can be cured at once, but they can be cured by discipline.

— Oswald Chambers

# Break Up Your Fallow Ground
## Hosea 10

Continuing the botanic metaphor, Israel is judged as an empty vine in this chapter. The Jewish nation bore some refreshing fruit for the Lord during those early years together in the wilderness, but that was not the situation now (9:10). Hosea rightly assesses: *"Israel empties his vine; he brings forth fruit for himself"* (v. 1).

Centuries earlier, Asaph spoke of Israel as a vine brought out of Egypt that had once flourished because of God's care, but because of the nation's unfaithfulness had been repeatedly trampled on by invaders (Ps. 80). Hosea employs the same imagery and message for the Northern Kingdom here, as will Isaiah, Jeremiah, and Ezekiel in later warnings against the Southern Kingdom (Isa. 5:1; Jer. 8:13, 12:10-13; Ezek. 15). This prophetic choir resounded God's assessment of the Jewish nation: Israel was a worthless vine/vineyard because of its fruitless disposition towards God.

Israel had lush foliage, but its fruit was worthless because it was self-produced for itself, and was not from God or for God. At a superficial glance, the vine appeared prosperous and healthy, which characterized Israel economically and politically during the reign of Jeroboam II, the era of Hosea's preaching. The more God blessed Israel materially, the more she became self-absorbed, yielding corruption. God's vine had produced nothing valuable to Him – it was empty from His perspective and should be uprooted.

Jehovah would no longer tolerate the divided heart of His people. Their religious formalities towards Him (pictured in the altars) were as nauseating to Him as their sacred pagan pillars – He promised to tear down both (v. 2). It is impossible to live a holy life for God's glory unless single-hearted devotion guides the way. From Israel's inception, the Lord desired communion with a holy nation, not a double-minded, mostly-pagan people: *"Be ye holy; for I am holy"* (Lev. 11:44). Israel had forgotten from where they came, a pit of hopeless slavery, and why

God had delivered them from Egypt, to rescue them from Egypt's corruption to be His special redeemed possession.

Believers in the Church can also forget from where they came, both dead in trespasses and sin and enslaved to sin. Likewise, the Lord Jesus wants a spotlessly pure bride for Himself (Eph. 5:27), one that does *"abstain from the appearance of evil"* (1 Thess. 5:22). This means fully consecrating one's spirit, soul and body for God's purposes by abhorring evil in thought and deed. This means recalling that what the believer was positionally in Adam is dead and gone (Eph. 4:22; Rom. 6:6). All that we were before Christ is no more – we died with Him at Calvary. Because believers have been legally declared dead, they receive a new life – Christ-life through rebirth. Accordingly, we who have His life must endeavor to live daily as He would, which means we cannot pursue our own ambitions or lusts.

> *For the love of Christ compels us, because we judge thus: that if one died for all, then all died; and He died for all, that those who live should live no longer for themselves, but for Him who died for them and rose again"* (2 Cor. 5:14-15).

As Hosea is telling us, from God's perspective, a believer commits spiritual adultery when he or she lives a carnal life in lieu of a crucified life. It angers the Lord and summons His chastening hand to discipline on the believer. The Lord knows that we will be most joyful and fruitful while remaining on the "straight and narrow" way.

> *Adulterers and adulteresses! Do you not know that friendship with the world is enmity with God? Whoever therefore wants to be a friend of the world makes himself an enemy of God. Or do you think that the Scripture says in vain, "The Spirit who dwells in us yearns jealously"? But He gives more grace. Therefore He says: "God resists the proud, but gives grace to the humble." Therefore submit to God. Resist the devil and he will flee from you. Draw near to God and He will draw near to you. Cleanse your hands, you sinners; and purify your hearts, you double-minded* (Jas. 4:4-8).

James also reminds us that *"a double-minded man [is] unstable in all his ways"* (Jas. 1:8). Sadly, Israel was proving this true. Their lack of respect for Jehovah and His Law was obvious in their disregard for legal agreements and flippantly entering into litigation against each other for selfish gain (v. 4). When God's people venture away from the Lord, it always results in an unstable life and in failure of those things which matter for eternity.

Israel would discover this certainty too late – for judgment was coming and it would spread over the land like lethal hemlock. Hemlock is translated from the Hebrew *ro'sh*, which is also used to speak of an asp's deadly "venom" or "poison" (Deut. 32:33; Job 20:16). The thought is that death would spread over the entire land when Assyria invaded. Because Israel sowed corruption in the land, they would certainly reap what they had sown. Israel's political autonomy would be crushed and the Jews would comprehend too late the consequences of not fearing Jehovah (v. 3). The aftermath of judgment would be so harsh that they would also realize that no human king could rectify their situation – they were completely at God's mercy.

To eliminate any confusion on that matter, the prophet foretells particular events of the imminent Assyrian invasion, so that the Jews would be reminded later that their exile was under God's control (vv. 5-8). Jeroboam's golden-calf image at Bethel (Beth Aven) will be triumphantly carried away by Assyrian soldiers and presented to their king in Assyria; this will cause great consternation to the inhabitants of Samaria and the pagan priests (vv. 5-6). Either in its removal or after its transport to Assyria, the calf would *"be broken to pieces"* (8:6). The altar associated with the calf was destroyed.

Additionally, the prophet predicted that the king of Israel shall be cut off and the sacred high places and gardens for pagan worship will be destroyed. Briers and thistles shall spring up in their ruins (vv. 7-8). Utter despair will grip the hearts of Jewish survivors, who will beg the mountains and hills to *"Cover us!"* and *"Fall on us!"* What irony! In utter desperation these pathetic pagans cry out to the very mountains and hills on which they had erected shrines and altars to Baal to cover them.

To yearn for what is dreaded – death – instead of life under God's correction verifies the utter depravity of God's covenant people at this juncture. The full harvest of a God-shunning, self-willed, carnal life has now come to fruition and was deemed to be so miserable that it was not worth living. Similarly, those following the Antichrist during the Tribulation Period will become so disillusioned and distraught that they will beg for death in order to escape the Lamb's escalating judgments (Rev. 6:15-16, 9:6).

Hosea again refers to the grotesque conduct of the Gibeonites centuries earlier to pose an object lesson (v. 9). J. M. Flanigan explains:

> The story of Gibeah is a sordid one. It is a story of rape and murder which were the cause and prelude to fierce battles in which tens of thousands perished. The whole account is told in detail in Judges 19-20. The people ought to have learned that such iniquity must be, and would be judged, but since the days of Gibeah they had persisted in their sin with impunity. In the battle of Gibeah it is said that "they stood." The tribes of Israel remained and were not overtaken in the battle as were the perpetrators of the iniquity. The tribe of Benjamin was decimated and Gibeah was destroyed in those days. Should not Israel have learned the awful price to be paid for iniquity? But since the days of Gibeah they had continued in sin.[24]

Although initially all the tribes were appalled by the Gibeonites' lewd behavior, their example eventually became the pattern. Gibeonites were of the tribe of Benjamin, which was nearly eradicated by the ensuing Civil War. In fact, the Lord considered Israel's behavior now worse than guilty Benjamin in bygone days, for they had not learned from that example. Hence, the Lord promised to punish them with exile and captivity according to His timetable for *"their double sin"* (v. 10). This verse reminds us that though we choose our sin, it is God who chooses the consequences of our sin. The timing of His correction will be the best expression of His love and will be the optimal time to achieve our repentance and restoration.

Israel should have yielded to God's plan, which is likened to a trained heifer dragging a threshing board across grain (v. 11). This was a relatively easy task, plus the heifer received the benefit of feeding on some of the grain that had been separated from the chaff. However, stubborn Israel sought the much harder work of plowing. She preferred the heavy yoke of sin and suffering a hard life rather than yielding to the Master's design for her and enjoying a less stressful life with His approval and blessing. God would honor her choice; indeed she would plow hard and to utter exhaustion.

Verses 12-13 are a refreshing oasis of mercy in a wilderness of condemnation and despair. Despite Israel's clear guilt and God's anger towards His people after centuries of rebellion, God was still willing to offer them restoration and blessing through genuine repentance:

> *Sow for yourselves righteousness; reap in mercy; break up your fallow ground, for it is time to seek the Lord, till He comes and rains righteousness on you. You have plowed wickedness; you have reaped iniquity. You have eaten the fruit of lies, because you trusted in your own way, in the multitude of your mighty men* (vv. 12-13).

Their pursuit of righteousness would result in experiencing God's overflowing mercy, but this could not occur until the sin encrusting their hearts was broken away. To stress this point, Hosea employs an agricultural analogy of a farmer plowing hardened fallow ground. The phrase "fallow ground" is found only twice in the Bible: in this chapter as directed towards Israel, and also in the book of Jeremiah as declared to Judah: *"Break up your fallow ground, and do not sow among thorns"* (Jer. 4:3). Both Jeremiah and Hosea had similarly long prophetic ministries, though Hosea preceded Jeremiah by a century.

The Jews were a nation of shepherds and farmers. So when Hosea sternly warned them to plow up their fallow ground, they knew what he meant. Fallow ground is soil that was once cultivated, but now lies waste and is completely fruitless. The longer it remains uncultivated, the harder it becomes. In order for it to be made profitable again, it must be broken up with a plow; only then can it be planted again and made fruitful.

The purpose of the soil analogy was to call Israel to repentance. It would be better for them to plow up their own fallow ground (hearts) in response to God's word, than for God to enforce His word through the Assyrians without their cooperation. Choosing to cultivate righteousness ensures the child of God will reap the unfailing love and favor of God. However, Israel had lost the pliability of their hearts through longstanding wicked, deceptive, and selfish behavior; this hardened evil condition could no longer be permitted to continue.

If Israel did not repent, the Lord would bring Assyria to destroy their fortresses, dethrone their king, and decimate the land (vv. 14-15). Hosea even tells them the type of barbarity they would suffer at the hands of the Assyrians – infants would be dashed against the rocks before their mothers' eyes and then the mothers would be thrown on top of their shattered children (e.g. 2 Kgs. 8:12; Isa. 13:16). It was their choice, but their encrusted hearts would be plowed up and made fertile again towards God one way or another.

Jeremiah's message to adulterous Judah, though very similar to Hosea's, contained the additional warning against sowing among thorns (Jer. 4:3). In Matthew 13, the Lord Jesus likened the ground in which seed (identified as the Word of God) is sown to the spiritual disposition of human hearts. In the same parable the Lord used the imagery of thorny ground to describe how worldliness chokes out the impact of God's Word in a person's life (i.e. the acceptance of the gospel message). A similar spiritual consequence is true for believers also; lingering complacency to obey God's Word causes our hearts to become hard, cold, and dry; the only solution is to plow them up. Living under the shade of briars and thistles will block the light necessary for growth and fruit-bearing. It will amount to a wasted existence.

For revival to occur in the Church, we must be open to God's Word and shun worldliness. God's Word must penetrate our minds and take root before we can bear fruit. Revival must start in the Church before it can spill over and affect the unregenerate. If there was ever a time for spiritual revival within the House of God, it is now. Oh God, may it start with me!

*Will You not revive us again, that Your people may rejoice in You?*
*Show us Your mercy, Lord, and grant us Your salvation* (Ps. 85:6-7).

## Meditation

To have a faith, therefore, or a trust in anything, where God hath not promised, is plain idolatry, and a worshipping of thine own imagination instead of God.

— William Tyndale

The essence of idolatry is the entertainment of thoughts about God that are unworthy of Him.

— A. W. Tozer

69

Revival is a renewed conviction of sin and repentance, followed by an intense desire to live in obedience to God. It is giving up one's will to God in deep humility.

— Charles Finney

# Enduring Love
## Hosea 11

This chapter begins as the last one did, by contrasting Israel's early history with their present situation. Hosea, as inspired by the Holy Spirit, has shown that he cannot concentrate very long on the waywardness of his countrymen and their impending doom without reverting to the happier days of Israel's infancy (e.g., vv. 1-3). However, it must be noted, Hosea is not speaking first-person in this chapter; rather, the Lord is directly addressing Israel. William MacDonald notes that it is helpful to distinguish who is speaking in the final four chapters of the book to better understand the context of what is being said:

The Lord: 11:1-12:1
Hosea: 12:2-6
The Lord: 12:7-11
Hosea: 12:12-13:1
The Lord: 13:2-14
Hosea: 13:15-14:3
The Lord: 14:4-8[25]

The Lord begins by reviewing Israel's early years: *"When Israel was a child, I loved him, and out of Egypt I called My son"* (v. 1). While the primary focus of this verse is to remind Israel of God's past goodness and to call them to repentance, Matthew quotes verse 1 to affirm its messianic fulfillment. After Herod the Great's death, the Lord called His Son the Lord Jesus out of Egypt, where Joseph had fled with his family, having been warned in a dream to do so (Matt. 2:15). This is one of dozens of Old Testament prophecies pertaining to Messiah's first advent that is surreptitiously folded into the sacred page. However, with the light of New Testament revelation, the meaning of these prophecies becomes brilliantly visible.

The Lord loved the forming growing Jewish nation in Egypt as a son. He delivered Israel from his bondage in Egypt so as to enjoy communion with them through an everlasting covenant. The Lord then brought them into a fertile land where He could care and provide for the growing nation. However, in time, His people withdrew from Him to pursue and to worship other gods (e.g., Baals, v. 2). God sent His prophets to call them back to Him, but the more they pleaded God's longings for them, the further His people retreated.

This abandonment was despite God's tender loving care and goodness shown to His son. Like a good father, He had gently held His son's arms to teach him how to walk so he would not fall and hurt himself (v. 3). Through Israel's maturing years in the Sinai Wilderness and their entrance into Canaan, God sustained His people and lovingly cared for them (v. 4). Just as a good herdsman does not overdrive his stock, the Lord *"drew them with gentle cords, with bands of love."* Continuing the herdsman metaphor, the Lord did more than just care compassionately for Israel; He also gently removed the yoke of bondage from their necks. His people, like oxen that have plowed all day, were badly bruised when they were freed from Egyptian slavery, so the Lord carefully removed their yoke to avoid causing them needless pain.

Regrettably, Israel had grown up to be an ungrateful, rebellious son who needed correction. The rod of reproof would be the Assyrians (v. 5) who would put them back into their Egyptian situation of bondage, without returning to the land of Egypt. Because of Israel's obstinate refusal to return to the Lord, they would not enjoy God's goodness, but instead would be devoured by the sword and their cities would be destroyed (v. 6). Probably the best understanding of the allusive Hebrew language of verse 7 is that Israel had rejected God's pleas through His prophets and would suffer appropriately for their backsliding ways.

God's fervent passion for Israel and His aching heart for His wayward people is revealed in verses 8 and 9 with an intensity that few passages of Scripture can rival:

*How can I give you up, Ephraim? How can I hand you over, Israel?*
*How can I make you like Admah? How can I set you like Zeboiim?*
*My heart churns within Me; My sympathy is stirred. I will not execute*
*the fierceness of My anger; I will not again destroy Ephraim. For I*

*am God, and not man, the Holy One in your midst; and I will not come with terror.*

The Lord's four rhetorical questions demonstrate God's resolve to never permanently abandon Israel or completely destroy them in judgment, as He had Zeboiim and Admah with Sodom and Gomorrah in Abraham's day (v. 8, Gen. 14:2, 19:24-25). He promised not to punish Ephraim to this extent. Furthermore, though Ephraim would be severely punished, God would temper His wrath with mercy. This would ensure their continuation and the Lord's opportunity to dwell among them again as the Holy One, who transcends all that is fallible, for God is not a man (v. 9).

After their long exile is over, God will roar like a lion, powerfully drawing His now refined people home again (v. 10). At that juncture, a fearful awe of Jehovah will permeate their souls as when Moses first introduced them to Him at Mount Sinai (v. 11). Their flight from Assyria (the location) and from Egypt (picturing bondage) will be as swift as a flying dove.

Verse 12 (which is the first verse of chapter 12 in the Hebrew Bible) commences the final section of the book in which Hosea concludes the Lord's case against Israel. The prophet's closing statement squarely affixes guilt on the entire nation of Israel, although Ephraim is singled out as the chief offender. The Northern Kingdom was full of lies and deceit. Ephraim's utter hypocrisy and unfaithfulness was an affront to the wholly faithful One in whose essence is truth.

The latter part of verse 12 is rendered differently in various translations: *"But Judah still walks with God, even with the Holy One who is faithful"* (NKJV). *"Judah is also unruly against God, even against the Holy One who is faithful"* (NASB). Regardless of which meaning is correct, the central idea is that Judah, though unruly and worthy of rebuke, had not digressed from walking with the Lord to the degree that Ephraim had. Consequently, Judah would be tested and chastened by the Assyrians, but not utterly devastated as Israel would be.

Israel had rejected the tender and enduring love of God, as superbly revealed in this chapter and would suffer tremendous loss for doing so. However, a message of hope is also conveyed to Israel: Because of His covenant promises, God's heart still yearns for you; He cannot give up on you, but will do whatever it takes to secure your love and devotion again.

## Meditation

The love of God is greater far,
Than tongue or pen can ever tell;
It goes beyond the highest star,
And reaches to the lowest hell;
The guilty pair, bowed down with care,
God gave His Son to win;
His erring child He reconciled,
And pardoned from his sin.

Could we with ink the ocean fill,
And were the skies of parchment made,
Were every stalk on earth a quill,
And every man a scribe by trade;
To write the love of God above
Would drain the ocean dry;
Nor could the scroll contain the whole,
Though stretched from sky to sky.

— Frederick M. Lehman

# Israel Further Rebuked
Hosea 12

Israel's unfaithfulness to God was demonstrated in her domestic injustice (deceit and violence characterized the society) and by her foreign policy of seeking aid from other nations (e.g., Assyria and Egypt; v. 1). Both activities violated their covenant with God (His Law) and would prove to be as fruitless as pursuing the wind for nourishment. No matter what they tried to be satisfied with, apart from the Lord, they would remain empty – wind is a poor diet for a God-starving nation.

Although Hosea's ministry focused mainly on the Northern Kingdom, he sporadically warned Judah of following Israel's evil ways, as he does again in verse 2. God had a legitimate contention against the Southern Kingdom also, but would wait until the appropriate time to invoke corrective measures.

The prophet pauses from affixing guilt on Israel to again call her to repentance by reminding her of God's dealings with her forefather Jacob (vv. 3-6). God had informed Rebekah, Jacob's mother, that she would give birth to twin boys who would father two nations. At birth, the older son was hairy and red; thus, he was named Esau, meaning "hairy." During the birthing process, the younger son grabbed the heel of his older brother and was thus named Jacob, which means the "heel-catcher," or by implication "schemer" (v. 3; Gen. 25:26). This scene foreshadows the type of person Jacob would become. Indeed, later in his life he shrewdly acquired Esau's birthright in exchange for a bowl of bean soup (Gen. 27:35-36). Twenty years later, however, the schemer is faced with an unavoidable situation which threatens death on two fronts (Laban from the north and Esau from the south).

God graciously intervened through a dream to rescue Jacob from Laban, which left his brother Esau approaching from the south with 400 armed men. The news of Esau's approach unnerved Jacob, who immediately went into planning mode to try to resolve the situation peacefully through a goodwill gift of several hundred animals (Gen.

75

32:7). Jacob chose to meet imminent danger by his own devices – he did pray for God's help, but only after seeking to manage the situation himself. On this matter of dependence, C. H. Mackintosh writes: "We must be really brought to the end of everything with which self has aught to do, for until then God cannot show Himself. But we can never get to the end of our plans until we have been brought to the end of ourselves."[26]

On the eve of confronting Esau, Jacob isolated himself from his family to fret alone. The Lord, incognito, visited Jacob (Gen. 32:32). Apparently nothing was said, but the Lord initiated a wrestling match with Jacob, and Jacob was obliged to wrestle the unidentified man all night (v. 4; Gen. 32:24-25). Hosea refers to this theophany as an Angel (or Messenger) of God. When the Second Person of the Godhead appeared in Old Testament days, He was often referred to as "the Angel of the Lord," a title highlighting His messenger role. However, in the New Testament the Son became God's message to humanity and therefore is called the Word (e.g., John 1:1).

Both the Lord and Jacob desired something from the other. Jacob, nearly 100 years old, wanted a blessing from the Lord. The Lord wanted Jacob to be broken and yielded before Him. The Lord could have "pinned" Jacob at any time but did not choose to do so. The Lord was patient with Jacob and was willing to wrestle the whole night with him. What was the Lord's purpose in this? It was certainly not to defeat or destroy Jacob, but rather to teach him to be yielded and broken before Him. If the Lord has ever wrestled with you, it is for the same purpose – to obtain brokenness in order to bless you.

By divine skill, Jacob was crippled, making wrestling very difficult and painful (Gen. 32:32). Jacob, being disabled, resorted to the only tactic he had left, holding on to the Lord with all his might. It was at this moment that Jacob was blessed by God. Jacob had sent his family over the brook Jabbok while he remained on the other side alone. Ironically, Jabbok means "he will empty." Once Jacob's "will" had been broken and his self-dependence emptied, he then became a vessel fit for God's use. That day, Jacob received a new name, *Israel*, and a new walk, or rather a limp. The pain and the loss of mobility would be a constant reminder that he had wrestled with God and that God had won!

Hosea then reminded Israel that once Jacob returned to his homeland, God spoke with Jacob again to ensure that he returned to

Bethel where he had previously experienced the Lord God of hosts (v. 5; Gen. 35:1). Because Jacob had delayed in obeying the Lord's command to return to Bethel, his family suffered failure and harm (Gen. 34).

In his early days, Jacob was a heel-grabber, and because Jacob's descendants now held corrupt balances in their hands (alluding to dishonest business practices), they were following his example. The prophet was warning fraudulent Israel that the events in Jacob's life were about to be repeated unless the nation came to the end of themselves and relinquished control of their lives to God through complete obedience and faith.

If they did this, Hosea promised that God would help them in the same way He preserved and blessed their father Jacob: *"So you, by the help of your God, return; observe mercy and justice, and wait on your God continually"* (v. 6). God would not be fooled by mere lip service; true repentance would be evident by the paramount display of mercy and righteousness in the land.

Jacob labored fourteen years as a shepherd to secure his two wives Rachel and Leah. God was laboring also to secure the affection of His wife and with His assistance, Israel would return to Him in purity! C. A. Coates reminds us that the example of God and Jacob serving to secure a wife is brought over into the relationship of Christ and the Church:

> How Christ served when He delivered Himself up for the Church! And in sanctifying and cleansing her by the washing of water by the Word, He is serving that He may have His wife in suitability to Himself. He serves by means of the gifts He has given. If Israel [Jacob] for a wife kept sheep, it suggests to us that all the shepherd-service of Christ to His own has in view that He may have them as His wife. Whatever He does for us individually will ultimately work out in His having the Church for the satisfaction of His love, and in responsive affection to Him as His wife. The book of Hosea would raise the question with us whether His blessed service has had the present result of really securing us in wifely affection and devotion. Alas! Much of the Christian profession has taken on the character of the great harlot spoken of in Revelation 17.[27]

What Christ longs to hear from His Church and God yearns to hear from Israel is what their father Jacob said to the Lord on the day of his brokenness, *"I will not let You go"* (Gen. 32:26). Jacob had sought to be alone in misery, but after embracing the Lord, his soul clung to His presence and he was blessed. The Lord desired no less from Israel in Hosea's day, or from believers today!

To eliminate any confusion on the matter, Hosea describes how true repentance would be recognized in Israel: God's people would cease from defrauding each other and from proud self-sufficiency (vv. 7-8). There would be no dishonest scales found in the land and Israel's security would be in her God, not in her amassed wealth (much of which was obtained through duplicitous means). If His people persisted in rebellion and ingratitude, then the Lord promised to strip them of their resources and lead them back into the wilderness (referring to their previous post-Egyptian exodus experience; v. 9). There, the Lord would teach them through His prophets, by visions, and through a life-depending existence to trust in Him alone (v. 10).

This environment was just the opposite of their present situation. Hence the prophet rhetorically asks: *"Is there iniquity in Gilead? Surely they are vanity: they sacrifice bullocks in Gilgal; yea, their altars are as heaps in the furrows of the fields"* (v. 11; KJV). The prophet asks and promptly answers his own question to accentuate the fact that there was nothing but iniquity in the land. Gilead was a priestly city and a City of Refuge situated on the Eastern Plateau, while Gilgal, just west of the Jordan River, was the historical location in which God began with His people again under Joshua's leadership. Both cities were equally idolatrous and hence represented Israel's spiritual disposition on both sides of the Jordan. This sadly meant that God had to lead His people out of Israel and into a wilderness to prompt their brokenness. There they would again recognize Him as the one true God – their God!

Having revealed God's plan to extend mercy to Israel in the future, Hosea again reminds them of their forefather Jacob's humble beginnings. Jacob fled to Syria and there labored attending sheep to acquire a wife (through Laban's trickery Jacob was forced to labor for two wives). Later, his family was called back to Canaan, where the Lord again preserved Jacob from Laban's rage (v. 13). As time passed, Jacob's family relocated to Egypt because of a severe famine and was eventually enslaved. Yet, God was faithful to Jacob and delivered his descendants from Pharaoh through the prophet Moses.

F. M. Flanigan reminds us that the life of Moses also fits the pattern of humble beginnings and divine deliverance just affirmed in Jacob's life.

> Then there was the great Moses, but he too had been a fugitive, and he too had kept sheep (Ex. 3:1). There is an interesting play upon words in these verses. The word "kept" in the phrase "he *kept* sheep" (v. 12) is the same word as "preserved" in (v. 13), "by a prophet was he *preserved.*" In both places it is the Hebrew *shamar,* meaning to protect or guard. Just as the patriarch [Jacob] and prophet [Moses] had "kept" sheep, so had Jehovah "kept" the nation. How could they turn away from Him to lifeless idols, He who had led them like a flock (Ps. 77:20, 80:1)?[28]

While it was true that Israel's idolatry had provoked God to anger and there would be harsh consequences for their sin, the prophet's appeal to Jacob's and Moses' situation showed that there would be the opportunity for future deliverance (v. 14). This would occur when the nation was broken before God, just as Jacob and Moses were, and then sought God's help, just as both men did. The door of repentance permitting Israel's approach back to God was not locked, but in Israel's present spiritual state, there was no desire to find it, let alone to knock on it.

## Meditation

> Come, O thou traveler unknown, whom still I hold but cannot see,
> My company before is gone, and I am left alone with thee.
> With thee all night I mean to stay and wrestle till the break of day.
> My prayer hath power with God, the grace unspeakable I now receive
> Through faith I see Thee face to face, I see Thee face to face, and live.
> In vain I have not wept and strove; Thy nature and Thy name is love.
>
> — Charles Wesley

# Israel's Sin Is Stored Up
Hosea 13

Judah was the defining tribe of the Southern Kingdom, though Benjamin and Simeon dwelled there also. Likewise, Ephraim was the strongest tribe of the Northern Kingdom and unfortunately misused their principal position to lead the other tribes in the north into idolatry: *"When Ephraim spoke, trembling, he exalted himself in Israel; but when he offended through Baal worship, he died"* (v. 1).

Northern Israel's first king, Jeroboam, an Ephraimite, instituted a system of pagan worship honoring Baal to prevent the northern tribes from returning to Jerusalem to worship Jehovah as required by the Law. It was not long afterwards that Israel was full of various idols and images. Spiritually speaking, no matter how strongly one appears to be living for God, he or she will always finish badly if he or she departs from Him. Ephraim began as a strong leader able to defend its brethren, but in time they turned from the Lord and led the other northern tribes to do the same.

For the third time, Hosea mentions one of the chief offenses against God – the worship of the golden calf image erected at Bethel with its altar (v. 2, 8:4-5, 10:5). All those who lowered themselves to venerate this image by kissing it would be swept away in judgment. The prophet applies four metaphors to illustrate the brevity of life that an idolater under judgment could expect. He is likened to a passing morning cloud, to the morning dew, to chaff blown from the threshing floor, and to smoke from a chimney (v. 3). Israel was worthless chaff that God was about to blow from His threshing floor!

Again the Lord reminded Israel of their humble beginnings, and that without His deliverance and care they would have perished in Egypt. The Lord asserts that no one else could deliver them from death and bondage – He was the one true God (v. 4). But His care for Israel did not stop with the Exodus. He provided for His people in the wilderness, and then led them like sheep into the green pastures of Canaan and cared for them there (v. 5).

Sadly, once in this land full of milk and honey they became proud and self-sufficient and in time forgot the Lord: *"When they had pasture, they were filled; they were filled and their heart was exalted; therefore they forgot Me"* (v. 6). This was exactly what Moses warned the Israelites not to do once God brought them into Canaan: *"When you have eaten and are full, then beware, lest you forget the Lord"* (Deut. 6:11-12). He further warned, *"For the Lord your God is a jealous God among you, lest the anger of the Lord your God be aroused against you and destroy you from the face of the earth"* (Deut. 6:15). Instead of being filled with what was praiseworthy to God, the Jews were filled with their own pastures, that is, whatever they longed for and had previously murmured to God about in the wilderness. They had what they lusted for (i.e., what their souls really wanted) and hence did not need the Lord anymore.

Their ingratitude and desertion provoked the Lord's anger. He promised to be like a lion or a leopard that suddenly leaps on and tears its prey (i.e., the unprotected sheepfold of Israel), or like a sow-bear who fiercely attacks those threatening her cubs (vv. 7-8). Because of Israel's rejection, her divine Helper had become her foremost Antagonist (v. 9). As a result, the human political leader that they desperately wanted to deliver them from trouble was non-existent; only God could save them (v. 10).

Hosea illustrates this latter point through a brief history lesson. During the days of the prophet Samuel, Israel had also demanded a king to rule over them. This disappointed Samuel, who sought the Lord's counsel in prayer (1 Sam. 8:6). The Lord responded to His prophet's petition saying:

> *Heed the voice of the people in all that they say to you; for they have not rejected you, but they have rejected Me, that I should not reign over them. According to all the works which they have done since the day that I brought them up out of Egypt, even to this day – with which they have forsaken Me and served other gods – so they are doing to you also. Now therefore, heed their voice. However, you shall solemnly forewarn them, and show them the behavior of the king who will reign over them* (1 Sam. 8:7-9).

The rebellion of the people angered the Lord. As He explained to Samuel, the people were rejecting their almighty God and His goodness for a selfish, fallible human leader. Israel was still suffering from the

81

same ideology in Hosea's day. So the people were reminded that God appointed Saul as their king in His anger to teach them the repercussions of rejecting Him (v. 11; 1 Sam. 12:12). This verse may also refer to Jeroboam I whom God appointed to discipline them, but not to lead the northern tribes into gross sin (1 Kgs. 11:28-31). The latter part of verse 11, *"and took him away in My wrath,"* likely refers to God's removal of Israel's monarchies forever through the Assyrian invasion; King Hoshea was the last king of Israel (2 Kgs. 17:1-6).

Ephraim should not think that, because the Lord had not chastened them for over two centuries of idolatry, God had forgotten their sins. Not only did God possess a written record of these offenses, they had been "stored up" so to speak in a secure place to ensure that they would not be lost or forgotten (v. 12). It would be foolish for Israel to think that time erases wrongs. Humanly speaking, we forget details over time, but God's very existence is outside time and though He may choose not to remember confessed sin, He cannot forget anything!

Alas, Israel had not responded to the call for repentance and is likened to a stubborn baby who will not be delivered from his mother's womb despite her exertions (v. 13). The travail of the mother pictures Israel's future anguish and pain caused by Assyria, while the baby in the womb depicts Israel's stubborn, unrepentant nature which precludes God's deliverance. How foolish – for it will result in the death of both the mother and the baby. Regrettably, Israel had missed the appropriate time for repentance and as a result they would suffer death.

It is with this understanding that verse 14 must be interpreted; otherwise the verse would become a confusing interruption to the thematic flow throughout the chapter. Furthermore, how could benefits of redemption be reconciled with God's statement of having no pity on those dead in sin?

> *I will ransom them from the power of the grave; I will redeem them from death. O Death, I will be your plagues! O Grave, I will be your destruction! Pity is hidden from My eyes* (v. 14).

While it is true that Hosea has routinely shifted from assigning guilt to calls of repentance, and from pronouncing judgments to providing hope of recovery, the insertion of a double-thematic flip-flop in one verse seems unlikely here. With this premise, R. B. Chisholm Jr. explains what the poetic expression of verse 14 likely refers to:

The first two statements may be translated better as rhetorical questions implying a negative answer: "Shall I ransom them from the power of Sheol? Shall I redeem them from death?" The next two questions: "Where, O death, are your plagues? Where, O grave, is your destruction?" would then be appeals for death to unleash its "plagues" and "destruction" against Ephraim, not a triumphant cry of victory over death. Of course the Apostle Paul, writing under the inspiration of the Holy Spirit, applied the language of this text in the latter sense (1 Cor. 15:55-56). However, in that context Paul was drawing on the language of Scripture as traditionally understood (from the Septuagint); he was not offering a textual and exegetical analysis of Hosea 13:14.[29]

Obviously, the Lord would redeem Israel from death at a later date, but this verse affirms that at this time death is deserved. The prophet Jeremiah, writing a century later, does speak of Israel's redemption: *"For the Lord hath redeemed Jacob and ransomed him from the hand of him that was stronger than he"* (Jer. 31:11). God would deliver the Jews from the Babylonians later, but the Northern Kingdom would not be delivered from Assyria now. At this juncture, the Lord's compassion was removed; God was about to blow a hot east wind on Israel (speaking of the Assyrians) which would result in widespread atrocities against His rebellious people (vv. 15-16).

The Church is also a ransomed possession of the Lord; *"For you were bought at a price; therefore glorify God in your body and in your spirit, which are God's"* (1 Cor. 6:20). The Church, like Israel, is waiting for the culmination of her redemption in Christ. Paul acknowledges that Christ "gave Himself a ransom for all, to be testified in due time" (1 Tim. 2:6). Israel is waiting for Christ's second advent to establish His literal earthly kingdom; this will fulfill every aspect of the Abrahamic covenant. Then, the Jewish nation will be fully redeemed (i.e., Christ's shed blood will become effectual for her) and she will remain with the Lord forever.

The Church, however, is waiting to be instantaneously snatched away from the earth to be with the Lord in heaven in glorified bodies (1 Thess. 4:13-18; Phil. 3:21). In that event, the same phenomenal power which defeated the power of hell at Christ's resurrection will be exercised to resurrect believers from Satan's domain – the world. Paul wanted the Christians at Corinth to understand this important truth, saying, *"Who delivered us from so great a death, and does deliver us;*

*in whom we trust that He will still deliver us"* (2 Cor. 1:10). Likewise, to the saints at Ephesus he wrote:

> *The eyes of your understanding being enlightened; that you may know what is the hope of His calling, what are the riches of the glory of His inheritance in the saints, and what is the exceeding greatness of His power toward us who believe, according to the working of His mighty power which He worked in Christ when He raised Him from the dead and seated Him at His right hand in the heavenly places* (Eph. 1:18-20).

Positionally speaking, the believer has already died with Christ, but, practically speaking, the believer will be delivered through death at the rapture of the Church to be with Christ forever.

Hosea's rhetorical statements in verse 14 were not intended to instill hope at that time, but the timeless truth of Scripture is that God is the only One who can redeem those justified in Christ from the power of the grave and from death! Accordingly, every child of God will ultimately experience the power of God and will be brought through death and will then receive an incorruptible and immortal body (1 Cor. 15:51-52). This is our blessed hope!

## Meditation

Do not look to your hope, but to Christ, the source of your hope.

— Charles Spurgeon

I am still in the land of the dying; I shall be in the land of the living soon.

— John Newton (his final words)

# Turning and Healing
## Hosea 14

Thankfully, Hosea did not conclude his book with harsh judicial denunciations, scarcely interrupted in the last several chapters, but with a fresh call to repentance: *"O Israel, return to the Lord your God, for you have stumbled because of your iniquity"* (v. 1). Some people do stumble without falling, but Israel had stumbled in such a way that they were destined to hit the ground hard. Even though the Lord knew that Israel's deep-seated arrogance and wickedness would require stern judgment to change, He again summoned them to repent. God foreknew that this call would be ignored, but He wanted a future generation of Jews to understand how to return to Him and how much He loved them.

So Hosea, speaking to that chastened and despairing generation, tells them what genuine repentance looks like: *"Take words with you, and return to the Lord. Say to Him, 'Take away all iniquity; receive us graciously, for we will offer the sacrifices of our lips'"* (v. 2). A truly repentant sinner acknowledges the validity of God's Word by returning to God and by specifically confessing failure to conform to His Word, asking Him for forgiveness, and then expressing both appreciation for His forgiveness and a willingness to obey His Word in the future. This meant that the repentant Jewish remnant in the future would not trust in Assyria's assistance and would purge all their hand crafted idols. Through painful centuries they would learn that in their God alone *"the fatherless finds mercy"* (v. 3). H. A. Ironside explains the idea behind this future realization:

> Israel had been Jehovah's son, whom He had called out of Egypt. But they had forgotten Him, and done despite to His Spirit of grace. Therefore He had pronounced the Lo-ammi and Lo-ruhamah sentences upon them, as we saw in the beginning of the prophecy. Thus, when they return, they come in on the ground of pure grace and mercy. They come as "the fatherless," not to claim the rights of a child, but to be the subjects of that lovingkindness which is better

85

than life. How suited to the lips of the Remnant of the last days will be the words of this prayer![30]

To this repentant generation the Lord promised to extinguish His anger and again demonstrate His love by healing His once unfaithful people from their backsliding (v. 4). The solution to all Israel's sorrows was not self-deliverance, but to experience supernatural rejuvenation, which is likened to the morning dew which comes from above to refresh the grass and trees below (v. 5).

Both verses 4 and 5 begin with the Lord saying, *"I will."* Only the Lord could heal, refresh, restore, and bless His people in the land of Israel again. Furthermore, He would do it in such a way that the Jews would bless others through their agricultural prosperity (vv. 6-7). The Lord then suggests a number of foliage metaphors to express the benefits Israel will experience when they rest in and abide with Him: He says the Jewish nation will be beautiful, fragrant, fruitful, and will exceedingly increase in every imaginable God-honoring way.

Enjoying such a full existence the nation will gladly affirm, *"What have I to do anymore with idols?"* And Jehovah, observing this delightful scene, will affirm that He is like a tall, flourishing cypress tree carefully watching over His people and gladly sharing His fruit with them (v. 8).

The book concludes with a wise axiom which summarizes the theme of Hosea's messages to the Northern Kingdom: *"Who is wise? Let him understand these things. Who is prudent? Let him know them. For the ways of the Lord are right; the righteous walk in them, but transgressors stumble in them"* (v. 9). Simply put, the wise know that what God says is right, and it is what they must do to be blessed by God. The foolish reject God's Word and suffer His indignation.

Although Hosea's messages have been mainly directed at the Northern Kingdom, their backslidings portray all the failings of God's people in every age. Likewise, God's recovery method of reestablishing the wayward has not changed throughout the course of time. May all those who have wisdom and understanding learn from this account of God's dealings with Israel and ever yearn to enter into all His prerogatives!

Sadly, Israel ignored and rejected God's Law, the basis of their covenant with God, and His attempts to restore them to Himself. God's enduring love, however, would not be satisfied until through punitive measures, He had reinstated His people to a place of communion and blessing. This was the message illustrated to Israel so colorfully in the infidelity of Hosea's wife and also in her humbling and restoration – this would be Israel's story too!

When Christ returns to the earth, the spiritual blindness of the Jewish nation will come to an end. They will trust in the Lord Jesus Christ, their Messiah, the One they pierced two thousand years earlier and they will receive the Holy Spirit. All this to say that God is a covenant-keeping God and His marvelous plan for the Jewish nation is still unfolding and will be completed according to His sovereign purposes. God's love for the nation of Israel has never varied from the beginning, though her love for Him has waxed and waned through the centuries. Yet, in a coming day, the Jewish nation will be fully restored to God and will, with all saints forever, bask in His unchanging, forbearing love (Rom. 11:17-24). Then the entire world will witness the power of perfect, sacrificial, and abiding love that never gives up!

## Meditation

If you know that God loves you, you should never question a directive from Him. It will always be right and best. When He gives you a directive, you are not just to observe it, discuss it, or debate it. You are to obey it.

— Henry Blackaby

The Christian does not think God will love us because we are good, but that God will make us good because He loves us.

— C. S. Lewis

Love means to love that which is unlovable; or it is no virtue at all.

— G. K. Chesterton

# Joel

# Overview of Joel

## The Author

Joel was the son of Pethuel (1:1). Nothing else is known about him or his family, or where he resided. Joel's name means "Jehovah is God." Although not specifically stated, Joel's frequent references in chapters 2 and 3 to Judah, Zion, and Jerusalem seem to indicate that his ministry was mainly to the Southern Kingdom.

## Date

Because Joel does not mention any Jewish or Gentile kings, nor does he refer to Israel's enemies or well-known historical events in his prophecies, dating his book is difficult. The absence of Jewish kings' names in the text has caused some to conclude that the book was written in the era following the Babylonian exile. Many commentators, however, believe that Joel was among the oldest of God's writing prophets and lived towards the end of the ninth century B.C. This date would align with the reign of King Joash in Judah (835-796 B.C.) and perhaps, even as late as King Jehoash in Israel (798-782 B.C.). Gilliland presents the following argument as to why this is the best date for Joel's prophecies:

> First, the allusion in chapter 3 to the victory of Jehoshaphat in the Valley of Berachah would have been fresh in the memory of Jehoiada's contemporaries. That great victory over the enemies of Judah had happened only something like forty years previously (2 Chron. 20). Second, the enemies of Judah mentioned in Joel 3, the Phoenicians and Philistines (3:4), together with Edom and Egypt (3:19), are the very enemies which had, in the century before the time of Joash and Jehoiada, been a constant irritation to Judah and Jerusalem. The Egyptian Pharaoh, Shishak, had plundered Judah (925 B.C.) less than one hundred years before the commencement of Joash's reign. The rebellion of Edom had taken place less than twenty years before Joash came to the throne (2 Kgs. 8:20-22); about the same time, the Philistines, helped by the Arabians, invaded Judah and

inflicted heavy losses (2 Chron. 21:16-17). It may also be a further indicator of this earlier date that none of the later major foes of Judah, such as Assyria or Babylon, is mentioned in Joel.[31]

If this assessment is correct, Joel's prophecies would be the oldest among the Old Testament prophets and hence would establish a general eschatological framework on which all other inspired writers would build and further explain. As an example, both Peter and Paul quote Joel (Acts 2, Rom. 13) to explain God's dealings with Israel as relating to Christ. It is no surprise, then, that the last Old Testament prophecy that the Lord Jesus refers to, before ascending into Heaven, was Joel 2:28-29. The Lord reaffirmed God's promise to send His Spirit and that His disciples were to wait in Jerusalem for His coming (Acts 1:4-8). They obeyed the Lord and ten days later the Holy Spirit did indeed come upon them in Jerusalem, as recorded in Acts 2.

## Theme

The theme of Joel centers on the recurring expression of God's judgment of the wicked, "the Day of the Lord" (1:15, 2:1, 11, 31, 3:14). Joel employs this term more than any other prophet. In the first part of the book, the expression relates to the chastening of His people in the ninth century B.C. and God's calling them to repentance. In the latter part of the book, the Day of the Lord addresses a future day in which God will punish the wicked on the earth and work incredible feats to rescue His people from Gentile oppression. Joel uses the Day of the Lord in both a near-term and far-reaching fashion to proclaim God's message.

The Jewish nation was idolatrous and unrepentant, hence in the ninth century B.C. the Lord struck Israel with a locust plague to punish them (1:1-2:11). The prophet notes the uniqueness of this judgment to summon his countrymen to repentance (2:12-17). The latter section of the book speaks of the horrors of the Tribulation Period and the final restoration of Israel to commence the Kingdom Age (2:18-3:21).

## Outline

The Present Chastening (1:1-2:11)
A Call to Repentance (2:12-17)
The Promise of Renewal (2:18-27)
The Promise of the Holy Spirit (2:28-29)
The Future Day of the Lord – Israel's Final Deliverance (2:30-3:21)

# Devotions in Joel

# Has Anything Like This Happened Before?
Joel 1

Like Hosea, all that we know about Joel is his father's name, Pethuel (v. 1). As previously mentioned, Joel's name means "Jehovah is God." The prophecies of Joel are difficult to date as he references no monarchies or specific events to correlate with known history. As mentioned in the *Overview* section, many believe Joel's ministry occurred around the end of the ninth century B.C. If this assumption is true, Joel would be one of the oldest of the prophets. He would have prophesied just before King Jeroboam II sat on Israel's throne and about twenty to thirty years before the ministries of Hosea and Amos.

Joel's messages coincided with a devastating locust plague that impoverished much of Judah (1:1-2:1). The prophet uses the plague to indict and warn the Jews of their apostasy and call them to repentance. The plague is then used as a backdrop to explain God's future prerogatives to be accomplished in the Day of the Lord: purifying and restoring the Jewish nation to Himself, judging of the wicked (including Israel's enemies), and establishing Messiah's kingdom on earth.

The prophet begins by asking Israel's leaders and all the people a rhetorical question: *"Has anything like this happened in your days, or even in the days of your fathers?"* (v. 2). The obvious answer was "no." Even the oldest among them had never witnessed or heard of such a pervasive plague, one that would certainly be talked about for generations (v. 3). The point was that this was something completely new and that such an extraordinary measure could mean only one thing – God was trying to get their attention. Would they heed God's invitation or experience worse calamities?

The prophet identifies four successive waves of destructive locusts (chewing, swarming, crawling, and consuming) to portray the widespread devastation to the region's crops, vines, trees, and pasturelands (v. 4). Some commentators believe that the four distinct references relate to the stages of locust development from larva to maturity. However, it seems doubtful that all generations of countless insects would be at the same stage of development at the same time. Since the prophet does labor to identify four distinct periods of desolation, William MacDonald suggests that the four future world empires that would ravage Israel are in view: Babylon, Medo-Persia, Greece, and Rome.[32] This Gentile plague, so to speak, would end with Israel's final deliverance in the Day of the Lord.

Joel's opening section is imperative-enriched. Four of these commands: "Awake," "lament," "be ashamed," and "gird yourself and lament" form separate units of admonishment to different Jewish audiences: the drunkard (vv. 5-7), the land, perhaps speaking of all the people in the land (vv. 8-10), the farmers and vinedressers (vv. 11-12), and the priests (v. 13). The drunkards were to mourn for the locust had devoured the vines with the ferocity of a lion, even stripping the bark of the fig trees with their teeth (vv. 5-7). No vines meant no wine to be intoxicated by in the future.

R. B. Chisholm Jr. explains that the second command to lament actually pertains to the land. The land is personified as a virgin bride adorned in sackcloth and grieving over the death of her espoused husband (v. 8):

> The grammatical form of mourn in verse 8 (feminine singular) indicates that the addressee is neither the drunkards in verse 5, nor the farmers in verse 11 (both are addressed in the masculine plural). The land itself (2:18) or Jerusalem is probably addressed here, being personified as a virgin.[33]

*Bethulah* is the Hebrew word rendered "virgin" in verse 8, speaking of a young married woman still in the espousal phase of matrimony. This meant that she was under a marital covenant, but that the marriage had not yet been physically consummated. This new bride would have the highest and most joyful expectations of the future, and yet feel the deepest loss and have the most to mourn after hearing of her husband's demise. The illustration conveys the most comprehensive, unexpected loss and disappointment that could be imagined in human terms – such would be Israel's pain when the locust finished devouring the land. There would be no grain, oil, or wine in the land for the priests to offer to the Lord in daily sacrifices as required by the Law (v. 9). Additionally, Joel's overview indicates that there would be nothing in the land to sustain the people: *"the field is wasted, the land mourns; for the grain is ruined, the new wine is dried up, the oil fails"* (v. 10).

Obviously, the farmers and vinedressers expecting to rejoice at harvest time would lament because the locust had destroyed all the grain and fruit of the land (i.e., wheat, barley, apples, grapes, figs, dates, pomegranates, etc.; vv. 11-12). The priests would mourn in sackcloth, for they would lack the appropriate provisions to present grain and drinking offerings before the Lord (v. 13).

In the wake of such disappointment and calamity, Joel prescribes the appropriate response for the nation: they were to call "a sacred assembly" (a corporate fast) so that the leaders and common people could gather to seek the Lord through repentance (v. 14; Neh. 9:1-2).

## The Day of the Lord Is at Hand

Joel understood that the terrible locust plague was a precursor and sign of an even more horrific event that would devastate the entire world: *"Alas for the day!* **For the day of the Lord is at hand**; *it shall come as destruction from the Almighty"* (v. 15). H. A. Ironside explains the meaning of Joel's alarming appeal:

> The approaching day of the Lord is mentioned as an incentive to [fast and seek the Lord]. Not that the day of the Lord (which, in its full, prophetic sense, refers to the revelation of Jesus Christ to usher in the kingdom) was really to occur in their time; but as that day will be for the manifestation of all that has been in accordance with the mind of God, they were called upon to act then in the light of the day that was coming (ver. 16). In like manner are Christians exhorted to walk now in view of the day of Christ, when all our works shall be examined at His judgment seat. The all displaying light of that hour of manifestation should ever be shining upon our pathway that all our steps may be ordered in accord therewith.[34]

In the same way that the Church is to anticipate the Day of Christ (which speaks of the rapture of the Church and Judgment Seat of Christ), Israel was to live in respect to the Day of the Lord. To summarize, the Day of the Lord is an Old Testament term that speaks of those times when Jehovah intervened in a visible and powerful way to judge the wicked on earth. This meaning continues into the New

Testament and is further clarified to speak of the Tribulation Period and the Millennial Kingdom of Christ.

Peter tells us that *the Day of the Lord* and the Millennial Kingdom conclude with destruction of the earth (2 Pet. 3:10), and will be followed by *the Day of God*, often referred to as *the eternal state* (2 Pet. 3:12). Isaiah states that *"all the host of heaven shall be dissolved, and the heavens shall be rolled up like a scroll"* (Isa. 34:4). He later foretells that after the Millennial Kingdom, God will create a new heaven and new earth (Isa. 65:17) – a matter which John says occurs right after the 1000-year reign of Christ and the Great White Throne judgment of the wicked (Rev. 20:7-21:1).

During the Kingdom Age, Jerusalem will be the religious center of the world (Isa. 2:1-5). Christ will reign from there and all the nations will come there to praise, worship, and learn of Him. There will be no war or violence, only peace. All the earth will see the glory of the Lord Jesus (Isa. 60:18-20) and any nation opposing the Lord will be laid waste (Isa. 60:12). The Day of the Lord speaks of the era in which God will bring all this about. Ultimately, it will be Christ alone who will be exalted on earth.

Having summoned the nation to repent and sounded the alarm for failing to do so, Joel then returns to describing in verses 16-20 the aftermath of the locust plague. The goal of this review is to again assert his claim that a more terrible day was coming soon if the nation did not turn back to the Lord. If food was cut off now and every reason to be happy had vanished from the land because of the locust, think of how unbearable the situation will be during the Day of the Lord (v. 16). The plague was apparently accompanied by a drought, so that even the seeds that sprouted after the locust passed through soon shriveled in the hot sun (v. 17). Barns and storehouses were in shambles, meaning that there was no feed for starving livestock (v. 18).

Joel was not a coldhearted prophet who simply delivered God's word. He grieved over the wretched condition of his countrymen and the suffering of his people; hence, he pleads with God for mercy (v. 19). He likened the locust to a fire that had burnt up the entire countryside, and bemoaned the drought which had dried up streams and caused thirsty animals to pant for water (v. 20). Indeed, to be away from the Lord is to choose a dry, miserable, and fruitless existence, not worth living.

# Meditation

The day of the Lord is at hand, at hand;
Its storms roll up the sky;
The nations sleep starving on heaps of gold;
All dreamers toss and sigh;
The night is darkest before the morn;
When the pain is sorest the child is born,
In the day of the Lord at hand, at hand,
In the day of the Lord at hand.

— Charles Kingsley

# Sound the Alarm
Joel 2:1-17

Many of the Old Testament's prophecies against the nations coincide with Israel's final spiritual refinement and restoration to God as detailed in this chapter and in Ezekiel 36-39, Jeremiah 46-51, Daniel 7-8, and Zechariah 12-14. All these prophecies preview what is to come during and after the Tribulation Period. Believers in the Church Age should find interesting the events leading up to the fulfillment of these prophecies since the Church will be removed from the earth just prior to the Tribulation Period. Before reviewing the text, a brief overview of the Tribulation Period will be helpful in placing several of Joel's prophecies.

## Overview of the Tribulation Period
After all true Christians (i.e., those who had been born again and are indwelt by God) have been removed from the earth, the Antichrist will sign a peace treaty with Israel and be allowed to rule the world for seven years (2 Thess. 2:4-7; Dan. 9:27). God will pour out great wrath upon the earth at this time; Satan will attempt to gain as many followers as possible, slaughtering those who will not take his mark and pledge allegiance to the Antichrist (Rev. 12:12; 13:11-18). The holocaust during this time will be horrendous; the Lord Jesus said that if He should tarry longer than the appointed time for His return to the earth, humanity would be wiped out (Matt. 24:21-22). Considering the twenty-one specific divine judgments which occur at this time (Rev. 6-17), the Battle of Gog and Magog (Ezek. 38-39), the chastening of Israel (Rom. 9:27), and the Battle of Armageddon (Rev. 19), it is quite conceivable that seventy-five percent of the world population will die during the years of this epoch. Two-thirds of all Jews will be murdered during the Tribulation Period (Zech. 13:7-8), but God will protect a remnant of His covenant people from the Antichrist (Rev. 12:13-17) in

order to fulfill remaining promises to Abraham and David (Gen. 15:18-21; Ps. 89:3-4; Luke 1:32-33, 67-79).

Those martyred for choosing to worship God rather than the Antichrist will experience the first resurrection at the end of the Tribulation Period (Rev. 20:4). This miraculous event coincides with Christ's physical return to the earth to destroy the Antichrist, to judge and remove wickedness from the earth, and to establish His earthly one-thousand year kingdom (Rev. 20:4-6). The Day of the Lord includes the Tribulation Period (1 Thess. 5:1-5, 2 Thess. 2:3), and the Kingdom Age that follows (2 Pet. 3:10).

## The Day of the Lord Is Coming

Joel provides much more detail in this chapter concerning the subject he briefly introduced in the previous chapter – *the Day of the Lord* (1:15). He leaves the locust of chapter 1 behind to express what they represent in this chapter, future Gentile armies. The phrase *"before them"* in verses 3, 6, 10 nicely divides the first section (vv. 1-11) into four units before the prophet's call for repentance (vv. 12-17). D. Gilliland surmises that Joel's careful references to time in this chapter indicate that he is speaking about future events – events that could be avoided if Israel would repent and seek the Lord in time:

> One feature of the chapter to be carefully noted is its repeated notice of time. In the early verses there is a multiplication of future tenses. They describe something future from Joel's perspective. The invaders *"shall* ... leap"* (v. 5), they *"shall* run"* (v. 7), they *"shall* climb"* (v. 9), to note only a few. Then in verse 12 we have Joel's appeal "NOW." This brings us back to the prophet's own period. In the meantime, the total destruction threatened by this future attack can be averted by the evasive action of the present. NOW is the time for repentance. In the event of such true, heartfelt repentance, the promise of verse 18 will come into effect and "THEN" the Lord will have pity upon His repentant people.[35]

In the first unit, the Lord is likened to a Warrior-King summoning and leading His army into battle against the most vicious and enormous army to ever invade Israel (vv. 1-2). Moses used two silver trumpets to call the people together to repel invaders in the land (Num. 10:9). Interestingly, the Hebrew word for trumpet in verses 1 and 15 is *showphar* (shofar). This was the ram's horn that was blown to signal the fall of the walls of Jericho (Josh. 6:20). Perhaps, then, the use of the shofar in Joel 2 was to signal God's forthcoming victory over Israel's terrifying aggressors: *"Blow the trumpet in Zion, and sound an alarm in My holy mountain! Let all the inhabitants of the land tremble"* (v. 1).

Joel predicted that the attacking army will be so enormous that it will look similar to the dark, ominous clouds of locusts that previously covered the land (v. 2). The prophet then promises that after the Day of the Lord is over, no such army will ever assault God's holy mountain again (v. 2). This means that the battle prophetically referred to in this chapter and the one foretold in the next chapter are not historical conflicts, but even today, are still future. Clearly, the 200 million soldiers predicted to gather with the Antichrist for the Battle of Armageddon at the curtain call of the Tribulation Period would be a far greater number than any Assyrian or Babylonian invasion force that Israel had faced previously (Rev. 9:16).

In the second unit, the prophet describes the lush green land being overrun by hordes of locusts which rapidly consumed everything in their path like a raging wildfire (v. 3). Joel compared the swiftness of the locust to galloping horses (perhaps referring to advancing cavalry), and the noise of their wings to the sound of battle-chariots running over and crushing everything in their way (vv. 4-5). This may be a reference to tanks and other motorized armored vehicles of modern warfare.

The fearful sight and deafening noise of the invaders drained the color from the faces of Israel's inhabitants (v. 6). The hordes of locusts, which continue to picture the future army attacking Israel in the Day of the Lord, were unstoppable; they trampled over walls, invaded cities and homes with an uncanny systematized order, proficiency in movement, and unified purpose (vv. 7-9).

The invaders were so immense in number and so relentless in their advance that the earth quaked, the heavens trembled, and even the light from celestial bodies was obscured (v. 10). This is a poetic description of the cataclysmic upheaval in creation that will occur just before Christ's return to confront the Antichrist and his amassed army. The number of soldiers (saints) in the Lord's camp is also very great, but most importantly the One who executes His word is infinitely stronger than the advancing forces (v. 11). Hence, Joel concludes, *"For the day of the Lord is great and very terrible; who can endure it?"* The answer to this question is, only those who are on the Lord's side.

## The Call to Repentance

The only hope that Israel had against such an invincible army was to immediately return to the Lord. Accordingly, Joel pleads with his countrymen to return to the Lord in genuine brokenness and mourning:

*"Now, therefore," says the Lord, "Turn to Me with all your heart, with fasting, with weeping, and with mourning." So rend your heart, and not your garments; return to the Lord your God, for He is gracious and merciful, slow to anger, and of great kindness; and He relents from doing harm"* (vv. 12-13).

The repetition of "turn," "gather," and "sanctify" in Joel's message to Israel forms one of the clearest calls of repentance found in Scripture. The nation needed to collectively and genuinely acknowledge their sin, willingly turn from it, and commit to honoring God's Law again.

God's prophets often threaten His retribution for waywardness, but do not often speak of God's good character as a motivation for repentance. God is gracious, merciful, slow to anger, and full of kindness – this is why He longs to forgive those who confess their sin! If the Jews would return to the Lord in brokenness, they would learn what Jehovah was really like and experience full restoration, blessing, and honor. *"A man's pride will bring him low, but the humble in spirit will retain honor"* (Prov. 29:23). Both James and Peter proclaim the same truth: *"God resists the proud, but gives grace to the humble"* (Jas. 4:6; 1 Pet. 5:5). Joel wanted his countrymen to experience the fullness of God's character by expressing genuine humility and penitence.

True humility is selfless behavior that honors the Lord and longs to serve others. The Jews did not exhibit such a disposition towards God or their fellow man. The Lord wanted inward transformation, not the outward form of it; thus, He commands His people to *"rend your heart, and not your garments."* To be broken before the Lord is to be a qualified recipient of His grace. Our failures should lead to personal brokenness, which should then cause us to cast ourselves upon the Lord in a way that we were hesitant to do beforehand. Our victories, won by His grace, should prompt us to only praise His name! The outcome of testing, then, is that the believer knows and trusts the Lord with a greater patience and confidence than he or she had before. This is why the Lord longs for us to come to Him with all of life's burdens and also to seek Him to experience His mercy after failures.

The Lord Jesus gave this invitation: *"Come to Me, all you who labor and are heavy laden, and I will give you rest. Take My yoke upon you and learn from Me, for I am gentle and lowly in heart, and you will find rest for your souls. For My yoke is easy and My burden is light"* (Matt. 11:28-30). The disciple of Christ is to learn *Him!* This is the only passage in the New Testament where the Lord Jesus personally informs His disciples of what He is like and tells them that they should learn of Him. May we learn of Him and be like Him, for He is meek and lowly in heart. Believers learn of the Lord's gentle and humble spirit when yoked with Him in service, and they enjoy the peace of His presence when they rest in Him.

If the Jews would turn back to the Lord in humility and offer heartfelt grain and drink offerings, the Lord would cease chastening them in accordance with His sovereign timing (v. 14). So while it was possible that Israel's repentance could avert much of the travail that Joel was predicting, the Jews could not presume on God's mercy – they did not control God. E. B. Pusey uses an historical example to explain the meaning of Joel's statement, *"who knows if He will return and relent."*

> God has promised forgiveness of sins and of eternal punishment to those who turn to Him with their whole heart. Of this, then, there could be no doubt. But He has not promised either to individuals or to Churches that He will remit the temporal punishment which He had threatened. He forgave David the sin. Nathan says, *"The Lord also hath put away thy sin."* But he said at the same time, *"The sword shall never depart from thy house,"* and the temporal punishment of his sin pursued him, even on the bed of death. David thought that the temporal punishment of his sin, in the death of the child, might be remitted to him. He used the same form of words as Joel, *"I said, who can tell whether God will be gracious unto me, that the child may live?"* (2 Sam. 12:22). But the child died.[36]

Regardless of whether God would relent, Joel encourages his countrymen to trust in the merciful, longsuffering character of God and hope in Him no matter what the outcome would be. They should trust in Him because He had their best interests at heart.

Joel thought the best way to accomplish this was to have a congregational fast in Jerusalem where they would pray and lament before the Lord (v. 15). All the people, including elders, priests, children, and mothers with their infants; even those newly married should be in attendance (vv. 16-17). The prophet then instructed them how to pray if the nation did come together to humbly seek the Lord:

*Spare Your people, O Lord, and do not give Your heritage to reproach, that the nations should rule over them. Why should they say among the peoples, "Where is their God?" (v. 17).*

If prayed, this petition would indicate a legitimate concern for the honor of God's name, and that the Jews did not want His inheritance (themselves) becoming an object of scorn among the nations. Sadly, no such gathering occurred in Joel's day and God's people did become a reproach to the nations. In a future day, however, Israel will be broken and will draw near to the Lord in desperation, and He will powerfully deliver them from the Antichrist and restore His people to Himself. Then Israel will know unequivocally that Jehovah is the omnipotent, omniscient God who honors His Word at all costs!

## Meditation

The great thing in prayer is to feel that we are putting our supplications into the bosom of omnipotent love.

— Andrew Murray

God does not give us everything we want, but He does fulfill His promises, leading us along the best and straightest paths to Himself.

— Dietrich Bonhoeffer

Knowing God is more than knowing about Him; it is a matter of dealing with Him as He opens up to you, and being dealt with by Him as He takes knowledge of you. Knowing about Him is a necessary precondition of trusting in Him, but the width of our knowledge about Him is no gauge of our knowledge of Him.

— J. I. Packer

# Jerusalem Delivered and the Land Refreshed
Joel 2:18-27

Joel's call to repentance (2:15-17) marks a dramatic shift in the book. Previously, he mentioned all that the locust had and would eat; now he promises divine restoration of all the locust did eat. This parallelism is evident in several matched sets with the negative loss before the call to repentance being offset by the positive blessings afterwards. For example, weeping will be replaced with gladness, shame with honor, drought with the abundance of water, invaders with no invaders, etc. All this signifies the transition in verse 18 from God chastening His people to blessing them, and His tolerating the nations to judging them for their wickedness and their offenses against His people.

## Deliverance Promised

The prophet promised that if his countrymen approached God in humble repentance, *"then the Lord will be zealous for His land, and pity His people"* (v. 18). Furthermore, God would bless them by refreshing the land to satisfy all their needs; then they would no longer be a reproach among the nations (v. 19). Beginning with verse 20, we gain a deeper sense that the events Joel is foretelling reach far beyond the locust plague in Joel's day to the time of Israel's final repentance and restoration in the Tribulation Period. Then, a refined Jewish remnant will turn to and receive the Lord Jesus Christ; these Jews will be kept safe and secure during the time of Jacob's Trouble (Rev. 12:13-17).

We know from various prophecies that the Antichrist will desecrate the Jewish temple and put a stop to animal sacrifices at the midpoint of the Tribulation Period (Dan. 9:27; Matt. 24:15; 2 Thess. 2:3-7). This obviously means that a temple will have been erected and animal sacrifices, per the Levitical system, will have been reinstituted by that point. The Lord Jesus depicted this vain religious awakening as leaves shooting out from a fig tree that had been long dormant. Leaves may look good, but it is not the same as bearing spiritual fruit to the Lord. The Lord also said that the generation permitted to witness this event would also see His coming to the earth in glory (Luke 21:32). Today, many orthodox Jews are anticipating an imminent day when they will again perform the sacrifices as specified in the Mosaic Law.

Spiritual fruit can be produced only through spiritual rebirth which coincides with the Holy Spirit being poured out upon the Jewish nation. At the end of the Tribulation Period, the refined Jewish nation will receive the Holy Spirit. They will obtain spiritual life in Christ and will gladly worship Jesus Christ as Messiah (2:25-3:21; Zech. 12:10-13:1). This is what humble repentance, as Joel has been describing, will accomplish for Israel in a future day – ultimate and final deliverance. However, Israel in Joel's day had no intentions of sincerely confessing their sins and returning to the Lord.

## The Battle of Gog and Magog

In Joel 2, we learn that God will wipe out a brutal northern army invading Israel and that He will drive the remnant of this army out of Israel (vv. 20-21). This confrontation is referred to by Jeremiah (Jer. 31) and also by Ezekiel (Ezek. 38-39). Ezekiel names this the *Battle of Gog and Magog* and employs the Hebrew word *Rosh* to describe a specific people who will attack Israel during the battle of Gog and Magog:

*Now the word of the Lord came to me, saying, "Son of man, set your face against Gog, of the land of Magog, the prince of Rosh, Meshech, and Tubal, and prophesy against him"* (Ezek. 38:1-2).

*And you, son of man, prophesy against Gog, and say, Thus says the Lord God: "Behold, I am against you, O Gog, the prince of Rosh, Meshech, and Tubal; and I will turn you around and lead you on, bringing you up from the far north, and bring you against the mountains of Israel"* (Ezek. 39:1-3).

Generally speaking, Gog is thought to be the chief of the invaders, and Magog, his homeland. This understanding seems to explain the listing of Japheth's sons in Genesis 10: *"The sons of Japheth were Gomer, Magog, Madai, Javan, Tubal, Meshech, and Tiras"* (Gen. 10:2). Notice that *Gog* is not cited here, probably because *Magog* means "the land of Gog." Japheth's son may have been originally known as Gog, but the nation he founded was later referred to as *Magog*. *Gog* essentially means "high peak," which may refer to a mountain in Magog or may designate a dictator over the people there.

Who is the prince of Rosh? The Hebrew *rosh* may be translated as an adjective meaning "head" or "chief" as in the KJV and ESV or as a proper noun "Rosh" as rendered in the NKJV and NASV. Whether *rosh* further modifies Meshech and Tubal or refers to their broader social association is arguable. What we do know is that Gog, from the land of Magog (which may be Rosh), with its key centers of Meshech and Tubal will attack Israel. Meshech and Tubal may refer to two provinces of Asia Minor in the area associated with Scythians, rather than cities. Today, these people groups reside in the most eastern region of Turkey and Armenia, just south of the Caucasus Mountains.

Several factors suggest that Russia is the region from which the attack on Israel will originate. First, we know that Magog, Meshech, and Tubal were all sons of Japheth (i.e., the grandsons of Noah) who settled after the flood in a region just south of present-day Russia (Gen. 10:2). Second, the people of Rosh, Magog, Meshek, and Tubal are all situated directly north of Jerusalem (Ezek. 38: 6, 15) as one passes through Turkey and Georgia (which are between the Black and Caspian Seas). This will be the home of those who invade Israel for plunder during the Tribulation Period (Ezek. 38:12-13). Third, many of the nations listed as co-intruders with Gog have in recent years forged strong ties with Russia (Ezek. 38:5-6). William Kelly, writing in the late nineteenth century, states unequivocally that Russia would be involved in invading Israel in the future:

> Let me say here that according to Scripture there cannot be the slightest doubt that Russia is reserved to play a most important part in this great future crisis. ... Russia from its position in the northeast is known to seek the lead as suzerain over the eastern powers, acquiring influence politically, so as to be able to mold and guide those vast hordes of central Asia down to the south.[37]

Ezekiel identifies Togarmah, Gomer, Persia (Iran), Ethiopia, and Libya as siding with Gog. Togarmah refers to a people whose descendants now live in the far eastern portion of Turkey and Armenia. Gomer similarly refers to an ancient people called the Gimirrai or Cimmerians who resided in the same region southeast of the Black Sea (in or near Armenia). This means that Togarmah, Gomer, and Rosh all lie directly north of Israel.

Ezekiel tells us that the Jews will be dwelling safely in unwalled villages when Gog's armies come down from the north (Ezek. 38:8, 11, 14); they will be deceived into lowering their defenses while under the protection of the Antichrist's peace treaty (Dan. 9:27). This suggests that the timing of this battle is likely just prior to the Abomination of Desolation at the midpoint of the Tribulation Period (Dan. 7:8; Matt. 24:15). Joel addresses the Battle of Armageddon in the next chapter – there will be no escapees in that confrontation. Rosh's invading armies will be so enormous that Ezekiel likens them to a huge cloud that engulfs the entire land (Ezek. 38:9, 15, 16). Thankfully, with great fury and jealousy for His people, the Lord will intervene and defeat the military assault.

Joel and Ezekiel promised that the Lord will impede Rosh's invasion of Israel by destroying most of this army on the mountains of Israel and then drive surviving soldiers northward:

*Thus says the Lord God, "Behold, I am against you, O Gog, the prince of Rosh, Meshech, and Tubal; and I will turn you around and lead you on, bringing you up from the far north, and bring you against the mountains of Israel. Then I will knock the bow out of your left hand, and cause the arrows to fall out of your right hand. You shall fall upon the mountains of Israel, you and all your troops and the peoples who are with you; I will give you to birds of prey of every sort and to the beasts of the field to be devoured"* (Ezek. 39:1-4).

*But I will remove far from you the northern army, and will drive him away into a barren and desolate land, with his face toward the eastern sea and his back toward the western sea* (v. 20).

Joel may be speaking of the location where most of the northern army would be slain, that is, in Israel, which lies between the Mediterranean Sea to the west and the Dead Sea to the east. However, both prophets speak of God turning the northern army around during the battle of Gog and Magog. Certainly, Israel will not be a barren land at that time, for Rosh's invasion is to plunder the land (Ezek. 38:12-13). It seems more likely that the reference is to the region just north of Israel (between the Black and Caspian Seas) by which survivors of the routed army will return home.

Regardless which seas are meant, the incredible victory will provide testimony to the nations that the God of the Jews was again with His people and would be protecting them: *"Then they shall know that I am the Lord."* The incredible triumph over Rosh's armies explains why the Antichrist will be prompted to assemble such an enormous army against Israel at the end of the Tribulation Period. It will take all nations working together with all their resources to eradicate their greatest problem – Israel!

## Restoring the Years of the Locust

The Lord's spectacular intervention to protect Israel against the invading northern army will demonstrate that the Lord was in the midst of Israel again: *"Then you shall know that I am in the midst of Israel: I am the Lord your God and there is no other. My people shall never be put to shame"* (v. 27). This meant that after the Lord thwarted the Antichrist at the Battle of Armageddon (which is discussed in the next chapter), the Jews would never need to fear foreign raiders again.

The Lord would greatly bless His land (and their habitation) with rain and agricultural fruitfulness (vv. 21-24). In this fashion, the Lord would restore all that was lost through years of chastening, poetically expressed as *the years of the locust* (v. 25). God could not replace the years themselves, as if they never existed, but He would replace the lost productivity of the land. And Israel will be completely satisfied in the Lord and rejoice in the land's abundance (v. 26). The Jews will gladly praise Jehovah, for there is no One like Him, and He will not permit them to suffer shame ever again (v. 27).

## Meditation

> Lost years can never be restored literally. Time once past is gone forever. Let no man make any mistake about this or trifle with the present moment under any notion that the flying hour will ever wing its way back to him. ... It will strike you at once that the locusts did not eat the years—the locusts ate the fruits of the years' labor—the harvests of the fields. So the meaning of the restoration of the years must be the restoration of those fruits and of those harvests which the locusts consumed. You cannot have back your time. But there is a strange and wonderful way in which God can give back to you the wasted blessings, the unripened fruits of years over which you mourned. The fruits of wasted years may yet be yours. It is a pity that

they should have been eaten by your folly and negligence. But if they have been so, be not hopeless concerning them. "All things are possible to him that believes." There is a power which is beyond all things and can work great marvels.

— Charles Spurgeon
(*Truth Stranger Than Fiction*, May 30, 1886)

# I Will Pour Out My Spirit!
Joel 2:28-32

## The Holy Spirit Received "In Those Days"
As prophesied by several prophets, God instituted a New Covenant with His people that would give them eternal salvation, a new and clean heart, and allow the Holy Spirit to indwell them forever (Isa. 45:17-19; Jer. 31:31-40; Ezek. 34:23-28). With His own blood, Christ, as High Priest, sealed the New Covenant with the house of Judah and the house of Israel (Luke 22:20; Heb. 8:8). Hence, there is only one individual who can be Israel's Shepherd and King-Priest forever, the Lord Jesus Christ. In anticipation of His finished work at Calvary, God then could promise Israel through Ezekiel, *"A new heart also will I give you, and a new Spirit will I put within you"* (Ezek. 36:26).

Joel likewise foretells that the Jewish nation will receive the Holy Spirit, and a new heart (vv. 28-29). By His coming, God would put His Law deep inside His people forever and they would intimately know Jehovah as *"The Lord of Hosts"* (Jer. 31:33-35). Joel also states that the Holy Spirit would supernaturally equip the Jewish nation to both know and reveal the Lord to the nations:

> And it shall come to pass afterward that I will pour out My Spirit on all flesh; your sons and your daughters shall prophesy, your old men shall dream dreams, your young men shall see visions. And also on My menservants and on My maidservants I will pour out My Spirit in those days (Joel 2:28-29).

Peter quoted this portion of Scripture on the day of Pentecost to acknowledge that Joel's prophecy had been partially fulfilled (i.e., when Jewish believers were suddenly able to speak in various languages; Acts 2:17-21). Prophesying, dreaming dreams, seeing visions, speaking tongues, etc., will be evidences that the Holy Spirit has been received by Israel. The Holy Spirit will enable direct communication with God and the ability to express His will to others.

110

There are important implications of Peter's statements, which pertain both to the Church Age and the Tribulation Period.

**Concerning the Apostolic Age:** According to Acts 2:9-11, ten specific languages were heard in Jerusalem at the Feast of Pentecost, just after Christ's ascension into Heaven. This was the day the Church Age began (Acts 2:4; 1 Cor. 12:13). The Holy Spirit came to the believers as promised by the Lord Jesus, baptized them into the body of Christ, bestowed spiritual gifts on them, and enabled them to supernaturally serve the Lord and speak for the Lord. This event served two main purposes. First, it verified in the sight of the Jews that the apostles were continuing the ministry of Christ and were doing so by His power (Acts 2:22). Second, it served as a final warning to the nation of Israel to repent and turn to God through Christ. As a nation, they had rejected and crucified their Messiah, but, as individuals, they now had the opportunity to be saved. Unavoidable judgment was coming upon the nation of Israel and trusting Christ for salvation was the only way for them to obtain God's forgiveness.

In 70 A.D., that crushing judgment came. A vast Roman army of 70,000 soldiers, led by the future Emperor Titus, besieged and conquered Jerusalem. The temple, built in the sixth century B.C. was destroyed. There were to be no more offerings or sacrifices, no more Levitical priesthood, or the stench of humanized religion in the nostrils of Jehovah. Even to this day, although the Jews are back in their land and are a self-governing nation, they have no temple or priesthood to reinstate what God put away. This exactly fulfills what the writer of Hebrews said would happen – the Old Covenant had been replaced by a New Covenant and was therefore *"ready to vanish away"* (Heb. 8:7-13). The old system was completely put away about three to five years after this prediction.

These supernatural sign gifts (e.g. tongues) apparently diminished in normalcy during the Apostolic Age, as there is no mention of them in Scripture after 60 A.D. It is significant that over half the New Testament was written after this timeframe. Although the New Testament does record the names of many Jews who did turn from Judaism to Christ, Israel, as a nation, rejected Him and will continue to do so until His second advent at the end of the Tribulation Period (2:18-3:21; Isa. 11:1-16; Ezek. 36:16-38; Zech. 12:10).

This explains why Peter, inspired by the Holy Spirit, slightly modified the Hebrew text of Joel 2 when quoting it to his countrymen on the day of Pentecost. For example, when explaining the timing of God's pouring out of the Holy Spirit, Peter exchanged "afterward" to "in the last days," thus denoting a future time when Messiah would return to earth to reestablish Israel and end "the times of the Gentiles." Peter was affirming that Pentecost was only a foretaste of better things to come for the Jewish nation in the Kingdom age, when God pours out His Spirit on all flesh. Joel tells us that this event will be accompanied by supernatural signs in the heavens; that did not happen at Pentecost.

**Concerning the Day of the Lord:** The timing of the pouring out of the Holy Spirit is stated: *"it shall come to pass afterward"* (v. 28). This event relates to God dwelling among His covenant people again to bless them and to restore all that was lost through their years of chastening (vv. 26-27). After the battle of Gog and Magog (likely in the mid-portion of the Tribulation Period), the nations will know that the Lord is with Israel, and Israel will know it too! The second implication of the pouring out of the Holy Spirit pertains to the 144,000 sealed Jewish witnesses identified in Revelation 7. These evangelists may well be equipped with the gift of tongues as they spread the Kingdom Gospel message through Israel and then the world during the Tribulation Period. As in the early Church Age, this would both signal to Israel that judgment was coming and would provide the means for Jews to convey the gospel to all people groups in their own language.

This activity is in keeping with how the sign of the unknown tongue is used throughout Scripture – as a warning to the Jewish people of imminent judgment. Moses told the people that if they rebelled against the Lord, He would punish them through a nation whose language they would not understand (Deut. 28:49). This meant that God would use an army from a distant land instead of a neighboring nation. Isaiah warned idolatrous Israel by imposing this sign just prior to the Assyrian invasion (Isa. 28:11-12), and Jeremiah referenced it as a final warning to Judah of imminent judgment for the same deeply-rooted sin (Jer. 5:15). But the Jews ignored the warnings of Moses, Isaiah, and Jeremiah; the sign of the unknown tongue was issued and severe judgment ultimately came. Yet, this was not the last time God would use the sign of an unknown tongue to alert the Jews of impending judgment for their unfaithfulness.

While some Jews have come to faith in Christ and have received the Holy Spirit during the Church Age, the nation as a whole will not turn to Him until His Second Advent; this is the focus of Joel's prophecy. With Christ's Second Advent to earth, the spiritual blindness of the Jewish nation will come to an end. They will trust in the Lord Jesus Christ, their Messiah, the One they pierced two thousand years earlier (Zech. 12:10). In this spiritually fruitful state, the Jews will be known as the olive tree which provides a testimony of God's goodness to the entire world (Hos. 14:6; Rom. 11:17-24).

Although we see that individual Jews in the Old Testament were filled by the Holy Spirit in order to speak for the Lord or to serve Him effectively (e.g., Ex. 35:30-35; 1 Sam. 10:10), the nation as a whole has never been indwelt by the Spirit of God (Zech. 4:4-7). This will not happen until Christ's second coming to the earth (Isa. 59:21). Indeed, it is a subject frequently addressed in Scripture (Isa. 11:1-16; Hos. 3; Zech. 14:1-21; Rom. 11:7-25). God has issued many wonderful promises of Israel's future spiritual renewal and restoration to Jehovah, which is all accomplished by the pouring out of the Holy Spirit.

However, we cannot leave this section without noting two more important features of verse 28. First, the pouring out of the Spirit of God precedes the judgment of the wicked in the following verses. The Lord will clearly mark and seal with the Holy Spirit those who have chosen Him during the Tribulation Period (i.e., after the Church Age). This would include the 144,000 Jewish evangelists during the Tribulation Period, and the entire Jewish nation and Gentiles (surviving Tribulation saints) at its conclusion. This will ensure that the redeemed will not experience the Lord's wrath against the wicked nations in the Valley of Decision and the Judgment of Nations to follow.

The second feature of verse 28 of particular interest is God's promise to pour out His Spirit *"on all flesh."* J. N. Darby comments to the significance of the phrase "all flesh."

> It implies, as to its full accomplishment, the important fact that will take place at the end of this age, namely, that God will come out of the narrow circle of Jewish ordinances to act with regard to all mankind on the earth. This is already true morally by means of the gospel. But it will be true as to the government of God at the end. Christ, in coming down to the earth, came into the narrow fold [believers drawn from the lost sheep of Israel], and He led His sheep out of it, and called other sheep [Gentiles] also to form them into one flock, saved, set free, and finding pasture [the redeemed]. ... God will, in fact, deal at length with all flesh in His governmental power (e.g., Isa. 40:5).[38]

"All flesh" means "all of humanity" (e.g. Gen. 6:12-13). Paul tells us in the Epistle of Ephesians that Christ made Jew and Gentile one in a spiritual Body that He was building called the Church (Eph. 2:11-22). Beyond this, there is a coming day when every person on the planet (i.e., at the commencement of the Kingdom Age) will be spiritually one with God, for everyone will have His Spirit. However, with the passing centuries during the Kingdom Age, many of their descendants will not receive the Holy Spirit. This reality will set the stage for the last great rebellion after Satan is loosened from the bottomless pit. This will occur at the conclusion of Christ's one-thousand-year reign (Rev. 20:7-10).

Christ will then defeat Satan and his amassed armies of the world, just prior to the destruction of the earth (Rev. 20:11, 21:1). This event is immediately followed by the Great White Throne judgment when all the wicked with Satan will be cast into the Lake of Fire (Rev. 20:12-15). Then, in the Eternal State, all the redeemed will possess glorified bodies and will always be one with the Lord, and sin will be no more!

**Concerning the Church:** Believers in the Church Age are also sealed by the Holy Spirit (Eph. 1:13) and are thus exempt from divine wrath. These believers in the Church Age responded to the gospel message and were removed from the earth before God began to work with His covenant people again during the Tribulation Period. Therefore, Christians are commanded to wait for Christ's imminent and sudden appearing in the clouds to translate them from the earth (1 Thess. 4:13-18), to receive glorified bodies (1 Cor. 15:51-51), to be escorted to heaven and to be examined by Christ at His Judgment Seat (Rom. 14:10-12). There they will be appropriately rewarded by Him (1 Cor. 3:11-15; 2 Cor. 5:10).

Consequently, the Church will not suffer God's wrath during the Tribulation Period. Rather, Christ promised: *"I also will keep you from the hour of trial which shall come upon the whole world, to test those who dwell on the earth"* (Rev. 3:10). For this reason the Church is to expect the imminent return of Christ who will deliver from the wrath to come all those who have been born again:

*Much more then, having now been justified by His blood, we shall be saved from wrath through Him* (Rom. 5:9).

*And to wait for His Son from heaven, whom He raised from the dead, even Jesus who delivers us from the wrath to come* (1 Thess. 1:10).

*For God did not appoint us to wrath, but to obtain salvation through our Lord Jesus Christ* (1 Thess. 5:9).

Therefore the Church must be taken from the earth to Heaven before Christ opens the first seal on the scroll (Rev. 6:1), initiating the Tribulation Period. Likewise, surviving tribulation saints and those Jews of spiritual Israel will be spared death when God judges the nations at the end of the Tribulation Period. God's wrath is against wickedness, not against His redeemed (Zech. 12:8-9).

## Just Before the Great and Awesome Day of the Lord

The prophet Malachi foretold that God would send the prophet Elijah again just prior to the Day of the Lord: *"Behold, I am going to send you Elijah the prophet before the coming of the great and terrible day of the Lord"* (Mal. 4:5). The Lord confirmed that the spirit of Elijah was in John, who faithfully called that nation to repentance before Christ began His ministry during His first advent (Matt. 17:11-13). Likewise, 144,000 Jews will be sealed and empowered by the Holy Spirit to again preach the Kingdom Gospel message just before Christ's second advent. Their mission will be similar to Elijah's previous ministry to apostate Israel; it is also possible that Elijah himself will be one of the two powerful witnesses spoken of in Revelation 11:3-14.

Joel then revealed additional signs that would directly precede Christ's second advent to the earth:

*And I will show wonders in the heavens and in the earth: blood and fire and pillars of smoke. The sun shall be turned into darkness, and the moon into blood, before the coming of the great and awesome day of the Lord. And it shall come to pass that whoever calls on the name of the Lord shall be saved. For in Mount Zion and in Jerusalem there shall be deliverance, as the Lord has said, among the remnant whom the Lord calls* (Joel 2:30-32).

Matthew confirms the same details over eight centuries later:

*For as the lightning comes from the east and flashes to the west, so also will the coming of the Son of Man be. For wherever the carcass is, there the eagles will be gathered together. Immediately after the tribulation of those days the sun will be darkened, and the moon will not give its light; the stars will fall from heaven, and the powers of the heavens will be shaken. Then the sign of the Son of Man will appear*

115

*in heaven, and then all the tribes of the earth will mourn, and they will see the Son of Man coming on the clouds of heaven with power and great glory. And He will send His angels with a great sound of a trumpet, and they will gather together His elect from the four winds, from one end of heaven to the other* (Matt. 24:27-31).

After seven years of devastating judgments, the entire planet will be in a pitiful condition (Rev. 6-16). Clouds of ash and debris in the atmosphere will block much of the sun's light from reaching Earth. The prophets foretold that God would show such great signs and wonders in the heavens that the terror of Jehovah would be felt on the earth. Rebels will dig in and resist the Jehovah calling card, but many will surrender themselves to Him and put their trust in His deliverance. Even with all these horrific signs announcing the Day of the Lord, earthly dissidents will still be surprised by the Lord's sudden appearance to judge them. Being numb to God's Word and authority, the lost are likened to a sleeping homeowner startled by a *"thief in the night"* (1 Thess. 5:2, 1 Pet. 3:10). However, those who call upon the Lord will not be frightened by His coming, but rather will yearn for it; certainly the refined Jewish nation will be expecting His intervention.

The next chapter addresses the defeat of the Antichrist and his massive army. Either just before or directly after that conclusive battle, the Lord will sound the trumpet and bring every Jew still alive on the planet back to Israel (Ezek. 39:28-29). Then the prophecy of Joel will be fulfilled:

*And it shall come to pass that whoever calls on the name of the Lord shall be saved. For in Mount Zion and in Jerusalem there shall be deliverance, as the Lord has said, among the remnant whom the Lord calls* (v. 32).

While it is true that anyone can call on the Lord and be saved, in its context, this verse is speaking of the Jewish people. Any Jew calling upon the Lord will receive His Spirit and be delivered from the wrath of the Antichrist. Then, redeemed, refined, restored, and delivered Israel, now fully indwelt by the Spirit of God, will ever be with the Lord!

# Meditation

The Lord will come! The earth shall quake,
The hills their fixed seat forsake;
And, withering from the vault of night,
The stars withdraw their feeble light.

The Lord will come! But not the same
As once in lowly form He came,
A silent Lamb to slaughter led,
The bruised, the suffering, and the dead.

The Lord will come! A dreadful form,
With wreath of flame, and robe of storm,
On cherub wings, and wings of wind,
Anointed Judge of humankind.

— Reginald Heber

# The Valley of Decision
Joel 3

Joel begins this chapter by informing us that the Lord will be in the process of gathering His covenant people scattered throughout the world back to Israel and that He will permit Israel to be surrounded and threatened by many nations one last time (v. 1). To be surrounded by many nations meant that many different tongues would be heard. As discussed in the previous chapter, this has been God's warning to Israel throughout the Old Testament and during the Apostolic Age to repent and receive His deliverance or suffer imminent calamity. This time, having no other choice to avert annihilation, Israel will heed the warning.

The ensuing great battle will occur in the *"the Valley of Jehoshaphat"* (v. 2), also referred to as *"the valley of decision"* (v. 14). These terms address what the conflict is about rather than pinpointing its location. Jehoshaphat means "the Lord judges" and that is exactly what will happen – God will render a decision and pass judgment on the wicked. It was in the valley of Berachah that God defeated an innumerable host of Edomites, Ammonites and Moabites to defend His people. Jehoshaphat, in obedience to the Lord, led the army of Judah (with singers praising God before him) out to this location to witness God's promised deliverance (2 Chron. 20).

Berachah means "blessing." Just as God delivered and blessed His people in Jehoshaphat's day, He will do so again in the valley of decision. The Lord Jesus will descend to the earth to war against the Antichrist and his armies in the valley of Berachah, also identified as Armageddon (Rev. 16:6), or literally in the Hebrew *har mageddon* – "the Hill Megiddo." The Valley of Berachah is connected with the region of Megiddo in the Jezreel Valley; though brief in duration, it is where the greatest battle in human history will be fought.

Ironically, in 1799 Napoleon stood at Megiddo just prior to losing the battle that ended his quest to conquer the East and rebuild the Roman Empire. Considering the enormous plain of Armageddon, he

118

declared: "All the armies of the world could maneuver their forces on this vast plain ...There is not a place in the whole world more suited for war than this...[it is] the most natural battleground on the whole earth."[39]

At the moment Christ returns to the earth, the prophet Zechariah tells us that the Jews will be fighting to defend Jerusalem, and the city will have been conquered by the Antichrist (Zech. 14:2-3). Christ will quickly deliver the Jewish people and will also judge the nations for harming them and seizing His land set aside for them (v. 2). In this way, God is working to refine and restore His covenant people while at the same time meting out justice on the wicked:

*For we know Him who said, "Vengeance is Mine, I will repay," says the Lord. And again, "The Lord will judge His people." It is a fearful thing to fall into the hands of the living God* (Heb. 10:30-31).

Zechariah informs us that Christ will land on the Mount of Olives, thus splitting the mountain in half, such that a river of water will flow to the east and to the west out of the newly formed ravine (Zech. 14:4-8). The returning Messiah will be King over the whole earth (Zech. 14:9). He will cause the Jews' oppressors to fight each other and then cause their bodies to dissolve where they stand (Zech. 14:12-13).

John provides the number of those soldiers gathered in the Jezreel Valley for the battle of Armageddon: 200,000,000 (Rev. 9:16). He then explains that the entire valley will become a giant winepress, for when Christ destroys this enormous army, their blood will freely flow out of the valley basin for 182 miles (Rev. 14:19-20). Birds of prey will be summoned to clean up the carcasses of the slain army. Hence, John calls the aftermath of this event – "the great supper":

*Then I saw an angel standing in the sun; and he cried with a loud voice, saying to all the birds that fly in the midst of heaven, "Come and gather together for the supper of the great God, that you may eat the flesh of kings, the flesh of captains, the flesh of mighty men, the flesh of horses and of those who sit on them, and the flesh of all people, free and slave, both small and great." And I saw the beast, the kings of the earth, and their armies, gathered together to make war against Him who sat on the horse and against His army. Then the beast was captured, and with him the false prophet who worked signs in his presence, by which he deceived those who received the mark of the beast and those who worshiped his image. These two were cast alive into the lake of fire burning with brimstone. And the rest were killed with the sword which proceeded from the mouth of Him who sat on the horse. And all the birds were filled with their flesh* (Rev. 19:17-21).

Christ's coming and subsequent victory will deliver Jerusalem from the Antichrist's invading armies. After the Battle of Armageddon, all those following the Antichrist will be gathered and killed – this is called the Judgment of Nations (Matt. 13:47-50; 25:31-46; Rev. 19:20-21). Those who did not take the Beast's mark or devalue or mistreat the Jewish people will be allowed to enter Christ's kingdom on earth (v. 3; Matt. 25:31-46; Rev. 14:9-11).

Besides following the Antichrist, Joel addresses why various nations were destined to be judged by the Lord when He does appear. The Phoenicians and the Philistines had profited economically from Judah's fall (v. 4, Ezek. 25:15, 28:20-24). Their offenses included seizing Israel's wealth and enslaving or selling Jews into servitude (vv. 5-6; Amos 1:6-9). These crimes will be fully recompensed now, for the Jews will be their masters and will put the Gentiles to service (vv. 7-8). This will conclude the times of the Gentiles, which, beginning with the Assyrian Empire, saw tens of millions of Jews sold into slavery or slaughtered (Rom. 11:25; Rev. 11:1-2).

While these prophecies may have been partially fulfilled through historical circumstances, in the context of the passage, the meaning is obvious – the Jews will have a position of dominance over the Phoenicians and Philistines, who here seem to represent all Gentile nations. Zechariah foretold that at the beginning of the Kingdom Age, ten surviving Gentiles will clutch the skirt of one Jewish man and say, *"We will go with you: for we have heard that God is with you"* (Zech. 8:23). Indeed, God will be with the Jewish nation, and the entire world will esteem them for it!

## A Call to War

No more rhetoric, it is time for war. Unidentified messengers are commanded by the Lord to summon all nations to prepare their weapons and gather for battle against Him:

*Proclaim this among the nations: "Prepare for war! Wake up the mighty men, let all the men of war draw near, let them come up. Beat your plowshares into swords and your pruning hooks into spears; let the weak say, 'I am strong.'" Assemble and come, all you nations, and gather together all around* (vv. 9-11).

How puny men think they can outsmart and outmaneuver the providential control of their omnipotent and omniscient Creator is beyond reason, but such will be this end-times scenario. The factories of the world will be busy assembling their instruments of war in order to mount their best efforts to overcome Israel. After the above charge went out to the nations, the Lord was requested to take action: *"cause Your mighty ones to go down there"* (v. 11). Perhaps this is the voice of God the Father directing His Son to return to the earth with the army to establish His kingdom (John describes this majestic scene in Revelation 19:11-21).

After this request, the Lord Himself commands the nations to gather before Him at the Valley of Jehoshaphat: *"Let the nations be wakened, and come up to the Valley of Jehoshaphat; for there I will sit to judge all the surrounding nations"* (v. 12). And there God will sit and patiently wait for rebel nations to assemble before Him. Humanity will bolster its mightiest accomplishments through the ages in the valley of decision. Then, the gavel will fall; sentencing and vengeance will be executed immediately.

In the broader sense, God will judge the nations in two phases, first the sickle will remove the ripened grain into His barn and then the ripened grapes will be trampled in His great winepress. This is exactly the imagery John employs in Revelation 14. In that chapter, the Lord Jesus (or a powerful angel representing Him) is told by a messenger from God's heavenly temple to thrust His sharp sickle into the earth to reap the ripened grain. The grain represents believers (refined Israel and Tribulation saints) who will be taken out of the coming judgment – these will enter Christ's kingdom (Matt. 13:36-43; Rev. 14:14-16).

The next command from the heavenly temple is to gather and crush the grapes of wrath in God's winepress at the Valley of Jehoshaphat (Rev. 14:17-19). The valley of Jehoshaphat will become the great threshing-floor of the Divine Winnower and the vast winepress of the Divine Winemaker – there He will separate those who are to share in His kingdom from those who will perish in everlasting torment.

While it is true that the Antichrist and his armies will be completely destroyed in the Valley of Jehoshaphat, the fact that both a harvest of grain and a harvest of grapes are mentioned seems to indicate that the wider judgment of all nations immediately follows, as it does in John's prophetic account of these events (Rev. 19:17-21). The Lord Jesus mentioned that the wheat (believers) would remain in the field (the world) with the tares (children of the devil) until the time of divine reaping arrived:

> *Let both grow together until the harvest, and at the time of harvest I will say to the reapers, "First gather together the tares and bind them in bundles to burn them, but gather the wheat into My barn"* (Matt. 13:30).

> *The enemy who sowed them is the devil, the harvest is the end of the age, and the reapers are the angels. Therefore as the tares are gathered and burned in the fire, so it will be at the end of this age. The Son of Man will send out His angels, and they will gather out of His kingdom all things that offend, and those who practice lawlessness, and will cast them into the furnace of fire. There will be wailing and gnashing of teeth* (Matt. 13:39-42).

Joel describes an innumerable host assembled in the valley of decision bent on eradicating Israel, but instead they will be intercepted by Christ and instantly vanquished (reaped from the world). When the Lord appears to destroy the Antichrist and his hordes, it will be as the angel told Daniel, *"He shall plant the tents of his palace between the seas and the glorious holy mountain; yet he shall come to his end, and no one will help him"* (Dan. 11:45).

The battle scene is cataclysmic:

> *Multitudes, multitudes in the valley of decision! For the day of the Lord is near in the valley of decision. The sun and moon will grow dark, and the stars will diminish their brightness. The Lord also will roar from Zion, and utter His voice from Jerusalem; the heavens and earth will shake; but the Lord will be a shelter for His people, and the strength of the children of Israel* (vv. 14-16).

*"Multitudes, multitudes in the valley of decision"* will be judged by the Lord! The great outcome of this immense slaughter is that the name of the Lord Jesus Christ is vindicated before His enemies and that the nation of Israel affirms Him as their divine Messiah: *"So you shall know that I am the Lord your God dwelling in Zion My holy mountain.*

*Then Jerusalem shall be holy, and no aliens shall ever pass through her again"* (v. 17). He will reign over Israel forever and rule the nations with a rod of iron – no invaders, marauders, or pagans will ever invade Israel again.

## The Kingdom Age

Having judged the wicked and secured Jerusalem and the land of Israel for His people, Joel describes the Lord's supernatural cleansing and renewing of the earth's ecosystem commencing with the Kingdom Age. The Lord will be established in His temple in Jerusalem and living water will rush forth to renew the entire planet, a scene that Ezekiel vividly describes in astounding detail (Ezek. 47:1-12).

> *And it will come to pass in that day that the mountains shall drip with new wine, the hills shall flow with milk, and all the brooks of Judah shall be flooded with water; a fountain shall flow from the house of the Lord and water the Valley of Acacias* (v. 18).

Isaiah describes conditions on the earth after Christ removes the curses placed upon it due to the fall of man. All the wicked will be judged, the wolf shall dwell with the lamb, the leopard with the kid, the calf with the lion; the lion shall eat straw, and the child shall play by the hole of the asp (Isa. 11:1-8). Joel says that the grape harvest will be so bountiful that it seems like wine is dripping out of the mountains. Livestock will flourish in this blessed environment where bubbling brooks and running streams never dry up, meaning that there will be plenty of milk also.

In contrast to the abundance of agricultural prosperity in Israel, those nations who exploited, abused, and murdered the Jews will suffer infertility and will be wastelands (v. 19). Egypt and Edom are named as representative culprits who committed such atrocities. Yet, we know from Zechariah 14:17-19 that individuals from Egypt who did not identify with the Antichrist will be permitted to enter Christ's kingdom. If these people come to Jerusalem to regularly worship the Lord, then He will overrule the calamity He initially imposed on the land and will provide abundant rainfall. Jerusalem will be the worship capital of the world and will continually enjoy the Lord's blessings from generation to generation throughout the Kingdom Age (v. 20). Edom will not be as fortunate, however, for that nation has already been blotted out forever, as predicted by Obadiah and other prophets.

Geographic locations on earth today, such as Jerusalem, Egypt, and Lebanon, will exist in the Millennial Kingdom (Isa. 60:13; Joel 3:18; Zech. 14:16-21), but obviously not in the new earth. The new heaven and earth will not be created until after the Kingdom Age is concluded, Satan's last rebellion on earth is quelled (Rev. 20:7-10), and the planet that we presently live on is obliterated (Isa. 34:4; 2 Pet. 3:10; Rev. 20:11). Then the Lord will rule in the New Jerusalem (a city measuring 1500 miles in all three dimensions) which will hover above the new earth and the Lord will be forever with His glorified people (Rev. 21).

The final verse of Joel's prophecy confirms that the Lord (at His second advent) will thoroughly and fully avenge the "blood" (v. 21). But who is being avenged and what blood is being spoken of? D. Gilliland suggests that this reference is to Lord purifying His people from their past defilement resulting from shedding the innocent blood of Christ at Calvary:

> The Jews said solemnly, as instigated by their leaders, *"His blood be on us and on our children"* (Matt. 27:25). Peter later charged them with the death of Christ: *"But ye denied the Holy One and the Just, and desired a murderer to be granted unto you; and killed the Prince of life, whom God hath raised from the dead"* (Acts 3:14-15). This bloodguiltiness was confirmed by Stephen when, referring to Christ as the *"Just One,"* he added, *"Of whom ye have been now the betrayers and murderers"* (Acts 7:52).[40]

The fact that two-thirds of the Jewish people die during the time of Jacob's Trouble, the Tribulation Period, (Zech. 13:8-9) does seem to indicate that God is pouring out His final retribution against His covenant people. They rejected and put to death the Lord Jesus Christ, God's incarnate Son and their Messiah – they admitted publicly that His blood was on their hands. Yet, the context of this passage clearly decrees that God is also vindicating the blood of His people, shed by Gentiles through the centuries. Whatever the offenses against innocent blood were – all will have been justly dealt with by Christ and in such a way that the nations will know that *"the Lord dwells in Zion"* (v. 21). It is this reality that guarantees that divine blessing, peace, and security will continue in Israel throughout the Kingdom Age.

# Meditation

Day of judgment! Day of wonders!
Hark! The trumpet's awful sound,
Louder than a thousand thunders,
Shakes the vast creation round!
How the summons will the sinner's heart confound!

At His call the dead awaken,
Rise to life from earth and sea;
All the powers of nature shaken
By His look, prepares to flee.
Careless sinner, what will then become of thee?

Horrors, past imagination,
Will surprise your trembling heart,
When you hear your condemnation,
"Hence, accursed wretch, depart!
Thou, with Satan and his angels, have thy part!"

But to those who have confessed,
Loved and served the Lord below,
He will say, "Come near, ye blessed,
See the kingdom I bestow;
You forever shall My love and glory know."

— John Newton

# Amos

# Overview of Amos

## The Author

Amos resided among the sheep-breeders of Tekoa, a remote location in the Southern Kingdom about ten miles south of Jerusalem (1:1). He also labored in the coastal plain or Jordan Valley of the Northern Kingdom as a seasonal migrant worker gathering sycamore fruit (7:14). Later in his life, God called Amos from his lowly occupations to prophetically warn the inhabitants of Bethel, a chief pagan center in the Northern Kingdom. Although he encountered opposition, Amos continued preaching God's word to those who needed to hear it (7:10-17). He was "burdened," which is the meaning of his name, to do so.

## Date

Amos delivered his messages to the Northern Kingdom during the reigns of Jeroboam II in Israel and Uzziah in Judah, about two years before an earthquake struck the region (1:1). Amaziah's accusations against Amos to King Jeroboam II align with the prophet's opening statement (7:10-13). Archeological and geological information has dated an 8.0 magnitude earthquake with an epicenter about 150 miles north of Israel in approximately 760 B.C. (see 1:1 analysis). Additionally, NASA solar eclipse calculations show two significant solar eclipses affecting Israel and much of the Assyrian Empire during the eighth century, the first in 765 B.C. and the second in 763 B.C. (see evaluation in chapter 8). Amos prophesied total or near-total solar eclipse(s) as a sign of imminent judgment against Israel (8:9).

While the date of the earthquake is only approximate, the mathematical dating of the solar eclipses is more precise. Given the Bible account, available scientific evidence, and the historical record that Jeroboam II reigned from 782 to 753 B.C. and Uzziah (Azariah) from 767-740 B.C., it seems likely that Amos' ministry was between 766 to 764 B.C. (probably ending before both solar eclipses, but at least before the second in 763 B.C.). The above information and the language of the text indicate that Amos' prophetic ministry was brief (perhaps less than a year).

About forty years after Amos's oracles were delivered to Bethel, God would enable the Assyrians to conquer the Northern Kingdom and to enslave and deport much of the population. The prophecies of Amos to the Northern Kingdom preceded Isaiah's and Micah's ministry to the Southern Kingdom by approximately twenty-five years. Hosea's lengthy ministry to Israel would have overlapped Amos' preaching by several years on either side.

## Theme

God had already punished Israel for her idolatry (4:6-11), but the Northern Kingdom had not yet renounced her idols and returned to the Lord. Amos was sent to warn Israel that if she did not repent soon, God would bring widespread death and destruction to the land, and Jewish survivors would be exiled. Sadly, Israel did not repent, and the Lord used the Assyrians to vanquish the Northern Kingdom. To this end, the prophecies of Amos and his contemporary Hosea to the Northern Kingdom are similar in focus. Yet, Hosea's ministry was more personal and Jewish in nature, whereas plainspoken Amos foretold God's judgments on surrounding nations also.

## Outline

The book of Amos consists of eight announcements of irrevocable judgments against Israel, Judah, and the surrounding nations (chps. 1-2), five messages affixing guilt and explaining why God's judgments against Israel were deserved (chps. 3-6), and five visions describing what these judgments would accomplish (chps. 7-9). A simplified outline for the book would be:

Declarations of Irrevocable Judgment (1:1-2:16)
Reasons for Unavoidable Judgment (2:17-4:13)
God Pleads With Israel to Repent (5:1-15)
Reasons for Unavoidable Judgment Continued (5:16-6:14)
Visions of the Inescapable Judgment (7:1-9:10)
Israel's Final Restoration (9:11-15)

# Devotions in Amos

## For Three and for Four
Amos 1

Amos was tending sheep in Tekoa, a town ten miles south of Jerusalem when he saw visions concerning Israel (Tekoa still exists today). These messages were then delivered to the Northern Kingdom during the reigns of Jeroboam II in Israel and Uzziah in Judah, about two years before an earthquake struck the region (v. 1).

### The Earthquake

The earthquake (v. 1) must have been a monster-quake, as the prophet Zechariah mentions it two and half centuries later in his prophecy relating to the Tribulation Period: *"Yes, you shall flee as you fled from the earthquake in the days of Uzziah king of Judah"* (Zech. 14:5). No other prophet, but Amos, specifically dates the commencement of his ministry in relationship to this earthquake. This suggests that not only did Amos' ministry begin two years before the quake, but also that it finished before it struck, otherwise his predictions about it (e.g., 6:11, 8:8, 9:1) would be after the fact.

According to *International Geology Review*, a major earthquake occurred in Israel in approximately 760 B.C. Archeologists Yigael Yadin and Israel Finkelstein date the earthquake at Tel Hazor to 760 B.C. based on stratigraphic analysis of the destruction debris.[41] Similarly, David Ussishkin arrives at the same date based on the "sudden destruction" levied on Lachish. According to Steven A. Austin, the magnitude of this earthquake may have been at least 7.8, but more likely as high as 8.2: "This magnitude 8 event of 750 B.C. appears to be the largest yet documented on the Dead Sea transform fault zone during the last four millennia." The epicenter of this earthquake may have been 200–300 km north of present-day Israel.[42] Geological and archeological evidence confirms that a massive earthquake struck Israel sometime in the mid-eighth century B.C. Amos was called to be a prophet two years before this upheaval occurred.

## God Roars

The prophet was summoned to warn Israel and surrounding nations that God was ready to fiercely judge their wickedness. To illustrate this point, the prophet likened the Lord to a stalking lion that roars to paralyze its prey with fear an instant before the lion pounces on and kills it (v. 2). God's roar, so to speak, would sound out from Jerusalem, would carry across Israel's pasturelands, echo loudly in Mount Carmel, and be heard in the threshing floors of Gilead, and even in distant lands as far away as Damascus (vv. 3-5).

The reverberating roar pictures the expanding reach of a severe drought moving across the region and withering all vegetation. God was signaling that an even greater calamity was imminent if those hearing His call to repentance did not respond (1:3-2:16). Besides the Northern Kingdom which had forsaken their covenant with Jehovah (2:6-16), Amos identifies seven other people groups surrounding Israel that had heard God's roaring: Aram or Syria (1:3-5), Philistia (1:6-8), Tyre (1:9-10), Edom (1:11-12), Ammon (1:13-15), Moab (2:1-3) and then the Southern Kingdom of Judah (2:4-5).

Amos states to each society that irrevocable judgment was coming before he identified their crimes, and declared the punishment they will receive. The phrase *"For three transgressions..., and for four"* commences each of the eight warnings just described. This poetic idiom conveys completeness as symbolized by the number seven (i.e., the total of three and four). Hence, Amos does not list each nation's sins, but rather mentions the final offense that prompted God to cease tempering His burning indignation with patient mercy (i.e., the sin that *tipped the scales,* so to speak). The exception to this practice is that the prophet lists all seven of Israel's sins in the next chapter. God's longsuffering disposition could no longer tolerate mounting offenses against Him – He must act to uphold righteous justice. His anger would burn hottest against Israel, for she was an idolatrous covenant-breaker.

## Judgment Against Damascus (vv. 3-5)

Damascus, the capital city of Syria, had often meddled in Jewish affairs (1 Chron. 18:5; Isa. 7:1) resulting in much harm to God's people. Amos explains why God would punish Damascus, *"because they have threshed Gilead with implements of iron"* (v. 3). Gilead was situated on the Eastern Plateau, the region given for an inheritance to the tribes of Reuben, Gad, and the half tribe of Manasseh. As Syria's king Hazael invaded *"all the land of Gilead"* (2 Kgs. 10:32-33), Amos has the entire region east of the Jordan in view.

The Syrians not only conquered Gilead, but also massacred many Jews by running over them with threshing implements. E. B. Pusey describes Syria's ruthless behavior:

> The instrument, Jerome relates here, was "a sort of wain [wagon or cart], rolling on iron wheels beneath, set with teeth; so that it both threshed out the grain and bruised the straw and cut it in pieces, as food for the cattle, for lack of hay." A similar instrument, called by nearly the same name, is still in use in Syria and Egypt. Elisha had foretold to Hazael his cruelty to Israel: *"Their strongholds thou wilt set on fire, and their young men wilt thou slay with the sword, and wilt dash their children, and rip up their women with child"* (2 Kgs. 8:12).[43]

Pulling threshing implements over people would both crush them and cut their bodies to shreds. Such brutality and devaluation of human life was a war crime that would not go unpunished. The Lord promised that Syria would be invaded, their cities would be captured and burned, their rebel king killed, and many of their inhabitants would be enslaved and exiled to Kir (vv. 4-5). The Assyrians, led by Tiglath-Pileser III, fulfilled this prophecy in 732 B.C.

## Judgment Against Gaza (vv. 6-8)

Three other major cities in Philistia (Ashdod, Ashkelon, and Ekron) are named with Gaza to indicate that God's judgment would be against all the Philistines, not just the inhabitants of Gaza. The Philistines dwelt directly to the west of the Judean foothills and had been the enemies of Israel since Joshua led the Israelites into Canaan (Judg. 3:1-4). During the era of the Judges, the Philistines had repeatedly attempted to expand their dominion by invading Jewish territory. The conflict raged back and forth for hundreds of years until King David subdued Philistia (2 Sam. 8).

Amos states that the long-bitter enemies of Israel were engaged in the slave trade. Philistine raiding parties ventured into Israel and captured entire Jewish communities, which were then sold to the

Edomites, also long-standing enemies of Israel (v. 6). These helpless captives were then sold in the slave markets of Edom and shipped all over the world. These barbaric activities broke apart families and resulted in lifelong bondage and abuse for their innocent victims.

The *Lord God*, an expression found nineteen times in the book of Amos, would ensure that the buildings, people, and rulers of these Philistine cities suffered complete desolation (vv. 7-8). The Assyrian invasion in the eighth century B.C. partially fulfilled this prophecy. Hezekiah also had a hand in ensuring Gaza's decline (2 Kgs. 18:8). But the prophecy was more completely achieved during the Maccabean period in the second century B.C. In fact, by the start of the first century B.C. Israel had regained its borders similar to those under King David.

## Judgment Against Tyre (vv. 9-10)

Tyre was Phoenicia's leading seaport. Through a treaty, Tyre enjoyed a peaceful, productive relationship with Israel during the days of David and then Solomon (1 Kgs. 5). However, Tyre would reap God's indignation *"because they delivered up the whole captivity to Edom, and did not remember the covenant of brotherhood"* (v. 9). Edom and Philistia were longstanding enemies of Israel, but Tyre betrayed their covenant with Israel by capturing Jewish communities and then selling off entire families in Edom's slave market. The Lord promised to burn Tyre's fortifications and palaces. The Babylonians captured the mainland portion of Tyre after a thirteen-year siege in 573 B.C. Alexander the Great constructed a causeway to the island with materials scavenged from the mainland portion of the city. He then captured Tyre's island fortress in 332 B.C. after a seven-month siege.

## Judgment Against Edom (vv. 11-12)

The Edomites were the descendants of Jacob's twin brother Esau, who settled south of Moab and just east of the Dead Sea. The sibling conflict that began after Esau sold his birthright to Jacob for a bowl of bean soup continued among their descendants. Edom was a heathen nation that loathed the Jews, their fraternal brothers (Ezek. 35; Obad. 15-16). Edom's long history of hostility to the Jewish nation (e.g., 1 Sam. 14:47; 1 Kgs. 9:26-28; 2 Kgs. 8:20-21) commenced as the Israelites were journeying to Canaan. At that time, the Edomites refused to allow the Israelites to pass through their borders, which added many more miles to their route (Num. 20:14-21).

It was for their longstanding hatred of the Jews, their distant kin, and for selling them into slavery that they would be punished: *"Because he pursued his brother with the sword, and cast off all pity; his anger tore perpetually, and he kept his wrath forever"* (v. 11). Edomites had actually assisted Nebuchadnezzar in defeating Judah (Jer. 25:12). Edom had sided with Babylon in the defeat of Egypt in 605 B.C., but in 593 B.C. agreed to be part of an alliance, which included Judah and other nations, to rebel against Nebuchadnezzar (Jer. 27:1-7). However, when Babylon came against Jerusalem in 588 B.C., double-crossing Edom switched sides again and assisted Babylon in brutally conquering the Jewish nation (Jer. 49:7-22). Their hatred for Israel was so malicious that the Edomites laughed and rejoiced when the Babylonians conquered Judah. Yet, their folly was judged when Nebuchadnezzar burned their cities and palaces as promised (v. 12). This fulfilled Hosea's prophecy that Edom's largest southern city, Teman, and her fortified stronghold in the north, Bozrah, would be destroyed.

## Judgment Against Ammon (vv. 13-15)

The people of Ammon descended from Lot through his youngest daughter; hence, they were kin to the Moabites. They dwelled just north of Moab on the eastern side of the Jordan River. Ammon and Israel had been in frequent conflict since the time the Israelites entered Canaan (Judg. 10:6-11:33; 1 Sam. 11:1-11; 2 Chron. 20:1-30).

Amos says that Ammon deserved judgment *"because they ripped open the women with child in Gilead, that they might enlarge their territory"* (v. 13). When exactly this abuse of helpless mothers and unborn babes occurred is not stated. But God's tornadic judgment would lash against the Ammonites; the capital city of Rabbah would be burned and their leaders exiled (vv. 14-15). This prophecy was fulfilled in 734 B.C. during the Assyrian conquest.

Ironically, Ammon would repeat this offense by seizing several cities belonging to the tribe of Gad after Assyria conquered the region and exiled many Jews in 722 B.C. (Jer. 49:1). Jeremiah foretold that their god, Molech, whom the Ammonites brought with them into Gad's inheritance, would be removed from the land (Jer. 49:3). The

Babylonian invasion in the sixth century B.C. fulfilled both Jeremiah's and Ezekiel's prophecies against Ammon (Ezek. 25).

## Application

The Lord's fiery indignation towards Damascus, Tyre, Gaza, Edom, and Ammon in this chapter demonstrates His animosity toward those who oppress His people and brutalize the helpless (especially for profit or by treachery). Moses reminded the Israelites, before they entered the Promised Land, that vengeance and recompense for wrongdoing was the Lord's business (Deut. 32:35). God's wrath against wickedness and injustice is not a distasteful aspect of God's character, as some think, but rather a manifestation of His holy perfection. God's goodness and righteousness are demonstrated in both welcoming the repentant sinner into Heaven and casting the proud rebel into Hell. The psalmist recognizes this truth and calls on the Judge of the earth to take vengeance on the pompous wicked who persecuted His people (Ps. 94:1-3). Having steadfast confidence that God will not forsake His people, but will surely punish all those who afflict them instills hope in the minds of the oppressed (Ps. 94:14-15).

In the New Testament, Paul quotes the previously mentioned command of Moses, but adds this instruction for believers in the Church Age:

> *Repay no one evil for evil. ... Beloved, do not avenge yourselves, but rather give place to wrath; for it is written, "Vengeance is Mine, I will repay," says the Lord. Therefore ... do not be overcome by evil, but overcome evil with good* (Rom. 12:17-21).

During the dispensation of the Law, God demonstrated man's sin and need for a Savior because no one could keep the Law (Rom. 3:20; Gal. 3:24). However, in the Age of Grace, believers have the indwelling Holy Spirit and are commanded to fulfill the greater intention of the Law – to love selflessly, for example, by giving to others in lieu of merely not stealing from them (Rom. 13:8-10). Acknowledging God's righteous standard is the focus of keeping the Law, but demonstrating His irresistible love in righteousness is paramount in fulfilling the Law – and this we must do to win the lost to Christ! Christians, therefore, should desire to pluck lost souls out of hellfire much more than they desire to get even for wrong done to them. As we see in this chapter, in a coming day, God will deal with all injustice!

## Meditation

Ye sons of Adam, vain and young,
Indulge your eyes, indulge your tongue,
Taste the delights your souls desire,
Loosen all your carnal fire.

Pursue the pleasures you design,
And cheer your hearts with songs and wine;
Enjoy the day of mirth, but know
There is a day of judgment, too.

God from on high records your thoughts,
His book records your secret faults;
The works of darkness you have done
Must all appear before the sun.

The vengeance to your follies due
Should strike your hearts with terror through:
How will you stand before His face,
Or answer for His injured grace?

— Isaac Watts

# God Is Weighed Down
## Amos 2

Amos pronounced judgment on five people groups in the previous chapter; he will address three more in this chapter: Moab, Judah, and Israel.

## Judgment Against Moab (vv. 1-3)

Like the Ammonites, the Moabites were also descendants of Lot (through his older daughter). They were an arrogant people with a history of conflict with the Jews reaching back to the days of Moses (the Moabites tried to impede the Israelites from entering Canaan; Num. 22-24). The Moabites greatly oppressed the Israelites under the reign of King Eglon early in the era of the judges (Judg. 3:12-30). What is striking about Amos' denunciation of Moab is that the stated crime was not against the Jews, but was that of desecrating the bones of Edom's king and burning them to powder (v. 1). D. R. Sunukjian explains both the ancient custom and the possible historical situation in which the offense occurred:

> In ancient times much importance was placed on a dead man's body being peacefully placed in the family burial site, so that he could be "gathered to his fathers" and find rest in the grave. To rob, disturb, or desecrate a grave was an offense of the highest order. Many surviving tombs contain inscriptions uttering violent curses against anyone who would commit such an outrage. Moab, in a war against Edom (perhaps the incident referred to in 2 Kgs. 3:26-27), drove their opponents back to their own territory, opened the royal graves, and burned, as if to lime, the bones of Edom's king.[44]

Such sacrilege affronted God, for the Moabites were showing their utter contempt for their fellowman who was created in God's own image. Whether in its vicious ancient form or its modern culturally-refined jargon, racism has always been a slur against God's character.

When one man thinks he is more valuable than another man, it is not long before God is dethroned by a spirit of malice. Unchecked, this self-exalting pride will enslave those less-esteemed and will ruin every intention God had for human brotherhood. In this sense, the sacrilege committed by the Moabites was no less offensive to God than the slave trade that the Phoenicians, the Philistines, and the Edomites were engaged in. Amos promised that invaders would attack Kerioth (perhaps referring to the capital city of Ar), burn it with fire, and exile its leaders. Like Ammon, Moab fell to the Assyrians in 734 B.C.

## Judgment Against Judah (vv. 4-5)

Thus far, Amos has levied judgments against various Gentile nations for defiling the world with sin and breaking their *"everlasting covenant"* with God (Isa. 24:5). God created the earth in perfection and put man in authority over it, but humanity has utterly ruined what God made. God's conditional covenant with Adam in Eden put him under stewardship (Gen. 2:16-17). Obedience ensured life with God in paradise, but disobedience would result in hardship and death (including spiritual separation from God). God reaffirmed His everlasting covenant with man, after destroying the wicked, to establish a new beginning for humanity with Noah's family (Gen. 9:16). Man was created for God's pleasure and to glorify His name (Rev. 4:11). When man rejects the truth that God has revealed to go his own way, he has rebelled against the foundational purpose for which he was created. The only thing that elevates people over any other part of creation is their relationship with God.

God's judgment pronounced against Judah was for the weightier sin of breaking a second "everlasting covenant" that God instituted specifically with Abraham, then Isaac, then Jacob and his seed (i.e., the Jewish nation; Gen. 17:7, 19, 28:13-14). This covenant made Israel unique among the nations, but despite their special privilege and honor, they broke their agreement with God: *"they despised the law of the Lord, and have not kept His commandments. Their lies lead them astray, lies which their fathers followed"* (v. 4). Instead of holding to the letter of the Law, Judah adopted a more abstract form of it which led them out of the truth and into idolatry. The Southern Kingdom was not as blatantly pagan as the Northern Kingdom, but they approached Jehovah in vain religiosity, while secretly revering the same false gods that had led their forefathers astray.

Amos promised that Judah would be burned and Jerusalem destroyed (v. 5). This was partially fulfilled when Assyria captured and burned dozens of Judean cities, but the fuller invasion was averted when a brief revival under Hezekiah occurred in 701 B.C. The Lord then intervened to protect Jerusalem and thwart the Assyrian conquest. However, during the next century Judah continued to stray spiritually and morally. God sent both Jeremiah and Ezekiel to foretell the destruction of Jerusalem by the Babylonians. This occurred in 586 B.C. and ended the autonomy of the Southern Kingdom.

Throughout the Bible, idolatry is shown to be a door leading directly to immorality. This is why John, in his parting exhortation to fellow believers, wrote, *"Keep yourselves from idols"* (1 Jn. 5:21). Idols in our hearts will eventually lead us into moral ruin, as it did Judah who became immersed in both spiritual and physical adultery. It is one thing to be a pagan; it is an entirely different matter to be a pagan after having known the one true God, having experienced His goodness, seen His glory, and received His promises. The worst part was that the Jews did not even miss Jehovah's presence – an offense worthy of immense judgment. God loved His people too much to allow them to continue living a vain existence. In application, we should recall that an idol is anything that draws us away from the Lord; believers should be on guard, especially against those things which are associated with the doings of our own hands.

## Judgment Against Israel (vv. 6-16)

The final and most profound denunciation is now uttered by Amos against the Northern Kingdom. Indeed, God would hold nations accountable for their wickedness, but Israel was guilty of willfully breaking God's covenant, despite receiving His immense blessings. When Amos addressed the other nations, he mentioned only their final crime (i.e., the seventh) which filled up God's cup of indignation causing Him to be moved from patience to retribution. However, with Israel, the prophet does not blush or hold back; he bluntly lists all seven of Israel's crimes which have particularly offended God.

- They coldly sold their own countrymen who could not pay their debts into slavery (v. 6). Honest people were not given adequate time to repay the silver they owed, and poor people were enslaved for the insignificant sum needed to buy their sandals. Such callous treatment of the poor violated the Law (Deut. 15:7-11).

- They perverted justice to exploit the poor (v. 7). Judicial courts and creditors were in league with each other to trample over the impoverished for profit. The perversion of justice for profit was an affront to God's Law which specifically protected the poor from such things (Ex. 23:6-8).

- They were sexually perverse (v. 7). No doubt many examples could be named, but Amos identifies only one offense to represent their overall immorality: A father and son were having sexual relations with the same girl (either with the same temple prostitute in pagan orgies or the same servant, possibly a concubine of the father). God created marriage as a sacred institution between one man and one woman, which protected the physical relationship that a husband and wife were to enjoy (Gen. 2:20-24). Any distortion of God's design for marriage is an insult to His holy name. For this reason, the Law provided many decrees to ensure that marriage remained honorable and that women were not taken advantage of through unlawful lusting (e.g., Ex. 21:7-9).

- They were seizing inappropriate collateral to secure loans (v. 8). Under the Law certain items could not be used as an earnest to fulfill a loan commitment because they were essential for daily affairs, or to protect from inclement conditions. For these reasons, a millstone could not be taken as a pledge because it was necessary for grinding (Deut. 24:6), nor could a poor man's cloak be kept overnight (Ex. 22:26-27). Disregard for God's Law in this manner was bad enough, but the Jews were placing the illegal pledges before their pagan altars, thus displaying their contempt for God's commandments.

- They were committing idolatry (v. 8). In addition to placing illegal pledges from the poor before their altars, the Jews were raising cups of wine during ceremonial feasts to their gods. The wine apparently was paid for by extracting loan penalties and interest from the poor who were hopelessly ensnared in their financial trap. The Law strictly forbade all forms of idolatry (Ex. 20:3-4), but Israel's sin was compounded by demonstrating disdain for Jehovah's special provisions to protect the poor.

Before naming the last two sins, Amos pauses to describe how the nation had spurned God's bountiful grace through acts of rebellion (vv. 9-10). Amos mentions God liberating them from Egypt and bondage, providing for all their needs during their wandering years in the wilderness, and then defeating the Canaanites to give them a land of their own. God demonstrated His loyalty to His people by granting them victory against even their most formidable opponents in Canaan, the Amorites. Yet, despite God's abounding grace, Israel responded in defiance against God. Amos names two more ways that their belligerence was witnessed (vv. 11-12).

- They told God's prophets not to prophesy. Israel did not want to hear Jehovah's word, thinking somehow that ignorance would remove their accountability to Him.
- They enticed those consecrating themselves to the Lord in Nazirite vows to violate their commitments by drinking wine. The epitome of rebellion is when man willfully turns away from God and wants everyone else who lives for Him to do the same. E. B. Pusey suggests why and how Israel tried to corrupt the Nazirites:

God "raised up Nazirites," as a testimony to them; they sought to make His servants break their vow, in order to rid themselves of that testimony. Their effort to destroy it is a strong proof of its power. The world is mad against true religion, because it feels itself condemned by it. People set themselves against ... the Church ... only when and because they feel their power on God's side against them. What people despise, they do not oppose. ... If the people in power had not respected the Nazirites, or felt that the people respected them, they would not have attempted to corrupt or to force them to break their vow. The word, "cause" them "to drink," does not express whether they used constraint or seduction. Israel's consciences supplied it. Yet since they "persecuted the prophets" and put them to death, it seems likely that Amos means that they used violence, either by forcing the wine into their mouths ... or by threat of death.[45]

Christ, the Light of the world, challenges saint and sinner alike to step out from darkness and to walk in accordance with divine truth. In so doing, the unregenerate sinner will find salvation of his or her soul and the saint will learn more of the peace of God which surpasses all understanding. Accordingly, God's light without God's grace would be

142

a miserable existence indeed, and thankfully God does not offer either exclusively from the other. As long as God raised up Nazirites in Israel, it meant that truth and mercy were still available – the door of repentance leading back to Jehovah was still open.

## God Is Pressed Under Israel's Sin

All these transgressions (and many more could be named) greatly wearied the Lord. The Northern Kingdom was not atoning for their sins through genuine blood sacrifices per the Law, so their offenses were just piling up, so to speak. Amos wanted Israel to realize how wearisome their sin was to God: *"Behold, I am pressed under you, as a cart is pressed that is full of sheaves"* (v. 13). Later, Isaiah would declare a similar assessment to the Southern Kingdom: *"You have burdened Me with your sins, you have wearied Me with your iniquities"* (Isa. 1:24). The psalmist earlier wrote that God was *grieved* by sin (Ps. 95:10), but Israel's present situation was beyond mere grief; it was a heavy burden to Him.

Having named Israel's sevenfold offenses that deserved God's indignation, Amos describes the perilous military campaign against Israel in terms of a sevenfold defeat: the swift, the strong, the warrior, the archer, the infantry, the cavalry, even the bravest warrior will be overcome in battle; they will try to flee, but there will be no escape (vv. 13-16). This prophecy was fulfilled during the Assyrian conquest; Samaria, the capital city of Israel, fell in 722 B.C.

As Amos shows us, Scripture employs a variety of allegories so that we can better understand how wearisome willful sin, rebellion, and misplaced devotions are to God. Amos describes the injury to God in terms that we can identify – Israel's idolatry was crushing His heart under a cart fully loaded with grain. The wonder of the gospel is that a heavy-hearted God caused the object of His love – His sinless Son – to be sin for us, that we might have our burden of sin removed (2 Cor. 5:21). Thankfully, in a coming day, God will no longer be wearied and grieved by our sin. Nor shall we!

## Meditation

Years I spent in vanity and pride,
Caring not my Lord was crucified,
Knowing not it was for me He died on Calvary.

143

*Door of Hope*

By God's Word at last my sin I learned;
Then I trembled at the law I'd spurned,
Till my guilty soul imploring turned to Calvary.

Now I've given to Jesus everything,
Now I gladly own Him as my King,
Now my raptured soul can only sing of Calvary!

Oh, the love that drew salvation's plan!
Oh, the grace that brought it down to man!
Oh, the mighty gulf that God did span at Calvary!

— William R. Newell

# Revelation and Responsibility
Amos 3

Having concluded God's *roaring* indictments (1:2) against His own people and the surrounding nations, Amos delivers in this chapter the first of five personalized messages to Israel (chps. 3-6). Through these oracles he will assert Israel's guilt and the necessity of their punishment.

Israel was brought out of Egypt to enjoy a unique relationship with God through a covenant that placed them under greater responsibility (v. 1). The prophet's main point in his first message is that God did not afford Israel special privileges and benefits without accountability for covenant failure. For this reason, God treated the Jews differently than other people groups: *"You only have I known of all the families of the earth; therefore I will punish you for all your iniquities"* (v. 2).

God relates to the Jewish nation through a covenant of love (Ezek. 16:1-10). He promises not to deal with her as an enemy to be eradicated, but rather will instruct her through warfare and exile concerning the error of her ways (Isa. 27:8). Throughout Scripture we see that when God chooses to bless through revealing Himself, it always puts the recipient under more obligation. This coherent connection is the subject of verses 3-8.

Since Amos was God's prophet, if Israel ignored Amos' warnings, Israel would suffer irrevocable judgments! Amos then asks seven rhetorical questions that reasonably connected two things together to ensure Israel understood that divine revelation and responsibility could not be separated from each other.

- Two individuals do not agree to walk together, unless they have first talked with each other and agreed to do so (v. 3).
- A lion does not roar from his hiding place in the forest until he spots his prey (v. 4).
- A lion does not growl from his den, unless he is feasting on his prey (v. 4).

145

- A bird is not ensnared in a trap unless the trap has first been baited and set (v. 5).
- A tripped trap means something that was catchable triggered it (v. 5).
- When an alarm sounds to warn of advancing invaders, fear always results (v. 6).
- No calamity occurs which God does not permit (v. 6).

E. B. Pusey comments on what it means for two to walk together given the context of verse 3:

> This is an appeal to the conscience which feels itself parted from its God; *"so neither will God be with thee, unless thou art agreed and of one mind with God. Think not to have God with thee, unless thou art with God;"* as He says, *"I will not go up in the midst of thee, for thou art a stiff-necked people, lest I consume thee in the way"* (Ex. 33:3); and, *"if ye walk contrary unto Me, then will I also walk contrary unto you, and will punish you yet seven times for your sins"* (Lev. 26:4, 23). And on the other hand, *"They shall walk with Me in white, for they are worthy"* (Rev. 3:4). God cannot be agreed with the sinner who justifies himself.[46]

John explains that to remain in fellowship with God, a believer must continue to walk with God in the light of divine truth:

> *This is the message which we have heard from Him and declare to you, that God is light and in Him is no darkness at all. If we say that we have fellowship with Him, and walk in darkness, we lie and do not practice the truth. But if we walk in the light as He is in the light, we have fellowship with one another, and the blood of Jesus Christ His Son cleanses us from all sin* (1 Jn. 1:5-7).

A willingness to walk according to revealed truth brings happy fellowship with God and with other believers. We must have light to walk safely. When we choose to walk in the dark, we are inviting injury – the chastening hand of God. God is light, that is, His very character defines what is righteous. God will not, and indeed cannot, walk in darkness; that would offend His holy nature. Therefore, if we desire to have fellowship with Him, we must continue to live out revealed truth –

this is synonymous with walking with Him (i.e., walking in the Spirit; Gal. 5:16).

The Lord Jesus said of Himself: *"I am the light of the world. He who follows Me shall not walk in darkness, but have the light of life"* (John 8:12). The ultimate test of whether someone has truly trusted Christ for salvation is whether they continue in sin (i.e., the practicing of whatever displeases the Lord). A true child of God does not persist in sin (1 Jn. 3:9); a child of light does not blatantly walk in darkness. Why? Because a true believer longs for God's abiding presence and fellowship. Not only are there deep longings to be with God, but a profound remorse when under the conviction of the Holy Spirit should lead a true child of God to repentance and restoration.

Listen to Paul's medley of exhortations concerning the walk of the believer: do not walk as fools (Eph. 5:15), the way you formerly did (Eph. 5:8), or the way the Gentiles walk in the vanity of their minds (Eph. 4:17); walk as children of light (Eph. 5:8). In other words, don't be foolish; walk according to the truth, not in the darkness as before. The Lord Jesus promised that if we obey His commandments, He will manifest Himself to us in deeper fellowship (John 14:21). In order to walk with the Lord, we must be in agreement with Him on the matter of sin. For *"can two walk together except they be agreed?"* (v. 3). Surely, light has no communion with darkness; thus, may each of us walk with God according to divine truth and in moral integrity.

God, who keenly felt the loss of communion with His people, wanted them to joyfully walk with Him in the light, but they refused. His efforts to rectify the situation had not brought Israel back to Him; therefore, it was time for sterner measures.

A sovereign God is ultimately responsible for all calamities that occur, though He may not be the one doing the work (sometimes He permits others to do the work, e.g., Satan). He may also choose not to intervene in nature to preclude disasters, which occur as the fallout of original sin. Amos' point was the rebellion against God's revealed will must end with harsh consequences (v. 7). When God illuminates the path for us, it is foolish to venture into the shadows of humanism and the satanic darkness that rules the world: *"A lion has roared! Who will not fear? The Lord God has spoken! Who can but prophesy?"* (v. 8). God is a communicating God and He had not left Israel destitute of the truth; it had been sounded (roared) out through the prophets, including God's warnings against dismissing it.

In ironic poetry, Amos invites emissaries from Philistia and Egypt (Israel's bitter enemies) to take a position on the mountains above Samaria as witnesses to the repression, the brutality, the injustice, and the thievery in the land (vv. 9-10). These sins were flagrant abuses of God's law and He promised to punish Israel by ruthless invaders (the Assyrians) who would slaughter them (v. 11). Only a small remnant would survive the holocaust as pictured by a shepherd rescuing from a lion's jaws a few parts of a mostly devoured sheep (v. 12). Those in Samaria should not relax on their beds and couches after listening to false messages of assurance, but rather they should heed Amos' warnings, for God was roaring at them.

Besides foretelling the great Assyrian slaughter in Israel (the house of Jacob), Amos also said that Jeroboam's southern sanctuary in Bethel would be utterly destroyed (vv. 12-13). The altars associated with the golden calf would be cut down. Samaria's booming commerce would be ruined and the summer and winter mansions of Israel's affluent would be demolished (v. 14). Because Israel had thumbed her nose at God's will, as expressed by His prophets, severe judgment was unavoidable.

## Meditation

> This act of self-will on the part of the creature, which constitutes an utter falseness to its true creaturely position, is the only sin that can be conceived as the Fall.
>
> — C. S. Lewis


> Sin is a violation of moral light, a refusal to conform to what is known and perceived.
>
> — Gordon Olson

# Resisting Correction
## Amos 4

Amos likens the high-society women of Bashan to well-fed, unruly cows that were prone to intoxication (v. 1). Bashan, on the Eastern Plateau located east of the Jordan River, was known for its superb grasslands and lucrative cattle enterprise. In ridiculing the husbands of these plump, pampered women, the prophet does not use the normal Hebrew word for husband, but that of a master (*'adown*). Instead of rightly leading their wives as God intended, these men were docile servants responding to their wives' extravagant whims. Sadly, their luxurious lifestyle was at the expense of the poor.

God solemnly swears by His own holiness that every one of these high-society women will be judged (v. 2). The Assyrians would create so many breaches in the city wall that the captives would be led straight out of the ruins, instead of through the city's gates (v. 3). These snobby women would be tightly hooked together with ropes and marched single file into captivity. Those who resisted would be skewered with larger hooks or harpoons and be yanked along. The corpses of those succumbing to their wounds would be abandoned at Harmon. Harmon may refer to Mount Hermon on the northern tip of Bashan, which was on the route to Assyria. How ironic that these women, like the fattened cows of Bashan, would be slaughtered in their own land.

Genuine worshipers were instructed by Scripture to come to the sanctuary in Jerusalem to honor the Lord through sacrifices, tithes, and offerings of thanksgiving (Ps. 96:8-9, 100:2-4). Because Israel's gifts were for show and their praise devoid of true esteem for God, Amos sarcastically invites Israel to go to their pagan sites in Bethel and Gilgal to worship (v. 4; see 5:5). Additionally, he caustically instructs them to offer their sacrifices with leaven to better represent the true sinful state of their hearts (v. 5). Leaven represents sin throughout Scripture and was prohibited in burnt meal offerings. Continuing the mockery, Amos told these vain worshipers to offer their tithes every three days, instead of every three years as required by the law to assist the poor (Deut.

14:28-29). What Israel had grown to love – vain religiosity – is what God thoroughly disdained.

## Israel Scorned God's Correction

The final portion of this chapter addresses Israel's willful rejection of God's correction. Moses told the Israelites what would happen for failing to honor God's covenant and for continuing rebellion – a series of sevenfold increasing punishments (Lev. 26:14-39; Deut. 28-29).

*And after all this, if you do not obey Me, but walk contrary to Me, then I also will walk contrary to you in fury; and I, even I, will chastise you seven times for your sins* (Lev. 26:27-28).

Amos reviews these seven corrective measures: hunger and famine (v. 6), drought (vv. 7-8), blight and mildew (v. 9), locust (v. 9), disease and pestilence (v. 10), military defeat (v. 10), and widespread devastation (v. 11). It must be noted that before Moses threatened the above repercussions in Leviticus 26, he first affirmed God's blessing for obedience: *"If you walk in My statutes and keep My commandments, and perform them ..."* (Lev. 26:3). For their faithfulness, God's goodness could be expected in the following ways:

- Seasonal rainfall to ensure a bountiful harvest of fruits and grains (Lev. 26:4)
- Peace and safety from wild beasts and from invasion (Lev. 26:5-6)
- Invincibility in driving out the inhabitants of Canaan (Lev. 26:7-8)
- Many children (Lev. 26:9)
- Fulfillment of the land covenant originally promised to Abraham (Lev. 26:9)
- The Lord's abiding presence (Lev. 26:11-12)

The matter of disobedience is then addressed in the remainder of Leviticus. The Lord promised waves of chastening judgments with increasing severity leading to complete destruction of Jewish society if not heeded. Amos confirmed exactly what Moses said would happen. Yet, five times in this chapter the prophet discloses God's anguish over Israel's stubborn waywardness; they had not responded favorably to

His correction: *"Yet you have not returned to Me"* (vv. 6, 8, 9, 10, 11). For example, God had chastened them with hunger (clean teeth meant empty stomachs; v. 6) and then a drought that made drinking water and food scarce (v. 7), but still they would not repent.

Consequently, the intensity of chastening continued to increase, but no matter what God did, He could not get the attention of His people, let alone regain their affection. Even after permitting some of Israel's cities to be completely decimated by foreign armies, the nation would still not return to Him: *"I overthrew some of you, as God overthrew Sodom and Gomorrah, and you were like a firebrand plucked from the burning"* (v. 11). Only because of God's mercy had the nation escaped obliteration; Israel was like a burning stick pulled out of the fire.

In response to Israel's defiance, Amos issues one of the most chilling decrees in Scripture: *"Prepare to meet your God, O Israel"* (v. 12)! God's patience had run its course and now Israel would meet God in battle, so to speak, and experience the final blow of His reproving rod. The One who had fashioned the mountains and the wind would cover the entire land with an ominous cloud of death and destruction (v. 13).

The full brunt of God's chastening hand came against Israel through the Assyrians and, a little over a century later, against Judah through the Babylonians. However, God would honor His covenant with the Jewish nation and start with them again at the dawning of the Persian Empire. Israel would learn again the first lesson of their infancy at the bitter waters of Marah in the Wilderness of Shur:

> *If you diligently heed the voice of the Lord your God and do what is right in His sight, give ear to His commandments and keep all His statutes, I will put none of the diseases on you which I have brought on the Egyptians. For I am the Lord who heals you"* (Ex. 15:25-26).

The Lord would again teach His people this simple principle: obedience brings blessing, but disobedience results in punishment. Every child of God has the same choice: *"Be ye therefore followers of God, as dear children"* (Eph. 5:1). *"As obedient children, not fashioning yourselves according to the former lusts in your ignorance"* (1 Pet. 1:14). *"For whom the Lord loves He chastens"* (Heb. 12:6). There truly is only one way for a child of God to be happy in the Lord Jesus Christ – to trust and obey!

## Meditation

When we walk with the Lord in the light of His Word,
What a glory He sheds on our way!
While we do His good will He abides with us still,
And with all who will trust and obey.
Trust and obey, for there's no other way,
To be happy in Jesus, but to trust and obey.

— John H. Sammis

# Israel's Obituary
Amos 5:1-17

The third and fourth oracles of Amos to Israel are contained in this chapter. The overall theme of both messages is that God's judgment against Israel's immorality, social injustice, and idolatry were unavoidable, but individuals could still repent and live.

## The Prophet's Lament
The prophet invites his countrymen to listen to his lament over their demise (v. 1). How shocked would you be if, while strolling down a sidewalk in your hometown, you heard a grief-stricken friend reading your obituary aloud to a somber-looking crowd gathered to hear it? Under Jeroboam II, Israel's affluence was at its apex. Desolation and death were not on her mind, and yet the prophet was speaking as if it had already happened. No doubt Amos' dirge had a jaw-dropping effect on his happy-go-lucky audience.

Amos likened Israel to a maiden in the vibrancy and vigor of her youth who suddenly suffered a violent death in her own land (v. 2). Having been abandoned by God, her corpse lay unattended. There was no one who could restore her to life – her prime years would never be lived out. Her armies, dispatched to protect her, would be slaughtered; only one in ten of her soldiers would survive the confrontation (v. 3).

## Individuals Called to Repent
Amos stated in chapter 2 that God's judgment against the nation of Israel was irrevocable; yet, God was still willing to offer mercy to individuals who would genuinely return to Him. To this end, God beckons the wayward: *"Seek Me and live"* (v. 4) and *"Seek the Lord and live"* (v. 6). However, those seeking Him could not do so by engaging in pagan rituals at Bethel or Gilgal, or even at the patriarchal shrine in Beersheba (located in Judah). True worshipers must seek him inwardly through repentance (v. 5). True repentance would be evident

153

by remorse for sin and a lifestyle that now pursued holiness and good works (vv. 14-15). God's indignation would be a holy fire that would consume all who practiced paganism, perverted justice, and rejected His righteousness in the land (vv. 6-7). The only opportunity to escape this divine inferno was to truly seek the Lord!

The prophet interrupted his denunciation of Israel to interject that God, who is sovereign over His creation, is quite capable of executing full retribution against the wicked (vv. 8-9).

He created the stars and placed the constellations in the heavens for man to observe (v. 8). No doubt as a shepherd watching over his sheep on a Judean hillside, Amos had often looked up into the canopy of infinite blackness to contemplate the courses of the stars. Amos specifically refers to the constellation of Orion and the configuration of Pleiades (also called *"the seven stars"* (KJV) or sometimes the "seven sisters") as an example of God's handiwork in the heavens.

The Lord used Pleiades and Orion as object lessons to confirm His sovereign rule over the constellations while interrogating Job: *"Can you bind the cluster of the Pleiades, or loose the belt of Orion?"* (Job 38:31). Within the Taurus constellation is a tight grouping of stars in gravitational lock called "Pleiades." Although this cluster contains many stars (about 440 light years away), only seven are discernible with the naked eye on a clear night. As stated in Job, these stars are bound together; they cannot pull apart from one another. However, the constellation Orion is composed of stars throughout our galaxy, and we know that the Milky Way is expanding. As the years roll by, Orion's belt is literally *letting out a notch*. This is a wonderful example of how God is *"upholding all things by the word of His power"* (Heb. 1:3).

The answer to God's question put to Job is the same point Amos was making to Israel; the God who arranges galaxies and controls the constellations also completely controls your destiny. Jehovah was the One who controlled the stars, the rising and the setting of the sun, and the hydrologic cycle that watered the earth, and also the crushing vengeance to be released against Israel (v. 9).

Having asserted Jehovah's supremacy in ruling over Israel, Amos resumes his condemnation of Israel's depravity which must result in the Creator's reprisal. Because many in Israel had become rich through judicial fraud (lying for a bribe), dishonesty, and oppression of the poor, the well-to-do loathed anyone committed to honesty, truthfulness, and justice (vv. 10-12). The corruption was so widespread in Israel that many thought the prudent course of action was just to keep quiet, and not try to confront what could not be changed and those who would revile you for doing so (v. 13).

Silence condones sin; those who wanted to survive the coming holocaust must side with God and stand against what He disapproves of:

> *Seek good and not evil, that you may live; so the Lord God of hosts will be with you, as you have spoken. Hate evil, love good; establish justice in the gate. It may be that the Lord God of hosts will be gracious to the remnant of Joseph* (vv. 14-15).

The wise understand that God knows their abilities, works, and thoughts; therefore, there are no excuses which can fool Him from accurately judging our motives and behavior, especially if we are willfully silent amid injustice. Believers are instructed to *"have no fellowship with the unfruitful works of darkness, but rather expose them"* (Eph. 5:11). Amos' point is that silence condones sin! William MacDonald explains why believers cannot be silent spectators of unrighteousness:

> When innocent people are being led off to gas chambers, ovens, and other modes of execution – when unborn babies are destroyed in abortion clinics – it is inexcusable to stand by and not seek to rescue them. It is also useless to plead ignorance. As Dante said, "The hottest places in hell are reserved for those who in a time of great moral crisis maintain their neutrality."[47]

Israel was in great moral crisis! Those who would side with God could not be silent against such social depravity; they must seek and love good which meant shunning, confronting, and hating evil. A God-fearing, Christ-loving, Bible-believing person, will pursue speech and behavior that reflects this commitment.

Sadly, Israel did not have such convictions, so Amos returns to his earlier lament, for their holy God was going to pass through the land and judge the unrighteous (vv. 16-17). Afterwards, corpses would be lying everywhere, and grief and despair would fill rural highways, fields, vineyards, and Israel's city streets. The slaughter would be so great that there would not be enough professional mourners available to attend all the wakes and funerals. Even farmers (who are not accustomed to such emotional theatrics) would be summoned to weep and wail for the dead. If only the dead, while they were alive, would have listened to the prophet's plea, *"Seek the Lord and live."*

## Meditation

> Once again the Gospel message
> From the Savior you have heard;
> Will you heed the invitation?
> Will you turn and seek the Lord?
> Come believing! Come believing!
> Come to Jesus! Look and live!

> — Daniel W. Whittle

# The Day of the Lord
## Amos 5:18-27

In the Old Testament, the term "the Day of the Lord" is restricted to the prophetic books of Isaiah, Jeremiah, Ezekiel, Joel, Amos, Obadiah, and Zephaniah for obvious reasons – it is a future event significant to the Jewish nation. Amos applies the term three times in his book (vv. 18-20); only Joel has more occurrences, with five. The Day of the Lord is the subject of Amos' fourth of five messages.

In verse 18, Amos pronounces the first of two "woes" in his book: *"Woe to you who desire the day of the Lord! For what good is the day of the Lord to you?"* A "woe" in Scripture is an abrupt expression of distress often associated with God's displeasure and imminent judgment. The Jews looked forward to the Day of the Lord, because they believed that God, at that time, would deliver Israel from Gentile oppression forever and fulfill His covenant with Abraham. Ironically, this understanding was correct, but Israel did not understand the painful implications of the Day of the Lord to her personally – *"it will be darkness, not light."* Because Israel was not walking with Jehovah in holiness, the Day of the Lord would cause tremendous shame and grief. William Kelly suggests that the Church should not repeat Israel's error of yearning for Christ's coming for the wrong reasons:

> One evil was then prevalent which the prophet particularly notices, the boldness with which the people said that they desired the day of Jehovah (vv. 18-20). This is indeed presumptuous sin, not to believe the gospel but so to brave the day of the Lord. It is not so uncommon. We may often meet with it in Christendom. Have you not heard men say, in the midst of the present confusion, while helping it on, "It is true that the condition of Christendom is awful, but there is one comfort, that the Lord is soon coming to put it all right." Is not this desiring the day of Jehovah in a sense not remote from what is denounced here? "To what end is it for you?" If there were separation practically from what His word condemns, and devotedness to the objects He enjoins on us, it would be another matter. For true, the day

157

of Jehovah can be an object of desire if our souls are free as far as our conscience knows. We may, as we ought, and must then love His appearing. Far from this being inconsistent with His will and word, it becomes us. If walking in obedience and holiness, we should surely desire it, but it is an empty and bold illusion to settle down deliberately in what is contrary to scripture, and then to talk of longing for the day of the Lord. This seems to be precisely the sin of Israel here denounced. It was an evident sham; not only a powerless word without force in the conscience, but the witness of heart-indifference to the will of Jehovah.[48]

Jeremiah refers to Israel's refining period in the Day of the Lord as the *"Time of Jacob's Trouble"* (Jer. 30:7) which would occur in *"the latter days"* (Jer. 30:24). The Lord Jesus said it would be a time of great tribulation, and that there had not been anything like it before on earth, nor would there be afterwards (Matt. 24:21). It is not a literal day, but a seven-year period in which Israel will suffer greatly; yet, God will deliver His covenant people out of distress to experience, for a thousand years, the full wonder of Christ's Kingdom on earth. The Day of the Lord then includes the Tribulation Period and the Kingdom Age.

The period of immense tribulation for the Jewish nation is first introduced to us as a *type* in Genesis. During the days of Joseph, a devastating seven-year famine affected the whole land; this pictures the future seven-year Tribulation Period that will ravage the entire planet. When used metaphorically, *Egypt* speaks of "the world" in Scripture. Just as the nation of Israel was protected and preserved by God in Egypt during this severe seven-year trial, it will also be protected from the Antichrist during the Tribulation Period (Rev. 12).

Israel had an incomplete understanding of the Day of the Lord, and hence erroneous expectations. To illustrate the point that the Day of the Lord will be darkness and not light, the prophet provides a parable (vv. 19-20):

*It will be as though a man fled from a lion, and a bear met him! Or as though he went into the house, leaned his hand on the wall, and a serpent bit him! Is not the day of the Lord darkness, and not light? Is it not very dark, with no brightness in it?*

Israel is the "man" in the story. No matter how hard he tried to flee danger, he could not escape death; likewise, there would be no safe haven for Israel to avoid God's judgment. This is the plain context of the analogy, but there may be a prophetic meaning to the illustration which relates directly to the Day of the Lord in the future also. Rabbi Davis of the Beth Elohim Messianic Synagogue provides a Messianic Jewish perspective of Amos' story:

> It is prophetic for today. The phrase "if a man did flee from a lion and a bear met him" meant there will be NO escape. It may be a description for this generation, for the Lion may represent Great Britain and the Bear, Russia. Great Britain became the possessor of Palestine and declared they would grant a Jewish homeland in the Balfour declaration but reneged on their promise and Jews literally had to fight the British to gain possession of their homeland. Therefore we have Judah's (Israel's) conflict with Britain. The next event will be when, as prophesized in Jeremiah [Jer. 31, also see Ezek. 38-39], Israel will have to fight Russia who will invade Israel. Then in verse 19 we have the "serpent" bit him, Judah (Israel). This probably represents the rebuilding of the Temple, for Israel will defeat Russia. It represents the Antichrist who will declare himself God, who goes into the Temple and declared that all should worship him. We see a description of that in Amos 9:11-12.[49]

Interestingly, England (and then the United Kingdom) has employed lions prominently in its royal coat of arms for over eight hundred years. The bear (specifically the Eurasian brown bear) has been the most recognized symbol of Russia for the past four centuries. For example, the bear was the emblem of the XXII Olympic Games hosted by Moscow in 1980. Obviously, the serpent is a biblical icon for Satan (Rev. 12:9).

As Rabbi Davis has suggested, Amos' story has a remarkable resemblance to present-day events leading into the Tribulation Period. After WWI, Palestine became a British Protectorate and Jewish immigration was restricted. But after the terrible holocaust during WWII (over six million Jews were murdered by Hitler's third Reich), the Zionist Movement gained strength. Many surviving Jews desired to return to their homeland to start over. But Britain opposed this influx because Russia was promoting the idea of a Jewish state. Many Russian Jews wanted to resettle in Palestine, but the possibility of a communist beachhead on the Mediterranean Sea was not desirable.

Britain warships were deployed to blockade Palestine and intercept Jewish immigrants. Tens of thousands were caught and detained. U.S. President Harry S. Truman was a strong proponent of a Jewish state, which helped pressure the removal of the blockade and ultimately Britain's complete withdrawal from Palestine on May 14, 1948. That same day, the United States recognized Israel as a Jewish state. Israel escaped the clutches of the Lion, so to speak.

As Ezekiel foretells, Israel will escape from the Bear, during the Tribulation Period, when Jehovah intervenes to destroy the armies of Rosh (Russia) who will invade from the north to despoil Israel (Ezek. 38-39). This is called the Battle of Gog and Magog (see discussion in Joel 2).

Satan will be represented in the world by the Antichrist during the Tribulation Period (13:1-10). While Israel is under his false-peace treaty (Dan. 9:27), he will commit the abomination of desolation in the temple. He will stop the Jewish sacrifices and commence a rapid slaughter of Jews who will refuse to revere him. The Antichrist will murder approximately two-thirds of all Jews worldwide (Zech. 13:8-9), but his most intense desire will be to conquer Israel (Dan. 11:40-45; Joel 3:1-16; Zech. 14:1-2; Rev. 16:16). Amos says that the serpent will attack subtly in the man's house after he secures the door and rests his hand on it. The Jews will think they are safe in their homeland, but it will be there that the serpent's venom will do its worst.

Clearly, Amos' main point to the Jews in his day was to stop thinking the Day of the Lord was light (good). It was going to be a time of great darkness (distress and suffering). As to the possible symbolism of the Lion and Bear in our day, it is plausible and the discussed pattern does fit within the biblical framework of future events concerning Israel.

## God Hates Religious Hypocrisy

The message Amos delivers to Israel in verses 21-27 is similar to what Isaiah will declare a few years later to Judah: the Lord was fed up with Israel's vain religiosity. He hated and despised their feasts (v. 21) and He would not accept their burnt, meal, or peace offerings (v. 22). Through His prophets, God voices His utter disgust for Israel's religious hypocrisy. Through Isaiah, He said, *"Wickedness and the solemn meeting I cannot bear"* (Isa. 1:13; JND). In the next verse He decrees, *"My soul hates"* (Isa. 1:14), referring to their devotionless sacrifices, offerings, feasts, prayers, and observances. The literal meaning of this phrase is, "I hate with all my heart!" The Jews were morally corrupt and spiritually bankrupt people that were using religion as a cloak to cover their sin. The nation was superficially observing the Law without understanding the real purpose of what they were doing. God had had enough – He wholly detested being associated with these phony doings of His people!

Having censured Israel's religious fanfare, which included their corrupt spiritual leaders, Amos appeals to individuals to repent and to seek the Lord. D. R. Sunukjian observes:

> In verses 23-24 the verbs "away" [take away; NKJV] and "let...roll" [let run down; NKJV] are singular, whereas in verses 21-22 the pronouns "your" and "you" are plural. This indicates a shift from national accusation (vv. 21-22) to individual invitation (vv. 23-24).[50]

The Lord was not interested in hearing any individual sing or play musical instruments before Him (v. 23), unless they first were committed to following justice and righteousness inwardly (v. 24). The Lord wanted to see compassion and devotion spring up out of a pure heart and then flow out as a mighty, ongoing stream of goodness to others. Israel's superficial piety and religious nonsense did not refresh Him or others – it was a spiritual facade.

Returning to denouncing Israel's religious hypocrisy, the Lord reminded His people that much of their history had been marred by the same corruption and vanity that they were engaged in presently. Even in the wilderness years of their infancy, they offered sacrifices to a golden calf, to Molech, and to other false gods (v. 25; Acts 7:39-43). They had lifted up shrines to false deities, put graven images on pedestals, and lifted up the star symbol of their god to venerate figments of their imagination all the while provoking the God of their covenant to jealousy and anger (v. 26).

Amos wraps up his message by announcing God's judgment on Israel for their religious hypocrisy – *"exile beyond Damascus"* (v. 27). Heading northeast out of Israel and beyond Damascus would mean their destination was Assyria. For a Jew, exile was a worse punishment than a military defeat with heavy casualties, for it meant that they would be estranged from the land of promise and from Jehovah who resided there. But this was the judgment that Jehovah, *"the God of hosts,"* had deemed appropriate and needful to chasten His people.

The Church would do well to heed Amos' warning to Israel. It is human nature to traditionalize that which has no importance to God to displace what does. If Amos or Isaiah were before us today, they would affirm that the Lord hates check-the-box Christianity with the same fervor that He hates vain Judaism. That which displaces true devotion to, and appreciation for, Christ with meaningless religious trinkets and habitual routines is loathsome to God. Beloved, He deserves much more than a quick prayer here, or a staged production there, or weekly pew-warming exercises by holy misfits. The Lord wants the real thing – blood bought, born again saints with clean hands and pure heart that are in awe of Him and love Him above all else!

## Meditation

I consider that the chief dangers which confront the coming century will be religion without the Holy Ghost; Christianity without Christ; forgiveness without repentance; salvation without regeneration; politics without God; and Heaven without Hell.

— William Booth

I wish Christianity were more productive of good works ... I mean real good works ... not holy day keeping, sermon-hearing ... or making long prayers, filled with flatteries and compliments despised by wise men, and much less capable of pleasing the Deity.

— Benjamin Franklin

Let your religion be less of a theory and more of a love affair.

— G.K. Chesterton

# Complacency and Extravagance
Amos 6

In his fifth and final message, Amos asserts why Israel deserved divine punishment. So far the prophet has charged the North Kingdom with legal injustice, exploiting the poor, idolatry, religious hypocrisy, moral ineptness, and docile male leadership. In this chapter Amos will rebuke Israel's proud complacency and extravagant indulgence and predict the fall of both the Northern and the Southern Kingdoms (vv. 1, 14).

Amos' second and last "woe" is reserved for the pompous and morally complacent of Zion (Jerusalem) and Samaria. Although referring to the capitals of both kingdoms in verse 1, the remainder of the chapter is addressed solely to Israel. Judah was initially warned because they were being influenced by Israel's pagan ways and had begun to kindle God's anger towards them also.

## Proud Complacency
Under Jeroboam II, Israel enjoyed a robust economy and maintained a strong army to protect herself from those who might want to despoil their riches. Being a model nation, so to speak, the people trusted their leaders to guide and protect them (v. 1). Amos warned Israel's proud leaders of their self-sufficiency and against feeling invincible. He told them to look around and consider cities like Calneh and Hamath in northern Syria (Aram) and Gath in Philistia who similarly thought they were dominant and secure (v. 2). But Assyria conquered these Syrian cities in 854-846 B.C. and Syria had taken Gath in 815 B.C. Likewise, Israel should not be too high on themselves; they were no better prepared to fend off invaders than these kingdoms, and Israel's cities and territory were inferior to those that had been conquered.

Israel was therefore foolish to trust in their own ability to thwart the evil day: *"Woe to you who put far off the day of doom, who cause the seat of violence to come near"* (v. 3). D. R. Sunukjian suggests that Amos' prediction of *"the seat of violence to come near"* was fulfilled just prior to the day of their doom:

> "A reign of terror" aptly describes the last years of Israel's history before her captivity by Assyria (2 Kgs. 15:8-17:6). In the 31 years after Jeroboam II, Israel had six kings, three of whom seized power by political coup and assassination. The fear and violence in this period is reflected in the atrocities of 2 Kings 15:16.[51]

Even before the Assyrians invaded their land, Israel would taste the bitter fruit of a frivolous, morally-depraved society. Unbridled sin eventually leads any society into a runaway disaster.

## Extravagant Indulgence

While Israel's leaders had the respect of the common people, they did not have God's favor. They slept in ivory beds and sprawled out on soft couches while gorging themselves with the finest cuisine and guzzling bowls of wine, all the while dabbing themselves with precious ointments and perfumes (v. 4). Comparing themselves to David, these leaders even thought of themselves as accomplished musicians; they sang their own songs to each other, which further bolstered their egotistical folly. The self-exalting, self-focused attitudes of Israel's leaders in Amos' day were similar to what Christ confronted centuries later. The Lord Jesus said of them:

> *To what then shall I liken the men of this generation, and what are they like? They are like children sitting in the marketplace and calling to one another, saying: "We played the flute for you, and you did not dance; we mourned to you, and you did not weep." For John the Baptist came neither eating bread nor drinking wine, and you say, "He has a demon." The Son of Man has come eating and drinking, and you say, "Look, a glutton and a winebibber, a friend of tax collectors and sinners!" But wisdom is justified of all her children* (Luke 7:31-35).

The Lord likened the Pharisees to children in the street dancing to their own piped songs. Anyone who did not join them was rejected. John lived a simple existence while preaching in the wilderness. The Pharisees accused the Lord of extravagant living because He ate and drank with those He came to save. Yet, the attack on their lifestyles was merely an excuse to reject their divine messages. As Amos would demonstrate, those who live for the Lord will never be able to please Pharisees; they only danced to their own music! He was not distracted by their criticism or the rejection of his message. Rather he ignored their opposition and kept to the work that God gave him to do. When faced with pharisaical pride, this is a good example for us to follow also.

Israel's leaders had lulled themselves into a pampered, self-absorbed existence with no care for those they governed or for the imminent collapse of Joseph (speaking of the Northern Kingdom; v. 6). H. A. Ironside suggests that God's disdain for Israel's self-focused complacency should alarm every believer today:

> Are we not in grave danger of living to please ourselves, rejoicing in our possessions, and forgetting the breach of Joseph? – Forgetting the unhappy state of the assembly, indifferent to the breaches made by self-will, and which have so dishonored the Lord, the Church's glorified Head? Surely true love to Him will result in exercise of soul as to the present state of that which is so precious in His sight. Such exercises will lead to searching the Scriptures, and judging all in their light; to seeking to walk individually in "the old paths" in which the people of God have walked, even if one has thus to walk alone. But, withal, there will of very necessity be a manifestation of that "love to all the saints" which should characterize everyone who enters in any degree into the truth that "there is one Body, and one Spirit."[52]

But there was no such love in Israel for the covenant-body; rather, the rich aggressively oppressed the poor to sustain their plush lifestyle. Amos promised that Israel's high-minded, self-centered leaders who survived Assyria's campaign would be among the first to be exiled from their homeland (v. 7). That would silence their singing and put an end to their sumptuous revelry.

## Disaster Ahead

Because of Jacob's (Israel's) pride, the Lord swore an oath on His high title "Lord God" to destroy his luxurious palaces, which Israel believed to be safe havens (v. 8). Israel's high society had been built by oppressing the poor, and God promised to utterly smash it. Much of Israel's populace would be slaughtered by the Assyrians, but even if individuals could hide and escape the invasion, they would die of pestilence – there was no escaping God's judgment (v. 9).

In the aftermath, there would be so many corpses littering the land that normal burial practices will be ignored; dead bodies will have to be burned. If family members enter a house to retrieve a relative's corpse and find other survivors, they will tell those still alive not to mention the name of the Lord, lest they inadvertently cause Him to take notice of them (v. 10). There is a certain insanity that accompanies sin, and thinking that anyone could escape the scrutiny of an omniscient God by merely ignoring Him is the epitome of stupidity. Amos said that very few would escape God's wrath, for the homes of rich and poor alike would be demolished throughout the land (v. 11). Smashing even the little houses to pieces may be a direct reference to the great earthquake which occurred in approximately 760 B.C. (1:1).

Amos then offers two metaphors to depict the ludicrous depravity of Israel's leaders: a horse galloping on rocky crags which would surely break its legs and die, and a farmer attempting to plow the same rocky bluffs who would utterly fail in the task and likely damage his equipment and injure his oxen. Yet, Israel's vain and perverse leaders had *"turned justice into gall, and the fruit of righteousness into wormwood"* (v. 12). Israel's courts often sided with evil for the sake of profit instead of with what was just and righteous. This is unseemly. Such injustice poisons a society and ultimately leads to its demise.

Amos' indictment against Israel would be good for Western societies, established on a Christian heritage, to consider today. Many such *developed nations* have civil laws which directly oppose the moral constraints of the Ten Commandments which were to guide Israel's conduct. In the United States, for example, it can be reasonably argued that all of God's Ten Commandments have been undermined by civil law. Is our advanced culture any better than ancient Israel's, when freedom of speech permits the public disdain of God's name? When abortion allows the slaughter of millions of unborn babies, and bankruptcy laws endorse theft? When adultery and divorce are socially glamorized? When coveting is promoted through a bombardment of advertising schemes? Indeed, our carnality is more sophisticated, but it is nonetheless abrasive to God's holiness.

Under Jeroboam II, Israel's military enjoyed a string of victories and had reclaimed much of their land east of the Jordan (the cities of Lo Debar and Karnaim are named; v. 13). Israel's inhabitants were high on success and feeling invincible. Yet, Amos told them not to rejoice, for the Lord God of Hosts was going to raise up a nation that would decimate the entire region from *"Hamath to the Valley of the Arabah"* (v. 14). Lebo-hamath represented the northern boundary of Canaan promised to Israel (Num. 13:21), while the Valley of Arabah was the basin just south of the Dead Sea. When the Assyrians came, they would conquer all of Israel and portions of Judah as well.

It seems likely that Amos may have pronounced the city of *Lo Debar* as *Lo Dabar*, which in Hebrew means "nothing." The point is that all man's accomplishments, apart from God's blessing, count for nothing. All the economic prosperity and military successes that had prompted Israel's haughty ease and extravagant indulgences were coming to an end. All their great endeavors and achievements were nothing more than a fleeting, self-proclaimed hurrah; nothing they did had any lasting value or counted for eternity!

## Meditation

Therefore Thou alone, my Savior,
Shalt be All in all to me;
Search my heart and my behavior,
Root out all hypocrisy.
Restrain me from wandering on pathways unholy
And through all life's pilgrimage keep my heart lowly.
This one thing is needful, all others are vain;
I count all but loss that I Christ may obtain.

— Johann H. Schröder

167

# Locust, Fire, and a Plum Line
## Amos 7

In chapters 3-6 Amos delivered five messages that thoroughly presented God's case against Israel as covenant-breakers. Having substantiated the reasons Israel's punishment was warranted, the prophet transitions in chapters 7-9 to what will be accomplished through God's judgment. This information was conveyed to Amos in the form of five visions. God's severe chastening of the Northern Kingdom was unavoidable, but Amos kept the door of repentance cracked open for individuals who would humble themselves and return to the Lord. The Northern Kingdom was doomed, but those who would put their confidence in Jehovah could still be rescued from the coming desolation.

## First Vision – The Locust

The Lord showed a vast swarm of locusts that God had brought against Israel after the first crops of the early spring harvests had been gathered (v. 1). The king was entitled to his portion of the harvest before the people gathered for themselves. Amos knew that if the locust consumed the latter harvest, there would be no food in Israel to sustain the people – their starvation would be unbearable. He therefore passionately interceded for Israel, and the Lord, moved by His prophet's prayer, relented (v. 2). The Lord could not forgive Israel's sin without repentance, but He chose to chasten them in a different way as a result of Amos' prayer (v. 3).

One of the present ministries of Christ in heaven is to be our legal representative, or advocate, before the Father (1 Jn. 2:1). This is a special comfort for all believers, especially knowing that Satan slanders us before God's throne day and night (Rev. 12:10). Although the English word "advocate" is translated only once from the Greek New Testament, the same Greek word *parakletos* is often rendered "comforter," as in the references to the Holy Spirit in the Gospel of

John. The role of an advocate or a comforter is to plead the case of another person in a court of law – to be a legal intercessor. As pertaining to Christ, *Thayer's Greek Dictionary* defines the meaning of *parakletos* as "Christ's pleading for pardon of our sins before the Father." When does Christ plead our case? Is it when we acknowledge and confess our sins? No, 1 John 2:1 affirms that Christ's advocacy occurs *if* we sin, not *when* we confess our sins, even though we certainly should confess them. In other words, Christ is our Advocate at all times, not just when the believer fails. It is our Advocate's presence in heaven and not His plea per se that provides every believer with assurance of their positional standing before God. Thankfully, we have a High Priest and Advocate in Heaven who continues ongoing intercession for the wayward.

It is in God's nature to show mercy, so He appreciates those who will stand in the gap between a holy God and rebellious sinners. Amos followed the example of Abraham, who interceded for wicked Sodom (Gen. 18), and of Moses who interceded for the errant Israelites (Ex. 32). As a result, the Lord, who only threatened to send the locust plague to prompt Amos' intercession, did not punish His people in that way. So whose will was done on this particular day – God's or Amos'? The answer is both. Amos' faithful prayer simply affirmed God's sovereign plan for Israel that day – *"'It shall not be,' said the Lord"* (v. 3). But God appreciates those who remind Him of His Son by interceding for others to whom He longs to show mercy, but who do not deserve it. May we be willing also to stand in the gap for those undeserving of God's mercy that both the best outcome for the wayward and the most glory for God can be achieved.

## Second Vision – Fire

In the second vision the Lord showed Amos an immense and terrifying fire sweeping through Israel. A severe drought had dried up the rivers, streams, and even the underground aquifers, so the people had no means of extinguishing the inferno that was rapidly devouring the entire land (v. 4). The outcome of this vision would be even worse than the first, as the people would be without adequate drinking water and food, and even shelter would be scarce. For a second time Amos pleads with the Lord to relent, and as in the first vision, the Lord says, *"This also shall not be"* (vv. 5-6). At this time, God would not use the locusts, nor a blazing inferno to punish Israel.

These visions clearly reflect God's justified wrath over Israel's sin, but also His merciful character which tempers His wrath to wonderfully express the fullness of His character – completely righteous, just, and holy, but also gracious, longsuffering, and merciful. Hence, this is another wonderful outcome of prayer – those who engage in intercession are blessed by witnessing the fuller nature of God.

## Third Vision – The Plumb Line

A plumb line, which consisted of a line with a weight on one end, was a building tool used to ensure that walls were constructed vertically straight. It was also used to check existing walls for settling degradation. Tilting stone walls were dangerous and needed to be torn down and reconstructed to prevent a sudden collapse. Centuries earlier, God had initially constructed the Jewish nation with the Law as their plumb line (v. 7). However, when God rechecked Israel, that same moral tool indicated that Israel was badly tilted, and needed to be dismantled and brought down (v. 8). Before Amos had an opportunity to intervene again in prayer, the Lord explained that this vision was irrevocable. He was bringing a foreign army against Israel to tear down the high places and pagan shrines and to smite His idolatrous people with a sword and to exile the survivors – Israel would be dismantled (v. 9).

This vision shows us that though God appreciates our intercession on behalf of others, there is a limit to what He will act on. Sin is offensive to God's holiness and must be punished – there will always be consequences for sin, for it is outside His will and therefore lacks His blessing. Amos, understanding this aspect of God's character, does not try to intervene for Israel. In considering the matter, he was likely thankful that in God's mercy only some of the people would be consumed by the sword, rather than the whole nation perishing in the aftermath of a locust plague or conflagration.

## Amaziah's Complaint Against God's Servant

Amos was speaking to a spiritually despondent people who were locked into a perverse state of mind. Not surprisingly, they rejected the prophet's message. Amaziah, a pagan priest at the worship center in Bethel, complained to King Jeroboam II concerning Amos' preaching:

*Amos has conspired against you in the midst of the house of Israel.*
*The land is not able to bear all his words. For thus Amos has said:*
*"Jeroboam shall die by the sword, and Israel shall surely be led away*
*captive from their own land"* (vv. 10-11).

Amaziah told Amos to leave Bethel and to return to Judah; the apostate priest forbade him to preach at the king's house (temple) again (vv. 12-13). The insult *"there eat bread"* implied that Amos did not work for an honest living, but sold his prophecies, like a fortuneteller, for profit. Since the king and the sanctuaries were specifically mentioned, and Amos did not reveal the first and second visions, Amaziah is apparently responding to Amos' third vision.

Amos responds to Amaziah's impertinent demands by sharing his personal testimony to explain how a common laborer became God's spokesman (vv. 14-17). Amos says that he was not a prophet's son (nor had he attended a prophet's school) and therefore had no training for such a ministry (2 Kgs. 2:1-5). He previously labored as a shepherd and a gatherer of sycamore fruit. However, one day *"the Lord took"* him from his duties and commanded him to *"Go, prophesy to My people Israel"* (v. 15).

Amos' testimony to Amaziah is an excellent example for us to follow when we are attacked by those rejecting God's message. The prophet humbly declares what he had been, what he was made by merit of grace, that he had not assumed the prophetic office by hereditary right, nor by personal choice, but in necessity to obey God's command who inspired and sent him.

Amos was a laboring man whom God called to an entirely new kind of work. The Lord usually provides greater opportunities for service when His people are faithful to what they have already been asked to do, or are doing what they know they should do (Luke 16:10-11; Acts 13:1-3). There is no example in Scripture of the Lord calling a lazy person to serve Him. Elisha was plowing behind twelve yoke of oxen when he received his call through Elijah. Gideon was threshing wheat, and Moses and David were shepherding sheep when God beckoned them to service. Four of the disciples were fishing when they were told by the Lord Jesus, *"Follow Me."* The Lord calls working people to serve Him and Amos had proven himself a faithful laborer.

H. A. Ironside suggests that those years laboring as a shepherd and in orchards were not wasted years but were beneficial and enhanced his prophetic ministry:

> Not only were they years in which he listened to the voice of God speaking to his own soul, but in them he was acquiring experience, and an insight into men and things which would be invaluable to him later on. Again and again in his public utterances he uses figures, or illustrations, which show how closely and thoughtfully he had observed the many things, animate and inanimate, surrounding him in his early life.[53]

However, Amaziah did not esteem Amos' calling or accept his vivacious sermons, but rather he publicly opposed the prophet. Consequently, the Lord had a two-part message for Amaziah: First, the pagan priest was confronted by his own words that were in contradiction to God's command, *"Do not prophesy against Israel, and do not spout against the house of Isaac"* (v. 16). Second, Amos foretold that when his message (vv. 8-9) was fulfilled, Amaziah and his family would not be spared because he had rejected God's word (v. 17). He would be stripped of his office and property and exiled to eat unclean food and die among the heathen in a foreign land. To survive, his wife would be forced to earn a living as a prostitute in their hometown, and all their children would be slain by the invading Assyrians. All of this personal devastation could have been avoided, if only Amaziah had heeded Amos' call in chapter 5 to repent and had returned to the Lord. But he did not. Therefore his family would be amid the mass of misery in Israel – there was no escape.

The writer of Hebrews reminds believers that it never ends well when God's people harden their hearts against His express will:

> *For we have become partakers of Christ if we hold the beginning of our confidence steadfast to the end, while it is said: "Today, if you will hear His voice, do not harden your hearts as in the rebellion"* (vv. 14-15).

The Lord desires that the redeemed should experience the fullness of His salvation, His abiding presence, and His good favor. As the psalmist proclaims, this is what God wanted for Israel: *"Surely His salvation is near to those who fear Him, that glory may dwell in our land"* (Ps 85:9). Sadly, Amaziah's disposition was representative of the entire nation; Israel did not want God's goodness or His word, and consequently God's judgment was imminent. His glory would be demonstrated in the land, but not through salvation. Amos' preaching and prayers could not change this outcome, but perhaps there were a few lost sheep in Israel that heeded his message and were spared death.

The decisive call throughout Scripture is that *"now is the accepted time; behold, now is the day of salvation"* (2 Cor. 6:2). God's offer of deliverance should never be spurned, for there may never be another opportunity to receive mercy!

# Meditation

Be Thou my Judge, O righteous Lord,
Try Thou mine in-most heart;
I walk with steadfast trust in Thee,
Nor from Thy ways depart.

O search me, Lord, and prove me now;
Thy mercy I adore;
I choose Thy truth to be my guide,
And sinful ways abhor.

— A Paraphrase of Psalm 26

# Summer Fruit and Silence
Amos 8

The fourth of Amos' five visions is recorded in this chapter.

## The Fourth Vision – The Vision of the Summer Fruit

The Lord appeared again to Amos and asked him what he saw, implying that there was something for him to see – a vision (v. 1). The prophet answered, *"a basket of summer fruit"* (v. 2). This was the correct answer, and the Lord confirmed its meaning: *"The end has come upon My people Israel; I will not pass by them anymore"* (v. 2). Amos did not just say a basket of fruit, but of "summer fruit," which, as D. R. Sunukjian explains, refers to the last ripe fruit of the year:

> "Ripe fruit" (NIV) *qayis* was "summer fruit" (NKJV) or "end-of-the-year fruit" – the last fruit of the season, fully ripened, with a short edible life. "Ripe time (*qes*) was "end time" or "cutting time" – "the reaping time" of death.[54]

The basket of fully ripened fruit would need to be eaten quickly before it spoiled. This implied that Israel's time was up; judgment was looming over the last harvest of the season. Soon the songs in the temple would be replaced by wailing for the dead, whose bodies would litter streets. When the mourners did momentarily pause to ponder why God had permitted such devastation in Israel, only silence would be heard (v. 3). No new message from the Lord to Israel would be necessary at that time. Rather, survivors should consider the one Amos had delivered to them previously (i.e., his message contained in this chapter should be considered then).

His sermon was addressed to those *"who swallow up the needy, and make the poor of the land fail"* (v. 4). The prophet is then quick to indict Israel's businessmen with unethical and fanatical practices (vv. 5-6): unethical because they were fudging the scales on goods sold, cheating their customers on the money exchange rates, and selling substandard merchandise (e.g., mixing soiled grain with the good and selling it as all good); fanatical because they resented religious observances interrupting their commercial enterprises and they mercilessly sold the poor into slavery whenever they could not pay their debts, even trivial sums (e.g., the price of a pair of sandals).

The Lord was fully aware of what commercial Israel was doing and the financial atrocities they were committing against the poor. Therefore, He swore *"by the pride of Jacob"* not to forget any of their evil works (v. 7). *The Pride* [or Excellency; KJV] *of Jacob,* like the *"the Strength of Israel"* (1 Sam. 15:29) is a title for God in association with His covenant people. The God who does not forget wicked deeds would recompense the entire land for swelling up in pride.

Judgment culminating with the Assyrian invasion would be ushered in by unusual phenomena and natural disasters. For example, Amos predicted an earthquake; *"shall the land not tremble for this"* (v. 8). The Northern Kingdom would experience severe agitation like the turbulent swells of the Nile River (v. 8). This analogy likely describes an imminent earthquake, suggests E. B. Pusey:

> The prophet represents the land as heaving like the troubled sea. As the Nile rose, and its currents met and drove one against the other, covered and drowned the whole land like one vast sea, and then sank again, so the earth should rise, lift up itself, and heave and quake, shaking off the burden of man's oppressions, and sink again. It may be, he would describe the heaving, the rising and falling, of an earthquake. Perhaps, he means that as a man forgets all the moral laws of nature, so inanimate nature should be freed from its wonted laws, and shakes out its inhabitants or overwhelms them by an earthquake, as in one grave.[55]

As the Nile does not flow through Israel, we understand that Amos is using poetic expressions to describe the desolating upheaval coming to Israel. This meant that the time for repentance had passed and widespread bitterness and mourning could not be averted. Geological and archeological evidence shows that an earthquake with an estimated magnitude of 8 occurred in the mid-eighth century B.C. (see chapter 1 for this evaluation). In the next chapter, Amos describes the massive destruction caused by this earthquake (9:1).

## Solar Eclipse(s)

Additionally, Amos foretold that the sun would appear to set although it was midday (v. 9). This heavenly spectacle(s) would also confirm that the prophet's words were true and that God's judgment against Israel was imminent (v. 10).

The solar eclipse(s) foretold by Amos did occur shortly after delivering his messages. The National Aeronautics and Space Administration's (NASA) solar eclipse model reveals that there were only two near-total solar eclipses that affected Israel in the entire eighth century B.C.[56] The first occurred on Feb. 10, 765 B.C. and had a *Greatest Eclipse* (GE) center of latitude 43N and longitude 32E (in the Black Sea) and had a total eclipse path-width of 362 km. The second occurred on June 15, 763 B.C. and had a GE center of latitude 39N and longitude 54E (the eastern edge of the Caspian Sea) and had a total eclipse path-width of 204 km.[57]

The 765 B.C. solar eclipse had an 83% obscuration (i.e., the portion of sunlight blocked by the moon) in Israel, while the 763 B.C. solar eclipse (which trekked over the heart of the Assyrian Empire) had a 90% obscuration in Israel. Israel has a latitude 31N and longitude 35E. The 765 B.C. eclipse occurred mid-morning and lasted 2 hours and 39 minutes in Israel. The 763 B.C. eclipse also occurred mid-morning and lasted 2 hours and 43 minutes in Israel. For two, nearly total solar eclipses to be seen in Israel in a two-year period is extremely unusual – no doubt these disturbances reminded the apostate nation of Amos' prediction.

Archeological evidence also confirms that in 763 B.C. the Assyrian capital of Nineveh was totally blacked-out by a solar eclipse. A cuneiform tablet of an Assyrian Chronicle preserves the names of the annual magistrates for the year corresponding to 763–762 B.C. It reads: "Revolt in the citadel; in [the month] Siwan [equivalent to May–June], the Sun had an eclipse." Apparently, the insurrection in the city of Ashur, now known as Qal'at Sherqat in Iraq occurred at the same time of the eclipse.[58]

Returning to the NASA eclipse model, we also know that on April 4, 778 B.C. a midday solar eclipse occurred with 61% obscuration in Israel. And then on November 8, 771 B.C. a midday solar eclipse occurred with 50% obscuration in Israel. These are the only other, somewhat significant solar eclipses to occur in Israel during the eighth century B.C. prior to Amos' ministry. This means that the Jewish generation Amos was speaking to would have understood the meaning of his prophecy, as partial eclipses would have preceded his messages by less than a dozen years. The next significant solar eclipse to affect Israel after Amos' ministry was not until March 14, 711 B.C. It had a 65% obscuration.

If the above calculations are correct, it is likely that Amos began preaching shortly after King Uzziah (Azariah) took the throne of Judah in 767 B.C., and he finished no later than early 763 B.C. A prophetic ministry between 766 and 764 B.C. seems most likely. The solar eclipse(s) would precede an era of great mourning in Israel (v. 10). So many would die that everyone would be lamenting, all would be wearing sackcloth, and men would shave their heads bald. The ripened summer fruit would indeed perish quickly.

## Divine Silence

God's silence to Israel, likened to a famine in the land, would accompany His judgment. No matter how hard the people sought an explanation from Him, none would be given. His prophets had already declared what the people needed to know, yet they did not heed it (vv. 11-12). Even if those full of vitality, fair virgins and young men, walked throughout the entire land they would find no new revelation from the Lord (v. 13). J. Hay describes how Jewish young people will languish sadly because of this spiritual void:

> Here are young lads and girls experiencing spiritual debilitation, without as much as a syllable from heaven to ease their plight or to satisfy their yearnings. No crumb would fall from the master's table; there was no one to dip the tip of their finger in water to cool their tongue. Their desolation was complete. Drift and departure on the part of their fathers had left them casualties.[59]

The suffering of the next generation because of parent's despondency has been a recurring travesty throughout human history. May the Church learn from Israel's mistake – spiritual negligence today impairs tomorrow's children!

Those who had worshiped the gold-calf idols of Samaria and of Dan, and had visited the pagan shrine in Beersheba will not hear anything from the Lord despite their appeals. Their gods brought shame to Israel and their worshipers were destined to fall and not rise again (i.e., they would die in the Assyrian invasion).

177

Famine, drought, pestilence, locust, fire, earthquakes, invaders, and even death are all painful consequences of waywardness, but God turning a deaf ear to those He loves is to be feared even more than physical suffering. God spoke to these idolaters in their time, but He will be silent towards them in His eternity.

## Meditation

Silence at the proper season is wisdom, and better than any speech.

— Plutarch

God's silence should cause us to seek what He has already revealed!

— Warren A. Henderson

# God's Avenging Sword
Amos 9

The final chapter of the book contains Amos's fifth and final vision.

## The Fifth Vision – God's Avenging Sword

In this vision Amos saw a large congregation gathered in Bethel at the pagan sanctuary. Perhaps this feast and sacrifice was the one Jeroboam instituted in Bethel on the fifteenth day of the eighth month (1 Kgs. 12:31-33). As the king of Israel approached the altar with his sacrifice, Amos saw the Lord already standing before the altar with a sword in His hand (v. 1). The time had come to put an end to the evil temple and altar and to judge His idolatrous people worshiping there. Matthew Henry reminds us:

> Wherever sinners flee from God's justice, it will overtake them. Those whom God brings to heaven by his grace shall never be cast down, but those who seek to climb thither by vain confidence in themselves will be cast down and filled with shame. That which makes escape impossible and ruin sure is that God will set his eyes upon them for evil, not for good.[60]

The narrative foretells a twofold sentence against these pagans: First, either the Lord suddenly smote the temple with His sword or He used a great earthquake (1:1) to cause the door posts and the foundation stones of the pagan temple to shake violently, resulting in its total collapse. Its occupants were buried under the rubble. Second, those who survived would be slaughtered by the Assyrians – God would see to it that none would escape His wrath. William Kelly comments to the ominous imagery that Amos is describing in verse 1:

> It is no longer a question of sprinkling the lintels of the door with the blood of the paschal lamb. Now, on the contrary, it is His own people who are the object of inevitable destruction. Jehovah is not viewed

179

here as staying His hand and passing over His people, neither does He judge others in His displeasure; He is punishing not the Egyptians or the Gentiles, but Israel. A solemn sight and sound![61]

God's sword was now raised against His condemned people. Verses 2-4 whimsically portray their failed attempts to escape His judgment. Whether, hypothetically speaking, they were exiled to a foreign land, or tried to hide in the dense forests of Mount Carmel, or in the bottom of the sea, or in depths of the grave or even in the heights of heavens, God would hunt them down and execute them. Because the God of Israel ruled over all creation, He guaranteed that every pagan in the land would be destroyed by His sword one way or another (vv. 5-6). The One who caused mountains to quake and flatten and churned up the seas is the God who rules over every aspect of the earth's existence, including the lives of the wicked.

Next, Amos confirms God's sovereign control over the nations and His determination to show wayward Israel no special favor because of His covenant; the Jewish nation was going into exile (v. 7). Since God causes nations to rise and fall as He wills, He is certainly able to lead Israel in and out of captivity to achieve what is best for His people. As a holy and just God, He must place on Israel the covenant curses for disobedience as promised through Moses. Having stated God's judicial impartiality, Amos issues three separate verdicts of doom against Israel (vv. 8-10):

*Behold, the eyes of the Lord God are on the sinful kingdom, and I will destroy it from the face of the earth* (v. 8).

*For surely I will command, and will sift the house of Israel among all nations, as grain is sifted in a sieve* (v. 9).

*All the sinners of My people shall die by the sword, who say, "The calamity shall not overtake nor confront us"* (v. 10).

These statements alone would be the final blow for the Jewish nation, but the first and second decrees are followed by a message of hope for repentant individuals: *"Yet I will not utterly destroy the house of Jacob"* (v. 8) and, *"Yet not the smallest grain shall fall to the ground"* (v. 9). Not one righteous grain (a repentant Jew) would be lost during the forthcoming sifting judgment. Indeed, God would spare a remnant of Israel; He must do so to honor His covenant with the Jewish patriarchs. On this appeasing note of ultimate restoration Amos closes his book (vv. 11-15).

## Israel to Be Restored

The final five verses will be fulfilled during the Kingdom Age under Messiah's rule. Having appropriately punished the Jewish nation for idolatry, Jehovah will regather His covenant people back to the land of Israel and will reestablish David's kingdom (v. 11). The Messiah, being a descendant of David, will rule the entire nation; there will not be a Northern and Southern Kingdom. Moreover, all Gentiles (as represented by Edom) who did not follow the Antichrist during the Tribulation Period will enter the Kingdom Age and be abundantly blessed by Israel's Messiah (v. 12).

James, the half-brother of Christ, cited verses 11-12 during the Jerusalem Council (Acts 15) to prove that God desired to bless the Gentiles through Christ also. Gentiles in the Church Age could be saved in the same way as Jews were, by believing the gospel message, not by conforming to the rituals of the Law, such as circumcision. The Law still served as a moral guide to show sin, but the Gentiles were never under it, and the Jewish nation was no longer under its judicial sway. In the Kingdom Age, both Jewish and Gentile believers together will enjoy the blessings of Christ!

During Christ's Millennial Kingdom, the divine curses levied on the earth because of original sin will be lifted and nature's full productivity will be restored for all to enjoy (v. 13; Rom. 8:21-22). A handful of seed casually scattered on a mountaintop will produce a great harvest (Ps. 72:16), longevity will be restored to humanity, weapons will be used as agricultural implements (Mic. 4:3), and a spirit of peace and tranquility will engulf the earth, including all wildlife (Isa. 11:6-10).

Amos says that the harvest will be so plentiful that those plowing will have to slow down to permit the reapers time to gather all the grain, and those planting in the vineyards will have to give way to those gathering and processing grapes (v. 13). The goodness of the Lord, poetically speaking, will flow down from the mountains and will ooze out of the hills – the entire planet will be an agricultural wonder.

The Lord will regather all surviving Jews in the world to the land of Israel to receive their inheritance by tribe (v. 14; Ezek. 39:28-29;

47:13-48:35). Israel's cities will be rebuilt and God's covenant people will enjoy the rich bounty of the land. No invaders will ever disturb the Jews again, for God will plant them in the land during the Kingdom Age and no one shall pluck them out again (v. 15). The God of Israel is sovereign over His creation and His covenant people and He has sworn to do all that Amos has prophetically declared, for it is *"the Lord who does this thing"* (v. 12).

## Meditation

> God moves in a mysterious way
> His wonders to perform;
> He plants His footsteps in the sea
> And rides upon the storm.
>
> Deep in unfathomable mines
> Of never-failing skill
> He treasures up His bright designs
> And works His sovereign will.
>
> His purposes will ripen fast,
> Unfolding every hour;
> The bud may have a bitter taste,
> But sweet will be the flower.
>
> Blind unbelief is sure to err
> And scan His work in vain;
> God is His own interpreter,
> And He will make it plain.

— William Cowper

# Obadiah

# Overview of Obadiah

## The Author

Although about a dozen others share his name in Scripture, nothing more about the prophet Obadiah is revealed to us. Obadiah's name means "servant of Jehovah."

## Date

Like the prophet Joel, Obadiah does not mention any Jewish or Gentile kings during his prophetic ministry or any specific events that would assist us in dating this brief narrative. Because no Jewish monarchies are identified, some prefer a sixth century B.C. date shortly after the destruction of Jerusalem. However, the prophet's warning not to repeat the offenses of the past would be meaningless if the Babylonians had already decimated the region. Others believe that Obadiah prophesied shortly before the fall of Jerusalem and that both Jeremiah and Ezekiel then quoted him in their works (Jer. 49:7-16; Ezek. 25:12-13).

Many commentators believe that Obadiah lived in the ninth century B.C., during the reign of King Jehoram and was the oldest of the writing prophets, with the possible except of Jonah (848-841 B.C.). The date of the prophecy cannot be confirmed, but this author favors the older date as the sins of Edom against Israel had piled up for centuries and were ripe for judgment. Additionally, no rebuke is given to Israel or Judah for idolatrous practices. Yet, such warnings abound in all prophetic books written in the eighth, seventh, and early sixth centuries B.C., which address Israel to some extent. The books of Jonah and Nahum are strictly addressed to Nineveh and do not address Israel. Yet, Obadiah, while pronouncing judgment on Edom, has only blessings to declare for Israel – no rebuke whatsoever.

## Theme

Obadiah is the shortest book in the Old Testament and the third shortest in the Bible. This brief oracle has a concentrated theme that foretells the doom of proud Edom, a nation fathered by Jacob's twin brother Esau. The prophet's message closes by prophesying Israel's future deliverance and blessings. Jacob and Esau's descendants followed in the same hostile behavior that the two brothers expressed towards each other as recorded in Genesis. When was Obadiah's prophecy fulfilled? It can be argued that partial fulfillment occurred during the Assyrian conquest of the eighth century B.C. and then the Babylonian invasion in sixth century B.C. Complete fulfillment happened in 70 A.D. under the Romans.

Prophets following Obadiah utter more specific judgments against Edom. Isaiah foretold that Edom would be oppressed by Assyria (Isa. 21:11-12). Edom did pay tribute to Assyria (Tiglath-Pilesar in 734 B.C. and Sargon II in 711 B.C.). Ezekiel, in the sixth century, tells us why God was angry with the Edomites – they had assumed Israel was a nation no different than any other. This conclusion challenged the importance of God's Word and His special relationship with the Jewish people (Ezek. 25:8). Furthermore, Edom's sin was great because they had actually assisted Nebuchadnezzar in defeating Judah after agreeing to be Judah's ally against Babylon (Ezek. 25:12; Jer. 27:1-7, 49:7-22). Ezekiel said that Edom's actions were motivated by hate and revenge (Ezek. 25:12). Obadiah's book, then, is the first of several condemnations of Edom in Scripture.

## Outline

The Doom of Edom Foretold (vv. 1-9)
The Reasons for Edom's Judgment (vv. 10-16)
The Future Deliverance of Israel (vv. 17-21)

# Devotions in Obadiah

# Faithfulness in Captivity
Obadiah

The book commences with these words: *"The vision of Obadiah; thus says the Lord God concerning Edom."* The prophetic books of Amos, Micah, and Nahum begin in a similar fashion. Old Testament prophets not only heard the Lord, but often saw through visions the messages that they were to convey to God's people. Obadiah was to summon the nations to battle against Edom: *"Arise, and let us rise up against her for battle"* (v. 1). The Edomites were the descendants of Jacob's twin brother Esau, who settled in the region south of Moab and east of the Dead Sea.

Although more is said later, Obadiah reveals the underlying reason for Edom's judgment in verse 3:

*The pride of your heart has deceived you, you who dwell in the clefts of the rock, whose habitation is high; you who say in your heart, "Who will bring me down to the ground?"*

Edomites greatly esteemed their wealth and accomplishments. They had fortified themselves in the mountains of Seir and thought they were invincible. The prophet likens Edom's self-deception to an eagle soaring up into the heavens to construct her nest among the stars and then pompously saying, *"Who will bring me down to the ground?"* But the God who hates pride (Prov. 6:16-17) answers Edom's haughty question, *"I will bring you down"* (v. 4). Edom would be brought low and be despised by the nations (v. 2).

## Edom's Judgment
Edom was proud of her wealth (v. 6), her foreign alliances, (v. 7), her wisdom (v. 8), and her military might (v. 9). Whereas a thief

striking at night and gatherers of grapes at harvest time do not rob or reap everything, Edom's invaders would strip their land bare (vv. 5-6). Though proclaiming to be wise, Edom was unaware of the fact that her allies were deceiving her through trade agreements and political alliances to covertly overcome and despoil her (v. 7). *"'Will I not in that day,' says the Lord, 'even destroy the wise men from Edom?'"* (v. 8). The result would be that Edom's warriors would be dismayed, Edom's soldiers and citizens would be slaughtered, and their capital city Teman would be destroyed (v. 9). In demonstrating His hatred of pride, everything that Edom valued and boasted in God promised to take away.

God's actions against conceited Edom should cause us to consider Solomon's wisdom on the matter of pride: *"The fear of the Lord is to hate evil, pride and arrogance, and the evil way"* (Prov. 8:13). *"By pride comes nothing but strife"* (Prov. 13:10). *"Pride goes before destruction and a haughty spirit before a fall"* (Prov. 16:18). *"A man's pride will bring him low, but the humble in spirit will retain honor"* (Prov. 29:23). The Edomites' self-confidence and arrogance would cause their undoing, and it will result in ours also if we repeat their sin.

## Edom's Crimes

Obadiah first identifies Edom's sinful heart attitudes (vv. 10-12), and then her offenses against Judah (vv. 13-14). From the very beginning, the Edomites loathed the Jews, their fraternal brothers. Ezekiel refers to this as *"an ancient hatred"* (Ezek. 35:5) that began after Esau (the father of Edom) sold Jacob (the father of Israel) his birthright for a bowl of bean soup. Since God had promised to curse all nations that would curse the promised nation (Abraham's seed), Edom was doomed from the beginning (Gen. 12:3). Edom's *ancient hatred* of the Jews had caused them to commit many atrocities against God's people. Consequently, none of the prophets offer Edom a promise of future restoration.

The prophet then lists Edom's specific crimes. When Israel was invaded and despoiled, Edom looked with indifference at the suffering of their distant kin and even boasted over Israel's trouble (vv. 11-12). Then afterwards, Edom raided Israel, looting and slaughtering escaping survivors (vv. 13-14; Ezek. 35:6-10). True, Jehovah had to chasten His people, but proud and brutal Edom sought to profit from their calamity and in doing so went too far. Therefore, the Lord was going to severely punish Edom.

Motivated by covetousness and hatred for centuries, the Edomites had inflicted much suffering on God's covenant people. Obadiah affirms that in the same ruthless way the Edomites had treated Israel, God would recompense them when He judged all nations in the Day of the Lord (vv. 15-16). See Joel 2 for a detailed discussion on the Day of the Lord. In the end, Edom *"shall be cut off forever"* (v. 10) and *"no survivor shall remain of the house of Esau"* (v. 18).

Indeed, no descendant of the Edomites can be identified on earth today. They were ruled over by the Babylonian and Medo-Persian Empires. The latter pushed them from their homeland into the southern hill country of Judah. In 126 B.C. the Jews conquered and forced the Edomites remaining in their land to convert to Judaism. When Jerusalem was destroyed by the Romans in 70 A.D., the Jewish population was dispersed among the nations and any evidence of this once vast nation that might have still remained was lost. Edom is indeed desolate forever! William Kelly sees a principle here in God's dealings, given His patience in permitting Israel to suffer Edom's cruelty for so many centuries before avenging His covenant people:

> The greater the patience of God, the worse man behaves in presence of His goodness and patience, so much the more tremendous must be the judgment when it comes. This we may read in the ultimate history of Edom.[62]

## Israel Blessed

Jehovah promised to avenge Edom's cruelty with the same measure of hatred and jealousy they had shown Israel. In this sense, Edom is an object lesson warning all Gentile nations – God will hold every nation accountable for how they treat Israel. When the Lord returns to establish His kingdom, all nations of the earth will be judged accordingly (Matt. 25:31-46). God loves His covenant people despite their unfaithfulness; woe to any nation that abuses them. It is His plan to completely restore the Jewish nation to Zion in holiness and give to them the possessions of those who oppressed them (v. 17). In this sense, Israel will be the flame that will utterly consume the stubble of Edom in the future (v. 18).

All that was taken from Israel by the nations will be returned to the Jews with much more in the Kingdom Age. All Jews worldwide will return to the Promised Land to commune with their Messiah (Ezek. 39:28). Those Jews living in the Negev, in southern Judah, will inherit the mountains of Esau (i.e., Edom; v. 19). Jews in the Judean foothills (the Shephelah) will move into the fertile plain of Philistia. Even the small tribe of Benjamin will extend its borders east of the Jordan River (v. 19). Returning Jews will also inherit land as far north as Zarephath and the Negev in the south (v. 20). Specific tribal boundaries and national borders during the millennial reign of Christ are described in Ezekiel 47:13-48:29.

This brief book closes with a promise: *"The deliverers will ascend Mount Zion to judge the mountain of Esau, and the kingdom will be the Lord's"* (v. 21; NASB). Judges in Jerusalem will oversee those who live in the mountains of Esau, but all will be under Messiah's rule, for it is His Kingdom. W. L. Baker provides this application for us to consider as we ponder the book of Obadiah:

> Obadiah presents a powerful message. It shows what happens to those who reject God's Word and His grace, rebelling in foolish pride. During Edom's prosperity many in Israel could have asked, *"Why do the wicked prosper?"* (Ps. 73:3). But the voice of Obadiah comes thundering through the pages of the Old Testament, and is echoed in the New: *"Do not be deceived: God cannot be mocked. A man reaps what he sows"* (Gal. 6:7). Obadiah's words underscore the fact of God's justice. *"For we know Him who said, 'It is Mine to avenge; I will repay.' ...It is a dreadful thing to fall into the hands of the living God"* (Heb. 10:30-31). One who responds in obedience to the grace of God has everything to gain, but a person who spurns His grace in pride has everything to lose.[63]

## Typological Fulfillment

Besides judging their barbaric atrocities against Israel, why were the Edomites destined to lose their distinctiveness as a people? The answer originates in Exodus 17 and is then confirmed elsewhere in Scripture: the Edomites represent something which continues to oppose God and must therefore be eliminated. After crossing the Red Sea, the Israelites were brought into the wilderness by Moses. There they suffered an unprovoked attack by the Amalekites (Edomites). Amalek was the grandson of profane Esau, *"who for one morsel of food sold his birthright"* (Heb. 12:16). Consequently, both Esau and Amalek are used in Scripture to picture the lusting flesh which continues to, war against God's people.

So why will the Edomites not have an inheritance in the Kingdom Age: Why do they have no future identity as a people? This is a fair judgment for the nation's sins and it is symbolically fitting because the Edomites picture the flesh, which is in opposition to God (Gal. 5:17). God desires believers to *"make no provision for the flesh to fulfill its lusting"* (Rom. 13:14). This mindset is vital to victorious Christian living: *"For if you live according to the flesh you will die; but if by the Spirit you put to death the deeds of the body, you will live"* (Rom. 8:13). The stench of carnal flesh is what the Lord wants to remove from us; it will have no place in His kingdom, and neither will the Edomites. No wonder, then, the Lord said, *"Esau I have hated, and laid waste his mountains and his heritage for the jackals of the wilderness"* (Mal. 1:3).

## Meditation

Matthew Henry likens Edom's carnal opposition to God's covenant people to the hostility against the Church today. His point is that what is of the flesh cannot overcome that which God favors:

All the enemies of God's church shall be disappointed in the things they stay themselves on. God can easily lay those low who magnify and exalt themselves; and will do it. Carnal security ripens men for ruin, and makes the ruin worse when it comes. Treasures on earth cannot be so safely laid up but that thieves may break through and steal; it is therefore our wisdom to lay up for ourselves treasures in heaven. Those that make flesh their trust, arm it against themselves.[64]

— Matthew Henry

# Jonah

# Overview of Jonah

## The Author

Jonah is probably the best known of the Minor Prophets because the narrative is his personal story rather than merely a record of pronounced judgments. In actuality, the prophet Jonah uttered only one prophecy and it related to Nineveh at that time. Yet, the book is distinctly prophetic in that it reflects God's future dealings with Israel's unspiritual attitudes and it presents a type of Christ's resurrection, which the Lord Jesus confirms. Jonah is one of four prophets that the Lord Jesus referred to during His earthly ministry (Matt. 12:41); the others were Elijah, Elisha, and Isaiah.

Jonah was from Gath-Hepher in Galilee and his father was Amittai. We also know that he had an active prophetic ministry prior to being summoned to Nineveh (2 Kgs. 14:23-25). Jonah's name means "dove," which symbolizes peace in Scripture. Given his antagonism towards Nineveh, Jonah was a strange dove, that is, messenger of peace. Though initially Jonah was an unwilling foreign missionary, his warning of coming judgment was well-accepted by the inhabitants of Nineveh. Consequently, God's mercy rather than His wrath was received.

## Date

Jonah lived during the reign of King Jeroboam II and actually prophesied that Israel's boundaries would expand under his leadership, which they did (2 Kgs. 14:25). Jeroboam reigned in Israel from 793-753 B.C. Jonah would have been a contemporary of Hosea and Amos. The timing of the great earthquake (approximately 760 B.C.; see Amos 1), two severe famines in 765 and 759 B.C., and the total solar eclipse which trekked across the heart of the empire on June 15, 763 B.C. (see Amos 8) may have been phenomena that psychologically rattled the Assyrians and caused them to heed Jonah's warning. If this assumption is true, Jonah's ministry in Nineveh would likely be shortly after these events (e.g., 759-755 B.C.).

## Theme

Although God wanted to show mercy to the inhabitants of Nineveh if they would heed Jonah's message, that is not the primary emphasis of the book. Rather, God's rebuke of Israel's superficial religiosity and their callous concern for perishing Gentiles is paramount, as is God's loving care to nudge His servant on to maturity.

Accordingly, Jonah does not hesitate to reveal his disobedience to God's expressed will, his punishment for doing so, his miraculous deliverance, and his restoration to fruitfulness. He then informs us of the positive outcome of his ministry and how the Lord also dealt with his ungodly attitudes. While tens of thousands of souls were spared death through Jonah's preaching, the forbearing and forgiving nature of God is wonderfully expressed in His dealings with His wayward prophet.

It is observed that *Elohim*, translated "God," occurs fifteen times in the book, and *Yehovah* (Jehovah), rendered "the Lord," is found twenty-five times. In His mercy and sovereign sway over nature, God saves pagan sailors, a heathen city, and a prophet from his own hardened heart. All this to say that the book of Jonah is rich testimony of Jehovah God's goodness!

## Outline

The Disobedience of Jonah (1:1-11) – Jonah Rebels
Jonah's Prayer While in a Great Fish (1:12-2:10) – Jonah Prays
A Great Revival in Nineveh (3:1-10) – Jonah Preaches
God's Mercy and Rebuke (4:1-11) – Jonah's Anger

# Devotions in Jonah

# Going "Down"
Jonah 1

Jonah was from Gath-Hepher in Galilee and his father was Amittai (v. 1). Jonah was already serving as God's prophet (2 Kgs. 14:23-25) when one day he received new marching orders from the Lord: *"Arise, go to Nineveh, that great city, and cry out against it; for their wickedness has come up before Me"* (v. 2). The Lord was mindful of Nineveh's increasing wickedness and He was poised to judge that city, but not without first providing a warning and giving them the opportunity to be delivered. Nineveh was an ancient city, first built by Nimrod (Gen. 10:11), and then becoming the capital city of the Assyrian Empire during the eighth and seventh centuries B.C.

## Fleeing God
Jonah was not at all sympathetic to God's compassion for Israel's enemy; he therefore did not respond to God's directive favorably: *"But Jonah arose to flee to Tarshish from the presence of the Lord. He went down to Joppa, and found a ship going to Tarshish; so he paid the fare, and went down into it, to go with them to Tarshish from the presence of the Lord"* (v. 3). Jonah did not simply ignore God's command; he was determined to get as far away from Nineveh as possible. He journeyed to Joppa (which is on the outskirts of modern-day Tel Aviv) and booked passage on a ship to Tarshish. The exact location of Tarshish is debated (e.g., Spain or Britain), but it certainly was to the far west and the end of the world, so to speak, for Jonah.

A ship full of pagans was a strange place for a Jewish prophet. His Jewish dress and features must have aroused some suspicion. The fugitive quickly boarded the ship and withdrew from sight into the lowest level of the ship. But no matter what dark hole Jonah scurried into, he could not hide from God.    Rather than journeying northeast on the path of righteousness set before him, Jonah headed west, away from his calling. In fact, he was willing to go much farther than the 550 miles to Nineveh in the opposite direction to avoid God's command altogether. The idea of being a prophet to the Gentiles was distasteful enough (unless condemning them), but the idea of preaching to Israel's ruthless enemy in a way that might preclude their judgment was unacceptable, for Jonah knew that, if he preached to them and they turned from their wickedness, God would show mercy to them (4:2-3).

Jonah did not want the Ninevites to receive God's forgiveness; he wanted God to wipe them out for their brutality to Israel. Although we are not told why Jonah acted against God, racial hatred and the desire for revenge seem likely motives. All this to say that God's dealings in the book of Jonah are as much about God working to refine His prophet as averting judgment of sinners in Nineveh.

## God Pursues

The Lord's response to Jonah's rebellion was decisive: *"The Lord sent out a great wind on the sea, and there was a mighty tempest on the sea, so that the ship was about to be broken up"* (v. 4). The experienced mariners knew by its sudden development and swelling intensity that this was no natural storm. This realization caused each one to consult his god/idol for answers: *"Then the mariners were afraid; and every man cried out to his god, and threw the cargo that was in the ship into the sea, to lighten the load. But Jonah had gone down into the lowest parts of the ship, had lain down, and was fast asleep"* (v. 5). Jonah sought to escape the heavy burden of his guilty conscience through slumber. Instead of being wearied in service for God, Jonah was exhausted by his own disobedience and did not discern the peril that he was in. His sleep, as H. A. Ironside explains, pictures his dull spiritual perception and ineptness, having willingly erred from the path of righteousness.

> All on the ship are at once aroused – at least all save the miserable man for whose sin the storm has come. He is sound asleep; having gone down into the sides of the ship – insensible to the anxiety and distress he has been the means of bringing upon so many others who had no share in his evil way. What a picture of one who has taken the first wrong step, and, though discipline has begun, is sleeping on in self-complacency, utterly unconscious of the fact that the hand of the Lord has been stretched out against him!

This is the hardening through the deceitfulness of sin, concerning which the apostle warns us.[65]

In fear for the lives of his crew and himself, the captain woke Jonah from his sleep and begged him to consult his God also (v. 6). No doubt the captain wondered how any man (especially a non-seafaring man) in his right mind could be comfortably asleep in a ship being pounded by a fearsome tempest. Jonah's slumber pictures his spiritually complacent, unperceptive, and powerless state. James tells us that there is only one remedy for believers locked into that sorrowful state of mind: *"Draw near to God and He will draw near to you. Cleanse your hands, you sinners; and purify your hearts, you double-minded"* (Jas. 4:8). James also says that a double-minded man is unstable in all his ways (Jas. 1:8). So it should be no surprise, then, that the pagan captain of the ship had more sense than Jonah about their perilous situation.

W. W. Fereday draws an important distinction from the text concerning the type of deep rest the obedient enjoy in contrast to the shallow and brief rest of the disobedient.

> The path of obedience is the path of blessing. Peace and communion are found therein. Disobedience and self-will may seem to prosper for a time, but He who loves us infinitely will not suffer His own to continue thus. Disaster ensues from His all wise chastening hand. In the midst of the storm, while others were praying, Jonah was sleeping. Conscience was being stifled by his self-will. How different with the Lord Jesus! When the storm burst upon the Sea of Galilee, He slept peacefully in the stern of the vessel. As the perfect Man of faith, He could repose His weary head, assured of the Father's care. His sleep astonished the disciples as much as Jonah's sleep astonished the heathen mariners, but how great the contrast between the fugitive prophet and the Man Christ Jesus![66]

While others recognized their peril and were praying, Jonah was oblivious to the danger he was in. Then, after being awakened and learning of their situation, the prophet still had no mind to pray. In stubborn superiority he had set his course away from God, and prayer was consequently out of the question. G. C. Willis cautions us not to repeat Jonah's mistake, for we too can fall prey to our own pride and cease following the Lord:

Do not think, dear reader, that Jonah was any worse than we are today. The story before us is only an illustration of how very far from God even a saint and a prophet, one who has been used of God to do His work, may get. Even the sight of death itself did not break down the barrier that Jonah's sin and pride had raised between God and his heart. True, the barrier was all on his part, but he would not humble himself to turn to God and cry for mercy.[67]

This was no ordinary gale, and as it continued to intensify, the sailors cast lots to identify the deity-offending culprit. God permitted an accurate casting of lots and Jonah was rightly identified as the guilty party (v. 7). The fearful mariners asked Jonah five questions to ascertain the reason for the storm: *"For whose cause is this trouble upon us? What is your occupation? And where do you come from? What is your country? And of what people are you?"* (v. 8). Jonah honestly answered them, though his actions were inconsistent with his explanation: *"I am a Hebrew; and I fear the Lord, the God of heaven, who made the sea and the dry land"* (v. 9). Indeed, Jonah was a Hebrew and his God was the Creator of all things, but Jonah apparently did not fear Him enough to obey His commandment to go to Nineveh. Reverential fear, devotional awe, and unwavering lordship all walk together.

The Lord Jesus warned believers not to enthrone themselves and reject Him as their Lord: *"But why do you call Me 'Lord, Lord,' and not do the things which I say?"* (Luke 6:46), or to put it in the modern vernacular, "Don't call Me Lord if you are not going to do what I say." Normally, when Scripture speaks of the will of God, it explicitly states what it is. There is no mystery about it; God has declared to us His general will for our lives. Consequently, the more pertinent question becomes, not what the will of God is for my life, but will I obey the revealed will of God for my life? The Lord Jesus says, *"If you love Me, keep My commandments"* (John 14:15). Obedience to the Lord Jesus practically proves our love for Him. A lack of love for the Lord will be shown through an unyielded spirit and through disobedience. There is such an intimate tie between genuine love for the Lord and obedience to the Lord that Paul bluntly states, *"If any man love not the Lord Jesus Christ, let him be Anathema* [eternally condemned]" (1 Cor. 16:22). Jonah knew God's will concerning Nineveh, but Jonah believed he had a better plan for Israel's enemy.

While the pagan sailors would not understand what it meant to love and obey the true living God, they did know that Jonah was wrong to flee from his God. The sailors then wanted to know how to remedy their life-threatening situation caused by Jonah's rebellion:

*Then the men were exceedingly afraid, and said to him, "Why have you done this?" For the men knew that he fled from the presence of the Lord, because he had told them. Then they said to him, "What shall we do to you that the sea may be calm for us?" For the sea was growing more tempestuous* (vv. 10-11).

Jonah's answer was honest and selfless, but not God-honoring, *"Pick me up and throw me into the sea; then the sea will become calm for you. For I know that this great tempest is because of me"* (v. 12). Jonah understood that the storm was his fault and he was willing to suffer the consequences, even death to preserve those he put at risk. Jonah may have thought that death was preferable to preaching to Israel's bitter enemy and seeing God show mercy to them.

However, Jonah's solution was not God's solution. The Lord did not want a dead prophet, but a broken and yielded one to represent Him to Gentiles. The men, not willing to throw Jonah overboard, rowed hard towards the land, but the wind and likely the tide were against them, plus the tempest continued to gain strength (v. 13). Finally, these desperate and exhausted seamen concluded that everyone would be lost if they did not do what Jonah had said. Through the entire ordeal the sailors were gaining appreciation for Jonah's God, so they beseeched Him and God honored their prayer:

*We pray, O Lord, please do not let us perish for this man's life, and do not charge us with innocent blood; for You, O Lord, have done as it pleased You." So they picked up Jonah and threw him into the sea, and the sea ceased from its raging. Then the men feared the Lord exceedingly, and offered a sacrifice to the Lord and took vows* (vv. 14-16).

Jonah's statement was correct, that the storm had resulted from his disobedience. The moment he was cast into the sea, it dissipated instantly. This unnatural event proved to the mariners that Jonah's testimony was correct – his God was *"the God of heaven, who made the sea and the dry land."* Not only is our amazing God able to correct

His wayward prophet through a supernatural gale, but He does so in such a way to turn the heart of pagans towards Him in worship also. The sailors had petitioned their own false gods, but none of them could do what Jonah's God did in a moment. The narrative shows God's compassion for His errant prophet, for the wicked people in Nineveh, and also for a few frightened pagans sailing on the Mediterranean Sea. Truly, as Paul proclaims, He is the God of the Gentiles also (Rom. 3:29). The entire incident shows how God can reach the most remote soul with the truth, and, through the most unusual means, see him or her saved. No one is beyond God's reach, and His mercy is exceedingly abundant!

The Lord had no intention of permitting His prophet to drown in the sea: *"Now the Lord had prepared a great fish to swallow Jonah. And Jonah was in the belly of the fish three days and three nights"* (v. 17). Jonah had been preserved in the storm, and now he was spared from the sea. God had a purpose for his life – Jonah was going to Nineveh via a great fish!

There are various tales of sailors surviving encounters in the mouths of various kinds of whales and even being swallowed for a time and being recovered alive hours later. There is no means of verifying these tales (most are old whaling stories), and surely some are fictitious. From a natural perspective, a man would have to survive both the teeth and crushing forces of the lower jaw, fit through the esophagus, receive enough air to breathe, and then not be digested by acidic gastral juices in the whale's stomach. Such a naturalistic phenomenon is extremely improbable; however, when God prepares something to accomplish His purposes, such as a great fish swallowing a drowning man to keep him alive, no naturalistic explanation is required. Jonah's deliverance was no freak act of nature, but a miracle.

The Creator and Sustainer of all things is quite capable of moving beyond natural limitations to do as He pleases. Jonah's deliverance was miraculous and cannot be authenticated by modern experience or knowledge, nor should it be demeaned by the same. Believers simply do not need a whale of a story to believe the biblical account of Jonah's deliverance. Scripture records the story of Jonah for us to appreciate, and the Lord Jesus verified that it was true – end of story!

## The Sign of Three Days and Three Nights

Jonah is a type of Christ in many respects. First, like Christ, Jonah was from Galilee (Gath-Hepher was only three to four miles from Nazareth). Second, the Jewish leaders were in error when they said to Nicodemus: *"Search and look, for no prophet has arisen out of Galilee"* (John 7:52). In their proud religiosity, the Pharisees probably ignored Jonah because he preached to Gentiles; they simply could not bear the thought that God's grace should benefit publicans and sinners. Likewise, the Sanhedrin despised Jesus from Galilee and His mission. Third, the Lord referred to the "three days" Jonah was in the belly of the great fish to foretell His death, burial, and resurrection. However, our Lord tasted death in all its appalling reality as the righteous judgment of God against sin, your sin and mine (Heb. 2:9), whereas Jonah suffered for his own disobedience.

Hence, the Lord Jesus offered a prophetic sign to the Pharisees: *"For as Jonah was three days and three nights in the belly of the great fish, so will the Son of Man be three days and three nights in the heart of the earth"* (Matt. 12:40). Later, the Lord further clarified the exact meaning of His earlier statement about His own resurrection: He would be *"killed, and be raised up **on the third day**"* (17:23; NASB), but also be *"killed, and **after three days** rise again"* (Mark 8:31). The Lord Jesus implies that these are interchangeable expressions though appearing contradictory to us. In fact, most references speaking of the resurrection declare that it would occur **on** the third day (Matt. 17:23, 20:19; Luke 9:22, 18:33) or **in** the third day (John 2:19-22). The Lord Jesus used Jonah as a type to signify to the Pharisees what was going to happen to Him: three days and three nights Jonah was in the belly of a great fish, likewise for three days the Son of Man shall be in the earth (the grave).

Matthew 27:63 shows that the Pharisees understood the Lord's vernacular concerning His resurrection. He said, *"After three days I will rise again,"* but they asked for a guard to the secure the tomb **until** the third day. If the term "after three days" were not interchangeable with "the third day," the Pharisees would have asked for a tomb to be guarded for four days, but they did not do so.

The term "one day and one night" was a Jewish idiom for indicating a day, even when only a part of a day was indicated. Scriptural examples of this understanding include:

- Joseph imprisoned his brothers for three days, but released them on the third day (Gen. 42:74).

- While David was pursuing an invasion force that had left Ziklag in shambles, he found an Egyptian who had been left behind in a field because he was sick. He was faint because he had not eaten bread or drank water *"for three days and nights,"* but in the next verse he tells David that he was left three days earlier, not four (1 Sam. 30:12).

In summary, the idiom "three days and nights" and the expression "three days" were commonly used interchangeably. It would be no different than a woman expressing that she was in her ninth month of pregnancy, which could describe one day after eight months of being pregnant or up until her due date.

## Going "Down"

Notice that as Jonah tried to flee the will of God, he went "down": *"down to Joppa"* (v. 3), *"down into the lowest parts of the ship,"* and had *"lain down, and was fast asleep"* (v. 5). Later he was cast *down* into the sea by the sailors and the prophet acknowledges, *"I went down to the moorings of the mountain"* (2:6). For the believer, pursuing things that are outside God's revealed purposes will always result in a downward out-of-control spiral into carnality, worldliness, and destruction. Sin is a product of unbelief, that is, choosing human reasoning over God's revealed Word, and that is exactly what Jonah did. He went his own way (literally away from the Lord) to resolve his perceived difficulty.

Similarly, the Lord had given Abram the land of Canaan for an inheritance, but, because of a famine, he abandoned God's protection and provision and ventured to Egypt (a symbol of the world) to resolve his difficulty. Hence, Scripture speaks of Abram going *"down"* to Egypt (Gen. 12:10), and when he forsook Egypt, Scripture speaks of him *"going up out of"* Egypt (Gen. 13:1). When pilgrims of God venture "down" into Egypt, a selfish desire to explore the world system for aid and comfort is represented, while "coming out" of Egypt pictures their reliance on God's faithfulness for the same.

Abram's trip *down* to Egypt was a costly lesson. Jonah would also learn that escaping into the world to avoid the hardship of doing God's bidding never ends well. But by God's grace Jonah would not be digested by a great fish; instead he would be transported in the direction he needed to go and would be vomited up on dry land to do what he knew he must (2:10).

Warren Wiersbe comments on God's manifold wisdom and grace in working with His wayward and spiritually despondent prophet:

> Jonah lost God's voice, for now God had to speak to him in a storm. He lost his spiritual energy and went to sleep in the hold of the ship. He lost his power in prayer, and even his desire to pray. The heathen were praying, but Jonah was sleeping. He lost his testimony with the men on the ship, and he lost his influence for good, because he was the cause of the storm. He also almost lost his life. But how patient and long-suffering the Lord was with him.[68]

Each of us was born after the flesh, but those born of God need not live after the flesh any longer (Rom. 6:2). It is God the Father's earnest desire that His children live up to His Son's moral likeness; He pleads with us, *"Be ye holy; for I am holy"* (1 Pet. 1:16). He is jealous about our allegiances to other things, ideologies, and people (Ex. 34:14). Whatever prevents Him from being first-place in our affections provokes Him to take corrective action (Rev. 2:4-5). The prophet Jonah experienced this truth firsthand after acting in his flesh against the expressed will of God.

In a practical sense, a believer who chooses to live after the flesh is daring God, "Do You still love me enough to correct me?" The answer is, "Yes, He does" (Heb. 12:6). For this reason, the writer of Hebrews warns his audience that, *"since we are receiving a kingdom which cannot be shaken, let us have grace, by which we may serve God acceptably with reverence and godly fear. For our God is a consuming fire"* (Heb. 12:28-29). Likewise, Paul exhorts those at Corinth: *"Therefore, having these promises, beloved, let us cleanse ourselves from all filthiness of the flesh and spirit, perfecting holiness in the fear of God"* (2 Cor. 7:1). May each child of God understand the lesson that Jonah learned the hard way – to trust in one's flesh always disappoints the Lord and leads us into a chastening storm.

## Meditation

Ironically, hardhearted Pharisees rebuffed the Lord Jesus' messianic claims by saying to Him: *"Will the Christ come out of Galilee?"* (John 7:41). *"Are you also from Galilee? Search and look, for no prophet has arisen out of Galilee"* (John 7:52). Clearly, they had forgotten that Jonah was from Galilee. Spiritual blindness clouds human reasoning, perverts logic, and distorts our perception of reality. This is why, in spiritual matters, man must ignore sight-based faith and our mutable feelings, and must simply trust God at His Word; this is true faith and the only kind that pleases God (Heb. 11:6). God rewards true faith by opening our eyes to deeper spiritual truth; naturally speaking, we cannot understand the things of God without His help (1 Cor. 2:9-13). The Lord Jesus told His disciples, *"Know the truth, and the truth shall make you free"* (John 8:32). Whether one is a sailor, a Ninevite, a wayward prophet in the eighth century B.C., a lost sinner, or a child of God today, embracing God's truth by faith is the only way to experience His freedom and peace.

# Coming "Up"
Jonah 2

In the previous chapter, the Lord gained the *body* of his rebellious prophet – sequestered in a great fish. In this chapter, the Lord will labor to win over Jonah's *mind* as he meditates on the Psalms, on his situation, and on the cost of disobedience. In chapter 3, the Lord will have Jonah's *obedience,* and then the transforming work of the prophet's *heart* will commence in chapter 4. The entire book is a testimony of God's powerful work in transforming a rebel child of God into a fruit-bearing saint that exhibits God's character and is solely motivated for the glory of God. Jonah's story illustrates that God is as concerned about the character and disposition of His servants as He is for the heathen nations.

It is ironic that the pattern of deliverance in chapter 1 is repeated in chapter 2. First, there was a crisis at sea (1:4, 2:3-6). Second, a desperate prayer to Jehovah (1:14, 2:2, 7). Third, those who prayed were delivered from drowning (1:15, 2:6). Fourth, the saved sacrificed and offered vows to the Lord (1:16, 2:9). Both the pagan mariners and the rebel prophet were delivered from death in the same way.

## Jonah's Prayer
Jonah began to pray from the stomach of a great fish, perhaps a mammal such as the sperm whale (v. 1). He does not petition the Lord to rescue him, but rather offers praise and thanksgiving for saving him from drowning. His dark, putrid imprisonment reminded him of a grave, so he rejoices that God heard his cries *"out of the belly of Sheol"* (v. 2). In similar poetic language, David likens the time when God fashioned his inward parts in the darkness of his mother's womb to being *"in the lower parts of the earth"* (Ps. 139:13-15). Jonah was entombed in the fish, but alive.

Jonah's reference to Sheol (i.e., the grave) is not literal – Jonah did not die, but in every way imaginable the belly of the fish was like a grave. Even the Lord Jesus used Jonah's experience to foretell His own death, burial, and resurrection, as explained in the previous chapter. Furthermore, Jonah did not petition the Lord to save him from this watery grave, but rather he accepted his punishment and fate. This is a lovely picture of the Lord Jesus' full willingness to face the horrors of Calvary in accordance to His Father's will. Jonah's punitive drowning for his own rebellion is a shadow of the divine judgment Christ, as an innocent substitute, would bear for human rebellion. Prophetically speaking, David likened the judgment at Calvary to Jonah's experience in the deep: *"Deep calls unto deep at the noise of Your waterfalls; all Your waves and billows have gone over me"* (Ps. 42:7). As far as the Ninevites were concerned, it would seem as if Jonah had passed through death and experienced resurrection – which is the essence of the gospel message (1 Cor. 15:3-4).

Jonah knew Scripture, as he quotes or alludes to a number of the Psalms in his contrite prayer from the fish's belly:

Verse 2: Ps. 18:6, 31:22, 86:13, 88:1, 120:1, 130:1, 142:1
Verse 3: Ps. 42:7, 88:7
Verse 4: Ps. 31:22
Verse 5: Ps. 18:4, 69:1-2, 116:3
Verse 6: Ps. 116:4
Verse 7: Ps. 18:6, 69:13
Verse 8: Ps. 31:6
Verse 9: Ps. 3:8, 116:17-18

Jonah's prayer highlights the importance of committing Scripture to memory, for it is not always possible to pull out and read a pocket Bible during a temptation or trial. Jonah had no opportunity to read Scripture in his murky dismal environment, but he still could delight in God's Word and be sustained by it.

Obviously, Jonah recorded his prayer after being expelled from the fish, so his terrifying account is infused with praise and thanksgiving. Recalling the ordeal, Jonah recognized two important truths: First, it was God who cast him into the sea. Second, the sea's powerful billows and waves would have overcome him, if God had not prepared the great fish to swallow him:

*For You cast me into the deep, into the heart of the seas, and the floods surrounded me; all Your billows and Your waves passed over me* (v. 3).

He continues to speak of his near-drowning experience in verses 5 and 6. With sea vegetation wrapped around his head and amidst the swirling currents, he sank down towards the floor of the sea, even among the mountains that were there.

Jonah's statement in verse 4 shows contrition and repentance: *"Then I said, 'I have been cast out of Your sight; yet I will look again toward Your holy temple.'"* The prophet realized that his present banishment and isolation were consequences of his disobedience. Thankfully, Jonah did not faint beneath the discipline of the Lord, but looked up to God and counted on His grace, and as a result was blessed. In faith, he knew that he would again be before God in His temple. Whether Jonah was referring to God's heavenly throne room after death (speaking of his eternal security) or the temple in Jerusalem after his restoration (speaking of earthly communion) in verse 4 is debatable. Regardless, Jonah understood that at that very moment he still had access to his omniscient, omnipotent God through prayer (v. 7). H. A. Ironside suggests that Jonah's restoration and access to God pictures Israel's future restoration to the Lord in the Kingdom Age.

> His soul would have fainted within him, but he remembers the Lord, and is assured that his prayers shall be heard, and shall penetrate His holy temple. He is here in the place that the future remnant of Israel shall be in, in their experience, when the blindness of the present condition has passed away; afar off, yet, in accordance with the prayer of Solomon, looking toward the temple of Jehovah, though in ruins, as in the day that Daniel opened his windows toward Jerusalem (vv. 6-7).[69]

Indeed, dispensationally speaking, Jonah pictures Israel's failure to be God's witness of righteousness to the nations. The Jewish nation is at present cast into the sea of Gentiles (e.g. Rev. 17:1, 15), but is being marvelously preserved by God to be spiritually revived in a future day when they will superbly represent God to the nations (speaking of the Kingdom Age). Jonah would be preserved in the sea, just as God will preserve the nation of Israel throughout the time of the Gentiles (Rom. 11:25).

Jonah did not and would not follow the idolatrous course of his countrymen; he knew the only source of mercy was Jehovah and that *"those who regard worthless idols forsake their own mercy"* (v. 8). The KJV renders verse 8: *"They that observe lying vanities forsake their own mercy,"* which would include worthless idols and more. The pagan seafarers on Jonah's ship had found this to be true, and they experienced God's deliverance. Now Jonah had proved it to himself through experience also. Jonah had forsaken his own mercy when he sought the lying vanity of self-rule, thinking he could flee from God's presence and sovereign control of his life. Self-exaltation and idolatry spring up from the same depraved heart.

Knowing that he had not fulfilled God's purpose for his life also meant that the prophet would be preserved for that reason. He believed then that eventually he would be able to return to the temple in Jerusalem to offer praise and whatever he had vowed to the Lord (v. 9). Jonah's longing to be before God in the temple of Jerusalem is remarkable, as he was born of the ten tribes who turned away from God's sanctuary in Jerusalem to worship at pagan centers in Bethel and Dan (1 Kgs. 12:25-33). Despite this religious confusion of his day, Jonah's heart was to be with God, that is, to be where God had chosen to commune with His people.

There is a sense throughout this chapter that Jonah is being led along by the Lord into utter brokenness. The prophet prays and he vows sacrifices, but it is not until he comes to a complete end of himself and declares *"salvation is of the Lord"* (v. 9) that the Lord intervenes on his behalf. The offense and consequences of human sin cannot be remedied by human effort! This is true for the conversion of sinners and the repentance and restoration of wayward saints – salvation is of the Lord! Vowed sacrifices and prayers without such a heartfelt realization would be nauseating to the Lord (Isa. 1:11-17). That he is not completely done with self-rule is evident later, but Jonah's progress is sufficient for now and thankfully Jonah has a patient Teacher.

## Mountains in the Sea

Jonah's statement about there being mountains on the bottom of the sea could not be proven in his day, but we know it is true today. We often think that Mount Everest (rising some 29,035 feet above sea level) is the tallest mountain on the planet. However, that honor belongs to Hawaii's Mauna Kea. Mauna Kea is only 13,796 feet above sea level, but it begins rising off the ocean floor nearly three and a half miles below the ocean's surface. Mauna Kea, when measured from the ocean floor, reaches a height of 31,796 feet.[70] It is one of many mountains extending up from the ocean floor and one of the few viewed above the ocean's surface.

Mauna Loa is also found in the Hawaiian Islands and rises some 13,677 feet above sea level. Because of its vast base, Mauna Loa is considered the most voluminous mountain on the Earth. Much of the sea floor has yet to be explored, but we now know that mountains and even mountain ranges are plentiful (the Atlantic Ocean contains an undersea mountain range 10,000 miles long). Jonah declared long ago what modern science now understands to be accurate.

## Jonah's Journey

After a three-day journey, God commands the great fish to vomit Jonah on dry land (v. 10) – presumably on the coast of Phoenicia. If Jonah's great fish was a sperm whale, which can grow more than fifty feet in length and can dive for two hours to depths of a mile, how far could the whale have traveled in three days? Sperm whales can cruise comfortably over great distances at 3 knots, and can increase to 12 knots when chased.[71] This means Jonah could have traveled some 250 miles underwater via a whale!

Jonah initially fled southwest to Joppa from Gath-Hepher in Galilee, a journey requiring three or four days on foot. In Joppa the prophet boarded a ship heading west to Tarshish. However, for two reasons it seems that the ship had not ventured but a few miles from shore when the storm struck: First, Jonah, tired from his sixty-mile journey, went directly down into the boat and fell asleep and then the captain woke him up shortly thereafter and the storm was already raging (1:6). Second, the men knew where the shoreline was and attempted to row back to it to escape the tempest (1:13).

If this assumption is correct, then the three-day journey in the fish must have been to carry Jonah northward to assist him in completing his mission at Nineveh. This means that Jonah could have been set ashore near Tyre where he could head straight east to Damascus and then follow the main trade route through Hamath and Haran to Nineveh. Or the fish could have taken him as far north as Cyprus. If he was put ashore east of Cyprus, the prophet would have had a 45-mile walk to Hamath, requiring two or three days.

The distance from Jonah's hometown of Gath-Hepher to Hamath was 190 miles, and, given Sabbath rests, would have taken Jonah about two weeks to travel there, had he not rebelled. So the Lord, via whale, could have transported Jonah to Hamath (over one-third of the way to Nineveh) more quickly than if Jonah had walked there from Gath-Hepher.

If this hypothesis is accurate, the text bears out a lovely application to Jonah's deliverance and journey. While it is true that we choose our sin, God chooses the consequences of our sin; God does not want our failures to be final. Practically speaking, falling is not what makes one a failure, but wallowing in self-pity – choosing to stay down does. *"For a righteous man may fall seven times and rise again, but the wicked shall fall by calamity"* (Prov. 24:16). The Lord wants us to learn from our mistakes, to rise up in His grace and step forward with a revived tenacity to serve Him. Jonah indeed left the sea a chastened and humbled man.

One of the marvelous aspects of God's doings is that He is able to work wonders whether or not His people labor with Him or against Him. Through Jonah's failure, God accomplished many incredible feats:

- A violent tempest suddenly occurred.
- The lot accurately fell on Jonah.
- The sea became calm after Jonah was thrown overboard.
- A boatload of pagans worshipped Jonah's God.
- A great fish was commanded to swallow Jonah.
- The fish did not digest Jonah, but kept him alive.
- The fish transported Jonah three days and vomited him up on shore.
- Jonah's attitude was changed and he was restored to God.
- All the above likely occurred without delaying God's plans for Nineveh.

Jonah witnessed what God could achieve when he worked against Him; the prophet would soon learn what magnificent things God could do when he labored with the Lord. God has sovereign purposes that must be accomplished. May we remain in the center of His doings, which will be for His glory and our good. Oh Lord, help us to want only what You want!

# Meditation

Take my life, and let it be consecrated, Lord, to Thee.
Take my moments and my days; let them flow in ceaseless praise.
Take my hands, and let them move at the impulse of Thy love.
Take my feet, and let them be swift and beautiful for Thee.

Take my will, and make it Thine; it shall be no longer mine.
Take my heart, it is Thine own; it shall be Thy royal throne.
Take my love, my Lord, I pour at Thy feet its treasure store.
Take myself, and I will be ever, only, all for Thee.

— Frances R. Havergal

# A Message for Nineveh
Jonah 3

After being expelled on dry land, the word of the Lord came to Jonah a second time (v. 1): *"Arise, go to Nineveh, that great city, and preach to it the message that I tell you"* (v. 2). Jonah's response to God's command this time was much different: *"So Jonah arose and went to Nineveh"* (v. 3). Even from the Mediterranean shores near Hamath, the journey to Nineveh would still be over 400 miles. If Jonah was put ashore near Joppa, the journey would be over 600 miles. Regardless, the trek to Nineveh would have required several weeks on foot. As about an inch of Jonah's normal hair color would have been visible on his head and in his beard, he would have been bizarre-looking, no doubt a scary spectacle preaching in the streets of Nineveh.

The capital of the Assyrian empire was a massive city, by Jonah's account *"a three-day journey in extent."* Jonah did not delay in preaching the simple message God had given him: *"Jonah began to enter the city on the first day's walk. Then he cried out and said, 'Yet forty days, and Nineveh shall be overthrown!'"* Nineveh was a sprawling city, but how are we to understand Jonah's testimony that it took him three days to work his way across it? A review of archeological and historical evidence will be helpful in answering this question.

Nineveh was situated on the eastern bank of the river Tigris about fifty miles from its mouth (approximately 250 miles north of Babylon). The ancient walls of Nineveh form a rectangular shape approximately 1 mile by 3 miles enclosing an area of about 1,875 acres. Archeologist Donald J. Wiseman concludes that, even in the days of Sennacherib, Nineveh was never more than three miles across and was protected by an inner wall having a circumference of about 7.5 miles.[72] The city's inner wall had fifteen gates and measured about 100 feet high and fifty feet wide (though variable in width). An outer wall also enclosed smaller towns and fields.[73] G. Smith asserted that the circuit of the inner wall is about 8 miles, and Captain Jones, who made a trigonometrical survey in 1854, estimated that, allotting to each inhabitant 50 square yards, the city may have contained 174,000 inhabitants [i.e., within the inner wall].[74] If the area inside the outer wall is considered, Nineveh could have supported an even larger population of several hundred thousand people.

Obviously, it would not take Jonah three days to walk less than three miles or even eight miles around the inner wall (if Jonah was speaking of the city's circumference). So how are we to understand his statement *"a three-day journey in extent."* It seems likely that Jonah began preaching to those in the western suburbs of Nineveh immediately, and then continued to move inward and eastward, pausing and preaching along the way to ensure everyone heard God's message. Jonah's lurid countenance and bleached hair must have stunned the Ninevites as they heard his somber message. It took Jonah three days to pass through the streets of Nineveh.

It may be that Jonah preached God's message in Nineveh only for those three days and then departed. Given his ill-will towards the Ninevites and the fact that the news of his message spread through the city quickly, it does not seem likely that he needed to preach the entire forty-day period. Additionally, to keep preaching a forty-day message would cause confusion if Jonah was still proclaiming it, say, for thirty-nine days. If Jonah did take up temporary residence at a remote location outside the city (prior to the conclusion of the forty days), there can be little doubt that the Ninevites knew where he was and that he was watching them to see what would happen.

## Forty Days

Why not four days until judgment instead of forty? In Scripture, *forty* is the number of *probation* and *testing*. For example, Moses' forty-day stay on Mount Sinai provided an opportunity to test the Israelites – would they obey God's Law? Then the Israelites were tested forty years in the wilderness. The Lord Jesus was tested forty days in the wilderness after His baptism. Nineveh would also be given forty days to consider Jonah's message before judgment fell, which meant that God desired them to repent and was giving them time to do so. It is likely that Jonah understood the significance of the number forty in his message, though a reprieve from judgment may not have been directly communicated to the Ninevites.

Peter informs us that God *"is longsuffering toward us, not willing that any should perish but that all should come to repentance"* (2 Pet. 3:9). Likewise Ezekiel declares: *"I have no pleasure in the death of the wicked, but that the wicked turn from his way and live"* (Ezek. 33:11). Isaiah calls our attention to the fact that God's anger and subsequent wrath are not part of His primary work: *"that He may do His work, His strange work; and bring to pass His act, His strange act"* (Isa. 28:21; KJV). God's anger prompts His secondary (unusual) work. It is not that righteous wrath is less noble than divine love, for each necessitates the other, but God would rather shower His people with blessings than be angry with them. God's anger leading to acts of judgment is a necessary aspect of God's sovereignty, but His usual and normal work arises from His gracious, loving nature. God delights much more in provoking repentance and restoration, than invoking wrath and destroying in death those He longs to experience eternal life.

## Nineveh Turns From Evil

Jonah's message foretelling the total destruction of Nineveh spread through the city like wildfire; all social classes responded to it and put on sackcloth and fasted (v. 5). The people *"believed God;"* this does not mean that they became worshipers of Jonah's God, but rather by faith they believed the message of Jonah's God. Jonah may have included the fact that their wickedness had come up to God in heaven and could no longer be tolerated (1:2). Even the king, after hearing Jonah's warning, humbled himself by putting on sackcloth and sitting in ashes (v. 6). He then issued the following decree:

> *Let neither man nor beast, herd nor flock, taste anything; do not let them eat, or drink water. But let man and beast be covered with sackcloth, and cry mightily to God; yes, let everyone turn from his evil way and from the violence that is in his hands. Who can tell if God will turn and relent, and turn away from His fierce anger, so that we may not perish?* (vv. 7-9).

Jonah's message contained no provision for escaping God's wrath, nor, given the prophet's disposition towards his enemies, did he likely imply one. However, the king believed that if God saw the city's contrition and repentance for their wicked behavior, perhaps He would change His mind. No doubt the prophet looked on with amazement at more than a hundred thousand pagans responding to his simple message – even putting sackcloth on their animals. It is a true work of God when *"the greatest to the least"* within an entire city cry out to God for mercy!

Given the timeframe of Jonah's ministry (as discussed in the *Overview* section), it seems likely that Ashur-dan III was king of Assyria at this time. His reign was from 772-754 B.C. What factors may have contributed to the Ninevites' acceptance of Jonah's message? These were highly superstitious people and a rash of natural phenomena and calamities in the Assyrian Empire no doubt had raised their heathen anxiety:

- A solar eclipse with 80% obscuration in Nineveh on February 10, 765 B.C.
- A severe famine in 765 B.C.
- A total solar eclipse in Nineveh, June 15, 763 B.C.
- A massive regional earthquake in approximately 760 B.C.
- A severe famine in 759 B.C.
- Rebellions in various Assyrian cities in 758 B.C.[75]
- A Jewish man with bleached skin and hair, having been spewed out by a great fish, who came to warn them.

Dagon, the fish-god was widely revered in Mesopotamia and the eastern Mediterranean coast (Judg. 16:23-24; 1 Sam. 5:1-7). Archeologists have found several images of Dagon in Ninevite excavations, meaning that when Jonah arrived in Nineveh out of the sea via a great fish, he immediately had their attention. Henry Clay Trumbull explains this point:

> What better heralding, as a divinely sent messenger to Nineveh, could Jonah have had, than to be thrown up out of the mouth of a great fish, in the presence of witnesses, say on the coast of Phoenicia, where the fish-god was a favorite object of worship? Such an incident would have inevitably aroused the mercurial nature of Oriental observers, so that a multitude would be ready to follow the seemingly new avatar of the fish-god, proclaiming the story of his uprising from the sea, as he went on his mission to the city where the fish-god had its very center of worship."[76]

If the Ninevites, rattled by recent calamities and celestial signs, were responding to Jonah as an extension of Dagon, instead of as Jehovah's prophet, that would explain why there was no lasting revival in Nineveh. Simply fearing reprisal for doing what one knows is against his or her conscience, without appreciating the One who judges all wickedness, is not true repentance. Genuine repentance fully agrees with God on the matter of sin and its just punishment, pleads for His forgiveness, and shows a change of heart by ceasing the evil and doing what God says is good. The Ninevites had obeyed Jonah's message and turned from their wickedness, which was the initial reason God told Jonah that He was going to judge them (1:2).

However, simply trying to follow one's conscience is not the same as a spiritual conversion. For example, after her accusers departed, the Lord Jesus told the woman caught in the act of adultery: *"Neither do I condemn you; go and sin no more"* (John 8:11). She had not asked to be forgiven of her sins, and it was not time for her to be judged for her sins, so the Lord merely warned her not to continue in sin. Then the Lord said, *"I am the light of the world. He who follows Me shall not walk in darkness, but have the light of life"* (John 8:12). Trying not to sin is not the same as receiving light and life in Christ and following Him. The Ninevites turned from wickedness in fear, but they did not turn to Jehovah to receive forgiveness and more truth to walk in. Their king's humble response merely granted them more time before God's wrath would ultimately fall, and it did fall about 150 years later – Nineveh was destroyed by the Babylonians.

## God Relents

It becomes obvious in the next chapter that Jonah did not want Nineveh to respond to his message and was hoping that God would still crush them. Thankfully, God was more compassionate than His prophet towards this heathen city: *"Then God saw their works, that they turned from their evil way; and God relented from the disaster that He had said He would bring upon them, and He did not do it"* (v. 10). *"God saw their works,"* which as James tells us is evidence of true faith: *"Faith by itself, if it does not have works, is dead"* (Jas. 2:17). The Ninevites clearly had not gone as far as the mariners in worshiping Jehovah, but they had, in faith, responded to the truth that Jonah had revealed to them.

The reason that God was going to judge them then was removed; therefore, God relented from punishing Nineveh. The Gentiles' response to Jonah's message would serve to rebuke those Jews in Israel who had been rejecting God's repeated warnings of coming judgment through Hosea and Amos. The Gentiles who did not know Jehovah heard and immediately obeyed His word, but God's covenant people had been adamantly rejecting it.

In light of God's immutable nature, how do we understand verse 10 and other verses that seem to indicate that God changes His mind about judging sinners (e.g., Gen. 6:5; Ex. 32:12; 2 Sam. 24:16)? God often does not fully disclose His will to humanity, in order to test His people or to provide them with service opportunities they would not have had otherwise. For example, Israel deserved God's wrath for making and worshipping the golden calf. Yet, God gave Moses the opportunity to voluntarily intercede on their behalf, so that He could extend mercy to His covenant people, which He did.

Likewise, God wanted to show mercy to the city of Nineveh if they would repent, but if God had revealed His full intentions to Jonah, his prophet may not have preached to his enemies at all. When it seems as if God is changing His mind in Scripture, it actually means He is more fully declaring His sovereign will after certain necessary events have occurred. This ensures the maximum benefit to both His imperfect servants and to those to whom He wants to demonstrate mercy. God's ways are truly above understanding: when a rebellious Jonah was cast into the sea, God saved a boatload of pagans and when a repentant Jonah was spewed out of a fish, God saved an entire heathen city!

## Meditation

> Some people do not like to hear much of repentance, but I think it is so necessary that if I should die in the pulpit, I would desire to die preaching repentance, and if out of the pulpit I would desire to die practicing it.
>
> — Matthew Henry

> The Christian who has stopped repenting has stopped growing.
>
> — A. W. Pink

> Repentance, not proper behavior or even holiness, is the doorway to grace. And the opposite of sin is grace, not virtue.
>
> — Philip Yancey

# An Angry Prophet
Jonah 4

Jonah became angry after he discerned that God had relented from punishing the Ninevites (probably because the forty days had passed) and he ventured eastward from the city (v. 1). He built a temporary shelter, likely having a vantage point overlooking the city, and waited to see what the Lord would do. While he certainly did not want the Ninevites to live, he may have also felt that his integrity as a prophet had been tarnished because what he said would happen had not come about.

This scene is one of the most striking features of the book – a true prophet of God observing an entire city of perhaps several hundred thousand people be more affected by God's Word than the messenger who delivered it. Thankfully, although Jonah was in a sour frame of mind, he did not lose sight of his relationship with God. He therefore prays to the Lord, but only in grace can his self-focused statements be labeled a prayer:

*Ah, Lord, was not this what I said when I was still in my country? Therefore I fled previously to Tarshish; for I know that You are a gracious and merciful God, slow to anger and abundant in lovingkindness, one who relents from doing harm. Therefore now, O Lord, please take my life from me, for it is better for me to die than to live* (vv. 2-3)!

Jonah's four I's, two me's, and one "my," in contrast to referring to the Lord four times in his prayer indicates that Jonah had withdrawn into himself for answers. He understood God's character (even quoting Ps. 48:14), but did not want to have His mind on the matter. Beloved, it is dangerous to quote Scripture in a way that spites God's goodness and ignores His will. The child of God should always want what God wants and then desire to know why He does what He does.

Jonah confirms what we have suspected, but has not been said until now. He previously rebelled against his calling because he knew that Jehovah was a merciful God and he wanted the Ninevites punished, not forgiven. Now the worst possible thing had happened – the Ninevites had humbled themselves and turned from evil. Jonah keenly felt that this was his fault.

Coldhearted Jonah wanted Israel's enemy slaughtered, not spared – he did not want God to show them mercy. We all have experienced Jonah's frustration to some extent, for our flesh simply cannot understand the grace of God! It is beyond our comprehension. Thankfully, we have all eternity to be shown *"the exceeding riches of His grace in His kindness toward us in Christ Jesus"* (Eph. 2:7).

Having betrayed his countrymen (from his point of view), Jonah requested that the Lord would take his life. Death would deliver him from bearing the shame of delivering Israel's nemesis. In the belly of the fish, he wanted to live despite what might happen in Nineveh, but somehow watching the Ninevites actually obey his message was a worse situation – now he just wanted to die.

## The Question

Sometimes a well-worded question appealing to the conscience is better than an explanation. The Lord responds to Jonah's prayer with such a question, *"Is it right for you to be angry?"* (v. 4). The implied answer was "no," but the Lord permitted Jonah to work the matter over in his mind. The Lord's entire message to Jonah, in fact, consisted of three questions: with the first being posed twice.

In many respects, Jonah's attitude pictured the spiritual demeanor of the Jewish nation; they had forgotten that they were to be God's lampstand to the nations. Having experienced God's mercy and goodness, they should have wanted others to benefit from it also. Yet, at this juncture, Jonah is offended by God's mercy, even though he had earlier received God's unmerited forgiveness for blatant rebellion. In his estimation, the Ninevites were so evil that they did not deserve God's clemency. But what Jonah had forgotten was that no one deserves God's mercy, nor is He obliged to forgive the guilty. The prophet's callous attitude is hence demeaning to God's character. Jonah apparently thought that he possessed a higher knowledge than God did, and had a better sense of justice and fairness than He did. Righteous Job failed in a similar fashion.

How long Jonah actually preached in Nineveh is unknown, but after he finished delivering God's message he probably left the city to see what would happen at the set time. Now that the forty days had passed and Nineveh was not destroyed we read, *"So Jonah went out of the city and sat on the east side of the city. There he made himself a shelter and sat under it in the shade, till he might see what would become of the city"* (v. 5). He probably erected a simple lean-to structure that was open on the east and west sides so that he could view the city and enjoy some cross ventilation and shade during the hottest part of the day. Even though he knows that God has granted mercy to Nineveh, he is determined to sulk for a while to see if the Lord will change His mind.

## The Plant and the Worm

Besides a well-posed question, a good illustration is also an effective teaching technique to prompt reason. The Lord used an object that Jonah appreciated (because it brought him comfort) to rebuke his pitiless attitude toward lost souls:

> *And the Lord God prepared a plant and made it come up over Jonah, that it might be shade for his head to deliver him from his misery. So Jonah was very grateful for the plant. But as morning dawned the next day God prepared a worm, and it so damaged the plant that it withered. And it happened, when the sun arose, that God prepared a vehement east wind; and the sun beat on Jonah's head, so that he grew faint. Then he wished death for himself, and said, "It is better for me to die than to live"* (vv. 6-8).

If Jonah constructed a lean-to out of tree branches such that he could see the city to the west, it would not provide him shade during the morning and late afternoon. God had caused a plant with dense foliage to quickly grow during the night (v. 10) and to provide shade for Jonah (apparently from the morning sun). Jonah greatly appreciated this plant for the relief it brought him. But overnight, the Lord prepared a worm to damage the plant so it withered. Cutworms, for example, are the larvae of several species of night-flying moths which cause this type of damage. They are called cutworms because they cut down young plants as they feed on stems at or below the soil surface. The damage occurs within a few hours and the plant dies. Jonah's plant may have been a castor-bean plant which has large leaves and grows quickly up to a height of twelve feet, but also withers quickly if damaged.

In chapter 1, the Lord "prepared" a fish (1:17) for instructive purposes, and in this chapter He "prepares" a plant, a worm, and a vehement east wind. It was a cloudless morning. A hot, dry east wind pummeled Jonah and quickly withered the plant. Jonah grew faint and again wished he could die. The Lord asked Jonah a second time, *"Is it right for you to be angry,"* but then added *"about the plant?"* And Jonah quickly justified himself, *"It is right for me to be angry, even to death"* (v. 9)! The object lesson was to contrast Jonah's concern for his own creature comforts as compared to the spiritual welfare of all the souls of an enormous city. He was as angry (even unto death) over the loss of the plant as of the sparing of the city. Summing up the matter, J. G. Bellett writes:

> The prophet's delight in the gourd is but the faint reflection of the Lord's delight in the mercy that visits the creatures of His hand. ... And if Jonah would fain have the gourd spared, he must allow repentant Nineveh to be spared. Out of his own mouth he shall be judged: Jonah shall witness for the Lord against himself... The withered gourd teaches him how the blessed Lord, the Creator of the ends of the earth, the Lord of the cattle on the thousand hills, whether in Assyria or Judea, delights in His creatures, the works of His hands, finding His rest and refreshment in the mercy that spares them, when they repent and turn to Him.[77]

Because Jonah held selfish attitudes towards Nineveh and the plant, he became deeply frustrated that his expectations were not met. God's expectation for Nineveh had been accomplished, but that was of no interest to Jonah. The Lord now explains with a parting question the illustration which has so angered his prophet:

> *You have had pity on the plant for which you have not labored, nor made it grow, which came up in a night and perished in a night. And should I not pity Nineveh, that great city, in which are more than one hundred and twenty thousand persons who cannot discern between their right hand and their left – and much livestock? (vv. 10-11).*

How admirable is God's patience with his stiff-necked prophet! Jonah's anger resulted from the loss of a shading plant that he benefitted from for only one day and for which he did not labor at all. If he had been a gardener who had planted the seed, watered, and nurtured the plant for a long time in order to enjoy its beauty and benefit, perhaps it would have been right to be disappointed. But Jonah had done none of these things and yet was angry because his needs were not being satisfied.

In contrast, Jonah should consider how God felt over an entire city of lost souls that He had created and sustained for many years to bring Him pleasure, yet they were now so wicked that God contemplated destroying them. The hurt to God's own heart in the matter was not even comparable to Jonah's loss of the plant that he had not even labored for. Jonah's preaching had been the catalyst for causing creatures whom God loved to honor Him.

Notice God mentions His concern and care for the animals of Nineveh that would have been destroyed also. In their humility, the Ninevites had put sackcloth on their cattle. One can only imagine that humorous sight, but God looked on the matter with favor because it was further evidence of faith in His message. If people really believe in a life and death message, they do not hold back from responding, but do all that they can to avoid death. The gospel of Jesus Christ is indeed such a message: *"He who believes in the Son has everlasting life; and he who does not believe the Son shall not see life, but the wrath of God abides on him"* (John 3:36). There can be no riding the fence when the eternal destination of a soul hangs in the balance. Complacency is foolishness when desperation demands earnestness.

The burden of God's heart and all He yearned to accomplish did not compare with Jonah's petty selfishness – Jonah had no reason to be angry. Jonah thought that God was absurd to spare Nineveh, but it was actually Jonah who was irrational. God was not selfish (like His prophet), but He was genuinely concerned for the welfare of others.

## Nineveh Spared

How many people lived in Nineveh? Some commentators think that the reference to 120,000 persons speaks of the entire population who were totally ignorant of spiritual matters. Others believe that the reference is to the children who had not reached an age of moral understanding. If the latter be true, the population of Nineveh may have been as many as 600,000. In the next century Nineveh would become the largest city on earth.

Sadly, the revival in Nineveh was short-lived for reasons explained in the last chapter. In 745 B.C., about ten to fifteen years after Jonah's visit, the Assyrian Empire began a brutal quest for world domination under Tiglath-pileser III. He invaded northern Israel and deported many Jews to Assyria. In 722 B.C., Sargon II completed the long siege of Samaria that had been initiated by Shalmaneser V. Jonah may have witnessed Assyria's invasion of Israel. But as Amos and Hosea had already prophesied, Assyria was God's chastening rod for His people. Israel, having the Law, would not turn from their wickedness, while Nineveh, which was ignorant of God's ways, did for a time do what was right in God's eyes.

Judgment would come to Nineveh, when God's purposes for Assyria were accomplished. Man has no choice in being a part of God's plan, but as a moral and a conscious being, he has every choice in how he will answer God's call and be used within God's unfolding design. Whether or not we yield to His call, God will be glorified through our choices; He will use us either as vessels of mercy prepared for glory, or as vessels of wrath fit for destruction (Rom. 9:14-23). God prepares yielded vessels for glory and rebellious vessels to receive His wrath. The Assyrians chose to be the latter.

In the next century God would summon the prophet Nahum to deliver a second warning to Nineveh. The city would be destroyed by the Babylonians about one hundred and fifty years after Jonah's visit. God would use the Babylonians to punish wickedness throughout the region and specifically His wayward people in Judah.

## The Closing Question

Jehovah has the last word, as indeed He always must have; hence, Jonah ends his book with God's question without recording his response to it. At that time the prophet was in no frame of mind to answer properly, but it is doubtful that he could have so vividly penned this testimony depicting his own wrong attitudes without having grasped the meaning of the Lord's lesson. On this point J. N. Darby writes:

> It is sweet, after all, to see Jonah's docility in the end to the voice of God, manifested by the existence of this book, in which the Spirit uses him to exhibit what is in the heart of man, as the vessel of God's testimony, and (in contrast with the prophet, who honestly confesses all his faults) the kindness of God, to which Jonah could not elevate himself, and to which he could not submit.[78]

Jonah's disposition towards the Ninevites at this time reflected Israel's disaffection for God and for those things that mattered to Him. Instead of being a testimony of God's goodness and holiness to the nations, they were ensnared in vain religiosity. One purpose of Jonah's testimony was to awaken the Jewish people to their missionary calling (Isa. 49:3).

No doubt Jonah was hoping that the final inquiry would assist his countrymen to learn what he had through the same probing question. Should not God have pity for the lost souls who will perish without His grace? And it is with that thought that the book abruptly closes; Jonah must answer God's challenge for himself, just as we also must answer it for ourselves. W. W. Fereday explains how this question applies to believers in the Church Age:

> When the Lord Jesus was on earth, there were two occasions when the compassion of His heart specially went forth. In Matthew 9:36, He felt for the people's spiritual need. The land was full of religious leaders, but the people were unfed. *"When He saw the multitudes. He was moved with compassion, because they fainted, and were scattered abroad, as sheep having no shepherd."* In Matthew 14:15, He was concerned about their temporal need. He *"saw a great multitude, and was moved with compassion toward them."* Thousands of hungry men, women, and children were around Him with nothing obtainable in the wilderness. But His disciples did not share the distress of their Lord. Indeed, they urged Him to send the multitudes away, regardless of consequences. The pressure of the people annoyed them, and interfered with their comfort! A great lesson is here! We live and serve in the midst of a suffering creation, and the suffering increases with the growing violence of men: but are our hearts really moved by the serious universal need? God's heart yearns over the masses, young and old, but do our hearts yearn in sympathy with Him? It is terribly possible to become formal and stereotyped in our service, and thus to serve out of harmony with the One who has sent us. Let us seek to keep near the heart of the God of infinite compassion.[79]

God told Jonah to *"Arise, go to Nineveh"* (1:2) and later the Lord Jesus commissioned His disciples, *"Go therefore and make disciples of all the nations"* (Matt. 28:19). The Greek text literally reads, "Having gone on your way therefore" (Wuest). There was no doubt in the Lord's mind that the disciples would obey His command. Likewise, God knew that Jonah would go to Nineveh and be a testimony for Him there, despite his initial resistance.

In this sense, Jonah pictures the nation of Israel which was to be a lampstand to the world of God's grace and righteousness, yet they failed miserably. However, in a future day their resistance to Christ and His message will be overcome and they will represent Him in the power of the Holy Spirit to all nations. Today the Church is to display the greatness of God to a lost world and to principalities and powers (Eph. 3:10). How are we doing? May we fulfill the Great Commission (Matt. 29:19-20), train the next generation to do the same (Eph. 6:4), and pray that they will continue to walk with the Lord and answer His call.

## God's Call

The book of Jonah reminds us that God is summoning every man, woman, and child to be part of His eternal purposes. Whether or not we hear God calling depends on the openness of our ears; whether or not we answer the call depends on the yielded condition of our heart. Nowhere in Scripture does God constrain anyone to surrender against their will. He kindly invites, graciously petitions, and mercifully warns, but He does not force Himself on anyone. As Lord of all, and Creator of all, He certainly is able to interject His will into ours, but then our actions become robotic gestures lacking the luster of love. We demonstrate adoration for God by obeying His call and commands (John 14:15).

God speaks to His children in the quietness of His presence, but each believer is free to depart from this privileged realm of communion to go his or her own way. Jonah determined to escape to Joppa and put out to sea rather than preach God's message to hostile Nineveh as commanded. God did not force Jonah to submit to His will, but He did put Jonah in such a desperate situation that Jonah wished he had obeyed. From the belly of a huge fish Jonah repented of his sin and at that moment divine communion was restored.

The irresistible love of God can only be experienced by answering His invitation to know Him. Our understanding of God's plan and our commitment to live it out will be directly proportionate to the extent that we have known and experienced Him. The Lord Jesus said, *"He who has My commandments and keeps them, it is he who loves Me. And he who loves Me will be loved by My Father, and I will love him and manifest Myself to him"* (John 14:21). Continued submission to divine

227

truth is the pathway to intimately experiencing and knowing God in deepening degrees. It is this consistent contact with God's nature that results in our comprehension of His wondrous design for our lives. The extent to which we respond to His invitation and have contact with God's nature will ultimately determine our wherewithal to know God, to express His nature to others, and to adhere to His calling for our lives.

## Meditation

My contact with the nature of God will shape my understanding of His call and will help me realize what I truly desire to do for Him. The call of God is an expression of His nature; the service which results in my life is suited to me and is an expression of my nature. ... Service is the overflow which pours from a life filled with love and devotion. ... Service is what I bring to the relationship and is the reflection of my identification with the nature of God. Service becomes a natural part of my life. God brings me into the proper relationship with Himself so that I can understand His call, and then I serve Him on my own out of a motivation of absolute love. Service to God is the deliberate love-gift of a nature that has heard the call of God. Service is an expression of my nature, and God's call is an expression of His nature.[80]

— Oswald Chambers

# Micah

# Overview of Micah

## The Author

Micah, whose name means "Who is like the Lord?" was from Moresheth situated about twenty miles southwest of Jerusalem (1:1). Micah employs a number of wordplays in his literary style, even once to his own name, *"Who is a God like You?"* (7:18). He prophesied to the Southern Kingdom during the reigns of Jotham, Ahaz, and Hezekiah, which meant he was a contemporary of Hosea and Isaiah. Although from a small, rural town, most of Micah's prophetic ministry was uttered in Jerusalem.

## Date

As just mentioned, Micah delivered his messages during the reigns of three Judean kings who ruled from 740–687 B.C. Micah's and Isaiah's prophetic ministries were concurrent, but Isaiah's began before and ended after Micah's. Given the content of his prophecies, it is generally thought that Micah's ministry ended early in Hezekiah's reign, probably before the king's miraculous healing and the great Assyrian defeat occurring in 701 B.C. About 150 years later, Jewish leaders referred to Micah's prophecies to confront Jeremiah's messages (Jer. 26:18).

## Theme

Micah announced judgments to come which would ensure the establishment of the kingdom of God on earth. Some of these predictions have been fulfilled, but others relate to the Kingdom Age and are yet future. As Micah and Isaiah were contemporaries, some of their prophecies are identical (e.g. Micah 4:1-3 as compared to Isaiah 2:1-4). Micah is quoted five times in the New Testament and one of those occurrences was by the Lord Jesus. Micah's most known prophecy was to foretell the birthplace of the Jewish Messiah – Bethlehem Ephrathah (5:2).

The blatantly idolatrous Northern Kingdom was poised to be judged and conquered by Assyria. The Southern Kingdom, to whom Micah ministered, was politically, morally, and spiritually weak. The Lord would use the Assyrian conquest as a chastening rod to awaken Judah out of their despondent condition. While there were brief times of revival under Hezekiah and Josiah, overall the Southern Kingdom continued to decline, which warranted, as Jeremiah, Isaiah, and Habakkuk warned, the destruction of Jerusalem by the Babylonians about a century after Micah's ministry.

## Outline

Although Micah mentions the coming decimation of the Northern Kingdom, he mainly addresses the religious hypocrisy of the Southern Kingdom and forewarns of God's chastening hand. To this end, the book consists of three messages, each commencing with an exhortation for Judah to "hear" and to "listen" to what the Lord had to say:

Condemnation and Captivity (1:1-2:13)
Rebuke and Future Restoration (3:1-5:15)
Pleading, Confession, Mercy, and Praise (6:1-7:20)

# Devotions in Micah

# Judgment Is Imminent
Micah 1

The book commences with these words, *"The word of the Lord that came to Micah"* (v. 1). The message he received pertained to both Samaria, the capital of the Northern Kingdom, and Jerusalem, the capital of the Southern Kingdom. This meant that all twelve tribes of Israel should listen to and heed his oracles. Micah was from Moresheth Gath, a town situated about twenty-five miles southwest of Jerusalem (vv. 1, 14). Micah delivered his messages during the reigns of Jotham, Ahaz, and Hezekiah, who ruled in Judah from 740–687 B.C.

## Jacob's Judgment

Micah summons the inhabitants of the earth to hear God's case against His covenant people (v. 2). The Lord was ready to leave His high throne in heaven to render judgment on Israel, whose pagan shrines and altars were throughout the high places of the land. Therefore, poetically speaking, God would trample down the mountains of Israel, causing them first to melt like wax in a fire and then to pour down the slopes like a flashflood after a cloudburst (vv. 3-4). The meaning of Micah's description is clear: God was going to judge "Jacob" in such a way as to remove all of her idolatrous centers.

"Jacob" is cited eleven times in the book. Nine of those times, as in its first mention in verse 5, the name refers to the entire Jewish nation. Clearly, the second reference in verse 5 is tied to Samaria to depict the Northern Kingdom only, as Jerusalem and Judah are addressed separately. The actual patriarch is referred to in 7:20. Micah affirms in his opening statement what the remainder of the book will explain – both Jewish kingdoms were idolatrous and, accordingly, would be severely punished per the Law of Moses (Deut. 27-28).

233

Both "sin" and "transgression" occur together in verse 5, as they do again in 3:8, 6:7, and 7:18. Sin is that which offends God, but a transgression is a willful action contrary to God's commandments. By engaging in idolatry, Israel had knowingly violated the first three of the Ten Commandments (Num. 20:3-7). Furthermore, the child sacrifices and the immoral pagan rituals associated with Jacob's religious hypocrisy breached the sixth, seventh, and eighth commandments (Num. 20:13-15). Jacob had sinned with his eyes open and now would be openly shamed before the nations. The Northern Kingdom would be judged first (vv. 6-7) and then the Southern Kingdom (vv. 9-16).

## Israel's Destruction

The capital city and stronghold of Israel would become a heap of rubble (v. 6). After a three-year siege, Samaria was conquered by Assyria in 722 B.C. – its ruins today bear witness to the validity of God's word. All those engaging in idolatry would be slain and all Israel's pagan centers where she prostituted herself with various lovers would be destroyed (v. 7; Hos. 5:3-5). Because Israel was carried away in heathen rituals, such as temple prostitution, God would give them what they yearned for among the pagans in Assyria: *"For she gathered it from the pay of a harlot, and they shall return to the pay of a harlot"* (v. 7). The sad irony was that those who survived the Assyrian invasion would be exiled as slaves to a foreign land that was full of the idols they had lusted after.

## Lamenting for Judah

Micah lamented over the incurable wound that God inflicted on Jacob as if it had already happened (v. 8). To weep, wail, and discard clothes and shoes were all signs of intense grieving and mourning. As one of the faithful few, Micah's groans for his suffering countrymen would be like the wailing of a jackal or the mourning of an owl (KJV; NIV) or an ostrich (NKJV; NASB). These creatures live in isolation and in barren places. Furthermore, the jackal and the owl are rarely seen because of their nocturnal instincts. E. B. Pusey provides further insight into these expressions of anguish:

> Not only would he, representing them [the faithful remnant], go bared of all garments of beauty, as we say "half-naked" but despoiled also, the proper term of those plundered and stripped by an enemy. He

speaks of his doing, what we know that Isaiah did, by God's command, representing in act what his people should thereafter do: *"Wouldest thou that I should weep, thou must thyself grieve the first."* Micah doubtless went about, not speaking only of grief, but grieving, in the habit of one mourning and bereft of all.

The cry of jackals and ostriches, as heard at night, is very piteous. Both are doleful creatures, dwelling in desert and lonely places. The jackals make a lamentable howling noise, so that travelers unacquainted with them would think that a company of people, women or children, were howling, one to another. "Its howl," says an Arabic natural historian, "is like the crying of an infant." ... Jerome: "As the ostrich forgets her eggs and leaves them as though they were not hers, to be trampled by the feet of wild beasts, so too shall I go childless, spoiled and naked." Its screech is spoken of by travelers as "fearful, affrighting." "During the lonesome part of the night they often make a doleful and piteous noise. I have often heard them groan, as if they were in the greatest agonies."[81]

Only a few righteous Jews, as represented by Micah, would escape the coming judgment, but they would keenly feel the pain of their brethren regardless. God would use the Assyrians to inflict a near fatal wound on Jacob, even pushing southward into Judah to the very gates of Jerusalem (v. 9). This portion of Micah's prophecy was fulfilled in 701 B.C. Although Jerusalem did not fall during the Assyrian invasion, Sennacherib's Prism, discovered in the ruins of Nineveh in 1830, claims that the Assyrian king conquered forty-six Judean cities:[82]

As to Hezekiah the Jew he did not submit to my yoke I lay siege to forty-six of his strong cities walled forts and to the countless small villages in their vicinity. I drove out of them 200,150 people. Himself I made a prisoner in Jerusalem his Royal residence like a bird in a cage.

The divine chastening, that began with the Assyrian conquest in 701 B.C. to awaken the Jews in Judah to their abhorrent spiritual condition, would continue until Jerusalem was destroyed by the Babylonians in 586 B.C.

*"Tell it not in Gath"* in verse 10 refers to David's statement after learning of King Saul's demise – he did not want the Philistines to hear the news and rejoice in Saul's death (2 Sam. 1:20). Micah reapplies

what David said with a different application – he did not want the Philistines to hear about Assyria's victories in Judah. Nor should Gath weep, otherwise other nations would hear about the devastation in Judah. Micah then employs several clever wordplays to emphasize the desolation caused by the Assyrian army in Judah (vv. 11-16). J. A. Martin explains these paronomasias.

> Micah told the people of Beth Ophrah (meaning "house of dust") to roll in the dust, in an expression of their grief (Jer. 25:34). When attacked by Assyria, Shaphir (meaning "beautiful or pleasant") would become the opposite of its name – a town of nakedness and shame. In Hebrew Zaanan (*sa'anan*) and come out (*yasah*) are related words; in contrast with their city's name, the Zaananites would not dare go outside their city walls because of the warfare. Nor would anyone go to Beth Ezel (meaning "house of nearness or proximity") for protection, for that town would itself be in mourning and in need of help. In Maroth (which sounds in Hebrew like the word for "bitterness") people would writhe in pain while waiting for relief from Jerusalem. But no relief would come because the destruction would go all the way to the gate of Jerusalem (v. 9).

> Sarcastically Micah urged the citizens of Lachish (*lakis*), which sounds something like the word for a team (rekes) of horses, to get a chariot ready for escaping from the Assyrians (Lachish was known for its horses). But their escape attempt would be in vain. ... Lachish was *"the beginning of sin."* [Apparently] Lachish influenced Jerusalem toward idolatry.[83]

In a satirical expression of giving, Moresheth Gath (Micah's hometown) would be bestowed as a parting gift by Jerusalem to the Assyrians (v. 14). The town of Aczib when conquered by the Assyrians would fulfill the meaning of its name "deceptive," for it would not be able to provide assistance to Israel's king as anticipated. Sennacherib the conqueror would go against Maresah, whose Hebrew name *maresah* sounds similar to the Hebrew word for "conqueror" (*hayyores*). Maresah means "possessor," and ironically it would be the Assyrians that possessed Maresah (v. 15).

As David escaped to Adullam to hide from Saul, "the glory of Israel," speaking of Judah's leaders, would also be fugitives there. Sadly, many children would be taken captive and exiled to Assyria as slaves. This will cause great mourning throughout Judea and many will shave their heads to express their grief (v. 16). A Hebrew-speaking audience would have understood Micah's wordplay to emphasize how widespread Assyria's invasion would be into northern Judah. The enemy would come to the gates of Jerusalem, but no further (v. 9), and that is exactly what happened in 701 B.C. (Isa. 36-37). It is God who controls the empires of the world to accomplish His purposes, including the chastening of His people.

## Meditation

A providence is shaping our ends; a plan is developing in our lives; a supreme and loving Being is making all things work together for good.

— F. B. Meyer

God will not lightly or easily lose His people. He has provided well for us: blood to wash us in; a Priest to pray for us, that we may be made to persevere; and, in case we foully fall, an Advocate to plead our cause.

— John Bunyan

# Ruined, Beyond All Remedy
## Micah 2

Micah, continuing his first message, utters the first of two "woes" in his book. The Hebrew word *howy*, rendered "woe," is a passionate lament, usually an expression of despair and recognized guilt which anticipates imminent disaster. One can almost see Micah slowly shaking his head while saying, "Oh Israel." Micah's woe is pronounced against those Jews who lay awake at night devising evil schemes and wicked acts to do the next day (v. 1). Solomon often contrasted the ways of the wicked and their sure demise with the deeds of the righteous and their blessed life:

> *The wicked man does deceptive work, but he who sows righteousness will have a sure reward. As righteousness leads to life, so he who pursues evil pursues it to his own death. Those who are of a perverse heart are an abomination to the Lord, but the blameless in their ways are His delight* (Prov. 11:18-20).

Apart from God, man will always do that which displeases his Creator: *"the soul of the wicked desires evil"* (Prov. 21:10). Thankfully, those who delight in the Lord will also experience His delight: *"But mercy and truth belong to those who devise good"* (Prov. 14:22). Moral behavior where self is preeminent and the welfare of others is ignored will lead to the demise of a society, not to its beneficial development, for *"righteousness exalts a nation, but sin is a reproach to any people"* (Prov. 14:34). Moral relativity devolves human society into chaos, while the pursuit of divine righteousness leads to prosperity – God's blessing. Ultimately, a society's conduct is a direct reflection of their attitude towards God, and where God is not revered, man will not prosper. Such was the state of Israel in Micah's day, says H. A. Ironside:

Their state of soul at this time was wretchedly low; consequently their apprehension of divine things was so dulled that they had lost the power to distinguish what was of God and what was of man. It is ever thus when people do not walk in obedience to revealed truth. They lose the power to distinguish truth from error, and may, under the deadening influence of the deceitfulness of sin, do the most outrageous things, and calmly announce that they were for the glory of God: yea, and be deeply grieved if their high pretensions are not recognized and bowed to.[84]

Accordingly, Micah's woe is well placed on the wayward Jewish nation and on us too, if we defy God's rule and good intentions for us.

In Micah's day, the Jewish elite were driven by a self-promoting, materialistic fervor that did not regard the personal rights and needs of others, especially the poor (vv. 2-3). The Lord had liberated their forefathers from their bonds in Egypt to enjoy a commonwealth that ensured every family would have a lasting inheritance in a new land. But the wealthy were using their resources to defraud and steal from others what the Lord had given as a perpetuating inheritance.

Accordingly, the Lord would strip them of their assets and the perverse legal system that permitted such crookedness to occur (vv. 4-5). Then the proud, affluent Jews would suffer the same debased condition they were inflicting on others. Moreover, as humiliated slaves, they would be a spectacle of ridicule to surrounding nations.

Next, Micah rebukes the false teachers in Judah that were leading the people away from the Lord and into deeper sin (vv. 6-11). God's prophets often foretell future events (both the good and the bad), but mostly the Lord used these men to summon the nation to follow the Lord. They warned and rebuked evil doings, while false prophets, to ensure their own acceptance and welfare, conveniently told the people what they wanted to hear.

Sadly, there are many preachers in Christendom today who engage in the same type of professional heresy. They are more concerned about their own prosperity than the good of God's people. As in Micah's day, these false teachers resist those speaking the truth: The Hebrew in verse 6 is obscure; the NASB and the Darby translations probably render the intended meaning the best:

*Do not speak out, so they speak out. But if they do not speak out concerning these things, reproaches will not be turned back* (v. 6; NASB).

*Prophesy ye not, they prophesy. If they do not prophesy to these, the ignominy will not depart* (v. 6; Darby).

The false prophets did not want to hear God's word, but God's prophets spoke it anyway and, even if they did not, Israel's shame would not be negated. So it is foolish to think that silencing God's messengers somehow would undermine His plans for Israel. These false prophets demeaned the character of a holy God by surmising that a good God would never be so angry that He would judge His people so harshly (v. 7). This is the type of message carnal people rehearse in their own ears: "I can do what I want and God will not judge me because He knows my weaknesses and imperfections!" "God is tolerant and will forgive me, for we all make mistakes!" etc.

God's holy character and attributes are perfectly and consistently demonstrated in all that He does. Thus, we learn about God by observing what He does, how He accomplishes what He purposes to do, and why He was motivated to do what He does. What God does is a direct reflection of His character; He can do nothing against His holy nature. Our God is loving, merciful, gracious, faithful, holy, jealous, just, and wise. All of God's characteristics are holy and none are compromised in any of His actions. In other words, everything God is, is what He does. A. W. Tozer explains:

All of God's acts are consistent with all of his attributes. No attribute contradicts any other, but all harmonize and blend into each other in the infinite abyss of the Godhead. All that God does agrees with all that God is, and being and doing are one in him. The familiar picture of God as often torn between his justice and his mercy is altogether false to the facts. To think of God as inclining first toward one and then toward another of his attributes is to imagine a God who is unsure of himself, frustrated and emotionally unstable, which, of course, is to say that the one of whom we are thinking is not the true God at all but a weak, mental reflection of him badly out of focus.[85]

Accordingly, God is completely satisfied with all that He does. His love does not overpower His holiness. His mercy does not ignore justice. His grace is not prompted by mere sympathy, but by what is best for those in need. Scripture tells us that God is good and does good (Ps. 119:68). God's holy character ensures that He must judge sin (Ex. 34:7). God would be unjust if He did not prosecute that which opposes His nature, as a lack of action against sin endorses wickedness. Clearly, the false prophets of Judah did not know God, and were not speaking for God. Therefore they adamantly opposed those who did – the same confrontation between workers of iniquity and God's servants continues today.

Micah rebukes the false prophets for misleading the people: *"Is the Spirit of the Lord restricted? Are these His doings? Do not My words do good to him who walks uprightly?"* (v. 7). *The Jamieson, Fausset, and Brown Commentary* provides this helpful explanation of verse 7:

> Is His compassion contracted within narrower limits now than formerly, so that He should delight in your destruction? Are these His doings? – that is, are such threatenings God's delight? Ye dislike the prophets' threatenings: but who is to blame? Not God, for He delights in blessing, rather than threatening; but yourselves who provoke His threatenings.[86]

Micah's message was not negative. It revealed how to enjoy a meaningful and joyful life. God longs to bless those who pursue righteousness. H. A. Ironside reminds us that if we are feeding on God's Word, we will be equipped by the Holy Spirit to overcome the challenges of life:

> God's words will ever "do good to him that walketh uprightly." Spiritual things "are spiritually discerned," and therefore only the upright and godly soul will find real profit and blessing in the Scriptures. But where there is exercise as to this, the Word will be found sufficient for all the needs of the pilgrim-path. There will never be a circumstance so trying, a crisis so serious, that the man of God will be left without furnishing unto all good works, if he be found feeding upon the truth. Scripture, with the Holy Spirit's enlightenment, is all that is required in every emergency.[87]

If the Jews returned to the Lord and lived uprightly, there would be no ill repercussions to worry about. However, the prosperity message of the false prophets was leading the nation away from God and into the hands of the Assyrians.

The Jews had become like an enemy of Jehovah. The affluent were flaunting their wealth as victors returning from battle. But their spoils of war were obtained by oppressing the poor. They displaced families by foreclosing on their homes, and enslaving mothers, separating them from their children, to resolve unpaid debts (vv. 8-9). E. B. Pusey suggests that these displaced women were largely widows:

> These were probably the widows of those whom they had stripped. Since the houses were theirs, they were widows; and so their spoilers were at war with those whom God had committed to their special love, whom He had declared the objects of His own tender care, "the widows and the fatherless." The widows they "drove vehemently forth," as having no portion in the inheritance which God had given them, as God had driven out their enemies before them, each "from her pleasant house," the home where she had lived with her husband and children in delight and joy.[88]

Only someone with a seared conscience could evict and enslave a widow and cast her children into the street for personal gain. In the Lord's estimation, Judah had become so defiled with such unrighteousness that she was *"ruined, beyond all remedy"* (v. 10). The only solution would be to scrap the Southern Kingdom, severely chasten them in a foreign land, and then restore them to the land after being purified from their idols and depraved ways. Yet, even this plan was tempered with mercy and would require two more centuries to complete.

Sadly, the flawed ethics of the Judean society readily accepted the misleading messages of the false prophets who promised plenty of *"wine and drink"* rather than divine affliction (v. 11). Many prophets were forecasting merrymaking times ahead and only a handful were calling the nation to repentance with warnings of imminent judgment. Carnal people love their sin and all that promotes sensual satisfaction, so God's message was widely ignored.

Micah then closes his first message with God's promise to gather His people back to Israel after their chastisement was completed and to lead them as their Shepherd and King:

*I will surely assemble all of you, O Jacob, I will surely gather the remnant of Israel; I will put them together like sheep of the fold, like a flock in the midst of their pasture; they shall make a loud noise because of so many people. The one who breaks open will come up before them; they will break out, pass through the gate, and go out by it; their king will pass before them, with the Lord at their head* (vv. 12-13).

Although grim and sorrowful times were ahead for Judah, all three of the prophet's messages conclude with the promise of their future restoration to God in the land. Just as a good shepherd leads his sheep out the sheepfold gate to green pastures and to be refreshed by still waters, God will break open the way and lead His covenant people into immense blessing. He will remove every obstacle – no Gentile nation will ever oppress His people again. The Lord will be their King and they will readily acknowledge Him as their head. While God would return Israel to the land from Babylon in the sixth century B.C., the complete fulfillment of this prophecy will not occur until the Kingdom Age. Then the Lord Jesus Christ will rule over, care for, and protect Israel forever.

## Meditation

God's compassion flows out of His goodness, and goodness without justice is not goodness. God spares us because He is good, but He could not be good if He were not just.

— A. W. Tozer

# Hating Good and Loving Evil
## Micah 3

Micah's first message foretold Judah's coming judgment and why. He tallied Judah's sins and warned that there was only one remedy if they did not repent and return to the Lord – invasion and exile. Only two verses in the first message promised future restoration and blessing (2:12-13). The prophet's second oracle is in contrast with his first in that after listing the sins of Judah's leaders in chapter 3, the remainder of his message foretells Israel's future blessedness. Chapter 4 highlights the blessings of the coming Millennial Kingdom and chapter 5 introduces the magnificent King who will rule Israel at that time.

Addressing both the Northern and the Southern Kingdoms, Micah minces no words in his indictment of corrupt leaders who were perverting justice and ruining the people (v. 1):

*You who hate good and love evil; who strip the skin from My people, and the flesh from their bones; who also eat the flesh of My people, lay their skin from them, break their bones, and chop them in pieces like meat for the pot, like flesh in the caldron* (vv. 2-3).

Because Jewish rulers hated good and loved evil, they failed to be good shepherds of God's sheep; rather, they were like hunters who kill and slaughter their prey. The description of removing the animal's hide and cutting up meat and bones into small pieces to prepare a stew depicted how God's people were being completely devoured, morally speaking, by their perverse leaders. When spiritual leaders do not pursue the Lord, they not only betray the Lord, but also those in their care. The worst kind of pride is spiritual pride. Whenever God's people settle into complacency and ease, there will always be an abundance of vain, self-confident men with high-sounding titles and ecclesiastical decrees. Such was the situation in Israel.

Micah says that there was a calamity coming (speaking of the Assyrian invasion) in which Israel's leaders would cry out to the Lord, but it would be too late; He would not answer them (v. 4). All those who led God's people astray would be harshly punished. Having addressed Israel's corrupt leadership, Micah turns his attention to pronouncing judgment on Israel's many false prophets (vv. 5-8). These prophets were motivated by greed, being concerned only with their own welfare. If the people took good care of them (put food in their mouths) they would prophesy tidings of peace, but if they were not fed well, then these false prophets threatened war (v. 5). But nightfall (picturing God's disciplinary retribution) was coming, and then these false prophets would suffer lingering darkness (judgment without God responding to their cries) and days of shame (vv. 6-7). Those who preferred darkness to light in order to practice their evil deeds and mislead others will suffer in their own delusions.

In contrast to the fabricated message of peace by the false prophets, Micah was empowered by God's Spirit to deliver a message of power, truth, and justice which warned the people to repent of their transgressions before it was too late (v. 8). He then appealed to Israel's rulers to listen to him (v. 9). Their leadership should have upheld God's justice and righteousness, but instead they permitted murder, took bribes, and governed in favor of those who paid them well (vv. 10-11). When their coffers were full, they spoke pleasantries such as, *"Is not the Lord among us? No harm can come upon us"* (v. 11). These so-called prophets were nothing more than con-artists and fortune-tellers. They spoke for profit, not for God.

While it was true that the Lord was among them, He was not Israel's good luck charm protecting them from danger. Rather, He was a holy God burdened by His troublesome people. The writer of Hebrews explains that a holy God must judge His wayward people:

*"Vengeance is Mine, I will repay," says the Lord. And again, "The Lord will judge His people." It is a fearful thing to fall into the hands of the living God* (Heb. 10:30-31).

In the coming days, all Israel would learn the validity of this statement. Micah promised that the land, including Jerusalem, would be turned upside down by His judicial plow and even His temple would be destroyed (v. 12).

## Meditation

The neglected heart will soon be a heart overrun with worldly thoughts; the neglected life will soon become a moral chaos.

— A. W. Tozer

Really great moral teachers never do introduce new moralities: it is quacks and cranks who do that.

— C. S. Lewis

Art, like morality, consists in drawing the line somewhere.... I say that a man must be certain of his morality for the simple reason that he has to suffer for it.

— G. K. Chesterton

# God's Mountain
## Micah 4

Having indicted Israel's rulers and false prophets and foretold God's chastening calamity coming to the region, Micah transitions to a positive theme of hope in this chapter. He reveals the tenor of the Kingdom Age (4:1-8), the events directly preceding it (4:9-5:1), and the King who will reign over it (5:2-15). Micah prefaces this section by stating when the Kingdom of God, depicted as a mountain, would occur – *"in the latter days."*

*Now it shall come to pass in the latter days that the mountain of the Lord's house shall be established on the top of the mountains, and shall be exalted above the hills; and peoples shall flow to it* (v. 1).

Hosea spoke of "the latter days" as the time when the unfaithful Jewish nation would be restored to Jehovah. Jeremiah says that this latter-day event occurs as an outcome of the *"Time of Jacob's Trouble"* (Jer. 30:7, 24). The Lord Jesus said it would be a time of great tribulation, and that there will not have been anything like it before on earth, nor would there be afterwards (Matt. 24:21). This is why Peter slightly modified the Hebrew text of Joel 2 when he quoted it to his countrymen on the day of Pentecost to explain the timing of God's pouring out of the Holy Spirit on the Jewish nation (Acts 2). Peter exchanged "afterward" for "in the last days" to denote a future time when Messiah would return to earth to reestablish Israel and end "the times of the Gentiles." Peter was affirming that Pentecost was only a foretaste of better things to come for the Jewish nation in the Kingdom Age, when God pours His Spirit out on all flesh.

To summarize, chapters 4 and 5 foretell Israel's complete restoration to the Lord in the Kingdom Age, which will occur directly after the Tribulation Period. Then *"the mountain of the Lord's house"* (v. 2; Isa. 2:2) will be above all mountains of the earth (i.e., God's kingdom will have worldwide acknowledgment and supremacy). Isaiah and Micah were contemporaries, and both prophets foretold God's glorious mountain on earth, speaking of Messiah's earthly kingdom.

When metaphorically applied in Scripture, mountains are used to symbolize governmental authorities or kingdoms (v. 1; Rev. 17:9-10). There was one instance during the latter days of the Lord's ministry in Decapolis that His divine essence was permitted to shine out of Him to picture exactly what Isaiah is alluding to in verses 2-5. The event is what we commonly call the "transfiguration." Matthew describes it:

> *Now after six days Jesus took Peter, James, and John his brother, led them up on a high mountain by themselves; and He was transfigured before them. His face shone like the sun, and His clothes became as white as the light* (Matt. 17:1-2).

In the preceding verse, the Lord Jesus had said, *"Assuredly, I say to you, there are some standing here who shall not taste death till they see the Son of Man coming in His kingdom"* (Matt. 16:28). For a brief moment the disciples were given a foretaste of the coming kingdom; they saw the intrinsic glory of Christ in a measure.

One can only imagine how the glory of the Lord appeared on a high mountain in a remote region and apparently at night (Luke 9:32-37). The transfiguration foretells a future day when Christ will rule the world and His intrinsic glory will be seen throughout the earth. When that kingdom is established, the word of God will go forth from Jerusalem and all nations will come to *"the house of the God of Jacob"* to see the glory of God and to worship Him (Isa. 2:3, 60:14, 66:10-18; Zech. 14:16-21). Indeed, the whole earth will be full of God's glory (Isa. 2:13, 2:2, 62:1-7). C. A. Coates notes the opposite pull of spiritual gravity, so to speak, during the Kingdom Age:

> The elevation of Jehovah's house is very strikingly presented in the opening verses of the chapter. We read of "the mountain," "the top of the mountains," "lifted up above the hills." "And many nations shall go and say, Come, and let us go up." Men will become sensible "in the end of days" that God's house is very elevated, but that it is attractive, and that it is worthwhile to go up to it. Indeed, it is said that "the peoples shall flow unto it," which seems to indicate a readiness to move under a law of attraction which draws upward. The natural law of gravitation is reversed, and this is what always happens when grace becomes operative in the souls of men. The tendency of

everything here is downward, for it is a fallen world, but when God moves in "the peoples," they will desire to flow up to what is of Him, and will realize that it is to be found in His house. This is true, in the principle of it, today.[89]

In the Kingdom Age, Israel will come to the temple in Jerusalem and be taught by the Lord how they should walk, and all Israel will obey Him (v. 2). No injustice, violence, or warring will be permitted in Christ's kingdom; it will be characterized by peace, prosperity, and righteousness (v. 3; Isa 2:4). Christ will reign over the nations and they will gladly yield to His rule, for His judgments are just and righteous. Such submission to the Lord will ensure that everyone can sit under his own vine or fig tree in utter security (v. 4). This future bliss refuted the counterfeit peace promised by false prophets in Micah's day because the Jewish nation did not yield to the Lord. Additionally, the Gentile nations were worshiping false gods in Micah's day, but as he just explained, that would not be the case when Israel was wholly walking with the Lord in the Kingdom Age (v. 5).

The Lord promised His covenant people *"in that day"*: *"I will assemble the lame, I will gather the outcast and those whom I have afflicted; I will make the lame a remnant, and the outcast a strong nation"* (vv. 6-7). Because of their spiritual lameness, the Jews had been scattered among the nations, but the Lord would gather a remnant back to Zion to rule over them and make them a strong nation. Furthermore, He would watch over them from Jerusalem, which He would establish as a bulwark and a high tower to watch over His people, as a shepherd observes his sheep from a high place (v. 8). J. M. Flanigan addresses the possible meanings of the "tower of the flock" expression:

> The "tower of the flock" is an obvious allusion to the watchtowers from which shepherds used to keep watch and guard over their flocks and in which they found shelter from the sun. This continues the metaphor of the shepherd and his sheep. Some think that here the tower of the flock is Jerusalem and some think that it may refer to the Temple, from which Messiah will oversee His sheep. Adam Clarke says, "I believe Jerusalem, or the temple, or both, are meant; for these were considered the stronghold of the daughter of Zion, the fortress of the Jewish people." Other expositors emphasize the Hebrew of the

words, *Migdal-Eder*, and point out that this was a place near to Bethlehem from which shepherds watched over their flocks.[90]

Regardless as to where the high location refers, the Lord will watch over and care for the sheep of His pasture (in Israel). The future gathering of Jews, now dispersed among the nations, back to Israel to be cared for by the Lord is a well-established prophecy in the Old Testament (Isa. 49:5; Jer. 23:3; Ezek. 39:28-29; Hos.1:11; Joel 3:1; Amos 9:1). Such prophecies repudiate Replacement Theology – clearly the Lord has wonderful future plans for the Jewish nation.

Having described the character of the Kingdom Age, the prophet pauses to foretell Israel's birth pangs in being delivered into that era of bliss (vv. 9-13). There would be sorrow and weeping when idolatrous Judah was exiled to Babylon, and afterwards there would be no king or counselor to lead them for some time (v. 9). Both Isaiah (Isa. 13 and 39) and Micah foretold that Babylon (v. 10) would conquer Judah and would lead enslaved survivors back to Babylon (camping in open fields along the way). This was an extraordinary prophecy because Babylon was not a powerful nation at the time and would not be in a position to overcome the Assyrian Empire for another century.

Micah also prophesied that the Lord would rescue His people from Babylon. Jeremiah predicted this deliverance would occur after 70 years of exile (Jer. 25:11-12). Isaiah even named the king and the people God would use to liberate the Jews from Babylon, Cyrus the Persian (Isa. 44:28-45:1). Much of what Isaiah predicts in Isaiah 40-48 pertains to this future liberation. Micah merely summarizes, *"There* [Babylon] *you shall be delivered; there the Lord will redeem you from the hand of your enemies"* (v. 10).

Moving further into the future, Micah foretells another divine deliverance which will occur when the Jews are living in Israel, but are surrounded by a host of invading nations (v. 11). These Gentile armies will be unaware that Jehovah has gathered them to His threshing floor, like sheaves of grain at harvest time (v. 12). This event is the Battle of Armageddon at the end of the Tribulation Period (see Joel 3 discussion). The Messiah, the Lord Jesus Christ, will return to the earth and will fight for His people (Zech. 14) and those in Jerusalem shall be victorious and the spoils of war will be dedicated to the Lord (v. 13).

God promised David that one of his descendants would sit on an everlasting throne (2 Sam. 7:16) – Jesus Christ is that descendant

(Matt. 1:1). Presently, the Lord Jesus resides on His Father's throne in Heaven (Rev. 3:21), and though He does have the title deed to His kingdom, He will not return to the earth to establish it until the Church Age, or the fullness of the Gentiles, is complete (Rom. 11:25). Then He shall be honored by not only the Jewish nation, but by all nations on earth, and, of course, by the glorified saints standing at His side.

## Meditation

The Lord unto His Christ has said,
"Sit Thou at My right hand,
Until I make Thine enemies
Submit to Thy command.
A scepter prospered by the Lord
Thy mighty hand shall wield;
From Zion Thou shalt rule the world,
And all Thy foes shall yield.

"Thou shalt subdue the kings of earth
With God at Thy right hand;
The nations Thou shalt rule in might
And judge in every land."
The Christ, refreshed by living streams,
Shall neither faint nor fall,
And He shall be the glorious Head,
Exalted over all.

— Henry S. Cutler

# Little Bethlehem
## Micah 5

Before describing the Ruler of the Millennial Kingdom to come, Micah returns to the incident identified in verse 9 of the last chapter – the fall of Jerusalem. When besieged by Babylon, Jerusalem will be the "daughter of troops" (v. 1). Micah sarcastically challenged the Jews to arrange their own troops to make Jerusalem as secure as they could. The prophet foretold that this would be a futile effort, for Jerusalem would fall and the judge of Israel would be captured and struck in the face with a rod. This speaks of Judah's leader being captured and humbled by Babylon.

Jeremiah tells us that when Zedekiah saw that Jerusalem was falling into Babylonian hands, he marshaled what soldiers he had left and fled eastward from the city. As Jeremiah had already predicted, he did not escape, but was captured in the plains of Jericho and brought before the Babylonian king. With Zedekiah watching, Nebuchadnezzar had the nobles of Judah executed and then he slew all of Zedekiah's sons. This horrific scene would be the last thing Zedekiah would witness, for his eyes were then put out, and he was chained and taken to Babylon (Jer. 39:4-7).

The prophet Isaiah foretold at length the sufferings of Christ to redeem those who would enjoy His kingdom with Him (Isa. 50-53). Some have suggested that verse 1 speaks of Christ's humiliation just before and during His crucifixion. While at first glance this seems plausible, biblical hermeneutics suggests that verse 1 does not speak of Christ for several reasons: First, the context of verse 1 pertains to an existing leader of Jerusalem being humbled by the Babylonians. Second, the one being humbled, Zedekiah, was in rebellion against God's revealed will; in contrast, Christ only did the will of the Father. Third, the Hebrew word *shaphat*, rendered "the judge of" in verse 1, speaks of Zedekiah's role in Jerusalem, whereas the One in verse 2 will be "the Ruler" (*mashal*) of all Israel. Fourth, Christ was not captured and beaten by Babylonian troops that had put Jerusalem in a long siege.

Fifth, the "But you" at the beginning of verse 2, marks a distinction between the near-term prophecy of verse 1 and the far-term prophecies in the remainder of the chapter.

## Messiah's Birth

Having foretold events that would happen to the Jewish nation prior to the Kingdom Age, Micah shifts his focus to the birth of Israel's future Deliverer (v. 2) and the work He will accomplish (vv. 3-15). The Messiah's birthplace would be the same as David's, Bethlehem of Ephrathah, located about five miles south of Jerusalem:

> *But you, Bethlehem Ephrathah, though you are little among the thousands of Judah, yet out of you shall come forth to Me the one to be Ruler in Israel, whose goings forth are from of old, from everlasting* (v. 2).

Israel's Messiah would be the eternal God incarnate – the One who literally stepped out of "the days of immeasurable time" or "the days of eternity" into time! At that time, the Son of God, the living Word, would take on flesh to become the Savior of the World (John 1:1, 14, 3:16). Micah's declaration is a strong affirmation of the deity of Christ, who would be born of a virgin (Isa. 7:14) in the small town of Bethlehem in Ephrathah of Judah.

But since there were not thousands of towns in Judah, how are we to understand the phrase, *"little among the thousands of Judah"*? E. B. Pusey answers this question:

Literally, "small to be," that is, "too small to be among" etc. Each tribe was divided into its thousands, probably of fighting men, each thousand having its own separate head (Num. 1:16; 10:4). But the thousand continued to be a division of the tribe, after Israel was settled in Canaan (Josh. 22:21, 22:30; 1 Sam. 10:19, 23:23). The "thousand" of Gideon was the meanest in Manasseh (Judg. 6:15). Places too small to form a thousand by themselves were united with others, to make up the number. So lowly was Bethlehem that it was not counted among the possessions of Judah. In the division under Joshua, it was wholly omitted. From its situation, Bethlehem can never have been a considerable place.[91]

As there was also a town called Bethlehem in Galilee, naming the county, Ephrathah, ensured that there would be no confusion as to which small town Micah was speaking of. Luke records the story of Joseph and Mary venturing from Nazareth to Bethlehem to take part in a census, and that Mary gave birth to the Lord Jesus in a lowly stable in Bethlehem (Luke 2:4-11).

When the Magi from the East came to Jerusalem seeking the one born king of the Jews, the priests and scribes rightly identified the birthplace of the Messiah as Bethlehem (Matt. 2:3-6). When the Magi did not return to tell Herod the Great that they had found the Jewish Messiah, the king had all baby boys two and under in the region slaughtered to remove any rivals to his throne. However, Joseph was warned in a dream to escape into Egypt with his family, which he did (Matt. 2:15). After Herod's death, Joseph returned to his hometown of Nazareth and that was where the child Jesus was raised. This created confusion in the minds of the religious leaders because Jesus claimed to be the Messiah, yet he was from Nazareth, not Bethlehem.

Thankfully, the information about the Messiah's first advent is contained in the whole of Scripture, which the spiritually-blind Jewish authorities ignored. For example, Hosea wrote: *"When Israel was a child, I loved him, and out of Egypt I called My son"* (Hos. 11:1). While the primary focus of this verse is to remind Israel of God's past goodness and to call them to repentance, Matthew quotes Hosea to affirm its messianic fulfillment: After Herod's death, the Lord called His Son, the Lord Jesus, out of Egypt, where Joseph fled with his family, having been warned to do so.

Additionally, Isaiah identifies the region from which the promised Deliverer would come, the tribal lands of Zebulun and Naphtali (Isa. 9:1). Christ's hometown of Nazareth was in Zebulun's territory, and Naphtali composed much of Galilee where the Lord spent most of His earthly sojourn. Hence a great light was afforded to those residing in Zebulun and Naphtali (Isa. 9:2; Matt. 2:2). Since Matthew quotes Isaiah and directly applies his prophecy to the ministry of the Lord Jesus in Galilee, we can be assured that this is Isaiah's meaning (Matt. 4:13-17).

Through the prophets, God the Father painted a portrait of the coming Messiah, so that when He arrived, Israel would recognize Him. He would be born of a virgin (Isa. 7:14), from the tribe of Judah (Gen. 49:10), the seed of David (2 Sam. 7:12-13), and in Bethlehem of Ephrathah (Mic. 5:2), but would live in Egypt for a time (Hos. 11:1), before being raised in Nazareth in Zebulun (Isa. 9:1; Matt. 2:23). These six prophecies alone would greatly limit the number of individuals who could possibly claim to be the Messiah. With the addition of another sixty-three specific Old Testament prophecies pertaining to Christ's first advent, the probability that anyone would fulfill all sixty-nine major prophecies, by chance, is estimated at one chance in 5.32 x $10^{72}$ attempts.[92] Jesus Christ did fulfill each of those prophecies, emphatically proving that He was God's Messiah, the Savior of the world.

## Bethlehem – "House of Bread"

The birthplace of Christ, Bethlehem, means the "house of bread" and wonderfully represents the work of Christ in saving sinners, as He Himself explained:

> *Then Jesus said to them, "Most assuredly, I say to you, Moses did not give you the bread from heaven, but My Father gives you the true bread from heaven. For the bread of God is He who comes down from heaven and gives life to the world." Then they said to Him, "Lord, give us this bread always." And Jesus said to them, "I am the bread of life. He who comes to Me shall never hunger, and **he who believes in Me** shall never thirst. But I said to you that you have seen Me and yet **do not believe** (John 6:32-36).*

> *Most assuredly, I say to you, **he who believes in Me has everlasting life**. I am the bread of life. Your fathers ate the manna in the wilderness, and are dead. This is the bread which comes down from heaven, that one may eat of it and not die. I am the living bread which came down from heaven. If anyone eats of this bread, he will live forever; and the bread that I shall give is My flesh, which I shall give for the life of the world (John 6:47-51).*

Christ came down from heaven as God's means to give eternal life to those who would believe on Him and His redemptive work accomplished at Calvary. Eating God's bread of life is synonymous with exercising faith in the gospel message preached by Christ – He is heaven's house of living bread!

The narrative of Genesis 35:16-20 wonderfully depicts in metaphoric form the two advents of Christ, which Micah is foretelling. Jacob departed from Bethel to travel to Ephrath. During this journey,

Rachel entered into hard labor to deliver her second son. This son was born at Bethlehem and was named "Benoni" by Rachel just before her death, but Jacob renamed him "Benjamin." Jacob then buried Rachel at Bethlehem and set a pillar upon her grave. In this messianic portrait, Jacob represents God the Father, Benjamin, the Lord Jesus, and Rachel, Benjamin's mother, the nation of Israel. Bethel means "house of God," Ephrath means "a place of fruitfulness," Bethlehem means "house of bread," Benoni means "son of my sorrow," and lastly, Benjamin means "the son of my right hand." Now, let us put the prophetic story together.

The Son left the house of God (Heaven), was born in Bethlehem of a Jewish virgin (Luke 2:15), and thus became "the bread of life" offered to mankind for eternal life (John 6:35). His earthly ministry transpired after leaving His home in Heaven, but before presenting a fruit harvest of souls to God through the work of His cross (Isa. 53:10-11). He was born to be the man of sorrows (Isa. 53:3), but after Calvary, the Father raised Him up to the seat of honor at His right hand (Heb. 1:3). To reaffirm that God had not forgotten His covenant to restore and bless Israel (Rom. 11:26), a pillar was erected on Rachel's grave. Historically, pillars were erected to visually acknowledge a covenant (Gen. 28:22, 31:45). The Lord Jesus sealed the New Covenant with His own blood. Christ and His work are clearly revealed through the birth of Benjamin at Bethlehem. Someday, Israel will not only eat of the bread of life, but will also honor the Son on God's right hand – the Lord Jesus Christ!

Little Bethlehem of the Old Testament wonderfully foreshadows precious truths concerning Christ's advents. In Genesis 35 and Micah 5, a **Son** is born, as just discussed. In Ruth 2, a **Savior** (i.e., a Kinsman Redeemer) and the Lord of the harvest appears. In 1 Samuel 16, a **Sovereign** is anointed (the Shepherd and King of Israel). While the Son, the Savior, has already come to seek and save the lost, the latter aspect of Christ's rule will not be realized until the Kingdom Age.

## Messiah's Kingdom

Having foretold the birthplace of Christ, Micah begins to address Christ's second advent in verse 3:

*Therefore He shall give them up, until the time that she who is in labor has given birth; then the remnant of His brethren shall return to the children of Israel.*

Isaiah also connects both advents of Christ in his prophecies (Isa. 9:6-7, 61:1-2). Micah's prophecies concerning Israel fall into three distinct segments: First, because Israel rejected Christ at His first advent, the Jewish nation will be set aside and dispersed. They are presently waiting, just as a mother must carry a child through the long gestation period before delivery can occur. Second, there will be a hard and drawn out labor and delivery process, which pictures the intense suffering that Israel will endure during the Tribulation Period. Third, Israel will be delivered when Christ returns to rescue and regather His people to be with Him in Israel (v. 3). J. N. Darby summarizes the dispensation ramifications concerning Israel in verse 3:

Israel is given up to judgment, forsaken of God, in a certain sense, for having rejected the Christ, the Lord. But now she who travails has brought forth. Afterwards, the remnant of the brethren of this first-born Son, instead of being added to the church (Acts 2), return unto the children of Israel. The Christ is not ashamed to call them His brethren, but at this period they no longer become members of His body. Their relation is with Israel. This is the position in which they are placed before God.[93]

In the Kingdom Age, the Lord will shepherd the Jewish nation to ensure her security, and His majesty will be known throughout the earth (v. 4). When the Lord Jesus previously walked upon the earth, He exhibited God's character for everyone to see, but few appreciated His majesty. Each page of the gospel accounts is saturated with the sweet aroma of Christ's divine nature. The wisdom of His teaching, the power of His grace, and the splendor of His miracles declare His glory! All His speech, His gestures, and actions perfectly represented the character of God (John 5:19, 8:29, 14:6, 17:6). Christ's own character serves as a living exhortation for us to follow; may we learn of Him and be more like Him (Matt. 11:28-30). John summarizes the matter well: *"And the Word became flesh and dwelt among us, and we beheld His glory, the glory as of the only begotten of the Father, full of grace and truth"* (John 1:14).

In the future, the Lord Jesus will be Israel's peace because He will conquer and subdue all Israel's enemies, as portrayed by the reference to Assyria. Assyria, the land of Nimrod, was the dominant Gentile power at the time of Micah's writing (vv. 5-6). This victory would ensure that Israel would overcome her enemies and have plenty of leaders to rule with Christ during the Kingdom Age. The reference to *seven* and then *eight* leaders is not to be taken literally as fifteen in total. Rather, one number followed by the next is a Hebrew literary form expressing completeness or adequacy. Additionally, seven is the perfect number of completeness in Scripture, so more than seven again conveys the thought of more than abundantly adequate for the task. See Job 5:19, Psalm 62:11-12, and Amos 1:3 for other examples of this type of Hebrew expression.

During the Kingdom Age, Israel will be completely nourished and refreshed by the Lord, not through any human effort, as symbolized by the dew and the rain which only God controls (v. 7). Being fully sustained and empowered by God meant that Israel would be as powerful as a lion against any adversary (vv. 8-9). Furthermore, the Lord will teach His people to fully trust Him for protection and security; hence, He will destroy the warhorses, war-chariots, and military strongholds throughout Israel (vv. 10-11).

What Israel will learn during the Kingdom Age is what the Church should relish today, that is, deep satisfaction and complete security are found in Christ alone. He is the believer's nurturing rain and dew in the dry seasons of life. Christ is our bulwark of strength when we are tempted to defend ourselves against injustice and wrongdoing.

Much of what Eliphaz said against Job was incorrect, but he did put his finger on the weak spot in Job when he said to him: *"Is not your reverence your confidence? And the integrity of your ways your hope?"* (Job 4:6). Job was a righteous man, but not a perfect man. He would learn that it was not his perseverance in well-doing that would secure his livelihood and enjoyment in life; rather, such things were controlled by the God whom Job worshiped. Let us be careful not to adore what we have, what we are doing, or what we have done; God could blow it all away with one puff of air (Hag. 1:9). Our security, satisfaction, and prosperity are in Him alone, not in the relationships we establish, nor in our accomplishments, nor in our stockpiled resources, and definitely not in the organizations to which we belong.

To conclude his second message, Micah foretold that the Messiah would purge from Israel all idols and anything else that had to do with pagan worship (vv. 12-14). Moreover, He will rule the nations with a rod of iron; anyone not submitting to His authority would reap His wrath (v. 15). The kingdom of Christ will be pro-Israel and those not revering Him or esteeming His covenant people properly will suffer His displeasure! This message would be a great encouragement for the dispersed Jewish people as they wait through the arduous centuries for deliverance into the life of Christ and into His Kingdom.

## Meditation

Thy Kingdom come, O God,
Thy rule, O Christ, begin;
Break with Thine iron rod
The tyrannies of sin.

Where is Thy reign of peace,
And purity, and love?
When shall all hatred cease,
As in the realms above?

When comes the promised time
That war shall be no more –
Oppression, lust, and crime,
Shall flee Thy face before?

Over heathen lands afar
Thick darkness broodeth yet:
Arise, O Morning Star,
Arise, and never set!

— Lewis Hensley

# Testify Against Me
## Micah 6

Micah's final message commences abruptly as he transitions from the blissful but future Kingdom Age (chp. 5) to Israel's present pathetic spiritual condition. As in the opening of the book (1:2), the Lord summons Israel to stand before the mountains, depicting the various peoples of the world, so that God's case against her could be heard and validated by all (vv. 1-2). The Lord prosecutes His people Himself and opens with a question: *"O My people, what have I done to you? And how have I wearied you? Testify against Me"* (v. 3). The rhetorical question was to affirm God's complete innocence – He had shown Israel tender care and faithfulness throughout their history.

To prove this assertion, the Lord rehearses examples of His authentic guardianship of Israel since the days of her conception (v. 4). He had not only delivered His people from slavery in Egypt, but also had prevented Moab's king Balak and the false prophet Balaam from cursing them (v. 5). Throughout their long pilgrimage to Canaan, the Lord went before them every step of the way, even opening a way through the flooding Jordan River to conduct them safely to Gilgal.

The testimony of God's faithfulness (vv. 3-5) is now contrasted with Israel's apostasy through a series of hyperbolic statements designed to awaken Israel to the gravity of her infidelity. Micah asks:

*With what shall I come before the Lord, and bow myself before the High God? Shall I come before Him with burnt offerings, with calves a year old? Will the Lord be pleased with thousands of rams, ten thousand rivers of oil? Shall I give my firstborn for my transgression, the fruit of my body for the sin of my soul?* (vv. 6-7).

The prophet already knew that no sacrifice or offering would appease the Lord's anger over Israel's apostasy. Micah even used the extreme example of child sacrifice, which was forbidden, to illustrate the futility of somehow making restitution for their blatant idolatry and transgressions against God's Law. The prophet then told the Jews ("O man" which refers to anyone in Israel) what God did require of them: *"He has shown you, O man, what is good; and what does the Lord require of you but to do justly, to love mercy, and to walk humbly with your God?"* (v. 8). There need be no guesswork about it; God had revealed to them what would please Him. William MacDonald explains what God did not want from His people and how it would be possible to give to Him what He did want:

> What does the Most High seek in return for this [His goodness to man]? Not extravagant animal sacrifices! Certainly not human sacrifices! But justice, and mercy, and humility. Verse 8 describes what God requires; to obey this a person must have divine life. An unconverted person is totally incapable of producing this kind of righteousness.[94]

Only through repentance and conversion can an individual please the Lord. William Kelly explains that it is impossible to walk with the Lord until one has been converted through faith:

> But nobody does so [walks with God] until he is brought in as a converted soul and receives the grace of God in Christ. It is impossible to act justly and to be really humble before God, until we have turned to Him in faith. ... There is a real repentance formed in the soul first; and Israel will be brought into this. It is faith which produces real repentance and true humility; where faith was not, we find to the end of the chapter the solemn proof of evil manifested in both people and king.[95]

The same reality is true in the Church Age – no one can walk with the Lord without exercising faith in the gospel of Jesus Christ and experiencing regeneration by the Holy Spirit. He then empowers believers to repudiate sin and not be mastered by it. Paul explains in Romans 8 that the believer has received a new nature and that through the power of the Holy Spirit, this nature can control the believer so that his or her flesh nature no longer rules his or her life: *"For the law of the Spirit of life in Christ Jesus has made me free from the law of sin and death"* (Rom. 8:2). This results in a new war within each believer, a war between the old and new nature. *"Therefore, having these promises, beloved, let us cleanse ourselves from all filthiness of the flesh and spirit, perfecting holiness in the fear of God"* (2 Cor. 7:1). Thankfully this is a battle in which the believer can be victorious, for the power of the Holy Spirit is available to overcome our inherent depravity: *"Walk in the Spirit, and you shall not fulfill the lust of the flesh"* (Gal. 5:16). All this to say that believers in the Church Age can do what is good and just, can love mercy, and can humbly walk in the Spirit with their God!

## God's Rod

While saints in Micah's day were not indwelt by the Holy Spirit, God's grace and mercy were just as available to them as to believers today through repentance and confession of sin. Sadly, the nation would not yield to God's revealed will, nor acknowledge their sin to experience His reviving work in them. Without spiritual revival, they could not please God, but rather would live for themselves – this meant that God must punish His people. Micah therefore tells them that it would be wise to listen to this disciplinary lesson spoken through God's rod (v. 9).

To eliminate any confusion as to why God would punish His people, Micah again refers to their wicked practices. The rich were amassing wealth at the expense of the poor (often through violence; v. 12) and merchants were using a "short measure" (a smaller sized standard to measure dry goods) to cheat their customers (v. 10). It was also common business practice to use "wicked scales" (dishonest balances) to accomplish the same fraudulent outcome (v. 11). The Jewish populace had digressed into a lying and deceitful society who cared not for their fellowman, nor were the people concerned about the consequences of their sin (v. 12).

The only solution to such hardened depravity was severe, relentless chastening: *"Therefore I will also make you sick by striking you, by making you desolate because of your sins"* (v. 13). One cannot put a positive spin on such a sobering statement – God was, figuratively speaking, going to beat His people until they regained their senses, and returned to Him in humble repentance. He would first cause crop failures and deprive them of food. Their stores of grain would not sustain them because these stashes would be confiscated by marauders (v. 14). The prophet promised that their fields, olive groves, and vineyards would not benefit them no matter how much they labored in them (v. 15).

Wicked behavior results when God's people turn away from the Lord. The root cause of Israel's wickedness was that she had departed from God and from obeying His Law to embracing the statues of Omri and the ways of Ahab (v. 16). Omri and his son Ahab were the most evil kings of Israel. They plunged the Northern Kingdom into deep idolatry, and popularized the worship of the fertility gods Baal and Ashtoreth (or Astarte or Ishtar). Because Judah had followed the pagan practices of the Northern Kingdom, she also would experience ruin, captivity, exile, and the ridicule of the nations, just as Israel would. God would use the rod of Babylon on Judah and the rod of Assyria on Israel to accomplish this chastening.

## Meditation

> Lord of our life, God Whom we fear,
> Unknown, yet known; unseen, yet near;
> Breath of our breath, in Thee we live;
> Life of our life, our praise receive.
>
> Shine in our darkness, Light of light,
> Our minds illumine, disperse our night;
> Make us responsive to Thy will;
> Our souls with all Thy fullness fill.
>
> We love Thy Name; we heed Thy rod;
> Thy Word our law, O gracious God!
> We wait Thy will; on Thee we call:
> Our light, our life, our love, our all.

— S. F. Smith

# From Shadow to Light
## Micah 7

As a godly man and prophet of God, Micah felt keenly the depravity of the godless people he resided among. He felt like a hungry person venturing into a vineyard to find newly ripened grapes or into a grove to pick the first figs of the season, only to find all the fruit had already been picked clean (v. 1). The fruit of faithfulness that God appreciated had vanished from the land; instead violence and deceit engulfed the nation (v. 2). The morality of the Jewish people had degraded so far that treachery was rampant; no one could trust their neighbor, friend, spouse, or children to be loyal or to act with integrity (vv. 5-6).

The leaders ruled in favor of those who gave them gifts; judges accepted bribes and perverted justice, and the powerful schemed together to profit from those unable to defend themselves (v. 3). Even the best leaders still inflicted harm on the people like a brier, and the worst of them like the razor-sharp thorns of a thicket (v. 4). However, what Isaiah and Micah (God's true watchmen) were predicting would happen – all vile, deceitful rulers would be severely punished.

Micah, speaking on behalf of the faithful remnant, turns his thoughts from the depravity of his countrymen to the faithfulness of God (v. 7). Despite the perverse situation in Israel, he would hope and wait on the Lord, Israel's Savior. He would first chasten and refine His people to later restore them to Himself – He would turn the present darkness into future light (v. 8). This prophecy was partially fulfilled when Cyrus released the Jews to return home from Babylon and rebuild the temple in the sixth century B.C. But as that temple was destroyed in 70 A.D. by the Romans, we understand that there is yet a magnificent temple to come, the one that Ezekiel describes for us in great detail (Ezek. 40-47).

Having acknowledged the sad state of affairs in Israel, Micah chose not to affix guilt on his forefathers for negligence or to focus further on the failures of the nation's present leadership; rather he humbly identifies with the sins of the people and confesses them as his own: *"I will bear the indignation of the Lord, because I have sinned against Him, until He pleads my case and executes justice for me"* (v. 9). Micah was a godly man living for the Lord, but we do not see him praying as the proud Pharisee did: *"God, I thank You that I am not like other men – extortioners, unjust, adulterers..."* (Luke 18:11). Rather, a spirit of brokenness permitted Micah to look beyond the failures of individuals that he well knew, to own the failure of God's people as a whole.

Israel's sins were known among the nations, but Micah knew something about his God that the nations did not know – His longsuffering and covenant-keeping nature: *"He will bring me forth to the light; I will see His righteousness."* Indeed, hard times were ahead, but the prophet knew that God would restore His people in purity and in justice in a future day. The Jews would be restored to the Promised Land and Jerusalem would be rebuilt (v. 9). Then the nations will be ashamed for their treatment of Israel during her chastening years. They had even mocked the suffering Jews with the question, *"Where is the Lord your God?"* (v. 10). Any nation not honoring Israel in the Kingdom Age will be trampled down like a muddy street.

A believer who knows the character and greatness of the Lord is better able to discern the spiritual state of His people and to trust to Him what only He can accomplish. Micah was not personally guilty of the moral or religious corruption of his day, but he did realize that as Jehovah's covenant people, they had failed to obey God's law and to declare His glory to the Gentiles. H. A. Ironside suggests that such a contrite attitude would liberate believers to pray as they should for the testimony of the Church today:

When we look around, and see the failure in the Church, the fleshliness and the worldliness that prevail on every hand, let us not be content to pass our judgment upon them, and lift up our hearts in spiritual pride...but oh, let us remember that we too are part of that Church which has failed. We cannot dissociate ourselves from other Christians; we have to take our place with them, and bow our heads in the presence of God and own that we have sinned. If we could remember this always, it would cure us of railing against the people of God who have less light than we have, or than we fancy we have.[96]

During the Kingdom Age, the Jewish nation, as ruled by the Messiah, will be the glory of God unto the nations. Israel's cities will be rebuilt, and her boundaries expanded (v. 11). People from sea to sea and mountain to mountain (i.e., nations worldwide) will come to Jerusalem to worship Christ (v. 12). Yet, before this utopia is established, the world will suffer a time of great upheaval during the Tribulation Period. *"Yet the land shall be desolate because of those who dwell in it, and for the fruit of their deeds"* (v. 13). William MacDonald offers this insight into verse 13:

> It should be noted that the Hebrew word translated "land" (*eretz*) can also mean "earth." Moffatt paraphrases along these lines also: "through all the world lies desolation in retribution for its pagan ways."[97]

The realization of Israel's travail during the Tribulation Period followed by the wonderful era of the Kingdom Age under Messiah's rule prompted Micah to pray. He asked the Lord to provide for His people in the same way a good shepherd cares for and protects his sheep: *"Shepherd Your people with Your staff, the flock of Your heritage"* (v. 14). This staff is no longer the rod of correction and inspection used for centuries on Israel, but rather the guiding and protecting rod of Psalm 23, *"Your rod and Your staff they comfort me."*

When the Jewish nation is regathered to Israel out of the nations by Christ, the prophet wanted the Lord to show them the same kinds of wonders they witnessed coming out of Egypt (v. 15). Such a feat will cause the nations that had previously oppressed Israel to be ashamed; they will realize that Christ is much more powerful than all their might combined (vv. 16-17). The will "lick the dust," that is, humbly surrender to the Lord or be crushed by Him.

Micah then eloquently declares God's long-suffering nature concerning the forgiveness of sins:

> *Who is a God like You, pardoning iniquity and passing over the transgression of the remnant of His heritage? He does not retain His anger forever, because He delights in mercy. He will again have compassion on us, and will subdue our iniquities. You will cast all our sins into the depths of the sea* (vv. 18-19).

Through the propitiation of Christ's sacrifice, God can justly deal with man's sin. He bleaches sin to remove its stain (Isa. 1:18), plunges it beneath the depths of the sea to behold it no more (v. 19), and completely removes sin's essence from any map of earthly recognition: *"As far as the east is from the west"* (Ps. 103:12). North and South may meet, but East and West never do. He eternally removes sin from our account and from His own remembrance. How a sovereign, omniscient God chooses not to remember confessed sin is a miracle beyond human comprehension. Though God chooses not to remember, the believer will find it helpful to recollect what mire he or she has been saved from through the blood of Christ. One should not feel guilt over what has been forgiven (Heb. 9:14), but remembering the terrible cost of our sin will provide an extra incentive not to return to what has grieved God, hurt others and brought nothing but misery and pain.

Since believers have a standing of righteousness in Christ, the purpose of confessing sin is to be brought back into fellowship with God. Our relationship depends upon spiritual birth into God's family, but our communion with Him depends upon our behavior.

*If we say that we have no sin, we deceive ourselves, and the truth is not in us. If we confess our sins, He is faithful and just to forgive us our sins and to cleanse us from all unrighteousness. If we say that we have not sinned, we make Him a liar, and His word is not in us* (1 Jn. 1:8-10).

The believer must endeavor to keep "short accounts" with the Lord Jesus. The moment wrong thoughts enter our minds or inappropriate actions are committed, we should quickly confess the sin and turn from the wrong behavior. Thankfully, through the finished work of Christ, God is quite capable of righteously dealing with man's sin.

The last verse of the book is a brief aspiration of confidence and praise to the Lord. Micah knew that God would do all that he had just prayed. He says to the Lord, *"You will give truth to Jacob and mercy to Abraham, which You have sworn to our fathers from days of old"* (v. 20). Micah was trusting in God's unconditional covenant with Abraham, which was confirmed to Jacob. God always keeps His word, so despite the entrenched darkness of his day, Micah set his mind on brighter and better days yet to come. There was still a door of hope for Israel!

When Christ returns, the spiritual blindness of the Jewish nation will come to an end. They will trust in the Lord Jesus Christ, their Messiah, and they will receive the Holy Spirit (Zech. 4:4-7). This will not happen until Christ's second coming to the earth. God is a covenant-keeping God and His marvelous plan for the Jewish nation is still unfolding and will be completed according to His sovereign plan. There is a day coming in which the Jewish nation will be restored to God and will provide a testimony of His goodness to the entire world (Hos. 14:6; Rom. 11:17-24). Then everyone will understand just how powerful the God of the Jews is and no one will dare say to them, *"Where is the Lord your God?"*

## Meditation

O Son of God, in glory crowned,
The Judge ordained of quick and dead!
O Son of Man, so pitying found
For all the tears Thy people shed!

Be with us in this darkened place,
This weary, restless, dangerous night;
And teach, O teach us, by Thy grace,
To struggle onward into light!

And by the love that brought Thee here,
And by the cross, and by the grave,
Give perfect love for conscious fear,
And in the day of judgment save.

— Cecil F. Alexander

# Nahum

# Overview of Nahum

## The Author

Nahum was from Elkosh, whose location is unknown (1:1). Some scholars identify it as Capernaum in Galilee (Jerome emphatically held this view), while others prefer the village of Elcesei (or Elkesi) in Judah between Jerusalem and Gaza. If this view is correct, Nahum may have been part of the Judean emissary that brought the annual tribute from King Manasseh to Nineveh, thus explaining his familiarity with the layout of the city as described in chapter 2. Another possibility is that Nahum was an Israelite captive in Assyria residing in the village of Elkosk (near modern day Al-Qush), located about 25 miles north of Nineveh.

Not being certain where Nahum's hometown was located does not hinder us from understanding his message concerning Assyria's capital city, Nineveh. Nahum's name means "comfort" or "consolation" and his message would comfort the nations, especially Judah (1:15), who had been oppressed and pillaged by the Assyrian Empire for centuries. No one else in the Old Testament shares Nahum's name.

## Date

Nahum delivered his messages against Nineveh approximately a century after Jonah preached against the city and witnessed the greatest revival in biblical history. His ministry occurred in between Ashurbanipal's capturing of the well-fortified Thebes (No-Amon) in Egypt (3:8) in 661 B.C. and the defeat of Nineveh by the Babylonians and Medes in 612 B.C. Since the Assyrian Empire was not weak at the time of Nahum's prophecy, a date prior to the death of Ashurbanipal in 627 B.C. seems likely. Many believe Nahum prophesied during the latter years of King Manasseh's reign in Judah. Manasseh paid annual tribute to Assyria and died in 643 B.C.

271

## Theme

Unlike most of the Old Testament prophetic books there is no rebuke of God's covenant people in the book of Nahum, although he does acknowledge that God used Assyria as an instrument to chasten them (1:12-13). Both Jonah and Micah preached against Nineveh. Jonah's message was concise: *"Yet forty days and Nineveh will be overthrown"* (Jon. 3:4). To Jonah's chagrin, the city's inhabitants humbled themselves and repented and God's threatened judgment was delayed approximately a century. God now prompts Nahum to lash out with fiery indignation towards Assyria and pronounce impending doom on the pagan empire that had raped the nations.

Nahum's message is pungent and offers no means of alleviation: *"'Behold, I am against you,' says the Lord of hosts, 'I will burn your chariots in smoke, and the sword shall devour your young lions; I will cut off your prey from the earth, and the voice of your messengers shall be heard no more.'"* (2:13). Nahum decrees the destruction of Nineveh, describes it, and then explains why it was deserved. The fall of Nineveh was also foretold by the prophet Zephaniah (Zeph. 2:13-15). Babylon's victory over the Assyrian Empire and the fall of Nineveh is recorded on the Tablet of Nabopolasar (the father of King Nebuchadnezzar).

## Outline

The Majesty of God (1:1-8)
The Certainty of God's Judgment (1:9-15)
The Fall of Nineveh Foretold (2:1-13)
The Reason for Destruction (3:1-19)

# Devotions in Nahum

# God Avenges His People
Nahum 1

The book commences with these words, *"the burden against Nineveh."* A century earlier, God, burdened by Nineveh's wickedness, had sent Jonah to warn them of imminent destruction (Jon. 1:1). The Ninevites responded humbly to that message and turned from their evil doings and God mercifully relented from destroying them. However, the city soon returned to their old ways. Hence *"the burden of Nineveh"* in the seventh century B.C. meant that God was ready to levy a heavy sentence against the wicked capital city of Assyria.

Additionally, we read *"the book of the vision of Nahum the Elkoshite"* (v. 1). The prophetic books of Isaiah, Obadiah, and Micah begin in a similar fashion. Nothing is known about Nahum, except that he was from Elkosh, whose location is unknown (see *Overview* discussion). He delivered his oracle against Nineveh about 100 to 120 years after Jonah had delivered God's message warning of the city's destruction.

In this chapter, Nahum prophesied that Nineveh, who had plotted against the Lord (vv. 9-11), would be destroyed (vv. 2-6, 8). Plotting against the Lord may refer to the brutal intentions of Sennacherib during the days of Hezekiah about forty to sixty years earlier. Obviously, Nahum's message concerning the doom of Nineveh would delight Jewish readers who had suffered much under Assyrian rule (vv. 12-15). In this respect, the Lord remained a refuge for all those who would truly trust in Him (v. 7).

The prophet commences his oracle by affirming that the omnipotent God of Israel was jealous for His people and would avenge those who had oppressed them beyond His intentions:

> *God is jealous, and the Lord avenges; the Lord avenges and is furious. The Lord will take vengeance on His adversaries, and He reserves wrath for His enemies; the Lord is slow to anger and great in power, and will not at all acquit the wicked* (vv. 2-3).

In referring to the majesty and power of God, Nahum conveys a message of confidence and hope to the Jewish people, says P. Harding:

> His irresistible power is vividly portrayed in His control over the mighty storms and earthquakes on earth which indicates how awesome and terrible His judgment is. None can escape or stand before His wrath and fury. Thus, over against the oppression and cruelty of the Assyrians, Nahum places before the people of God, in forceful terms, the majesty and power of God, showing His passion (v. 2), His patience (v. 3a), His power (vv. 3b-6), and His provision for them (vv. 7-8).[98]

God's vengeance flows from His holy and just character, meaning that all sin must be judged and crimes against those He loves must be avenged. Yet, such actions are fully orchestrated to accomplish His sovereign purposes and demonstrate the fullness of His holy character. William Kelly suggests that believers should mark God's character and behavior and then emulate them in daily living so that the unregenerate may observe what God is like:

> Now the believer has to imitate the character of God, for we must remember that it is our point as Christians. Anything else becomes self-righteousness. But there is nothing more important than being true to the character of God, who is our Father, whose nature we have now, who has revealed Himself perfectly in Christ. And we find this most beautifully in His servant Paul, who puts patience above all the other signs of an apostle. It is as eminently Christ-like as any quality man-ward. There is nothing that more thoroughly shows superiority to all that Satan can do.[99]

However, the flipside is also true. When those identifying with Christ fail to live out Christ's character in what they do, the Lord's name is demeaned before the lost and Satan gains a victory. For example, James reminds those who represent Christ on the earth today (i.e., Christians) to be impartial and just in their treatment of others and not be *"judges with evil thoughts"* (Jas. 2:4). God will avenge the oppressed in His timing; therefore, it is better to be mistreated and happy in the Lord than to be numbered with those who taint the Lord's name through corruption.

To ensure His audience understood why God must act against wicked Nineveh, Nahum first speaks of God's holy and just character, before stating what God would do. The prophet also reminds his audience that because God controls all things (e.g., the seas, the rivers, the hills, the mountains, and the earth's vegetation; vv. 4-5), there was nothing too hard for Him to accomplish. Since the earth convulses at His awesome presence, how could Assyria withstand His wrath?

Verse 6 then poses two rhetorical questions to emphasize this point: *"Who can stand before His indignation? And who can endure the fierceness of His anger?"* Obviously, no one nor anything can overpower God. All creation is subject to Him, including wicked Assyria who would soon experience His long-stored-up wrath. The prophet says, *"The Lord has His way in the whirlwind and in the storm"* (v. 3) and He was sending a Babylonian tempest to decimate Assyria.

Not all storms in life are destructive expressions of divine wrath, but all are for God's glory. He sends challenging, refining, and chastening situations into our lives to accomplish His purposes not possible through direct blessings. While enduring a distressing situation David wrote, *"I would hasten my escape from the windy storm and tempest"* (Ps. 55:8). If given a choice between enduring hardship with the Lord or having a life of ease, the flesh will pick the latter. It is so easy to run from our difficulties, unless we understand that God has His way in the storms of life and that if we flee prematurely, we are actually withdrawing from God's presence.

Accordingly, every devoted Christian is destined for trouble, but not for despair. *"Yes, and all that will live godly in Christ Jesus shall suffer persecution"* (2 Tim. 3:12). The Lord Jesus explained to His disciples, *"In the world you shall have tribulation: but be of good cheer; I have overcome the world"* (John 16:33). Prepare your mind for the struggles ahead (1 Pet. 1:13), and don't get bogged down in self-pity, grappling with despair when those forecasted and necessary storms of life arrive.

The Lord Jesus suffered a divine tempest of indignation while being the Sin-bearer for humanity. He experienced the fierceness of His Father's anger because of our sin, which necessitated His death at

Calvary. All God's anger soon to be released on Assyria, as foretold in the following chapters, is only a minute portion of the divine wrath poured out on Christ while He was nailed to a cross!

The Ninevites thought they were safe in their fortified capital city, but Nahum states that true security and protection are only found in the Lord:

> *The Lord is good, a stronghold in the day of trouble; and He knows those who trust in Him. But with an overflowing flood He will make an utter end of its place, and darkness will pursue His enemies* (vv. 7-8).

Those who trust the Lord will find Him good, a bulwark of strength, and completely trustworthy; those who reject Him will also find Him decisively strong and utterly faithful to His Word, but sadly, too late for them to be saved.

Nahum foretold how Nineveh would fall, in verses 8-10, by an *overflowing flood*. The Greek historian Ctesias in the fifth century B.C. records that while a drunken feast was going on, the flood-gates of the city were swept away by a sudden rise of the river, and the palace foundations were thus dissolved.[100] The specifics of how this happened will be discussed in the next chapter. It suffices here to acknowledge that the prediction came true.

Thanks to the Lord's deliverance of Jerusalem during the days of Hezekiah, the Assyrians were unable to conquer Jerusalem afterwards. Yet, they continued planning and plotting against the Jewish capital (v. 9). Nahum declares that anyone planning the demise of God's people was picking a fight with Him. He then stated that the capital city of Assyria, Nineveh, would never get a second chance to overcome Jerusalem, for its own destruction was imminent. The prophet predicts their fall:

> *For while tangled like thorns, and while drunken like drunkards, they shall be devoured like stubble fully dried. From you comes forth one who plots evil against the Lord, a wicked counselor* (vv. 10-11).

The meaning of *"while tangled like thorns"* is difficult to assert, but Elliott Johnson suggests that Nahum is employing a wordplay with synonymous emphasis in verse 11:

The entanglement of thorns refers to the confusion of the Ninevites when they were attacked in 612 B.C. ... This confusion, because of their drunkenness, resulted in complete disaster: the people were consumed quickly and fully like the burning of dry stubble. A wordplay is suggested by the similarity in sound between the Hebrew words for "entangled" (*cabak*) and "drunk" (*caba*).[101]

Because the Ninevites were mentally entangled by intoxicating drink and by fear, the Babylonian, Scythian, and Median armies would wreak havoc on them. The worthless, unnamed counselor (perhaps the Assyrian king then, or Sennacherib years earlier) who plotted against the Lord would not succeed. The Assyrian Chronicles end in 639 B.C. after the destruction of Susa, but the Babylonian Chronicles inform us that Nineveh fell in August 612 B.C. after a three-month siege. The Assyrian King Sin-shar-ishkun died during the siege (evidence suggests he killed himself just before the city was captured). Nineveh was plundered and burned, thus fulfilling Nahum's prophecy.

Next, the Lord uttered a solemn promise to Judah:

*Thus says the Lord: "Though they are safe, and likewise many, yet in this manner they will be cut down when he passes through. Though I have afflicted you, I will afflict you no more; for now I will break off his yoke from you, and burst your bonds apart" (vv. 12-13).*

Nineveh, the fortified capital of Assyria, had been invincible for centuries, but its days of oppressing the region, and especially the Jews, were coming to an end. Though, at that time, Nineveh was the largest city on the planet, it would be cut down and the Lord promised that it would not afflict His people anymore. Its vile people and false gods would be cut off and the Lord promised to dig their graves (v. 14). The devastation was so thorough that Nineveh was never rebuilt and in time its ruins became indiscernible. When the Greek historian Xenophon passed by the site two centuries later, he thought the ruins to be those not of Nineveh, but of the city Mespila once inhabited by the Medes.[102] Alexander the Great also passed near the ruins of Nineveh but did not recognize them. Interestingly, it was not until the mid-nineteenth century that any archeological excavations of Nineveh occurred – the ruins of the city were indeed well hidden (3:11)!

In contrast, the prophet described the exhilarating scene in Israel after learning of Nineveh's fall. Speaking as if it had already happened, messengers would traverse the mountains around Jerusalem bearing the good news of peace (v. 15). With the enemy destroyed, the Jews were to resume proper Levitical worship and feast days in gratitude to the Lord. The wicked city they feared had been destroyed and it would never threaten Israel again.

## Meditation

Not merely does God will to guide us in the sense of showing us His way, that we may tread it; He wills also to guide us in the more fundamental sense of ensuring that, whatever happens, whatever mistakes we may make, we shall come safely home. Slippings and strayings there will be, no doubt, but the everlasting arms are beneath us; we shall be caught, rescued, restored. This is God's promise; this is how good He is.

— J. I. Packer

# The Desolation of Nineveh
Nahum 2

In the previous chapter, Nahum serenely described God's forthcoming wrath on Nineveh in general fashion. Chapter 1 reads more like a preface in comparison to the vivid and expressive details of the attack, defeat, and plundering of Nineveh in chapters 2 and 3. The prophet's graphic portrayal of Babylon and Media's assault on the city effectively puts his audience right in Nineveh to witness her doom.

Foreseeing the impending attack on Nineveh by an unnamed aggressor, Nahum sounds the alarm for its inhabitants to shore up their defenses and ready themselves for battle (v. 1). The prophet's four commands: *"Man the fort! Watch the road! Strengthen your flanks! Fortify your power mightily"* convey prophetic irony. Nahum knew that even Nineveh's best efforts would not thwart God's annihilation of the city by Babylon's army.

Nahum interrupts his discussion of Nineveh's plight to tell Israel what the outcome of Nineveh's fall would mean to God's covenant people – the splendor and excellence of Israel would be restored: *"For the Lord will restore the excellence of Jacob like the excellence of Israel, for the emptiers have emptied them out and ruined their vine branches"* (v. 2). At that time, Israel was a ruined and emptied vineyard (Jer. 12:10; Hos. 10:1). Although the Jewish nation will not be fully rescued from Gentile oppression until the Kingdom Age, the destruction of the Assyrian Empire would end a ruthless and repressive tyranny. The downfall of Assyria meant that Israel would no longer have her grape vines trampled on (i.e., the despoiling of the Jewish nation would cease).

The prophet then describes the attackers' attire, their weapons of warfare and their ferocity in using them (vv. 3-4). Their shields were red (either because they were painted or were splattered with blood). The Babylonian military favored the color red, the Medes arrayed themselves in scarlet, so both would stand in contrast to the Assyrian's blue military dress. The attackers' long spears were swung violently (perhaps in a taunting display of power) and their metal chariots glistened in the sun as they moved, like lightning on the roads leading to Nineveh. After observing the approaching enemy, Nahum says the Assyrian king will station his troops on the walls of the city to defend it (v. 5).

About two and a half miles of the western wall of Nineveh was situated near the eastern bank of the Tigris River. The Khosr River and the smaller Tarbitzu River were tributaries of the Tigris and ran directly through the center of the city before joining the Tigris. The Tarbitzu (not shown on the map below) likely entered the city from the northeast (near the Halahhu Gate) and exited the city's west wall at the Mashki Gate (or the Gate of the Watering Places).[103]

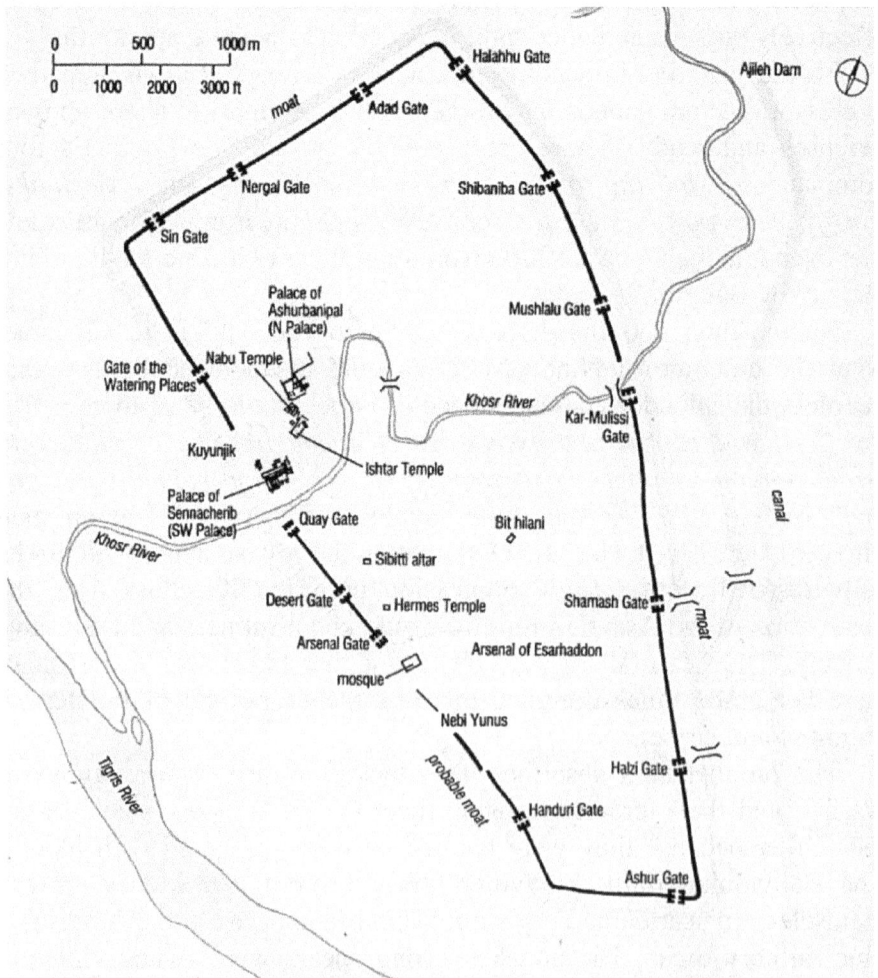

Scholars disagree as to what *"the gates of the rivers are opened"* means in verse 6. Some favor a metaphor pointing to invading troops pouring into the city, or God opening the floodgates of Heaven and causing a great flood which damaged Nineveh's wall. The Greek historian Diodorus Siculus (writing over five centuries later) tells us that the adjoining Tigris River was swollen and caused a 2.5-mile section of the wall to collapse.[104] While the span of damaged wall is obviously an exaggeration, excavations have shown a 1,200-foot section of Nineveh's wall to be missing. Yet, some experts question how the Tigris could have been so far out of its banks in August. Flooding normally occurred in the months of April and May, not in the dry season of August.

There is both historical and archeological evidence suggesting that something beyond a flooding Tigris may have contributed to the collapse of a section of Nineveh's wall. Nahum's prophecy seems to suggest that Nineveh's attackers either constructed dams or closed the gates of existing irrigation dams on the Khosr and Tarbitzu Rivers after initiating the siege. Then, when the reservoirs were full, the floodgates were suddenly opened or dams were destroyed to unleash a torrent of water which damaged the city's walls.

If a sudden rise in the Tigris River did occur, as Diodorus Siculus states, while there was low water levels in the city's canals (because the Khosr and Tarbitzu Rivers were blocked off), that would have created tremendous back pressure on the water gates protecting the city from flooding (as the moats on the Tigris side of the city would have been swollen). It seems possible then that Nahum's prophecy was literally fulfilled. The Lord caused an unusual summer rainfall to swell the Tigris River and to damage the city's walls. The damage may have been magnified by water held back and then released from the reservoirs by the attackers. Regardless of how the damage occurred, the breaches in Nineveh's wall were wide enough to permit enemy chariots to pass into the city (v. 4).

Diodorus Siculus also describes how the siege ended:

> There was an old prophecy that Nineveh should not be taken till the river became an enemy to the city. ... The river being swollen with continual rains, overflowed every part of the city, and broke down the wall for twenty furlongs [2.5 miles]; then the king, thinking that the oracle was fulfilled, and the river become an enemy to the city, built a large funeral pile in the palace, and collecting together all his wealth

and his concubines and eunuchs, burnt himself and the palace with them all; and the enemy entered at the breach that the waters had made and took the city.[105]

Many of Nineveh's inhabitants were slaughtered by the inrushing attackers; others were captured, enslaved, and exiled. Some scholars believe that the "she" in verse 7 speaks of the queen royal who was captured, publically stripped, and raped to bring the maximum dishonor to the Assyrian king and his throne. The Hebrew word `alah is translated *"she shall be brought up"* can confer a meaning of beasts mating (Gen. 31:10-12), which might describe the beastly treatment of the queen by victorious soldiers.

While this type of brutality would not be uncommon in ancient times, the "she" in verse 7 may not refer to the queen at all, but to the inhabitants of the city in general, who are referred to in the feminine gender in verse 10. Furthermore, all the Ninevites compose "the bloody city" (3:1) and are referred to as "the seductive harlot" (3:4); both are singular references. Regardless of who the "she" refers to, seeing their fate, Nahum prophesied that captured Assyrian women would beat their breasts to express deep mourning (e.g., Isa. 32:12) and would wail in distress. The prophet likens their lamenting to the soft, low and drawn-out calls of the mourning dove (v. 7).

Panicked Ninevites would try to flee their flooded city despite the warnings of officials to stay (v. 8). Seeing the scene prophetically unfolding before him, Nahum tells the invaders that it is time to despoil the gold, silver, and all treasures of the captured city (v. 9). The Babylonian Chronicles described the spoils taken from Nineveh: "Great quantities of spoil from the city, beyond counting, they carried off"[106] Nineveh's populace was afraid, defeated, and powerless against their plundering invaders (v. 10).

In satire, Nahum taunts the defeated Ninevites, asking, *"Where is the dwelling of the lions, and the feeding place of the young lions, where the lion walked, the lioness and lion's cub, and no one made them afraid?"* (v. 11). Assyria was once the prowling, ferocious lion which conquered and despoiled other nations, but now the lion's den was empty (v. 12). There was no lioness (queen), nor cub (royal prince), and no carcasses of prey (symbolizing acquired riches) to be found. The plural forms "lionesses" and "cubs" in verse 13 speak of a wider group of people, perhaps nobles, concubines, and other acquired people from foreign lands (e.g., eunuchs, servants, etc.). The king's den was now empty!

The prophet closes the chapter by reminding Assyria that their demise was decreed by Jehovah, the God of the Jews. He detested Assyria and boldly decreed, *"Behold, I am against you"* (v. 13). Those whom the Lord stands against will not prosper no matter how wealthy they are or how vast their army may be. They will suffer God's wrath and be vanquished. Nahum prophetically declares – Assyria is fallen!

## Meditation

Why do we calculate our forces, and consult with flesh and blood to our grievous wounding? Jehovah has power enough without borrowing from our puny arm. ... There is no attribute of God more comforting to His children than the doctrine of Divine Sovereignty. Under the most adverse circumstances, in the most severe troubles, they believe that sovereignty hath ordained their afflictions, that sovereignty overrules them, and that sovereignty will sanctify them all. ... Opposition to divine sovereignty is essentially atheism.

— Charles H. Spurgeon

# Woe to Bloody Nineveh
Nahum 3

While continuing the emotional intensity of the previous chapter, Nahum transitions from the demise of Nineveh to the reason it occurred – to punish a proud city for its immense depravity. The prophet pronounces a "woe" against the deceitful city that had shed much blood in the pursuit of wealth and territory (v. 1). Assyrian archeological evidence displayed in the British Museum confirms Nahum's epithet of "bloody Nineveh" to be accurate, says Gordon Franz:

> The city and the Assyrian Empire had a well-earned reputation for being bloody. Just a casual glance at the reliefs [a relief is a molding, carving, or stamping which stands out from the surface] from the palaces of Sennacherib and Ashurbanipal shows the "gory and bloodcurdling history as we know it" (Erika Bleibtreu, *Biblical Archaeology Review*; 1991, p. 52). There are reliefs with people being impaled, decapitated, flayed, and tongues pulled out. Other reliefs show the Assyrians making people grind the bones of their dead ancestors, and even vultures plucking out the eyes of the dead! One panel graphically shows their disrespect for human life. On it, a commander is presenting a bracelet to an Assyrian soldier who had decapitated the five or six heads at his feet. There are two scribes behind him recording the event. This bracelet, perhaps a medal of valor, is worth five or six lives! In Assyrian thinking, life was cheap.[107]

The numerous piles of dead bodies left in the wake of Assyria's conquest attested to her barbaric triumph, but now Nineveh, the bloody city, would experience the same carnage inflicted by her foes. E. B. Pusey rightly suggests that the city of Nineveh represents the capital of the world system under Satan's present control, which, being contrary to the things of God, must be destroyed:

> Nineveh, or the world, is a city of the devil, as opposed to the "city of God." Two sorts of love have made two sorts of cities; the earthly,

love of self even to contempt of God; the heavenly, love of God even to contempt of self. The one glories in itself, the other in the Lord. Amid the manifold differences of the human race, in languages, habits, rites, arms, dress, there are but two kinds of human society, which, according to our Scriptures, we may call two cities. One is of such as wish to live according to the flesh; the other of such as will according to the Spirit. Of these, one is predestined to live forever with God; the other, to undergo everlasting torment with the devil. Of this city, or evil world, Nineveh, the city of bloods, is the type.[108]

Hence, the city of blood, which began shortly after Nimrod's rebellion long ago, must be destroyed (Gen. 10:9-11). The prophet vividly describes the deafening sounds of chariots and cavalry charging into Nineveh to slaughter the besieged inhabitants (v. 2). Whip cracking on warhorses, chariot wheels roaring, swords and spears clashing, and infantry stampeding through the city's breached walls would have terrified the Ninevites. The Babylonian, Scythian, and Median armies would quickly overpower Nineveh's defenses.

The attack on Nineveh would be poetic justice – the bodies of the slain Ninevites would be piled throughout the city: *"There is a multitude of slain, a great number of bodies, countless corpses; they stumble over the corpses"* (v. 3). Nineveh was full of harlotries and sorceries. They had pursued demonic divination and witchcraft in an attempt to know the future and to gain victories over their enemies through enchantments (v. 4). However, it was not sorcery that had won Assyria's previous victories, but the God of Israel.

About a century earlier, Isaiah had likened the nations that Assyria conquered to grass on a flat housetop – effortlessly flattened. These countries were easily overcome because Israel's God had weakened those opposing Assyria, whom He was using to punish His own people for disobedience (Isa. 37:26-27). Despite Isaiah's decree, Jonah's somber warning, and then God's merciful reprieve about a century earlier, Nineveh was now thoroughly wicked and pagan – ripe for destruction.

As a poetic expression of shame, the Lord says that He would lift up the skirt of Assyria to reveal her shame and make her a spectacle among the nations (vv. 5-6). Jeremiah uses a similar expression when speaking of how God would punish and humiliate Judah for her idolatries (Jer. 13:26). While the Hebrew word for "filth" may refer to human excrement, it may also speak of anything detestable, such as the idols which the judged once gloried in (e.g., Jer. 13:27). Whatever the intended meaning, Assyria would be covered and choked by what was putrid to God. Beside continual burning, wailing, and darkness, Hell will also have a putrid nature to it – it is the place in which the *"worm does not die"* (Mark 9:44).

Assyria would be a vile spectacle to all. The once seductive and attractive harlot would suffer a fitting punishment – she would become destitute and filthy. No one would desire her or take pity on her. Proud Nineveh would be disgraced and brought to nothing.

Nineveh had conquered the Egyptian stronghold of Thebes in 663 B.C. Thebes was east of the Nile River about 500 miles south of the Mediterranean Sea. The Jews referred to Thebes as No-Amon. The Egyptians believe Thebes to be the city of the god Amun. In prophesying Nineveh's doom, Nahum asks, *"Are you better than No Amon that was situated by the River?"* (v. 8). The question implied that Assyria would not escape destruction any more than Thebes had.

Thebes was surrounded by both the Nile River and strategic waterways which were an effective barrier against invaders, much like Nineveh's surrounding moats and wall that was 100 feet-high and 7.5 miles long.[109] However, Thebes had fallen despite having the benefit of several near-allies (Ethiopia, Put and Lubim); Assyria did not have that advantage (v. 9). So if Thebes fell, given her greater advantage, Nineveh would surely be captured.

When Thebes was conquered, the Assyrians were ruthless. They openly slaughtered infants at the intersections of public streets; they cast lots to publicly enslave and shame the nobility, and then they exiled most of the inhabitants as slaves (v. 10). The Assyrian atrocities produced maximum hysteria among the surviving inhabitants of Thebes. Now that same level of indignity and violence would return on Nineveh (v. 11). The Ninevites would try to escape by hiding from the enemy or by remaining intoxicated; neither action would aid the defense of the city. The proud capital of Assyria would suffer the same fate as Thebes had, but even more quickly because Jehovah was against Nineveh.

Just as ripe figs easily fall into the mouth of a harvester who gently shakes the tree, Nineveh's defenses would be readily overcome by her attackers (v. 12). Seeing the overwhelming opposition and their gates now open to the enemy, the once brave Assyrian soldiers would lose their courage and become like defenseless women (v. 13). The water-damaged walls permitted the invaders to breach Nineveh's defenses, then to burn the city's gates, and take over the city. Nineveh had drawn water from wells during the siege and rebuilt walls damaged by the attackers, but in the end all their efforts were futile because God was against them (v. 14).

Verse 15 reads, *"There the fire will devour you, the sword will cut you off; it will eat you up like a locust. Make yourself many – like the locust! Make yourself many – like the swarming locusts!"* The first part of this verse is straightforward, but the latter half is more difficult to understand. P. Harding suggests two possible meanings of the twice-repeated phrase *"Make yourself many"*:

> The expression, used twice, "make thyself many," comes from one Hebrew word *Kabed* meaning to be heavy or weighty. The literal meaning is rarely used, but the figurative is used in a variety of senses. It is stated that here it is firstly in the masculine gender and then in the feminine. There are two suggestions as to the use of these two genders.
>
> 1. The masculine gender represents the inhabitants of Nineveh and the feminine pictures the city itself. The thought would then be that even though defenders were many and the city had many defenses, yet both would be destroyed.
> 2. The masculine gender refers to the advancing army and the feminine refers to Nineveh. Since the word "cankerworm" is used in relation to the enemies earlier in the verse and in the following verse, it is feasible that it could refer to them here. If this is the case, then the enemies are commanded to make themselves strong (weighty) to accomplish the overthrow of Nineveh.[110]

The meaning seems to be that the Babylonians, the Scythians, and the Medes would pour into the city with swords and with torches; they would be like an army of grasshoppers destroying everything in their path. The locust (the attackers) would also despoil the city of its vast wealth and then they would fly away with it (v. 16). In verse 17, Nahum applies yet another locust metaphor, but this one relates to fearful Assyrian guards and officials. Locusts settle down in the cool night air, but with the morning sun they suddenly fly away to eat. Likewise, Assyrian officials would abruptly try to flee from their calamity.

Nahum's final words read as a dirge for Assyria's king. He may be addressing Sin-shar-ishkun who died at the end of Nineveh's siege in 612 B.C., but it seems more likely that the prophet was speaking to Ashur-uballit II. Ashur-uballit II (who may have been Sin-shar-ishkun's brother) escaped Nineveh and established a new capital in Haran. He attempted to hold the Assyrian Empire together for three more years before its final demise in 609 B.C. Ashur-uballit II summoned Egypt, Assyria's former colony, and its forces under Pharaoh Necho II to travel northward to assist him. Godly King Josiah aligned with Babylon and Media and sought to intercept the Egyptian army, but was killed at Megiddo. However, despite Necho's assistance, the Assyrians were defeated and forced to retreat into northern Syria. The end of the Assyrian Empire had come.

Nahum says that during these final years the king would look out over his crumbling empire and take note of the vast number of dead nobles and leaders (v. 18). Many uncaptured survivors would be scattered among Assyria's mountains, wandering aimlessly without shepherds to guide them. The king would then realize that there was no healing for the empire; the wound inflicted on Nineveh by the Babylonians and Medes was mortal (v. 19).

Nineveh would be completely destroyed and never be rebuilt – a fact now confirmed by archeological evidence. All who heard this news would clap their hands and rejoice, for bloody, wicked Assyria deserved no pity.

The prophecies of Nahum remind us that God is faithful to render justice and punish the wicked according to His timetable. He does so to demonstrate His rightful position over creation, to uphold His righteous character for all to see, and to refresh those who are oppressed. God lifted up Assyria to chasten Israel for her idolatry and also punish other wicked nations (2 Kgs. 15:29, 17:3-18). But as Isaiah states, Assyria was lifted up in pride, going far beyond what God intended, and therefore was punished:

*Woe to Assyria, the rod of My anger and the staff in whose hand is My indignation. I will send him against an ungodly nation, and against the people of My wrath I will give him charge, to seize the spoil, to take the prey, and to tread them down like the mire of the streets. Yet he does not mean so, nor does his heart think so; but it is in his heart to destroy, and cut off not a few nations* (Isa. 10:5-7).

When Israel's chastisement was complete, God broke His self-exalting rod of discipline (Assyria) by taking up another instrument for His glory – Babylon. In the coming century, Jehovah would further refine His covenant people and fulfill His prophetic word to demonstrate His greatness over all nations and also over their false gods (Isa. 48:3-5). Nahum's detailed prophecies concerning the fall of Nineveh and the collapse of the Assyrian Empire clearly show who controls the rise and fall of human governments and controls nature itself (1:3-6) – the God of Israel! *"The earth heaves at His presence, yes the world and all who dwell in it"* (1:5).

## Meditation

If you take care of yourself and walk with integrity, you may be confident that God will deal with those who sin against you. Above all, don't give birth to sin yourself; rather, pray for those who persecute you. God will one day turn your persecution into praise.

— Warren Wiersbe

# Habakkuk

# Overview of Habakkuk

## The Author

Habakkuk's name means "to embrace" or "to cling." Through his prayerful interaction with God, Habakkuk learned to cling to God by faith, even when the prophet could not rationalize His ways. We are not told anything about Habakkuk's family or place of residence, but James Catron concludes that the prophet undoubtedly lived in Jerusalem:

> His prophecy does not say that he lived in Jerusalem, but it can be safely inferred that he did. His mention of the moral and social evils best fits Jerusalem (1:1-4). The fact that the prayer psalm (3:1-19) was for the choir director (3:19, NASV) implies that he lived in Jerusalem.[111]

## Date

Habakkuk does not mention any Judean king in his book, but he does note the rise of the Babylonian Empire which began in 626 B.C. The prophet apparently began preaching after the fall of Nineveh in 612 B.C., as there is no mention of the Assyrian Empire, but before Nebuchadnezzar's first invasion of Judah in 605 B.C. The poor moral state of Jewish society depicted in the first four verses does not fit well with godly Josiah's reign, but does under his successor King Jehoiakim. If these deductions are correct, that would place Habakkuk's prophecies between 609 and 605 B.C. A writing of three or four years earlier (towards the end of Josiah's rule) is also possible. In either case, the Babylonians had not achieved uncontested supremacy at the time of Habakkuk's writing and, in fact, were probably still friendly towards the Southern Kingdom (2 Kgs. 20:12-19).

## Theme

Habakkuk's oracle differs from other prophetic books in that no direct appeal to Israel or the nations is issued. Rather, the prophecy

293

records a dialogue between the Lord and Habakkuk, who is deeply grieved by the moral failure of his countrymen. The exchange does more for Habakkuk than just sustain him through a difficult time; it brings his heart into the tranquility of deeper communion with God and a willingness to rejoice in his God despite his circumstances. Commenting on this lovely outcome of the prophet's encounter, J. N. Darby writes:

> There is nothing finer than this development of the thoughts of the Spirit of God, the sorrows and anxieties produced by Him, the answer of God to give understanding and strengthen faith, in order that the heart may be in full communion with Himself.[112]

The religious revival which occurred under King Josiah did not have a lasting effect in Israel. Habakkuk, a man of strong faith, was perplexed, even outraged by the persistence of evil among God's people. Why did an all-knowing and holy God tolerate wickedness in His people? Why doesn't God take action to vindicate His name? This book assists believers who may doubt God's sovereign purposes because they cannot understand His ways at the time. Specifically, Habakkuk had difficulty understanding why God would use a more vile and wicked people (the Babylonians) to punish his fellow unruly countrymen. God reminds his prophet that His ways are above human reasoning. This meant that people's response to His revealed will would confirm their allegiance to Him: *"Behold the proud, his soul is not upright in him; but the just shall live by his faith"* (Hab. 2:4).

## Outline
Questions of a Perplexed Prophet (1:1-2:1)
Answers of a Sovereign God (2:2-20)
The Psalm of a Trusting Prophet (3:1-15)

# Devotions in Habakkuk

## Why Lord?
### Habakkuk 1

Isaiah, then later Habakkuk, Jeremiah, and Ezekiel, foretold that the Babylonians would invade and decimate Jerusalem, slaughtering many Jews and exiling others to Babylon as slaves. The first deportation of Jews to Babylon occurred in 605 B.C. and Jerusalem was later destroyed in 586 B.C. The Jews had failed to heed God's threats of disciplinary judgment and the time for His retribution had come. About eight years after this, God called Ezekiel to prophesy to a despondent and spiritually-hardened group of Jewish captives in Babylon, he himself also being exiled. Habakkuk's prophecies were likely uttered within four to eight years of the first deportation.

Jeremiah's message to King Zedekiah ensured that the king knew that Babylonian rule was God's will and to rebel against it would prompt God's fury (Jer. 21:1-22:9). In fact, Jeremiah had been foretelling the destruction of Jerusalem by the Babylonians for over a decade before Habakkuk sorrowfully prophesied the same calamity (Hab. 1:6-9). Yet, Zedekiah rejected God's Word and rebelled against Nebuchadnezzar anyway.

### Why Is Judah's Sin Not Being Judged?
Habakkuk's prophecy was called a "burden," which is derived from the Hebrew word *massa* meaning "that which is being lifted up or carried" (v. 1). The burdened prophet lifted up weighty questions to the Lord for answers. Peter tells us that believers in the Church Age are also to lift up their burdens to the Lord as Habakkuk did: *"Therefore humble yourselves under the mighty hand of God, that He may exalt you in due time, casting all your care upon Him, for He cares for you"* (1 Pet. 5:6-7). Casting and lifting up in prayer those things pressing on

our hearts is initially a laborious effort, but ultimately results in abiding peace.

Prayer is work, and the believer must always leave strength and time for prayer. The purpose of such praying is not to shift our loads so that we can better shoulder them, for that is an exhausting waste of time, but rather to release them to the Lord to deal with as only He can. The only way to be burden-free, as missionary Hudson Taylor learned in China, is to roll our cares onto the Lord.

> After receiving four letters about serious trouble developing in certain provinces, Taylor began whistling *Jesus, I am resting*. A missionary with him asked how he could do so. He replied, "Suppose I was to sit down here and burden my heart with all these things; that would not help them, and it would unfit me for the work I have to do. I have just to roll the burden on the Lord."[113]

Hamilton Smith reminds us that lifting up our burdens to the Lord in faith is not the same as grumbling in prayer or complaining to others about them:

> In the presence of all these sorrows the prophet groans in spirit, for God's word permits of a groan, but never a grumble (Rom. 8:22-27). Moreover, the prophet utters his groans to the Lord. Alas! Too often there is a tendency with us, as believers, to discuss among ourselves the failures of the people of God in such a spirit of bitterness that the groaning becomes mere grumbling, or complaining as to what God allows in His dealings with His people. Thus complaining words to one another may betray either a lurking spirit of rebellion against God, or an effort to exalt ourselves by belittling others. Good for us, if we escape these snares by pouring out the anguish of our spirits and the exercises of our souls before the Lord.[114]

The prophet was lifting up to heaven the burdens, that were perplexing and grieving his soul: "Why was wickedness going unchecked?" (v. 2). "Why did God seem disinterested in punishing His people for their evil doings and in helping the righteous?" (vv. 3-4). "Why was the Lord compelling him to observe unchecked evil day after day?" God's answer to Habakkuk's inquiries would enable the prophet to "see" and understand that God was very concerned with the welfare of the righteous and that He was going to punish the wayward.

Habakkuk's petition, a sincere complaint of sorts, is framed by two inquires:

First, "how long" refers to God's apparent lack of response to his prayers to judge the rampant plundering, violence, strife and contention that he was being forced to observe day after day (v. 3). It is noteworthy that idolatry was not mentioned in the prophet's list, no doubt a lasting benefit of the great revival during the days of Josiah. But overall God's covenant people at this time were carnal and prone to violence and injustice. Why had not God brought relief to the righteous?

Second, "why" is used in connection to God's apparent indifference to ongoing wickedness in Judah. "Why, Lord, do you tolerate injustice and wrongdoing?" Habakkuk will repeat these same two questions during his second inquiry of the Lord (v. 13, 2:6). From the prophet's perspective, the Law had no power to maintain the morality of his countrymen, and justice was completely sidelined by crooked rulers (v. 4).

Habakkuk probably felt as many Christians do today – it would be better to not see the deplorable state of the Church than to be constantly burdened by it and see no remedy for the worsening morality and lethargy. However, H. A. Ironside explains that such an attitude merely contributes to the problem:

There is grave danger, in the present, disordered condition of Christendom, that one who is able to see things in the light of the word of God may be similarly affected. Some there are who, quite conscious of the lapsed state of the Church and aware of the unholy influences at work, can yet be supremely indifferent to it all, manifesting thereby their lack of real heart for what so intimately concerns the glory of God and the welfare of His saints. Others, whose eyes have been anointed and whose consciences have been exercised by the Holy Spirit, are in danger of being unduly oppressed and disheartened by the rising power of the mystery of iniquity. Quick to see dishonor done to Christ and departure from the truth on the right hand and on the left, they are oppressed in spirit by the seemingly irremediable and distressing conditions prevailing. Needless to say, both are wrong. Indifferent, no truly exercised soul could or should be. But disheartened none need be, for all has been long since foreseen and provided for. It was so with Israel: it is so with the Church. No failure on the part of man can avail to thwart the purposes of God.[115]

Indeed, the Lord is building His Church and has wonderful plans for her. In a coming day, Christ shall present her to Himself as a pure, spotless bride and she will rule and reign with Him. Until then, may those who clearly see sin be burdened to pray for a reviving work of God that would invigorate the Church with holiness, devotion, and power. Let us not give up, nor think that God is not doing what we think He should. He will do all that He promises to do and all that will add honor and glory to His name.

## The Lord's Answer

Jehovah chose not to answer the prophet's inquiries in the manner posed to Him. Indeed, a sovereign God need not explain His actions, but in this case God wanted to reveal what He was doing and about to do, so that later His people would recognize His faithfulness in fulfilling His word. Throughout Scripture, the God of the Jews always keeps His promises!

It is therefore no surprise that the Lord's response to Habakkuk and to others was not what they expected. The "you" in verse 5 is plural, meaning that the entire nation was to look, watch, and be utterly astounded: *"Look among the nations and watch – be utterly astounded! For I will work a work in your days which you would not believe, though it were told you"* (v. 5). The expression *"in your days"* indicates that what God was about to do would occur during the lifetime of the prophet and of those living with him in Judah.

The Lord's resolution to remedy the injustice that Habakkuk had been complaining about would be so shocking that it would seem unbelievable even after God told them in advance what He was about to do. Indeed, even godly Habakkuk was greatly perplexed that God would chasten Israel through wicked Babylon (vv. 12, 17).

Paul quotes verse 5 in the New Testament, but associates its baffling meaning to what God had accomplished through Christ at Calvary to resolve Israel's sin and rebellion:

*Look among the nations and watch – be utterly astounded! For I will work a work in your days which you would not believe, though it were told you* (v. 5; Acts 13:41).

Although God's plan of salvation in Christ was prophesied throughout the Old Testament, He did not divulge the details of His redemption plan until after Christ's resurrection. If the wicked ones of this world had understood what God would accomplish by Christ's death and resurrection, the Lord Jesus would have never been crucified (1 Cor. 2:8-9). The idea of God judging His own innocent Son in the place of condemned sinners would be so astounding that no one would have comprehended it, until explained by the apostles in the New Testament. Habakkuk was baffled by God's plan to refine and deliver Israel through wicked Babylon. Likewise, centuries later, Israel, a nation ensnared by legalism, would be confounded by the message of the cross. The idea of complete salvation offered to them in grace through Christ was unimaginable.

The Lord planned to use the Chaldeans (Babylonians), a ruthless and quick-acting people, to punish Israel for her idolatry and evildoings (v. 6). In fact, God would use the Babylonians to sweep through the entire region to punish the wickedness of the nations (i.e., the known world at that time). God's chastening rod would be this terrible and dreadful people who, being a law and honor to themselves, were not obliged to abide by any recognized international authority or etiquette (v. 7). The Babylonians would be barbaric, high on themselves, and do whatever they pleased. Sadly, many today who deny their accountability to a sovereign Creator are marked by the same self-controlling, self-gratifying, and self-exalting disposition that characterized the Babylonians.

With vivid imagery, the Lord then describes the fury of the Babylonian army. Their warhorses were swifter than leopards and fiercer than wolves (v. 8). Their cavalry would attack and conquer Israel as suddenly as an eagle swoops down on its unsuspecting prey.

We might be tempted to think that only the devil and his demonic horde could inflict such venomous injury upon God's people; yet, is not Jehovah the Instigator and the One who permits all that unfolds against the Jewish nation? The same One who turned the hearts of the Egyptians to hate and mistreat the Israelites (Ps. 105:25) is also the One who will march the ruthless Babylonians through the gates of Jerusalem. Despite our short-sighted perception of the benefit of things, God is always working in all things to accomplish a greater good that will honor His name (Rom. 8:28)! Habakkuk suffered from tunnel vision, but as God widened his perspective, he was able to see by faith that God really did have the whole situation under control.

The Babylonians were bent on violence and their army would advance unhindered, like the hot desert wind out of the east, and they would take many captives (v. 9). The proud Babylonians were afraid of no one; they scoffed at kings, and ridiculed their fortifications (v. 10). They built siege ramps to pound and break through defenses. The Chaldeans were high on themselves – they believed "might makes right." And since no nation could impede them, their pride continued to swell and they assumed that they were being empowered by their pagan deities (v. 11).

However, their ignorant boasting was an offense against God, the One who had lifted them up as an instrument in His hand. Daniel tells us that Nebuchadnezzar, the king of Babylon, was puffed up in his own successes, when he pompously proclaimed: *"Is not this great Babylon, that I have built for a royal dwelling by my mighty power and for the honor of my majesty?"* (Dan. 4:30). He would soon learn that the God who had raised him up to deal with offenders would also put him down for his pride that God might be glorified. Likewise, in a future day, Jehovah would punish the entire nation for their vanity and brutality. But for the present, He would use Babylon to chasten and refine His covenant people and also to punish surrounding nations for their wickedness.

## More Questions

Habakkuk was baffled by the Lord's initial response to his inquiry as to why He seemed indifferent to His people's sin. The prophet responds with a mixture of confidence and bewilderment:

> *Are You not from everlasting, O Lord my God, my Holy One? We shall not die. O Lord, You have appointed them for judgment; O Rock, You have marked them for correction. You are of purer eyes than to behold evil, and cannot look on wickedness. Why do You look on those who deal treacherously, and hold Your tongue when the wicked devours a person more righteous than he? Why do You make men like fish of the sea, like creeping things that have no ruler over them?* (vv. 12-14).

The gist of Habakkuk's response is: How can a God having *"purer eyes than to behold evil"* use a barbaric people, who are viler than His own people, to punish them (vv. 12-13). Habakkuk reasoned that even in their backsliding, the Jewish people were more righteous than the

Babylonians. However, the prophet was wrong in his assessment of the situation. True, the Babylonians were more pagan and more wicked than the Jewish nation, but God's people had much more revelation and were under a covenant to be a holy people. To have been given much more light and then to choose to walk in darkness is more offensive to God than to have had limited light and still be ensnared by darkness. More revelation means more divine accountability – unto whom much is given, much is required (Luke 12:48). The Jews had ignored Jehovah's Law and He was rightfully angry with His wayward people.

The prophet accepted God's word and realized that the Jewish nation was on their own before their invaders. They would be like a school of fish darting erratically here and there without sound leadership to guide or protect them (v. 14). Yet, God would limit the severity of His judgment through the Babylonians to manifest His justice, but also to display His mercy.

Accordingly, Habakkuk could rejoice in the reality that Jehovah was a covenant-keeping God and would be Israel's ultimate Rock of security and strength. Even if God permitted the Babylonians to catch the Jews (like fish with a hook and line or by nets or dragnets; v. 15), He would not let them bring an end to the Jewish nation – *"We shall not die"!* Clearly the prophet understood Jehovah intended to refine His people, yet, why would God use such a foul rod of correction to accomplish this objective?

Two further objections are noted. First, the wicked Babylonians had no regard for the welfare of the nations (i.e., as fishermen, they showed no mercy on the sea of humanity they were harvesting). Second, the Babylonians would praise their own gods for their successes in despoiling the nations and enslaving those they conquered (v. 16). The wealthy Babylonian fishermen were relentlessly and systematically depleting the nations of resources and life, thus the prophet cries out to the Lord, *"Shall they therefore empty their net, and continue to slay nations without pity?"* (v. 17). Indeed, Babylon would go too far, and God would both limit their exploits and punish their ruthlessness.

The Lord gave Jeremiah, writing at the same time as Habakkuk, two reasons He would punish Babylon. First, God avowed, *"I will bring judgment on the carved images of Babylon"* (Jer. 51:47). God hates paganism; it robs Him of His rightful honor as Almighty God, Lord Supreme, and Creator of All. Second, He promised, *"I will repay*

*Babylon and all the inhabitants of Chaldea for all the evil they have done in Zion in your sight"* (Jer. 51:24). The Jews are the apple of God's eye, and Babylon had brutally treated His covenant people – beyond what was appropriate. Zechariah proclaimed that any nation which persecutes the Jews will ultimately be judged by God: *"For thus says the Lord of hosts, 'He sent Me after glory, to the nations which plunder you; for he who touches you touches the apple of His eye'"* (Zech. 2:8). Babylon would be no exception.

As we will see in the next chapter, understanding God's response to Habakkuk's questions is foundational in comprehending how God works to accomplish His purposes and to better His people. He told His prophet, *"The just shall live by faith"* (Hab. 2:4). It suffices here to say that trusting in God and His Word results in life, but pride and rebellion lead to death.

## Meditation

Oh, what peace we often forfeit,
Oh, what needless pain we bear!
All because we do not carry
Everything to God in prayer.

Are we weak and heavy-laden,
Cumbered with a load of care?
Precious Savior, still our refuge –
Take it to the Lord in prayer.

— Joseph Scriven

# The Just Shall Live by Faith
Habakkuk 2

The first chapter commenced with the prophet lifting his burdens to the Lord: Why was wickedness going unchecked? Why was the Lord not punishing evildoers and not upholding the righteous? The Lord responded by telling Habakkuk that He was aware of His people's sin and was about to severely punish them through a Babylonian invasion. Although delighted to know that God was not disinterested in Israel's doings, God's answer further perplexed Habakkuk. How could a holy God righteously use a people more wicked than the Jews to punish them? To Habakkuk it seemed wrong to permit the wicked to prosper at the expense of those more righteous (speaking of Judah).

Habakkuk did not have the answers, but knew the One who did. Like Habakkuk, we too must get alone with God to learn His mind and His ways. The Lord Jesus emphasized to His disciples the vital importance of watching and praying to accomplish the same outcome (Luke 21:36). Watching does not mean focusing on what men are doing or will do, but rather on how God will answer and direct our steps by faith. Waiting for answers is not wasted time; rather, intentional stillness before God leads us into deeper serenity and an understanding of God Himself (Ps. 46:10). H. L. Rossier suggests that Habakkuk's questions and willingness to wait for divine answers conveys a great confidence in his God:

> Simultaneously they contain an acknowledgment of ignorance and a strong desire to be taught by Him. He had felt it already before, but would soon fully realize that to know God's ways it is sufficient to know God Himself. Without this knowledge of His Person, all that happens in the world will forever remain an unsolvable mystery to us.[116]

Habakkuk had taken his inquiries to the high court of heaven and now he eagerly waited for a response. He was like a sentinel perched in a watchtower observing the horizon for the first hint of an invading army. P. Harding also compliments Habakkuk's determination to patiently wait to know God's word on the matter, and he encourages believers today to follow his example:

> Habakkuk is now no longer looking at the problem or the conditions but is looking to Jehovah and waiting to see what He will say to him. How good to look beyond the prevailing conditions to God and to wait to hear His voice in His word. One must believe that God is always faithful to His word and so, having committed any problem to Him, one must wait with expectancy and certainty for God's answer. The prophet viewed himself as a watchman upon the watchtower waiting with vigilance for Jehovah to speak to him.
>
> There are two Hebrew words translated "watch" in this verse, the first (*mishmeret*) indicating a place of waiting or observation, and the other (*sapa*) meaning the act of watching or of being alert. The figure of a watchman, looking from the heights of the tower into the distance, is intended to express the spiritual preparation of Habakkuk to receive the word of God. It involved withdrawing from mundane things and fleshly thoughts to wait upon God. How vital for believers today to learn this important lesson from Habakkuk.[117]

In stillness and alertness Habakkuk prepared his heart to receive God's word. While he waited anxiously for God's answer, he also thought about what his response might be, that is, *"what I will answer when I am corrected"* (v. 1). This statement indicates that although the prophet fully trusted the Lord, he was still wrestling with comprehending His ways. He longed for an answer that he knew would both correct his flawed human reasoning and enhance his appreciation for God. To pray, "Lord correct me when I am wrong and teach me what is lacking" indicates a faith that is settled in God's sovereignty.

Believers in love with the Lord Jesus do not want to err from God's best for them. Telling God that, though we do not understand what He is doing, we trust Him anyway because He is just, holy, and true is the essence of faith. If we ask the Lord to reveal the reasons for what He is doing, He may do so, but often the fullness of divine grace is revealed in time, so that we will have a greater wonder and appreciation for God's accomplishments.

A father can tell his seven-year-old daughter that someday, after years of watchful care over her, he hopes to give her away in marriage to a young man who will cherish her as much as he does. However, the daughter cannot understand the full ramifications of that statement without experiencing all the love, provision, and protection of her father in the years prior to her wedding day. Life's best lessons are learned in the journey with God, rather than in knowing how He has plotted our course in time.

The prophet had questioned God's method of chastening Israel, so he expected to be corrected by the Lord. Although nervous about God's response, Habakkuk was willing to receive God's reproof to better understand His mind. God honors such an attitude. Though waiting for God's response can be mentally fatiguing, we can have confidence that God will not leave His servants without instruction where there is an eager heart, a willing mind, and an exercised conscience (Luke 11:9). However, neither should we be surprised if His answers are not what we expect and not as complete as we would like. This just means God wants us to more fully experience Him through faith!

## The Lord Answers Again

Unlike the revelation posed by the phony gods of world religions, in various holy books, Jehovah does not speak in poetic gibberish and vague ideas, but with clarity and directness. The Lord tells Habakkuk to write down the revelation on clay tablets to preserve it for others to read, to understand, and to herald throughout the land (v. 2). Every prophecy issued by God has an appointed conclusion; some are immediate, some have a near-term fulfillment, while others will occur in the distant future. All prophecies of God are true, but some require more patience to be worked out according to God's timetable (v. 3). The Lord informed Habakkuk that such was the case with the prophecy that was to be written down:

> *For the vision is yet for an appointed time; but at the end it will speak, and it will not lie. Though it tarries, wait for it; because it will surely come, it will not tarry* (v. 3).

The application in time of what was appointed to happen (the fall of Babylon and the restoration of Judah) would be yet future.

The destruction of Babylon and release of exiled Jewish slaves more than seventy years into the future was such a prophecy (Jer. 25:11). The gist of God's message is in verse 4: *"Behold the proud, his soul is not upright in him; but the just shall live by his faith."* The Babylonians were high on themselves and full of conceit; they were ripe for divine judgment. The wicked naturally exalt themselves and pursue their own lusts whenever God in mercy delays their judgment (2 Pet. 3:3). In contrast to the condemned, the righteous seek to live humbly before God and to be guided by faith during such delays, *"for the just shall live by faith."* As William Kelly suggests, this exhortation forms a central doctrine in Scripture for godly living by those justified in Christ through faith:

> Success had great weight with the Jewish mind. They wondered at the prosperous career of the Gentile. But the prophet is explaining the enigma as Isaiah had done before. He insists that the only righteous man is the believer. It is not the justified but "the just," and this in order to keep up the link between doctrine and practice, as it seems to me. "The righteous shall live by his faith." It is the combination of the two points, that faith is inseparable from righteousness, and a righteous man from believing. The Chaldean saw not God, and had no thought of His purpose or His way. The Israelite would find his blessing in subjection to His word and confidence in Himself.[118]

Verse 4 is quoted three times in the New Testament to explain enjoying spiritual life in Christ through faith (Rom. 1:17; Gal. 3:11; Heb. 10:38). Romans emphasizes that those justified in Christ should be characterized by "just" behavior. The Galatian reference focuses on pleasing God by "living" in the resurrection power of Christ's life. The writer of Hebrews reminds us of the necessity of genuine "faith" to progress in the work of the Lord.

The message to Habakkuk (and to us too) is that trusting God and obeying His Word results in life (communion with Him), while pride and rebellion lead to death (separation from Him; Rom. 6:23). Habakkuk was not to trust his feelings or emotions, but rather to have faith in God and His choices: God would chasten Judah, judge Babylon, and in the process exalt His great name in all the earth. The greatest good is accomplished when man lives by faith and trusts God with his fate.

While the main thrust of Habakkuk's prophecy concerned the future chastening of Israel and the subsequent destruction of Babylon, the ultimate fulfillment of verses 3-4 relates to the second advent of Christ and Israel's final restoration. The writer of Hebrews quotes these verses with a slight modification:

> *For yet a little while, and He who is coming will come and will not tarry. Now the just shall live by faith; but if anyone draws back, My soul has no pleasure in him* (Heb. 10:37-38).

Notice that the apostle switches the neuter pronouns in Habakkuk's statement to the masculine to speak of Christ's future coming. At the time Hebrews was written, Christ had already suffered the terror of Calvary. The Lord Jesus had experienced death, burial, resurrection, and had been exalted to the Father's throne in Heaven. But that is not the end of the story; Christ is coming back in power and majesty. At His second advent He will put down all injustice and wickedness in the earth, obliterate Israel's enemies, and restore the Jewish nation to a place of honor in the Promised Land. The writer says that all this will happen in *"a little while."*

No doubt Habakkuk was thrilled to know God's near-term plan for refining Israel and destroying Babylon, but all that he deeply yearned for would not come to pass until Christ's second advent to the earth. Afterwards, God will no longer tolerate evil on the earth, nor hostility towards His covenant people. Israel will be greatly blessed in the land under Christ's rule. As H. A. Ironside explains, it was this era of future blessing that Habakkuk was to expectantly live for by faith.

> It was all-important that the lonely prophet look beyond and above what his natural eyes beheld, and thus would he endure "as seeing Him who is invisible." Likewise today, there is much to dishearten and discourage. But dark though the times may be, the man of God turns in faith to the Holy Scriptures, there to find the mind of the Lord. He acts on what is written, let others do as they may. His path may be a lonely one and his heart be oftentimes sad; but with eager, glad anticipation he looks on to the day of manifestation, and seeks to walk now in the light of *then.* Thus his eyes are opened to behold everything clearly, and he is able to estimate the pretensions of ungodly and spiritual men at their true value.[119]

True faith invigorates the soul with hope! Faith permits believers to discern and hold to the truth. Genuine faith enables God's people to humbly press on despite the toils of ministry, the contradiction of sinners, and the painful reality of living in a sin-cursed world. The proud, self-willed person will utterly fail in accomplishing anything for eternity, but not so for those justified in Christ and who live by faith.

## A Woeful Song

The Lord then describes the character of the Babylonians which deserved retribution. They were arrogant, greedy, restless drunkards who would not be satisfied until they had conquered all peoples and nations (v. 5). However, their insatiable appetite for power and riches would come to an end – God would smash the Babylonian Empire when His purposes had been accomplished.

Having stated clearly what would happen to proud Babylon, God conveys the remainder of His message in a satirical song having five stanzas. Each stanza contains three verses and is associated with a "woe" (vv. 6, 9, 12, 15, and 19). Old Testament prophets often employed this term as an expression of sorrow for a devastating event or anguish over a pending one. Those who had suffered Babylon's brutality would be encouraged by singing this taunting proverb describing God's denunciation and judgment of the Chaldeans (v. 6).

The first woe was levied because of Babylon's brutal abuse and selfish exploitation of the nations. The Chaldeans were not satisfied with a victor's fair spoils; they mercilessly plundered everything they could from those they conquered. They heaped up unimaginable wealth at the expense of their victims. How long would Babylon be permitted to rob the nations (v. 6)? God answers this rhetorical question with two empathetic statements posed as questions in verse 7: *"Will not your creditors rise up suddenly? Will they not awaken who oppress you?"* This implied that those whom the Babylonians had despoiled would rise up and strike back at Babylon – then those who had taken what was not theirs would become the booty of those they had previously despoiled. This revolt would punish the Chaldeans for their senseless butchery of victims and for recklessly ransacking the region and cities (v. 8).

The second woe was in rebuke of Babylon's self-indulgence and self-exaltation. Their foolish greed was fueled by the desire to be completely self-sufficient. Speaking poetically, they sought to erect a "nest on high" which would make them impervious to any possible calamity (v. 9). But such exaltation came at a terrible price, as it necessitated the *"cutting off many peoples"* and also because it was an offense against their own conscience (v. 10). Babylon's plush house was figuratively built on masses of dead bodies which would not be silent (v. 11). These victims of Babylon's gross brutality moaned and groaned for vindication, in the same sense that Abel's blood cried out to God for justice after he was murdered by Cain.

Having addressed Babylon's plunder in the first woe and her pride in the second, a third woe was spoken to rebuke her prolific iniquity. They had built their great empire through perversity and by the sweat and blood of enslaved people (v. 12). Any nation seeking to rise above others through crime, cruelty, and murder will ultimately fall because God does not approve of such things. Thus, *"the peoples labor to feed the fire, and nations weary themselves in vain"* (v. 13). All that Babylon had forced its slaves to build would become an altar and kindling for God's great judgment that would leave Babylon in ashes. In contrast to Babylon's brutal empire which afflicts, steals, and kills would be the Lord's empire during the Kingdom Age. In that day, *"the earth will be filled with the knowledge of the glory of the Lord, as the waters cover the sea"* (v. 14).

The fourth woe against Babylon is for her inhumane treatment of those she conquered. Babylon was like a drunkard that forces innocent people to be intoxicated in order to force them to do shameful things (v. 15). Many victims were stripped, raped, and made to take part in hideous and shameful lascivious acts. God promised that this dishonor would return on Babylon, for the nation would be made to drink of His cup of indignation (v. 16). Then her inhabitants would be exposed and disgraced in the same way they had shamed their victims. The violence done to Lebanon by Babylon is cited as an example of their brutality. Babylon deforested the nation, killed the wild animals inhabiting the forests, and then slaughtered the people in the cities (v. 17). The Chaldeans had ruined Lebanon and that was what was going to happen to Babylon.

The last stanza commences with a question rather than a woe (which follows in the next verse): *"What profit is the image?"* (v.18). Whether carved out of wood or shaped in a molten cast, what profit is a dumb idol? The pagan oracles attributed to such images were all lies because wood and metal objects, no matter how beautifully crafted, do not speak! Hence the final woe expresses God's condemnation of those who revere and serve lifeless images and reject the true, life-giving God (v. 19). This assessment of dumb idols and the condemnation of their worshipers is then contrasted with the Lord's sovereign position over all things, bringing the poem to its climax: *"But the Lord is in His holy temple. Let all the earth keep silence before Him"* (v. 20). Jehovah is not silent and He rules from His throne. His position as Creator, Sustainer, and Lord of all ensures that everyone will eventually answer to Him, and that the condemned will have no means of escaping His judgment.

Having pronounced five woes against Babylon, the song concludes its invigorating effect on Habakkuk (which will become more obvious in the next chapter). J. Ronald Blue summarizes the overall effect of God's message on the prophet:

> For Habakkuk, the message was clear. Stop complaining! Stop doubting! God is not indifferent to sin. He is not insensitive to suffering. The Lord is neither inactive nor impervious. He is in control. In His perfect time Yahweh will accomplish His divine purpose. Habakkuk was to stand in humble silence, a hushed expectancy of God's intervention.[120]

Many happenings within our world corrupted by sin will be senseless, distasteful, and hurtful. Believers need to spend less time trying to reason out the carnal actions of others, and more effort trusting God to work all things together for our good and His glory (Rom. 8:28). Habakkuk had said *"justice never goes forth"* (1:4), but that assessment was from his narrow, impatient perspective; it did not reflect the vantage point of an immutable, eternal, all-knowing, all-seeing God. Accordingly, Hamilton Smith reminds us that:

> God, in His appointed time, will deal in judgment with all the evil of the world. There may be a waiting time, which calls for the exercise of faith, but faith is sustained by the assurance that whatever takes place among men, the Lord is in His holy temple, the unfailing resource of His people.[121]

God will execute justice for every injustice committed. "Never" is a word that temporal worldlings should use sparingly, especially when it refers to God's sovereign doings. All things are under His eye and His control; what seems like never to us is merely a sigh in time to Him, for when we stand in humble awe of God and in hushed expectancy of His goodness and fulfillment of His promises, we too will break into jubilant worship and praise as the prophet does in the next chapter! True faith rejoices in God; it does not murmur against Him for what we do not understand or for what we think He should be doing.

## Meditation

Faith does not eliminate questions. But faith knows where to take them.

— Elisabeth Elliot

Faith is a deliberate confidence in the character of God whose ways you cannot understand at the time.

— Oswald Chambers

# Habakkuk's Doxology
Habakkuk 3

Habakkuk was burdened initially because God seemed to be unconcerned with Judah's unrestrained sin. The Lord graciously informed His prophet that He was not only aware of their wickedness, but also had been preparing an instrument to punish them – the Babylonians. Habakkuk was stunned by this revelation. How could a holy God use such a cruel, vile people, who were more depraved than His own people, to punish them?

The Lord's second response to Habakkuk's inquiry was a dirge that was to be recorded. This satirical song foretold Babylon's destruction. When Habakkuk learned of God's plan to chasten His wayward people with the intention of restoring them and also of destroying Babylon in the process, he bowed his head in reverence. He poses no more quandaries or protests; rather, the prophet concludes his oracles with a hymn of mingled praise, a passionate plea, and thanksgiving.

Verse 1 reads: *"A prayer of Habakkuk the prophet, on Shigionoth."* This title is similar to the headings of several Psalms (e.g., 17, 86, 90, 102). The meaning of *shigionoth* (see Ps. 7:1) is obscure, but indicates that Habakkuk wanted the song to have a proper rhythmic energy fitting for its jubilant content. The prophet desired that this lyric be sung in temple worship with musical accompaniment: *"To the Chief Musician with my stringed instruments"* (v. 19). As seen throughout the Psalms, proper music can assist the soul to express from the heart the worship that God rightly deserves.

Jehovah had revealed to Habakkuk His awesome plan to reprove and refine Judah and destroy Babylon, and the prophet was overwhelmed with awe – only God could have contemplated such a plan and would be able to bring it about. After exalting the Lord, Habakkuk submits his only request in the entire prayer: *"O Lord, revive Your work in the midst of the years! In the midst of the years make it known; in wrath remember mercy"* (v. 2). This twofold petition expresses the deepest longings of the prophet. He yearned to witness the greatness of God's power in accomplishing what He had promised to do to Israel and the nations and also to see the full measure of God's mercy in pardoning Israel afterwards. H. A. Ironside reminds us that though many suffer today for spiritual failure, this is no cause for the faithful to despair or to think God is not doing great things:

> It is unbelief, not godly subjection that leads saints to take ground like this. In so writing, one thinks of that movement which in these last days resulted from the recovery of much precious truth which had been treated as a dead letter for centuries. In the practical carrying out of that truth there has been undoubted failure of the most humiliating kind. As a result, God has permitted division and strife to take the place of happy unity and holy fellowship. All this is cause for brokenness and humiliation on our part, but not for utter discouragement. Whatever failure may have ensued, God and His truth abide! *"That which was from the beginning"* is still with us, that we may order our ways thereby. To make failure a reason for further unfaithfulness is to walk in self-will, and to lose the force of the very lesson that our God would have us learn. Like Habakkuk, we have reason to take a very low place indeed; but, like him too, we can count upon God to be with us in that low place.[122]

Though the hour be late, may we still count on Christ to do a reviving work in the midst of His Church. Glorification of those composing the Church is assured, but a revived Church would bring glory to Christ now.

> Revive Thy work, O Lord,
> Create soul-thirst for Thee;
> And hungering for the Bread of Life,
> Oh, may our spirits be!
>
> Revive Thy work, O Lord,
> Exalt Thy precious Name;
> And, by the Holy Ghost, our love
> For Thee and Thine inflame.
>
> Revive Thy work, O Lord,
> And give refreshing showers;
> The glory shall be all Thine own,
> The blessing, Lord, be ours.
>
> — Albert Midlane

313

Having stated his request in response to God's marvelous revelation to him, the prophet launches into a hymn of praise that recalls previous feats of God's magnificent power and mercy. Habakkuk refers to God's delivering His people from slavery in Egypt and leading them through the wilderness to the Promised Land to indicate his confidence that God will do something similar again. After God has chastened His people in Babylon, He will free them and bring them back into the Promised Land.

## God's Appearance and Majesty

With sublime language, Habbakkuk recalls how the Holy One came from Teman and Mount Paran to meet first with Moses and then, later, to deliver the entire Jewish nation from Egypt (v. 3). Historically speaking, Teman was a grandson of Esau, the father of Edom. Teman was a desert oasis in Edom, and may be used here to speak of the entire region south of the Dead Sea. Spiritually speaking, Teman represents the all-sufficient oasis that Jehovah was for the Israelites in the wilderness. He set a table in the wilderness for His people in which all their needs were satisfied and they enjoyed communion with the Lord (Ps. 78:19).

Mount Paran is associated with Mount Sinai (Deut. 33:2), and is located in the Wilderness of Paran west of Edom (Gen. 21:21; Num. 10:12, 12:16). The Wilderness of Paran was the area encompassed by the Wadi Paran and its tributaries and extended from about the midpoint of the Arabah Valley between the Dead Sea and the Gulf of Aqaba (or Elat), southwest to the Trans-Sinai Highway which went through the Wilderness of Paran (1 Kgs. 11:18). All this to say that the alternate use of Mount Paran for Mount Sinai means that Sinai should be located in the Wilderness of Paran.

This region south of the Promised Land is where God initially and majestically showed Himself to His people, dwelled with them, and worked great wonders among them. This wondrous time is contrasted with Babylon's invasion from the north which would cause death and destruction in Israel. God led His people in this southern wilderness for forty years to prepare them to enter Canaan. He used Jeremiah to warn them for forty years before removing them from Canaan through a Babylonian exile. Babylon would come from the north and bring chastening destruction. God originally met with His people in the south to show them His glory and splendor and to bless them. Hence,

Habakkuk's hymn contrasts the direction of these visitations with their diverse outcome for Israel (i.e., God's divine presence and blessing in the south with God's severe chastening by the Babylonians in the north). God went before His people to victoriously usher them into the Promised Land, and in the same way He will now crush them and remove them from the land in shame.

At Sinai, God's glory was likened to the brilliant radiance of the sun and to flashes of lightning; like a holy God, both manifestations are powerful and unapproachable (v. 4). To preserve the earth from destruction, God does not reveal the fullness of His power. However, even exercising constraint He is fully capable of moving over the earth and wiping out His enemies with various plagues, as demonstrated in Egypt through Moses (v. 5). The earth shudders in humility before its eternal Creator and the nations quake in fear of God's majestic presence (v. 6). For example, the Cushites and Midianites, who witnessed Jehovah's wrath on Egypt and the deliverance of His people through the opening of the Red Sea, trembled before Him (v. 7).

Habakkuk asks a series of rhetorical questions in verse 8 to transition from acknowledging God's awesome presence over His creation to how He moves to control it. His point is that God was not angry with His creation (e.g., the seas and rivers). He smote the Nile River and opened the Rea Sea, and later the Jordan River to display His power and ability to bless His people despite any opposition against them. God is spoken of as a great Conqueror moving across the land in His battle-chariot; nothing in nature could restrain Him from doing whatever He desired to do – especially the vanquishing of His enemies! His commands go forth like mighty arrows, which are unstoppable and always hit their mark with deadly accuracy (v. 9).

The mountains, the storms, the lightning, the seas, the rivers, the sun, the moon, indeed all of nature comprise a great choir that praises God's awesome presence and magnificent power (vv. 10-11). As a great Warrior walking among the nations, God would completely thresh the wicked to preserve His own people (v. 12). The preservation of the Jewish nation would safeguard the Messianic line, permitting the birth of Christ, the Anointed One, who would be Israel's ultimate Deliverer. God's decimation of Egypt to release His people from bondage would again be repeated in Babylon with the same superb result (v. 13).

Habakkuk recalls two instances of God's past warfare to acknowledge God's adequacy to accomplish this goal. First, God caused confusion and panic among Israel's enemies so that they slaughtered each other with their own weapons of war (v. 14). This pompous army had previously gloated over their poor, defenseless victims, but through divine manipulation the enemy slaughtered each other and became like those they sought to destroy. It is unknown what event in Israel's history this refers to, but these circumstances do describe Gideon's victory with only three hundred Jewish men over an innumerable Midianite army (Judg. 7). Second, God heaped up the water in the Red Sea to conduct His people to safety, then, poetically speaking, He trampled the Red Sea with His own horses to wipe out Pharaoh's pursuing army (v. 15).

The Lord had been showing Habakkuk His majesty in controlling creation as a victorious Warrior. The revelation passing before him of God's power demonstrated in Egypt, the Red Sea, at Mount Sinai, the Jordan River, and during the Canaan conquest (perhaps even into the period of the Judges) overpowered the prophet. Physically, his personal encounter with God had caused his heart to pound in his chest, his lips to quiver, and his knees to knock together – he felt as if he were ready to collapse (v. 16). However, spiritually, the prophet had been revitalized to serve God with greater fervor. Peace resided in his soul and he was determined to wait patiently for the invasion of Babylon and also for the calamity that Babylon would suffer afterwards, when God *"will invade them with His troops."*

As Peter says, Habakkuk girded his mind to prepare for the worst before the Lord's deliverance from Babylon would be realized (1 Pet. 1:13). Even if all the fruit trees, vineyards, olive trees, croplands, flocks, and herds in Israel were confiscated or destroyed by Babylon (v. 17), Habakkuk was determined to rejoice in his God despite catastrophic circumstances: *"Yet I will rejoice in the Lord, I will joy in the God of my salvation"* (v. 18). The joyful and contented attitude of Habakkuk in verses 17-18 is the same that Paul learned to adopt to best serve the Lord. He informs the Philippians:

*Rejoice in the Lord always. Again I will say, rejoice!* (Phil. 4:4).

*Not that I speak in regard to need, for I have learned in whatever state I am, to be content: I know how to be abased, and I know how to abound. Everywhere and in all things I have learned both to be full and to be hungry, both to abound and to suffer need. I can do all things through Christ who strengthens me* (Phil. 4:11-13).

Satisfaction, full joy, and contentment are found only in the Lord – knowing and experiencing Him makes life worth living. Through this awareness, Habakkuk now had the strength and sure footing of a deer climbing the steepest ridge. That is, he felt that in faith he could rise victoriously above the difficult circumstances ahead, and hope in the blessings that God would bestow to Israel after Babylon's fall (v. 19).

In the writings to the Corinthians, Paul related some of the incredible difficulties he faced in his ministry, but then concludes by declaring, *"As sorrowful, yet always rejoicing"* (2 Cor. 6:10). The Lord had miraculously delivered him from many life-threatening circumstances (2 Cor. 11:23-28). Paul also informed the Corinthians that though his labor among them had cost him personally, he had maintained a sense of gladness. Rather than complaining, Paul chose to rejoice while serving the Corinthians, knowing that in time they would be brought to maturity. Later, during his first Roman imprisonment, Paul chose to set his mind on those things in which he could rejoice, and thus he was not defeated by his harsh situation, but triumphed over it through faith.

Whether we are confronted by intense opposition, daily suffering, or the disappointing regression of the Church, we must learn to trust and rejoice in the Lord. In such times of distress, may we too recall to mind Nehemiah's charge to his distressed fellow countrymen: *"The joy of the Lord is your strength"* (Neh. 8:10). Rejoicing is a choice (Phil. 1:18), and it is a command (1 Thess. 5:16). Rejoicing in truth revives the heart of the redeemed and opens the way for God to perform the spectacular!

Habakkuk's declaration of love for the Lord in verses 17-18 is "one of the strongest manifestations of faith in the Scriptures," says C. I. Scofield. He then describes how exercising faith matured Habakkuk's devotion towards the Lord – his love "is not based on what he expects God to give him. Even if God should send him suffering and loss, he declares, he will still rejoice in the God of his salvation."[123] P. Harding encourages believers today to follow Habakkuk's example of rejoicing and resting in the Lord to experience the same kind of spiritual reviving that the prophet enjoyed:

It is possible for believers today to be so occupied with the problems of this life that they are robbed of the joy of the Lord. The vision that God gave Habakkuk of His greatness and purpose satisfied his heart and gave him tranquility. The closer one draws to the Lord and the more one is occupied with His word the stronger one becomes spiritually, and the more one is able to rest in the Lord and to rejoice in Him. The forces of evil might seem to be growing stronger, and iniquity might be increasing today, but remember that God is still on the throne. He will ultimately fulfill His purpose in destroying the powers of evil and bringing His people into eternal blessing. With this assurance the believer can rejoice in the Lord in every circumstance of life. Habakkuk found that, although he was weak in himself, he could be strong in the Lord. This can be the experience of every child of God.[124]

The God-fearing prophet began his journey burdened with complaints and seeking answers, but he concludes it by singing a doxology to his great God (v. 19). Once weighed down with burdens, Habakkuk had been transformed into a joyful prophet experiencing the blessings and power of God's presence in heavenly places. This is the great privilege of every child of God (Eph. 1:3, 2:6). God had said that *"the just shall live by faith"* (2:4) and indeed, the prophet had learned what John would later confirm as true: *"This is the victory that has overcome the world – our faith!"* (1 Jn. 5:4). Happy is the believer who rests by faith in Christ above, for He rules over all that happens below.

## Meditation

Though poor in this world's goods, though grieving the loss of loved ones, though suffering pain of body, though harassed by sin and Satan, though hated and persecuted by worldlings, whatever be the case and lot of the Christian, it is both his privilege and duty to rejoice in the Lord.

— A.W. Pink

# Zephaniah

# Overview of Zephaniah

## The Author

Zephaniah was the son of Cushi and the great-great-grandson of King Hezekiah (1:1). Zephaniah's name means "the Lord hides or conceals" (2:3). Nothing else is known about Zephaniah. Being a descendant of Hezekiah and a distant cousin of King Josiah, the author may have resided in Jerusalem.

## Date

Zephaniah prophesied in the days of Josiah (640-609 B.C.). Scholars are divided as to whether the book was written before or after the great revival in 622/621 B.C. This wonderful renewal occurred in the eighteenth year of Josiah's reign after God's Law was rediscovered and read to the king. Josiah was twenty-four years of age at the time.

The following evidence supports a date several years after the 622 B.C. revival: First, Zephaniah notes that Josiah's sons were wearing foreign clothes, which implies they were old enough to make a conscious decision to do so (i.e., young adults; 1:8). Josiah had four sons: Johanan and Eliakim were born in 634 B.C. by his wife Zebudah and Shallum (632 B.C.) and Mattanyahu (618 B.C.) by his wife Hamutal (1 Chron. 3:15; 2 Kgs. 23:31-36, 24:18). Given the age of the oldest sons, a writing date after 618 B.C. seems likely. Second, Zephaniah frequently quotes the Law throughout the book, which means that it had to have been rediscovered already. Third, Zephaniah's description of Judah's poor moral and religious condition agrees with Jeremiah's assessment just a few years prior to Babylon's first invasion in 605 B.C. (Jer. 8:2, 19:13). Apparently, the revival in Josiah's day was not widespread and did not have a lasting effect.

Jeremiah's forty-plus-year ministry began in the thirteenth year of Josiah's reign (627 B.C.). In his opening two messages Jeremiah extended an opportunity to Judah to repent and avoid invasion (Jer. 2-6); however, the prophet withdraws the option in his third message (delivered perhaps fifteen years later; Jer. 7). Since Zephaniah pleads with Judah to return to the Lord, the opportunity to avert captivity is still viable during the time of his ministry (i.e., prior to 612 B.C.). Additionally, Zephaniah predicts the fall of Nineveh and the Assyrian Empire, which did occur in 612 B.C. (2:13-15). Therefore, a date at least a couple of years prior to this event is warranted. For these reasons, an approximate writing date of 615 B.C. is suggested. This would be about seven years after the revival, ten years before the invasion of Jerusalem, and thirty years before its fall.

## Theme

The central theme of this book is "the Day of the Lord." Zephaniah employs this term more than any other prophet, except Joel. Concerning Zephaniah, C. I. Scofield writes:

> Stirred by the moral declension of his time, he foresaw the fall of Jerusalem which, in his inspired vision, became a figure of the day of the Lord. Not only so, but he also looked forward to the judgment of the Gentiles and the restoration of Israel in the Messianic kingdom.[125]

Zephaniah pleads with those in the Southern Kingdom to *"seek the Lord"* so that they might be *"hidden in the day of the Lord's anger"* (2:3). However, knowing that his countrymen would not seek the Lord, the prophet foretold the destruction of Judah and Jerusalem by the Babylonians (1:4-2:3, 3:1-7). However, the prophet promises that a believing remnant will return to Israel in the Kingdom Age to be greatly blessed and forever cared for by God. Then the Jewish nation will be honored and esteemed among the nations. Putting aside the many specific Messianic and Kingdom Age predictions and distinct decrees of judgment, this concise book harmonizes all the voices of the Hebrew prophets into a prophetic chorale.

## Outline

The Coming Babylonian Invasion (1:1-2:3)
Surrounding Nations to Be Judged (2:4-15)
The Deplorable Condition of Israel (3:1-7)
Future Judgment and the Kingdom Age (3:8-20)

# Devotions in Zephaniah

# The Day of the Lord Is Coming
Zephaniah 1

Zephaniah was the son of Cushi and the great-great-grandson of King Hezekiah (v. 1). The opening verse confirms the origin of Zephaniah's message: *"The word of the Lord which came to Zephaniah."* The books of Hosea, Joel, and Micah commence in a similar fashion. The prophet was to deliver a grave warning from Jehovah to his countrymen in Judah.

Zephaniah's message is similar in format to many prophetic messages in Scripture. The prophet begins by declaring that God's wrath was imminent, and he calls on the recipients of his message to repent. Then he promises God's favor to those who would heed his warning. After asserting God's judicial authority over the whole world (1:2-4), Zephaniah first addresses Jerusalem (1:4-2:3), then the surrounding nations (2:4-15), before warning Jerusalem a second time (3:1-7). The book closes with a promise of God's blessing and comfort for those responding to the prophet's warning, and a glimpse of Christ's coming kingdom (3:8-20).

## Worldwide Judgment

Zephaniah establishes God's supremacy over the earth and His authority to remove from it anything that has been corrupted by sin. God's promise, *"I will utterly consume everything"* in verse 2 must be interpreted with His later pledge to spare the godly remnant (3:9-13). The Hebrew word *acaph* rendered *"I will consume"* means "to gather for any purpose." In a coming day, God will gather all to Himself for evaluation; what is found unacceptable will be removed and what meets His approval will remain in His kingdom. The Lord Jesus conveys the same idea in the New Testament through allegories: After His second advent to the earth, He will separate the sheep from the goats (Matt. 25:31-46) and the bad from the good caught in the dragnet (Matt. 13:47-51) – only the righteous will enter His kingdom.

The order of this examination – man, land animals, birds of the air, and then sea-life in verses 2-3 – is exactly reversed from the original creation account of Genesis 1:20-26. Man was given authority over all that God created, and so humanity will have the highest accountability on judgment day. The reckoning is also referred to as the Judgment of Nations, which occurs directly after the Tribulation Period and just prior to the Kingdom Age. The Day of the Lord, which Zephaniah frequently mentions, includes the Tribulation Period (2 Thess. 2:1-10) and the Kingdom Age, which precedes the Day of God or the Eternal State (2 Pet. 3:10-12). P. Harding summarizes the intended emphasis of the prophecy:

> It is evident in this prophecy that the judgment predicted will culminate in the conversion of the nations and of Israel (3:9-13). This coming universal judgment will be as predicted in Revelation (6:12-17, 9:20-21, 16:1). There will be the most dreadful and fearful intervention of God in judgment upon the satanically inspired rebellion against God (Rev. 16:13-16) which will end with the manifestation of the Lord Jesus Christ and the destruction of all who are gathered against Him (Rev. 19:11-21). It has been pointed out that the tragedy of the present generation is that men are greatly concerned about global pollution, nuclear arms, and rogue countries, yet disregard the accurate and clear warnings concerning the coming wrath of God contained in His word (Matt. 3:7; Rev. 16:1).[126]

Indeed, those Gentiles ignoring God's warnings will be judged and then a refined Jewish remnant will be fully restored to God and blessed by Christ in His Kingdom. The Lord Jesus will remove all wickedness and defilement from the earth to commence the Kingdom Age. The admonition for Christians in the Church Age is to remember that this same holy God has taken up residence in every believer, and He demands nothing less than extreme purity. *"Be holy, for I am holy"* was as applicable to Israel then as it is for the Church today (1 Pet. 1:13).

## Why Jerusalem Would Be Judged

Having asserted creation's future accountability to its Creator, Zephaniah addresses the more pressing matter of Jerusalem's imminent doom (1:4-2:3). God was going to stretch out His hand over Judah to forcibly remove idolatry from the land (v. 4). Especially offensive was Baal worship among His people and also those who led them astray, namely, the pagan priests and corrupt Levitical priests. The coming Babylonian invasion and captivity would both punish these priests with death and purge the people's idols from Judah. God's plan was successful; when the surviving Jews returned from captivity seventy years later, they were idol-free and did not return to their former idolatrous ways.

The prophet then identifies three types of idolaters that would suffer God's judgment: First, those who worshipped stellar bodies (e.g., the stars, planets, and the sun) from their rooftops (v. 5), second, those who combined Jehovah worship with the veneration of Molech, the chief god of the Ammonites (v. 5; 1 Kgs. 11:33; 2 Kgs. 21:6), and third, those who were religiously indifferent (v. 6).

Though this latter group may not have been idolaters in practice, they were self-exalting nonetheless. To esteem oneself higher than the Creator is the worst kind of idolatry; it is self-enthronement and would not be tolerated. The Jewish nation had agreed to abide by God's covenant, which forbade the worship of anything or anyone, but Jehovah. The Lord's harsh dealings with Israel confirm that rebelling against the truth, diluting the truth, or ignoring the truth are never good options for the child of God. Sadly, much of Christendom today is controlled by human traditions that honor what God hates.

Zephaniah employs the first of nineteen references to "the Day of the Lord." Sometimes the phrase is shortened to "that day" or "the day." The theme of Zephaniah is the recurring expression of God's judgment of wickedness, "the Day of the Lord." Among the prophets, only the prophet Joel mentions this day more times.

The Day of the Lord is an Old Testament term that speaks of those times when Jehovah intervened in a visible and powerful way to judge the wicked on earth. This meaning continues into the New Testament and speaks of the Tribulation Period and the millennial reign of Christ. The Day of the Lord concludes with the destruction of the earth and the subsequent Great White Throne judgment (2 Pet. 3:10-13; Rev. 20). Zephaniah uses the expression to speak of both near-term (i.e., 6th and 5th century B.C.) and far-reaching (vv. 2-3) aspects of God's vindication, but the former is his main focus.

To this end, the prophet likens God as a priest preparing a peace offering, where Jerusalem is the sacrifice and the invited guests are the

Babylonians (v. 7). The Lord promised to punish not only idolaters but also Judah's carnal royalty who had led the people astray. The princes (Josiah's sons) boldly ignored the stipulated dress code in the Law by wearing the latest foreign fashions (v. 8). Jehovah had levied such ordinances to ensure that His people remained distinct among the heathen nations.

There are at least two good explanations of verse 9: First, the prophet is condemning those who rushed into another's home (i.e., they leaped over the threshold) to do violence to those inside or to plunder their possessions. Such a crime would be even more offensive if it was committed by a noble, who, while passing by someone's home, saw something he desired and quickly entered in to steal what he coveted. Second, the prophet is condemning idolaters; Dagon worshippers in Ashdod held to a superstitious practice of not stepping on the threshold (1 Sam. 5:5). Regardless of which explanation is meant, both pagans and those unjust rulers who oppress others would be executed by Babylonian invaders.

Because every level of Jewish society had become corrupt, God's judgment would affect the entire city – the stench of death would be everywhere. Wailing would be heard in the Fish Gate and in the Second Quarter (a District in the northern part of Jerusalem), and also in the hills of Acra, Moriah, and Opel within the city and as far south as Mount Zion (v. 10). The Second Quarter was located on the Hill of Acra and is where the prophetess Huldah once resided (2 Kgs. 22:14). The prophet then singled out the dishonest merchants in the market district, *"the inhabitants of Maktesh."* Maktesh means "hollow place" (Judg. 15:19), hence a depression between the hills in Jerusalem is implied. These fraudulent traders would also perish in the attack (v. 11).

Verses 10-11 speak directly of Nebuchadnezzar's future invasion of Jerusalem. The Fish Gate (later called the Damascus Gate) on the north side of the city was especially susceptible. Nebuchadnezzar would later enter Jerusalem through this gate.

Zephaniah then indicts the religiously indifferent along with the wicked. He vows that God will *"punish the men who are settled in complacency, who say in their heart, 'the Lord will not do good, nor will He do evil'"* (v. 12). God utterly detests spiritual complacency, as it eventually leads His people into compromise and then carnality. Men are accountable to God to set a good example of spiritual diligence for those that follow them. This is especially true in one's own family. A spiritually lackadaisical father, by example, implores his children to be apathetic also. Such silent neglect teaches children: There is no need to follow God. He is irrelevant. He does not care for you. He will not act on your behalf … man does not need God.

Charles L. Feinberg explains how the phrase *"settled in complacency"* would have been understood by his Jewish audience:

> The prophet predicts that the Lord will search out very minutely, as a man does with lamps, the most concealed wickedness. The punishment will fall after such a search upon those settled on the lees, a figure of speech which is proverbial for indifference and slothfulness (Jer. 48:11). Hard crust forms on the surface of fermented liquors when they are not disturbed over a period of time. Thus settled in their carelessness, they deny God's governing providence in the universe, His activity and agency in the world, as though He brought about neither good nor calamity. For such wickedness and impudence God will bring upon them the curses of the Law; they would enjoy neither their wealth nor their houses and vineyards (Lev. 26:32-33).[127]

The Jews had become like wine dregs which, if left undisturbed, become encrusted and fixed. Israel had become callous to the things of God and numb to His presence and Lordship. God's anger is always provoked when His people ignore, or are careless about, those things important to Him. God is never disinterested in the affairs of His people. The Jews were about to learn this to be true, but in a way that would strip them of everything they prized (i.e., their homes, land, and wealth; v. 13). Worldliness and materialism walk hand in hand with spiritual complacency.

Materialism is an ideology that has plagued God's people through the ages. The Lord Jesus warned His disciples not to be influenced by *"the leaven of Herod"* (Mark 8:15). Herod, a Jew, was in league with the Roman Empire, and was, therefore, a friend of the world (Jas. 4:4). For Herod and those like him, love for God and His Word had been supplanted by the love for materialism, fame, and political ambition. Little in one's life has value to God after a man or a woman has become mesmerized by earthly things, which must ultimately be lost and burnt up! This is why the Lord Jesus exhorted His disciples:

> *Do not lay up for yourselves treasures on earth, where moth and rust destroy and where thieves break in and steal; but lay up for yourselves treasures in heaven, where neither moth nor rust destroys and where thieves do not break in and steal. For where your treasure is, there your heart will be also* (Matt. 6:19-21).

Only what is invested for eternity has value to the Lord. On judgment day all else will be shown to be worthless and will be incinerated by the brilliance of God's holy presence (1 Cor. 3:11-15).

> He is no fool who gives what he cannot keep to gain what he cannot lose.
> — Jim Elliot

Through the Babylonians, the Lord did diligently search out those complacent Jewish leaders for punishment. After capturing Jerusalem, Josephus records that the Chaldeans thoroughly combed the city and found many Jewish nobles hiding in the city's sewer system. Zephaniah foretold that God would illuminate the hiding places of all the wicked, hence no one was escaping His justice.

## Jerusalem's Devastation Described

Having pronounced Jehovah's imminent judgment on Jerusalem and why God's wrath was deserved, the prophet then describes the devastation coming to Judah in the great Day of the Lord. Previously Zephaniah had warned that *"the Day of the Lord was at hand"* (v. 7). He repeats this threat for emphasis: *"The great day of the Lord is near; it is near and hastens quickly"* (v. 14). The Jews should not wait to get right with the Lord, because the opportunity for repentance would soon pass. Zephaniah's plea likely came about ten to fifteen years before the Babylonians ravaged the land, enslaving and exiling Judah's most promising young men.

In the day of His wrath, the Lord would blow His battle trumpet against the fortifications and high towers of Judah (vv. 15-16). Zephaniah says that the sight of the Babylonian army would strike agonizing fear among even the strongest of Jewish warriors (v. 14). The Lord promised to empower the Babylonians to breach the walls of Jerusalem and of other Judean cities to overcome and slaughter His people. Accordingly, God's day would be one of distress, devastation, darkness, and ruin.

So many Jews would be cut down that their blood would cover the streets like a layer of dust, and their rotting corpses would be heaped up in piles like dung (v. 17). In the aftermath, disillusioned survivors would wander the streets like helpless blind people. No amount of personal wealth could buy off their attackers' cruelty. Much of the Jewish population was wicked and idolatrous, and therefore appointed to slaughter. The intensity with which this was carried out increased with each of the three Babylonian invasions, until Jerusalem and the temple were completely destroyed in 586 B.C.

Zephaniah then closes his initial discourse in the same way he began, by acknowledging God's supremacy and authority over His creation (v. 18). God's wrath will be directed against all wickedness which robs Him of the rightful devotion and worship He deserves. Scripture repeatedly records God's resolve to remove all that hinders His people from experiencing the full joy and fruitfulness of being in communion with Him.

When God declared His Law to Moses at Sinai, He declared, *"I, the Lord your God, am a jealous God"* (Ex. 20:5). God is jealous over His people, which are His and to be His entirely. The same is true in the Church Age; Christ has purchased believers with His own blood and we are completely His (1 Cor. 6:20; 1 Pet. 1:17-18). We were once condemned sinners, but now we are one with, and alive with, Him forevermore. When we become devoted to other things rather than Christ, our misplaced affection prompts the Lord to righteous jealousy. He will then act to regain our attention, but this process usually has unhappy consequences for us. The Lord Jesus must remain the believer's first love, which means that all other affections must be a distant second (Rev. 2:4-5).

## Meditation

Only one life to offer
Jesus, my Lord and King;
Only one tongue to praise Thee
And of Thy mercy sing forever;
Only one heart's devotion,
Savior, O may it be
Consecrated alone to Thy matchless glory,
Yielded fully to Thee.

*Door of Hope*

Only one life to offer:
Take it, dear Lord, I pray;
Nothing from Thee withholding,
Thy will I now obey, my Jesus;
Thou who hast freely given
Thine all in all for me,
Claim this life for Thine own, to be used, my Saviour,
Every moment for Thee.

— Avis B. Christiansen

# Not a Pale-Faced Nation
Zephaniah 2

Having revealed that the terrible Day of the Lord was looming over Judah, Zephaniah comes to the reason for all he has said thus far – a call to repentance (vv. 1-3). It was not the prophet's intention to scare his countrymen into hopeless or foolish despair, but rather to frighten them out of their sinful ways.

## A Call to Repentance
It was not too late; there was still hope for Judah, if the people would come together and agree to turn from sin and live righteously before God (v. 1). In their present carnal condition, they were an *"undesirable nation"* (v. 1). The Hebrew word translated "undesirable" is *kacaph*, which means "to become pale." Shame over their wickedness and fear of God's coming judgment should have drained the blood from their faces, but it had not. The prophet told them that they were not *a pale-faced* nation, implying that they had no remorse over their sin or dread of God's retribution for their sin. Regrettably, they were quite content to remain in this pitiful spiritual state.

Therefore, Zephaniah pleads urgently with his countrymen to heed his warning before God's sickle cuts down the harvest (them) and the wind blows the chaff away. Then it will be too late to repent (v. 2). God's fierce wrath and jealous anger would not be tempered by His mercy much longer. The prophet's message was clear: "Today is the day of salvation – do not gamble on tomorrow. It may not come!"

True repentance is evidenced by changed behavior: *"Seek the Lord, all you meek of the earth, who have upheld His justice. Seek righteousness, seek humility. It may be that you will be hidden in the day of the Lord's anger"* (v. 3). Zephaniah promised that those who humbly responded to God's offer of forgiveness would be spared the full brunt of His wrath – they would be the *"meek of the earth."* No doubt the expression *"you will be hidden"* is a word play on the prophet's own name, which means "the Lord hides or conceals." When God hides His people, they are completely protected from harm. The psalmist rejoiced in the safety and tranquility of God's protective presence:

> *He who dwells in the secret place of the Most High shall abide under the shadow of the Almighty. I will say of the Lord, "He is my refuge and my fortress; my God, in Him I will trust"* (Ps. 91:1-2).

After Nebuchadnezzar conquered Judah, he permitted the poor to remain in the land to till the fields and attend to the vineyards (2 Kgs. 25:12). As Zephaniah promised, the humble were hidden and preserved by the Lord through the massacre. Those who heeded Zephaniah's warning would experience what the Lord Jesus later confirmed as a fundamental truth: *"Blessed are the meek, for they shall inherit the earth"* (Matt. 5:5).

There are always consequences for sin! Thankfully, God carefully chooses the repercussions of our sin to shape us and to honor Himself. As a whole, the Jewish nation would not heed Zephaniah's warning and therefore would be severely punished. However, those individuals who did repent of their sins would have God's protection and would survive the coming carnage. Those who did not respond to God's call to repent would perish; their urgent prayers in the day of God's wrath would be ignored.

Scripture repeatedly shows us that it is pointless to petition God for anything while persisting in sin. The child of God who does not seek God's face has no right to seek His favor. God chastens His people to bring them to repentance and to restore them to a state of blessing and fellowship with Him. Matthew Henry explains God's process of chastening to achieve restoration with His people:

> God is able to multiply men's punishments according to the numbers of their sins and idols. But there is hope when sinners cry to the Lord for help, and lament their ungodliness as well as their more open transgressions. It is necessary, in true repentance, that there be a full conviction that those things cannot help us which we have set in competition with God. They acknowledged what they deserved, yet prayed to God not to deal with them according to their deserts. We must submit to God's justice, with a hope in His mercy. True repentance is not only for sin, but from sin.[128]

Zephaniah knew that only through true repentance, and not just sorrowing over sin's consequences, would God's people experience spiritual refreshing. The prophet teaches us not to ignore sin, but to confess it to God immediately and to turn from it. If we fail to respond in this way, we have no cause to complain to God about the consequences of our stupidity. True repentance should never be repented of, for restored fellowship with God is a thing to be cherished (2 Cor. 7:10).

> True repentance has a double aspect; it looks upon things past with a weeping eye, and upon the future with a watchful eye.
>
> — Robert Smith

## Judgment of Surrounding Nations

Zephaniah transitions his attention from Jerusalem and Judah to pronouncing judgment on the surrounding nations (vv. 4-14). God's prophet first condemns Philistia to the west, then Moab and Ammon to the east, next Ethiopia to the south, and lastly Assyria to the north. Charles L. Feinberg explains why the Lord must punish the surrounding nations when He judges His own people:

> If the anger of the Lord sweeps as a storm through the land of His people, we may be certain that He will not wink at sin elsewhere. God cannot overlook sin in His people, but He will not allow the nations to afflict them without punishment. Nations from the four points of the globe are included to indicate again the universality of the judgment. The God of Israel is and always has been the God of the universe, the God of the nations.[129]

**Philistia Condemned**: The prophet names four of five chief cities in Philistia (Gaza, Ashkelon, Ashdod, and Ekron) to pronounce judgment on the entire nation (v. 4). The likely reason that Gath is not mentioned is because Uzziah and Hezekiah maintained that city in subjection (2 Kgs. 18:8; 2 Chron. 26:6). Zephaniah also includes in the forthcoming desolation those Cretans (the Cherethites) who had settled in the coastal regions of Philistia: *"I will destroy you; so there shall be no inhabitant"* (v. 5). The region would be so depopulated by the Babylonians that it would become pastureland for the flocks of the surviving Jewish remnant (vv. 6-7). This highlights God's providential care for those He loves and to whom He has pledged His love.

**Moab and Ammon Condemned:** Isaiah, Jeremiah, and Ezekiel likewise pronounce judgment on the Moabites and Ammonites. These nations dwelled just east of the Jordan River and were descendants of Lot through his two daughters. Zephaniah wastes no time indicting Moab and Ammon: *"I have heard the reproach of Moab, and the insults of the people of Ammon, with which they have reproached My people, and made arrogant threats against their borders"* (v. 8). No further specifics are supplied by Zephaniah concerning these charges, but Jeremiah does elaborate why these nations were a reproach to God.

Though Ammon forged an alliance with Judah during Zedekiah's final rebellion against Nebuchadnezzar, the nations had been in frequent conflict with each other since the time the Israelites entered Canaan. Jeremiah explains two main reasons Ammon would be judged by Jehovah (Jer. 49:1-6). First, Ammon had taken possession of several cities belonging to the tribe of Gad after the Assyrian invasion in the previous century. Second, the Ammonites were a proud people. They trusted in their vast wealth, gloried in their valleys, and felt they were invincible.

Jeremiah also devoted an entire chapter to explain why God would sternly punish the Moabites (Jer. 48). The Moabites had seized land from the Jews. They had overcome the Reubenites to possess much of their inheritance, including the cities of Nebo and Kiriathaim (Num. 32:37-38; Josh. 13:19). Because God detested Moab's moral depravity and pride, He promised to remove them from the land which belonged to Reuben.

*"Jehovah of Hosts, the God of Israel,"* now swore to make Moab like Sodom and Ammon like Gomorrah (v. 9). Afterwards, their lands would be overrun by weeds and salt pits, and the Jews would plunder them and again possess the land that was rightfully theirs. This is how the Lord responds to those who threaten and oppress His people (v. 10). Pondering God's providential care of the Jewish nation, despite all their shortcomings, caused Zephaniah to again assert God's supremacy over all nations and their pagan gods:

*The Lord will be awesome to them, for He will reduce to nothing all the gods of the earth; people shall worship Him, each one from his place, indeed all the shores of the nations* (v. 11).

This verse looks forward to the Millennial Kingdom, when all nations will honor the Lord Jesus Christ and will come to Jerusalem to worship the God of the Jews.

**Ethiopia Condemned:** Zephaniah's message is concise and pungent: *"You shall be slain by My sword"* (v. 12). A century earlier Isaiah also pronounced judgment against the ancient nation of Cush (from the Hebrew *Kuwsh*; Isa. 18:1). Cush occupied southern Egypt, Sudan, and northern Ethiopia. *Kuwsh* is often translated "Ethiopia" in Scripture, but, strictly speaking, Cush's boundaries went far beyond the modern borders of that country.

The Hebrew word *Kuwshiy* used by Zephaniah in verse 12 is derived from *Kuwsh*. In Isaiah's day, the Cushites had sent envoys to Israel with the objective of securing an alliance with Israel against the Assyrians. But Assyria was being used by God to chasten the idolatrous Northern Kingdom. Hence, Isaiah instructed the Cushites to return home rather than trying to stand in the way of Jehovah's sovereign care of His people (Isa. 18:3). No human alliance would defeat the Assyrians, but God would vanquish them at the proper time. The Cushites did not heed Isaiah's warning and judgment was coming.

**Nineveh and Assyria Condemned:** Zephaniah then foretold the destruction of Nineveh, Assyria's capital, and the fall of the Assyrian Empire (vv. 12-14). In 722 B.C., these northern invaders conquered Israel, enslaving and exiling many Jews. In 701 B.C. they returned to plunder much of the Southern Kingdom before the Lord intervened by slaughtering 185,000 soldiers in Sennacherib's army, thus abruptly ending his campaign. Now, Assyria would pay for all the atrocities they had committed. God was about to decimate Nineveh, leaving her ruins uninhabitable except for wild beasts and ravenous birds (vv. 12-13).

The city's inhabitants lived a carefree and self-gratifying lifestyle as they thought their city to be impregnable. The wall surrounding Nineveh was about 8 miles long, 100 feet high, 50 feet thick, and had 15 gates. Their perceived security and lack of want resulted in boasting, *"I am it, and there is none besides me"* (v. 15). But in 612 B.C. the

Medes and the Babylonians conquered the city and utterly destroyed it. Afterwards, those who passed by her ruins would shake their fists and hiss to express their contempt for Assyria's former pride and ruthlessness (v. 15). Commentary on Nahum chapter 2 contains the historical details of how Nineveh was conquered.

## Summary

Zephaniah tells us that the God of the Jews, as an expression of His love for them will be faithful to punish those nations who oppress His covenant people. However, Israel's covenant-relationship with Jehovah also demands that He chasten them for misplaced affections and for behavior affronting His holy character. Love for the Lord is proven through exercising choices that please Him and not doing what we know will grieve Him.

Speaking to His disciples, the Lord Jesus summed up the matter this way: *"If you love Me, keep My commandments"* (John 14:15) and *"He who has My commandments and keeps them, it is he who loves Me"* (John 14:21). Knowing what pleases God and doing it demonstrates love for Him. The Jewish nation was about to learn this fundamental truth again – the hard way.

## Meditation

Come to the Savior now, He gently calls thee;
In true repentance bow, before Him bend the knee.
Come to the Savior now, you who have wandered far;
Renew your solemn vow, for His by right you are;
Come, like poor, wandering sheep returning to His fold;
His arm will safely keep, His love will never grow cold.

— John Wigner

# I Will Restore
### Zephaniah 3

Having foretold God's judgment on nations to the west, east, south, and north of Judah, Zephaniah returns to predicting Judah's doom. The Jews had oppressed others through deceit and injustice; they had ignored God's Law, and were thoroughly polluted by paganism (v. 1). God had been longsuffering with His people, but they had not received His word or His correction. Because they did not know or trust the Lord, they did not have any reason to draw near to Him (v. 2).

It is absolutely important that believers continue exploring God's Word to learn more about Him and what He expects. Believers will not trust a God they do not know, let alone do what He says. Because the Jews had neglected God's Word, they had drifted into a superficial religiosity which did not value Jehovah or the things important to Him. In fact, they put a higher religious premium on their social traditions and heathen practices than on the edicts of Jehovah's Law (e.g., Jer. 7:17-20).

Zephaniah then lists God's grievances against Jewish civil and religious leaders. Speaking of their unjust and abusive behavior, the prophet likens the civil rulers to ferocious lions and the judges to a pack of ravenous wolves (v. 3). Additionally, he declares that Jerusalem's prophets were insolent liars and that her priests had polluted the sanctuary and done violence to God's Law (v. 4). In contrast to these corrupt civil and religious leaders, God is always righteous, exercises justice, and never does anything wrong; He is and always will be the Champion of the oppressed (v. 5).

Generally speaking, the moral and spiritual condition of any people does not rise above that of their leaders. Is it any wonder then that the state of Jewish society was so pathetic? Being governed by corrupt leaders, the Jews had been going their own way for so long that their consciences had become calloused. That is, they could do what they instinctively knew God disapproved of without feeling guilt or shame (v. 5).

Paul tells us that those who choose to worship creation or its creatures instead of the Creator are given over to a reprobate mind (Rom. 1:24-28). Instead of discerning the design and sophistication of creation and looking for the Designer, these pagans are content to glory in what they see (Rom. 1:21-23). Anyone committing such an offense deserves God's judgment: *"For the wrath of God is revealed from heaven against all ungodliness and unrighteousness of men, who suppress the truth in unrighteousness"* (Rom. 1:18). Without the Holy Spirit's work of conviction and enlightenment, such idolaters will remain in their depraved condition and the worst that is in man will be evident in their behavior (Rom. 1:27-31). The time of God's patience and pleading was nearly ended; He would have the devotion of His covenant people, even if it meant He had to harm them to awaken them to their spiritually depravity.

Just as God had acted in righteousness to severely judge other wicked nations, He would also uphold His holiness and justice concerning those who had willfully transgressed His Law (v. 6). Despite all of God's pleading through His prophets, the Jews would not repent, but zealously desired to continue in rebellious corruption (v. 7).

Verse 8 concludes the judgment portion of Zephaniah's book the way it began, by asserting God's universal judgment of all wickedness upon the earth. This verse previews the Tribulation Period in which God will powerfully judge and remove injustice and wickedness from the earth to establish a refined Jewish remnant with the full covenant blessings promised to Abraham long ago. The remainder of the chapter further explains this future day of blessing and restoration.

## Jehovah's Restoration

The "then" in verse 9 marks a major thematic change in Zephaniah's oracle – judicial wrath is replaced by immense grace. This time of divine blessing will occur during the Millennial Kingdom:

> *For then I will restore to the peoples a pure language, that they all*
> *may call on the name of the Lord,*
> *to serve Him with one accord* (v. 9).

Prior to the national rebirth of Israel in 1948, the Jews spoke Yiddish, an impure form of the Hebrew language. After 1948, however, the Jews adopted their ancient tongue, Hebrew, as their national

338

language. While exciting, this recent development is not what Zephaniah is predicting in verse 9. Rather, he is alluding to a time when the nation of Israel will receive the Holy Spirit and be able to praise God unhindered by any impurities of speech or conduct. In the Kingdom Age, audible expressions void of self-confidence and self-exaltation will precipitate from pure hearts.

All those who rebelled against God and followed the Antichrist will perish at the end of the Tribulation Period. The remaining Gentiles will be governed by Christ in righteousness and peace as they enjoy an earthly utopia free from the original curses caused by Adam's sin. During this wonderful era the nations will live and serve God in unity and all shall call on the name of the Lord (v. 9).

Zephaniah tells us that in a coming day God will finally get the portion that He deserves when Jewish and Gentile worshipers bring acceptable offerings to Him (v. 10). C. A. Coates writes, once His people have a pure language, that the first thing God will teach them is how to pray so that they can serve Him effectively:

> The first utterance of a pure language is when one can speak to God; to call upon God's name is a pure language. It is a first mark of a sovereign movement of God in the soul; thus a revolution is brought about. To obtain a link with God in calling upon His name is a revolution. "My Worshippers" – it is a beautiful expression, speaking of a certain class that God can regard as His people. We would like to be among them. It indicates a very definite desire to have something from God and for God. Those are the people we are to look out for; we are to follow with those that call on the name of the Lord out of a pure heart. And prayer must lead to service. *"That they may all call upon the name of Jehovah, to serve Him with one consent."* ...The result of prayer is a united desire to serve God for His pleasure.[130]

Those residing west of the Nile River (i.e., Egypt, Sudan, and Ethiopia) will be joined by the Jews, once scattered throughout the earth, to bring God offerings in Jerusalem (v. 10).

In that day (i.e., at the end of the Tribulation Period) the Lord will remove all the proud rebels from among His covenant people and then cleanse away their past shame (v. 11). Only the meek and humble will enter into God's Holy Mountain (His Kingdom) to enjoy His presence and continual blessings (v. 12). During the Millennial Kingdom of Christ, the Jews who are indwelt by the Holy Spirit will be cleansed of all wrong and deceitful behavior (v. 13). As a result, they will enjoy the care of Israel's great Shepherd, who will lead them into green pastures, and by still waters and in His rest. Likewise, their own flocks of animals will enjoy the same blissful conditions under Christ's care (v. 13).

How will restored Israel respond to such goodness? They will sing, shout praises, and rejoice in their God (v. 14). With their chastening over and all their enemies vanquished, the Jewish nation would finally enjoy the fulfillment of God's promises centuries earlier to Abraham (v. 15). Because Christ, the King of Israel, was in their midst, they were guaranteed peace and safety forever!

This reality is even confirmed by converted Gentiles during the Kingdom Age; they tell the Jews, *"Do not fear; Zion, let not your hands be weak"* (v. 16). Perhaps, after so many centuries of dispersal, oppression, and slaughter, it will be hard for some in Israel to really believe God will remain with them and bless them forever. But God's longings for Israel went well beyond just wanting to deliver her, care for her, and bless her; He wanted His people to know that He delighted in them:

> *The Lord your God in your midst, the Mighty One, will save; He will rejoice over you with gladness, He will quiet you with His love, He will rejoice over you with singing* (v. 17).

Indeed, God will save Israel, but beyond that, He will also enthusiastically sing over His people to express His love and delight in them (v. 17). William Kelly writes, "There is no finer description in the Bible of His complacent satisfaction when mercy has done all for the people that He loved."[131] A mother sings to quiet her baby so he can relax and fall to sleep. A husband and wife may share private musical expressions of love to reaffirm their commitment and intimacy to each other. But what will it be like for the Creator of all things to convey His tender affections to the redeemed in song? The prophet indicates that those experiencing this surreal melody will be unable to respond to it in words – they will simply choose to rest in their Beloved. What a gracious and loving God we have! He lavishes redeemed sinners with songs of tender affection despite all the heartbreak we have caused Him.

Zephaniah closes his oracle with a message of hope for the believing remnant of his day. Through seven "I will" statements, the Lord promises comfort and support to the faithful, despite the hard times ahead. When dispersed among the nations, the believing remnant would not be able to keep the Levitical feasts as the Law commanded; however, during the Kingdom Age, those past sorrows will be replaced with joyful celebrations in Jerusalem.

In his opening message, Isaiah rebuked the Jewish nation for their vain religiosity and impure motives for participating in Jehovah's feasts. Worship is burdensome when not motivated by joy, awe, and thankfulness. Under Christ's reign, all feasts in the Kingdom Age will be kept without any wrong motives, which had previously resulted in God's rebuke of His people (v. 18).

The prophet again speaks of a coming day when Israel's oppressors will not only be gone, but they will esteem her (v. 19). Both Isaiah and Zechariah tell us that the Jewish state of Israel will be the most esteemed nation on earth during the Kingdom Age (Isa. 60:12-15; Zech. 8:20-23). The Jews will again be in their land and will have possession of it. Their wealth will be restored and they will be honored and praised by all nations (v. 20). What Jew in Zephaniah's time would not be excited to hear how God would look beyond all their past failures to orchestrate such a wonderful ending to their mostly sorrowful history?

We conclude our study by pausing to consider the place Zephaniah's prophecies have in the wider scope of future events for the furtherance of God's glory. P. Harding summarizes:

The end of God's ways with Israel will be blessing for her, in spite of her failures. Israel's blessings and fame are earthly, the Church's are heavenly. Both will contribute to the glory of God and both will display the wonders of His grace. Throughout the prophecy the fact that God is light (1 Jn. 1:5 – intrinsically holy, righteous, and just) and God is love (1 Jn. 4:7-8 – showing grace and mercy) is demonstrated by His judgments and His salvation. Zephaniah's prophecy centers around judgment and particularly that of the Day of the Lord with no country or nation being exempt. Glimpses of His grace are given in the prophecy which ends with promised salvation and blessing, not only for Israel, but also for the nations. The salvation of the nations and their blessing are linked with those of Israel and both are only possible because of the finished work of the

341

Lord Jesus Christ. At Calvary He laid a righteous foundation that enables God to justify believers today, to bring salvation and blessing to Israel and the nations in a coming day, and to bring in a new earth and new heavens in which righteousness shall dwell.[132]

Despite the present darkness and hardships ahead, the redeemed go on with the Lord to enter into His rest and ultimately into their glorious inheritance. At present, believers are training for reigning, but one day our school days will all be done and the joy of what God accomplished in us will be ours forever.

# Meditation

Those times when you feel like quitting can be times of great opportunity, for God uses your troubles to help you grow.

— Warren Wiersbe

Teach us, O Lord, the disciplines of patience, for to wait is often harder than to work.

— Peter Marshall

# Haggai

# Overview of Haggai

## The Author

Haggai was a post-captivity prophet who had a powerful ministry that lasted only a few months. Haggai's name means "festive." The application of his name is not explained, but some scholars believe that he may have been born on a particular Jewish feast day associated with joy (e.g. the Feast of Tabernacles). He was a prophet to the governor Zerubbabel and the high priest Joshua (1:1), and to Jerusalem and Judah (5:1-2). Nothing is stated about his family lineage or hometown.

## Date

Haggai was a contemporary of Zechariah. Zechariah delivered his first two messages during the time that Haggai preached all four of his messages. Haggai's ministry lasted less than four months, but Zechariah's continued for several years. The older prophet Haggai's ministry began in August and concluded in December 520 B.C. (1:1, 2:1, 2:10, 2:20).

## Theme

The Jews returning from Babylon did complete the foundation for the new temple that Cyrus had commissioned them to build in 535 B.C. before abandoning the project because of opposition (Ezra 4:24). Fifteen years had passed without any progress on the temple. Haggai's ministry was specific; he was to rebuke and to inspire the Jews to complete God's house (Ezra 5:1). His ministry was successful, for the work resumed twenty-three days after his first message was delivered (1:1, 1:15). After motivating the people to begin the rebuilding project, Haggai also joined in the labor (Ezra 5:2).

## Outline

The First Message: A Warning to Rebuild the Temple (1:1-15)

The Second Message: A Promise of Greater Glory in the Temple (2:1-2:9)

The Third Message: A Priestly Inquiry to Show That Obedience Precedes Blessing (2:10-19)

The Fourth Message: A Messianic Prophecy Related to Zerubbabel (2:20-23)

# Devotions in Haggai

# Consider Your Ways
Haggai 1

Seven closely-linked Old Testament books describe the post-exilic circumstances of God's covenant people. Three historical books (Ezra, Nehemiah, and Esther) and four prophetic books (Daniel, Haggai, Zechariah, and Malachi) combine to provide a composite picture of the deplorable spiritual and social conditions of the Jewish nation at that time. Yet, despite these impediments, God was able to revive His people through a handful of faithful Jews who had not lost hope in Him.

## Overview

Just as there were three major deportations of Jews during the onset of the Babylonian captivity, there were also three major Jewish groups that returned to Jerusalem. Zerubbabel, under King Cyrus' authority, led approximately 50,000 Jews back to Jerusalem in 537-536 B.C. to rebuild the temple (Ezra 2:64-70). The second group of Jews numbering 1,772 men and their families was led from Babylon to Jerusalem by the scribe Ezra in 458 B.C. Ezra was tasked with teaching the people God's Law again. Thirteen years after Ezra departed for Jerusalem, a third group of approximately 2000 Jewish captives were led home by Nehemiah (445-444 B.C.). Nehemiah would oversee the rebuilding of Jerusalem's wall and infrastructure.

Preparations for rebuilding the temple began in 536 B.C. after the Jews had arrived in Jerusalem and erected an altar (Ezra 3:1-8). Under Zerubbabel's leadership, the temple foundation was completed and dedicated in 535 B.C., but the building program ceased sometime after that due to the efforts of the enemy to discourage and break down the resolve of God's people (Ezra 5:4-5). At the outset, the Jews rested solely on God's authority. When they first arrived in Jerusalem, the sufficiency of His Word was their battle-axe against opposition; that focus needed to be regained. What was God's solution to this situation? He called two prophets, Haggai and Zechariah, to reprove His people of sin and to motivate them to again begin the temple construction (Ezra 5:1). Their ministries were effective and the Jews again mobilized to complete the work. The temple was finished in 515 B.C., seventy-one years after Solomon's temple had been destroyed (Ezra 6:14).

Before meditating on Haggai's four messages, it behooves us to first remember the importance God places throughout Scripture on His earthly house. From the first temple constructed by Solomon, to the second built in the sixth century B.C., to the spiritual temple composed of believers in the Church Age, to the Millennial temple erected in the Kingdom Age, all have immense importance to the purposes of God, as each of these is God's abode among men. Hamilton Smith suggests that the spiritual implications of this have staggering ramifications for those who seek to honor the Lord:

> It follows that everything in God's house must take character from and be consistent with the One who dwells in the house. Thus the first characteristic of God's house is holiness, as we read, *"Holiness becomes Thine house, O Lord forever"* (Ps. 93:5). Further, everyone in God's house must be dependent upon God, and subject to His will. This dependence finds its expression in prayer; so we read, "Mine house shall be called the house of prayer for all people" (Isa. 56:7). Furthermore, if, in God's house, all are dependent upon God, then all in that house will be blessed by God; and the house in which man is blessed will be the place where God is worshipped.[133]

Regardless of what dispensation God's people may occupy, God's temple is to be a holy place that He may abide in and be refreshed by. Whether a building in the ancient days or in believers now, God desires a pure abode where there is no hindrance to fellowship, worship, or prayer. Jeremiah tells us that Solomon's temple had itself become an object of worship and therefore it was to be abolished. Ezekiel informs us that God's glory departed the temple just before He tasked the Babylonians with destroying it. Years have now passed and the idolatry of past Jewish generations has been dealt with. The time is ripe for God to send a prophet with an important message to His people. He was ready to start again with them, meaning it was time to erect a new temple so that all nations would know that Jehovah was residing with and blessing His people again.

So the temple from God's perspective, speaks of intimately abiding with His people, except when He cannot because of misplaced devotion and sin. This is why Haggai poses questions to the Jews as if Solomon's temple were still standing: *"Who is left among you who saw **this temple** in its former glory? And how do you **see it now?"** (2:3). For this reason, many of the older commentators favor that God is speaking of *"this temple,"* that is, a single holy temple (God's abode among His people), throughout the entire book. J. N. Darby concludes: "God ... will allow only a different state of the same house, and that was one of far greater glory."[134] William Kelly agrees:

> It is the same house in God's mind, as it is the same place. Let it be defiled, or even razed to its foundations and built again and again, still it preserves the character of unity the inspiring Spirit stamps on it.[135]

From the Jewish viewpoint, Solomon's temple was long gone, but although a building was destroyed, the yearnings of a covenant-keeping God to abide with His people had never been lost. Paul speaks of the same kind of loyalty in the Lord Jesus towards believers in the Church Age: *"If we are faithless, He remains faithful; He cannot deny Himself"* (2 Tim. 2:13). Rejoice dear believer, our Lord is always faithful, even when we are not! While the Spirit of Christ, speaking of the Holy Spirit (Rom. 8:9), cannot depart from believers in the Church Age, He may be grieved and quenched while abiding still (Eph. 4:30; 1 Thess. 5:19).

When under the Law during Old Testament days, sin resulted in broken communion with God and a loss of power and blessing, though a covenant relationship was still valid. May we then follow Paul's exhortation to Timothy and take heed to ourselves to know how we ought to conduct ourselves in the house of God, which is the church of the living God, the pillar and ground of the truth (1 Tim. 3:15).

## Haggai's First Message

Haggai received a message from "the Lord of hosts," a title of God found fourteen times in his book. On August 29, 520 B.C. he delivered his first message to Judah. The rebuke was addressed to the Jewish leaders Zerubbabel and Joshua:

> *In the second year of King Darius, in the sixth month, on the first day of the month, the word of the Lord came by Haggai the prophet to Zerubbabel the son of Shealtiel, governor of Judah, and to Joshua the son of Jehozadak, the high priest, saying, "Thus speaks the Lord of hosts, saying: 'This people says, "The time has not come, the time that the Lord's house should be built"'"* (vv. 1-2).

Zerubbabel, the grandson of Jehoiachin (1 Chron. 3:17-19), was the governor of Judah tasked by Cyrus to rebuild the temple. Joshua the high priest was the son of Jehozadak who was deported to Babylon after the fall of Jerusalem in 586 B.C. (1 Chron. 6:15). The people had decided that it was not time to rebuild God's temple (v. 2), so Haggai asks them a probing question and then warns them:

> *"Is it time for you yourselves to dwell in your paneled houses, and this temple to lie in ruins?" Now therefore, thus says the Lord of hosts: "Consider your ways!"* (vv. 4-5).

The prophet effectively confronts both the Jews' spiritual complacency and their pursuit of a comfortable standard of living in one statement. Apparently, materials earlier donated to build the temple had been used by the Jews to build themselves nice paneled houses, while God's house was in ruins. The prophet went on to inform the Jews that they were being economically penalized by God for their lethargic attitudes towards Him (v. 6). According to C. A. Coates, the application for God's people is straightforward:

> God would have His people to consider whether they are not giving a good deal of time to things which yield very little. There is a kind of eating which gives no satisfaction, and drinking which adds nothing to the inward man, and we may surround ourselves with things which bring no warmth to the soul, and what we earn may go into a bag with holes. These are striking figures of the result of seeking our own things. Christians on this line may get through life by the mercy of God, but it is a lean and empty and impoverished life compared with what it might have been.[136]

The Jews were laboring diligently and yet lacked because God was punishing them for disobedience (vv. 9-11). God was withholding rain, which was limiting their agricultural prosperity because of their negligence in erecting His house. Reduced productivity of their pastures and fields also meant that feed for their livestock was in short supply. Regrettably, they had drifted so far from the Lord that they had not even considered a spiritual explanation for their shortages. Hence, Haggai appeals to them again: *"consider your ways"* (v. 7). The prophet's message was blunt: If you want God's blessing in the land, you must obey His decree to rebuild His temple.

We in the Church Age do well to consider our ways also. For those of us who live in the affluent Western culture, the idea of trusting the Lord for our daily bread is a mostly untested theoretical concept. Little of our abundance is needed to supply our actual daily necessities and even less of it is used to feed and clothe the poor. Rather, our vast wealth is used to insulate ourselves against any conceivable mishap, to collect stuff we really don't need, and to indulge or pamper our flesh with thrills and creature comforts that last only a moment and waste valuable time. The prophet reminded the Jews that God could simply blow away everything they worked for with one puff of air (v. 9). Their personal investments meant nothing to Him; He valued their obedience and commitment.

Ponder for a minute all the resources we use to protect ourselves against potential calamities: we carry car insurance in case we have an automobile accident, home insurance for possible floods or fires, life insurance in case we die prematurely, medical insurance for when we might become ill. We cram piles of money into retirement accounts so that we can relax in our autumn years (if we live that long), and into educational accounts to insure our children and grandchildren get good educations (if they pursue one, that is). With religious smugness and callused hearts we close our selfish eyes to the needy while we empty our pocketbooks for trinkets, high-tech gismos, and tons of other dust collectors that count for nothing in the light of eternity. There is certainly nothing wrong with planning ahead, but the point is this: few Christians in our post-modern society actually rely on God for anything, let alone everything. No wonder the Western world has become a God-denying, self-centered culture; the cosmopolitan man has no need that he cannot provide for himself – he therefore surmises that he has no need for God.

The normal avenues of God's grace in human lives are blocked by our self-reliant measures, meaning that God must become increasingly more innovative to get our attention. He must work through some means for which we have not put up a financial defense and, thus, have no self-sufficiency. Such means might include: mental fatigue, incurable diseases, catastrophic disasters, a financial crisis, lingering wars, etc. As with the Jews in Haggai's day, the Lord is laboring to awaken the Church from its religious slumber today. The means by which the Lord is getting our attention are different because of our extreme self-sufficiency, but the fact that His blessings are restrained by disobedience is the same.

We too must pause to "consider our ways." We do not want to be engaging in any activity or speech which dethrones the Lord and exalts men. Sadly, we often just do not take time to ponder what God is telling us through His Word. We need to set aside quality time to explore and meditate on Scripture. What does the Lord have for me to live this day effectively for Him? In matters of revealed truth, our ignorance is not bliss; in fact, whether willful or not, it insults God (e.g. 2 Kings 22:13). The Lord guides those who are near and dear to Him into deeper truth and spiritual awareness.

The Jews were willing to fully sacrifice themselves for what God wanted them to do – build a dwelling place for God – His temple. In the Church Age, God's dwelling place is a living temple composed of believers, which is called the Church and forms His body (Eph. 2:19, 1 Tim. 3:15). The main two ways that the Church is built up are through evangelism (i.e., adding living stones to the structure; 1 Pet. 2:5) and then building up those who are a part of the spiritual structure (Eph. 4:12). Dear believer, are you willing to sacrifice yourself by evangelizing the lost and edifying those already saved? This effectual working of the Church is what is important to Christ:

> *That we should no longer be children, tossed to and fro and carried about with every wind of doctrine, by the trickery of men, in the cunning craftiness of deceitful plotting, but speaking the truth in love, may grow up in all things into Him who is the head – Christ – from whom the whole body, joined and knit together by what every joint supplies, according to the effective working by which every part does its share, causes growth of the body for the edifying of itself in love* (Eph. 4:14-16).

The Lord desires that every believer, as empowered by the Holy Spirit, do the work of ministry within the Body that he or she is called to do (Eph. 4:12). This will ensure that His temple, the Church, will bring Him the most glory! After Christ's death and resurrection, He could righteously take up residence within those who would receive Him and experience regeneration (John 1:12-13), but this was not possible in the Old Testament days. God could not dwell in His people, but He did desire to dwell as near to them as possible – thus a temple was required.

Having been awakened from their complacency, the Jews were now willing to sacrifice themselves to build God a house among them. Specifically, they were to go up into the mountains to hew wood and cut stones to obtain the necessary building materials to construct God's house (v. 8). God would delight in the finished project and be glorified in it among the nations. By constructing a new temple, the Jews would be telling the world that their God, Jehovah, was right in chastening them for their past idolatry and He was most worthy of their praise and worship.

What effect did Haggai's pungent preaching have on a comfortably slumbering nation? On September 21, 520 B.C., twenty-three days after delivering his first message, the work on the temple resumed:

> *Then Zerubbabel the son of Shealtiel, and Joshua the son of Jehozadak, the high priest, with all the remnant of the people, obeyed the voice of the Lord their God, and the words of Haggai the prophet, as the Lord their God had sent him; and the people feared the presence of the Lord. Then Haggai, the Lord's messenger, spoke the Lord's message to the people, saying, "I am with you, says the Lord." So the Lord stirred up the spirit of Zerubbabel the son of Shealtiel, governor of Judah, and the spirit of Joshua the son of Jehozadak, the high priest, and the spirit of all the remnant of the people; and they came and worked on the house of the Lord of hosts, their God, on the twenty-fourth day of the sixth month, in the second year of King Darius (vv. 12-15).*

It is rare in the Old Testament to see such a positive response to a prophet's rebuke, especially after only a single message. Besides this, it was evident that God's Spirit was at work in His people because of the widespread effect of Haggai's message. The governor, the priests, the prophets, and the general populace were all under conviction and were united in what had to be done (v. 12). What happens when God's people come together in unity, in reverential awe of God, and are willing to do whatever He says, no matter the cost? The devil cringes and redoubles his efforts to thwart whatever would honor the Lord's name.

Ezra confirms that there was immediate opposition to the sudden rebuilding effort after fifteen years of inactivity. Jewish adversaries accused the Jews of wrongdoing and petitioned Darius to suspend the work, but he only endorsed the activity. Furthermore, he commanded that resources be given to complete the construction effort and to supply Jewish sacrifices as well (Ezra 5:1-6:12). Because the Jews were unified, acted in faith, and had a mind to work, God blessed their efforts and the building project was completed within five years.

When believers are in communion with the Lord through willing submission, they will be in fellowship with each other and be able to serve the Lord together better. This truth carries over into the Church Age; therefore, Paul commanded fellow believers to *"keep the unity of the Spirit in the bond of peace"* (Eph. 4:3). The Holy Spirit is the only One who can create unity in the Church, and believers are the only ones who through carnal behavior and impure thinking can destroy that unity. If we are not in fellowship with God, it will be impossible for us to be in fellowship with each other or to serve the Lord in a cooperative way. His peace and blessing will be missing in all we attempt to do.

Plainly, Christendom in our day is becoming more apostate; however, H. A. Ironside suggests that this does not preclude us from maintaining unity with those who hold Christ and His word dear:

> So today, it is not possible to re-gather the whole Church of God in one outward visible unity. But it is possible for a feeble few to meet on the ground of the Church of God, refusing all sectarian names and ways, "endeavoring to keep the unity of the Spirit in the bond of peace." The last phrase must never be forgotten. When strife and discord come in, the unity of the Spirit is at once violated. It can never be forced. It is a practical thing, maintained alone as believers walk in the Spirit and recognize in each other all that is of God, while each one individually seeks to "follow peace with all men, and holiness, without which no man shall see the Lord."[137]

Thankfully, the Jews were now unified as a people and in one purpose – they were going to build God a temple. God wanted to go on with them afresh and they also wanted to go on with Him!

Even though the labor had commenced, the Lord moved Haggai to deliver three more messages and Zechariah to deliver his first message before the end of that same year. Haggai's confrontational ministry abruptly ended in December of 520 B.C., but Zechariah, who motivated the Jews with hope for the future, continued prophesying for two more years. Why did God's prophets keep preaching even after the Jews started rebuilding the temple? Because service for Jehovah was not enough; He also required a spiritual transformation of attitudes and behavior. Otherwise, His people would fail to properly represent Him among the nations after the temple was completed (Rom. 2:23-24).

In his initial message, Zechariah pleads with the people, *"Turn now from your evil ways"* (Zech. 1:4). Confronting sin among God's people is the first step towards spiritual revival. These messages caused the Jews to understand that God had justly chastened them in love and that they deserved it, but now it was time to go on with the Lord and to serve Him as a holy nation.

## Meditation

Revival is a renewed conviction of sin and repentance, followed by an intense desire to live in obedience to God. It is giving up one's will to God in deep humility.

— Charles Finney

# Greater Glory Shall Come
## Haggai 2

Haggai's first message began with rebuke, but ended with encouragement. He pleaded with his countrymen to consider their ways, but also reminded them of God's abiding presence. In his second message Haggai announced that God's temple would have a greater glory associated with it in the future (vv. 6-9). In his final two messages, Haggai will remind the Jews that no amount of obedience can undo one act of disobedience (v. 13), that God's seventy-year-rest judgment on the land had ended (vv. 18-19), and that in a coming era, Gentile oppression would come to an end (v. 22). The format of the prophet's final two messages dealt with their sin, which hindered them from living for God, and also inspired the Jews with hope (i.e. to anticipate what great things God would accomplish through them and for them).

## Haggai's Second Message (vv. 1-9)

The prophet's second message was directed to the entire Jewish nation on the twenty-first day of the seventh month (October 17, 520 B.C; vv. 1-2). Work on the temple had resumed about a month earlier and was progressing. Haggai begins this message by asking a series of rhetorical questions which would address the low esteem that the older Jews were ascribing to the scaled-down version of the temple they were constructing.

For most of the Jewish nation, the dedication of the temple's foundation some fifteen years earlier was a festive event, but for the ancients of the people, the smaller base was a bitter reminder of what had been lost fifty-two years earlier. For this reason Ezra tells us that while the majority shouted for joy and praised God for this accomplishment, others wept with loud voices (Ezra 3:11-13). Solomon's temple was enormous and had stood for over four centuries. The temple to be erected on the new foundation was in its shadow; it would suffice as a place to worship Jehovah, but in the estimation of the older generation the new temple would never hold the grandeur of Solomon's temple.

Dear believer, do not pass over this portion of Scripture without musing over the Lord's response to the thoughts of His people. Knowing exactly what the elders of Israel were thinking, God sends His prophet with a message of comfort and consolation. On this point, Edward Dennett writes:

> It is well for us to understand that even the feelings of the saints – feelings prompted in connection with the Lord's ways or service – are regarded by Him with tender concern. How many instances of this might be gleaned from Scripture. David says, *"Thou tellest my wanderings: put Thou my tears into Thy bottle: are they not in Thy book?"* Again, *"In the multitude of my thoughts within me Thy comforts delight my soul."* Also, *"Thou understandest my thoughts afar off."* And it was because the Lord Jesus entered into the feelings of His disciples that He said, "Let not your heart be troubled, neither let it be afraid." How different would be our daily lives if we were in the realization and power of this simple truth![138]

Haggai confirms that the new temple would be smaller than Solomon's temple (v. 3), but also that it would have a glory beyond that of the previous temple, which is alluded in verse 9. Despite its smaller size, God had great plans for His temple. For this reason, they should be strong and should continue working; God was with them in this endeavor (v. 4).

The Lord then reminds His people of the covenant He made with them at Sinai and that He was going to uphold His part of it. Just as His Spirit had accompanied them out of Egypt and had overcome Pharaoh's army, He would remain among them now to enable their work and to protect them from harm. This meant that there was no reason to fear any opposition to the construction effort (v. 5).

Why would the new temple be more glorious than Solomon's temple? Verse 9 answers this question in part: *"'The glory of this latter temple shall be greater than the former,' says the Lord of hosts. 'And in this place I will give peace,' says the Lord of hosts."* In short, the coming temple would have a greater glory than Solomon's temple. This may refer to either the millennial temple spoken of in verses 6-8 or it may be alluding to a future, glorious event which occurred in the

357

temple that the Jews were erecting at that time. Possibly both are in view, as there is an increasing glory associated with God's temple, from His perspective.

For example, the temple under construction would be greater because the Jewish Messiah, the Prince of Peace, would present Himself in *"this latter temple"* some five centuries in the future. John tells us that on the same day that Haggai issued this prophecy (i.e., the final day of the Feast of Tabernacles) that the Lord went to the temple to teach (John 7:28). We read that the Lord Jesus addressed the crowd at that time: *"On the last day, that great day of the feast, Jesus stood and cried out, saying, 'If anyone thirsts, let him come to Me and drink'"* (John 7:37).

So when the Lord Jesus entered the temple 2000 years ago, God did uphold His promise, *"I will fill this temple with glory"* (v. 9). Simeon confirms this perspective in his prayer after the Holy Spirit came upon him in the temple and while holding the baby Jesus in his arms:

> *Lord, now You are letting Your servant depart in peace, according to Your word; for my eyes have seen Your salvation which You have prepared before the face of all peoples, a light to bring revelation to the Gentiles, and the glory of Your people Israel* (Luke 2:29-32).

The glory of Israel, Jehovah's salvation (the literally meaning of Jesus' name) had now entered the temple constructed in the sixth century B.C. Then, about 38 years after Christ's coming, that temple was destroyed, meaning that no one else claiming to be Messiah could ever fulfill Haggai's prophecy.

With surety, then, we can proclaim to every Jew, "Your Messiah has already been in Jerusalem." Though His essential glory was veiled by flesh, Christ's divine moral glory was declared in Herod's temple on several occasions. The message He spoke was how to have peace with His Father through Himself. Though the offer of peace was extended to Israel in the temple in Jerusalem, the Jewish nation rejected it.

When Christ returns to shake the earth and to establish His Kingdom in Jerusalem (v. 6), a believing remnant of Israel will receive Him and will build Him a glorious temple dwarfing Solomon's. Again, God will uphold His word, *"I will fill this temple with glory."* Indeed, this temple will have even a greater glory associated with it than any other temples before it, because Israel and all nations will worship

Messiah there (v. 7; Ezek. 40-47). The phrase *"it is a little while"* in verse 6 does not mean this will happen immediately, but rather it could happen at any time that God chooses.

The Hebrew grammar in verse 7 (a feminine singular noun with a plural masculine verb) has led to differing opinions as to what *"the Desire of All Nations"* is referring to: *"'I will shake all nations, and they shall come to the Desire of All Nations."* The KJV and NKJV infer that the Messiah who comes will be the Desire of All Nations. Many of the modern Bible translations, however, imply that the nations will gladly render their desired things to the Lord. The NASB captures this idea: *"they will come with the wealth of all nations"* (v. 7; NASB). Obviously, the gold and silver of the nations (spoken of in verse 8) belongs to the Lord regardless. The point is that when Christ becomes precious above all things, this is what is valuable to God and such worshipers will freely adorn His house with glory and honor. C. A. Coates suggests that this is the meaning of "the Desire of All Nations":

> It refers to apprehensions and appreciations of Christ brought by the work of God into the hearts of His saints everywhere, so that Christ has become "the preciousness" to them. This is what has value before God, and He intends that it should all come to His house to enrich it with glory. So what God has in mind is not diminishing glory, but increasing glory. ... If God shakes the nations, it is with a view to what is precious coming to light as the glory of His house; it is that men and saints may be shaken out of settings that are not suitable to God's house, and brought as contributors of glory to that house.[139]

God's desire, then, is that the glory of His house increase, not decrease, and so it shall. The Jews saw only a smaller temple foundation and thus diminished glory, but God saw the greater reality of future things and knew the opposite to be true. The glory of the millennial temple would be far greater than of its predecessors.

Scripturally speaking, both the above understandings of "the Desire of All Nations" will occur in the Kingdom Age. Perhaps the prophet's ambiguity was by design to illustrate that those who desire the Lord give Him their desired things, that is, their best. The Jews in his day had an opportunity to dedicate their best efforts in labor for the honor and glory of God.

In speaking of these forthcoming events related to peace, Haggai ties Christ's first advent of filling the temple with glory (v. 9) with His second coming to shake the nations of the earth, to establish peace in Jerusalem and fill a future temple with glory (vv. 6-8). In His first advent He offered Himself a sacrifice to obtain the opportunity for Israel, and indeed humanity, to have peace with God. In His second advent to the earth, He will establish a kingdom peace, and all those who honor Him will enjoy it. Speaking of this event, the writer of Hebrews quotes Haggai 2:6, but then adds to further explain the future application that God's kingdom cannot be shaken:

> *He has promised, saying, "Yet once more I shake not only the earth, but also heaven." Now this, "Yet once more," indicates the removal of those things that are being shaken, as of things that are made, that the things which cannot be shaken may remain. Therefore, since we are receiving a kingdom which cannot be shaken, let us have grace, by which we may serve God acceptably with reverence and godly fear. For our God is a consuming fire* (Heb. 12:26-29).

The writer of Hebrews describes this future purifying judgment as a shaking away from the earth all that is undesirable. Indeed, the Lord Jesus will remove all wickedness and defilement from the earth to commence the Kingdom Age; all that does not honor Him will be removed – then those left will desire Him and will bring all that they desire to Him. The idea of a more glorious temple to come would inspire the Jews in Haggai's day to invest now into what would be! And we too, understanding the greater glory to come, should live for eternity now.

## Haggai's Third Message (vv. 10-19)

On the twenty-fourth day of the ninth month, Haggai received another word from the Lord (v. 10). The date would be December 18, 520 B.C., about two months after his last message. The Lord Jehovah instructed Haggai to ask the following questions of the priests (v. 11):

> *"If one carries holy meat in the fold of his garment, and with the edge he touches bread or stew, wine or oil, or any food, will it become holy?" Then the priests answered and said, "No." And Haggai said, "If one who is unclean because of a dead body touches any of these, will it be unclean?" So the priests answered and said, "It shall be unclean." Then Haggai answered and said, "So is this people, and so*

*is this nation before Me," says the Lord, "and so is every work of their hands; and what they offer there is unclean"* (vv. 12-14).

In the things pertaining to God, the book of Leviticus states that there were only three ceremonial classifications: holy, clean, and unclean. For example, the priests, their garments, the sacrifices, and the things of the tabernacle were specifically cleansed by blood and anointed with special oil in order to be declared "holy" before the Lord. The Israelites could not participate in any of the feasts or sweet-smelling sacrifices unless they were "clean." If "unclean," they were required to take specific actions to remedy the situation and become ceremonially "clean" again. For major issues, offerings were required, but for lesser and more common matters of uncleanness, one simply washed and remained isolated until evening.

"Holy" status could only be gained by divine imputation, usually through the means of blood purification and anointing oil. What God deemed holy was holy. Likewise a "clean" status was obtained only through the means which God set forth; this typically involved washing and waiting, or, depending on the type of uncleanness, blood purification. God labors to keep His people holy and clean, but man pollutes what God has accomplished (i.e., making that which is holy, unholy, and that which is clean, unclean). Haggai emphasizes this point to his fellow countrymen at a time when they had settled into spiritual complacency and materialism.

Ceremonially speaking, what is holy does not change what is not, but that which is unholy does influence what is holy. Having an altar and performing sacrifices did not make the Jews a holy people. In reality, they had made themselves unclean before Jehovah, and nothing they offered Him with defiled hands would be accepted. They were supposed to be building Jehovah a temple, but instead they used the resources supplied for that task to build themselves nice homes. Though they were performing religious gestures, the Jews had lost the joy, the privilege, and the status of a holy people. Haggai challenged them to cleanse their hands (i.e., to repent). They did so and a temple was quickly raised up against overwhelming opposition as a testimony of God's greatness. The prophet's message is a good one for us to consider also: Only those with "clean hands" can be as God's holy people among the nations.

The final portion of Haggai's third message reminded the people of the consequences of their past reluctance to obey the Lord and rebuild His temple (1:6-11). God had reduced the land's productivity through drought, blight, mildew, and hail in response to their disobedience (vv. 15-17). This adversity is then contrasted with God's agricultural blessing because of their obedience (vv. 18-19).

God began to bountifully bless the land of Israel again because the Jews had repented of their complacency and had begun rebuilding the temple. The exact day of this blissful transition is recorded in verse 18 – the twenty-fourth day of the ninth month, the day the temple foundation was completed. Apparently, more work was required after 15 years of neglect to ensure the temple foundation, first constructed by Zerubbabel, was now adequate and appropriate to erect the new temple on. The equivalent date on the Gregorian Calendar would be December 18, 520 B.C.

## Analysis of Jeremiah's Seventy-Year Prophecy

The prophet Jeremiah had earlier predicted the Jewish captivity and how long the land would be free of agricultural enterprises: *"And this whole land shall be a desolation and an astonishment, and these nations shall serve the king of Babylon seventy years"* (Jer. 25:11). Jeremiah confirmed a twofold seventy-year prophecy concerning the nation of Israel: there would be seventy years of Babylonian captivity and seventy years of rest for the land (v. 11; 2 Chron. 36:21). The seventy years of captivity began the very year that Jeremiah spoke the prophecy, coinciding with Nebuchadnezzar's first invasion of Judah and first deportation of Jews to Babylon in 605 B.C. The captivity portion of this prophecy was concluded seventy years later when the Babylonian empire fell to the Medes and Persians and the Jewish captives were freed by King Cyrus to return home in 536 B.C. This event was foretold two centuries earlier by Isaiah (Isa. 44:28-45:1). The prophet Daniel, who had been in that first group of captives, understood this event to be the fulfillment of Jeremiah's prophecy (Dan. 9:2).

The second portion of the prophecy of seventy years did not begin until Nebuchadnezzar's third invasion, when he besieged Jerusalem during King Zedekiah's reign. God commanded the prophet Ezekiel to record the exact date this occurred:

*Again, in the ninth year, in the tenth month, on the tenth day of the month, the word of the Lord came to me, saying, "Son of man, write down the name of the day, this very day – the king of Babylon started his siege against Jerusalem this very day"* (Ezek. 24:1-2).

There are differing opinions among scholars as to the exact date of the siege of Jerusalem, its capture, and its destruction. Although Scripture states that the city fell on the ninth day of the fourth month in the eleventh year of Zedekiah's reign, scholars are divided as to whether this refers to 586 or 587 B.C. Jeremy Hughes lists eleven scholars who preferred the first date and then eleven others who preferred the second date.[140] One's preference then affects the date the siege commenced. January 15, 588 B.C. is a widely accepted date for the start of the siege, while Sir Robert Anderson prefers December 13, 589 B.C. with the fall of Jerusalem in 587 B.C.

Why did the Lord want the exact date of the beginning of the siege of Jerusalem identified? It was because on that day all agriculture stopped in Judah and the seventy years of desolation which was prophesied by Jeremiah began (Jer. 25:11). The Babylonian army sowed fields with rocks, filled wells with debris, destroyed vineyards and fruit groves, and confiscated food stores outside Jerusalem. When Nebuchadnezzar surrounded Jerusalem with his army, the land began to enjoy its long overdue rest. There would be no planting or harvesting for the next seventy years.

One may wonder why the Lord would appoint a seventy-year cessation from agricultural work. The Mosaic Law commanded that the Sabbath day be set aside to rest and to honor God. The Jews, their slaves, and their beasts of burden were all to rest on the Sabbath day. Likewise, the Israelites were to honor a Sabbath year. Every seventh year, the fields, the olive groves, and the vineyards were to receive a full year's rest. Whatever grew naturally during this time was to be freely gleaned by the poor, and anything left would be God's provision for the beasts of the field. Certainly, the sabbatical year would remind the Jews that God owned the land they dwelled on and that they were merely stewards (Lev. 25:23).

This was God's Law for the land. Unfortunately, the Jews generally ignored the Sabbath year and, ultimately, God severely judged them by giving the land seventy years of rest. According to 2 Chronicles 35:14-21, the reason for the specific length of time was to exact the seventy years due to the Lord as His portion (i.e. one-seventh of the 490 years the Jews did not honor the Sabbath year).

Sir Robert Anderson in his book *The Coming Prince* initially dated the commencement of the land desolation judgment as March 14, 589 B.C., but he later revised it to December 13, 589 B.C. The seventy years of desolation ended, according to the prophet Haggai, when the foundation of the temple was laid on the base previously completed. Haggai recorded the exact day that the Lord lifted the forced agricultural rest:

> *Consider now from this day forward, from the twenty-fourth day of the ninth month, from the day that the foundation of the Lord's temple was laid – consider it: Is the seed still in the barn? As yet the vine, the fig tree, the pomegranate, and the olive tree have not yielded fruit. But from this day I will bless you* (Hag. 2:18-19).

This event occurred in the second year of Darius (v. 10). According to Anderson, the Jews who returned from Babylon began to enjoy the benefits of the land again on April 1, 520 B.C. [141]; however, in the tenth edition of *The Coming Prince* he revised this date to be December 17, 520 B.C.:

> Now seventy years of 360 days contain exactly 25,200 days; and as the Jewish New Year's day depended on the equinoctial moon, we can assign the 13th December as "the Julian date" of tenth Tebeth 589. And 25,200 days measured from that date ended on the 17th December 520, which was the twenty-fourth day of the ninth month in the second year of Darius of Persia – the very day on which the foundation of the second Temple was laid. (Haggai 2:18, 19.) [142]

The point is that God caused one prophet to record the exact starting date and another the precise ending date of the sabbatical period that the land would enjoy in order to prove that His Word stands sure for all time. Although today we do not know the exact date in which the seventy years of desolation began, if we use consistent parameters the duration of the prophecy can be validated. A Jewish year is 360 days (Rev. 12:6, 14, 13:5; Dan. 12:7), meaning that there are 25,200 days in 70 Jewish years (i.e. 70 x 360 days = 25,200 days). Thus, the seventy-year period of rest that started on a date in 589 B.C. (i.e., December 13, 589 B.C.) ended precisely seventy Jewish years later in 520 B.C., exactly when God restored the land to fruitfulness according to Haggai. God kept His word to His people to the day; on December 18, 520 B.C. the land would again have Jehovah's blessing. Just as Jeremiah predicted, and the writings of Ezekiel and Haggai verify, the land of Israel enjoyed seventy years of rest.

## Haggai's Fourth Message (vv. 20-23)

The prophet received a second message from the Lord on the same day as the previous one (v. 20).

This word from the Lord was addressed only to Zerubbabel, the governor of Judah:

> *I will shake heaven and earth. I will overthrow the throne of kingdoms; I will destroy the strength of the Gentile kingdoms. I will overthrow the chariots and those who ride in them; the horses and their riders shall come down, everyone by the sword of his brother* (vv. 21-22).

Through Haggai, the Lord had encouraged His people to rebuild the temple. Now the Lord encourages Zerubbabel to carefully lead those that He would protect and ultimately exalt among the nations. Jehovah promised to overthrow all Gentile armies to ensure a safe environment for His people to dwell in peace with Him. This prophecy alludes to the Kingdom Age and will be fulfilled at Christ's second advent.

At that time, God will put an end to Gentile rule. He will also fulfill His promise to David that one of his descendants would sit on his throne forever, speaking of the Messiah:

> *"In that day," says the Lord of hosts, "I will take you, Zerubbabel My servant, the son of Shealtiel," says the Lord, "and will make you like a signet ring; for I have chosen you," says the Lord of hosts* (v. 23).

In anticipation of this prophecy's fulfillment, the Lord had chosen Zerubbabel, a descendant of David, to continue his royal line, and thus he was a type of the Messiah to come. F. D. Lindsey explains the reference to Zerubbabel being a signet ring:

> The significance of comparing Zerubbabel to a "signet ring" (a seal of royal authority or personal ownership) is clarified by the imagery in Jeremiah 22:24-25. God said that if Jehoiachin (Zerubbabel's

grandfather) were His signet ring, He would pull him off His hand and give him over to Nebuchadnezzar. ...Zerubbabel's place in the line of messianic descent (Matt. 1:12) confirmed his representative role in typifying the Messiah.[143]

God was delighted to tell Zerubbabel, as a descendant of David, that he represented the coming Messiah. This means, as P. Harding explains, that the Lord Jesus is truly God's signet ring:

He is the executor of God's judgment upon the earth. He will administer the purposes of God when He comes back to reign. The term "My servant" belongs to Him in a special and unique way: *"Behold My servant, whom I uphold; Mine elect, in whom My soul delighteth ... He shall not fail nor be discouraged, till He hath set judgment in the earth: and the isles shall wait for His law"* (Isa. 42:1-4). He alone is the Perfect Servant who brought infinite pleasure and glory to God in His devoted service on earth: *"I have glorified Thee on the earth: I have finished the work which Thou gavest Me to do"* (John 17:4). He alone could say, *"I do always those things that please Him"* (John 8:29), and of Him alone could be said, *"He hath done all things well"* (Mark 7:37).[144]

Haggai completed his ministry in less than four months. He spoke four messages that changed the course of the Jewish nation. God's slothful and deprived people became zealously obedient and blessed servants of God. The prophet closes his book appropriately by exalting *"the Lord of Hosts."* The sovereign God of Israel and Creator of all things is very capable of bringing about all that He has promised to do. The new temple would be rebuilt and His glory would be witnessed there – in Christ. Later, all nations would seek to worship the Jewish Messiah in a temple in Jerusalem and from there He will rule the nations in righteous power. Then, the entire world will finally experience the peace of God in Christ!

## Meditation

Up, ye saints, arouse, be earnest!
Up and work while yet 'tis day;
Ere the night of death overtake you,
Strive for souls while yet you may.

— C. C. Luther

# Zechariah

# Overview of Zechariah

## The Author

Like Jeremiah and Daniel, Zechariah's prophetic ministry began at an early age – he was but a youth (2:4). Zechariah was a priest, the son of Berechiah, the son of Iddo the prophet (1:1). Zechariah is a common name in the Old Testament; twenty-eight men are referred to by that name. His name means "Jehovah remembers," and complements the focus of his ministry, which was to affirm that God had not forgotten His covenant people and, in fact, had wonderful plans for them.

## Date

Zechariah was a contemporary of Haggai. Zechariah delivered his first message about two months after Haggai preached his first message in August of 520 B.C. Like Haggai, Zechariah also delivered four different messages. Zechariah's second oracle was given three months after his first, followed by his third oracle about two years later; the fourth message is not dated.

## Theme

Without the fullness of Scripture, the eight visions recorded in the first six chapters would be difficult to interpret. The meanings of these visions align with prophecies recorded later in Zechariah's book and with now available historical information. No Old Testament prophet reveals as much about Christ, God's plan for Israel, and His judgment of the nations in such a short space as Zechariah does. Besides predictive messages to inspire hope in Israel (1:7-6:15, 9:1-10:12), the prophet also shares practical exhortations for godly living (1:1-6, 7:1-8:23).

Haggai had successfully aroused the slothful and self-seeking Jewish nation to action. Zechariah followed his ministry with messages of encouragement to bring the people into the power of Christ's coming in glory. On this aspect of Zechariah's ministry, H. A. Ironside writes:

He is largely occupied with the appearing of Messiah and His reign of righteousness. There is blessing in thus having heart and mind transported to the days of heaven upon earth. It is then that one is able to estimate aright the transitory glories of this present evil age. The hope of the Lord's coming has a purifying effect upon the lives of those held by it. *"Every man that hath this hope in Him purifieth himself, even as He is pure"* (1 Jn. 3:3).

The Church has lost much, therefore, by neglecting the study of prophecy. It should be borne in mind that while the prophets of the Old Testament do not speak of the assembly of the present dispensation, nevertheless those who compose the Body of Christ and the Bride of the Lamb may learn much that is for edification and blessing through Jehovah's word to Israel. Then too it should be enough for the devoted soul to know that Christ is to be the center of all that glory which is soon to be revealed. If He is concerned in it, all who love Him will find spiritual delight in tracing the steps leading up to His exaltation and the establishment of His kingdom.[145]

Well said, Mr. Ironside, and this author adds a hearty "Amen."

## Outline

A Call to Repentance (1:1-1:6)
Eight Visions to Console Jerusalem (1:7-6:15)
Answering the Bethel Delegation (7:1-8:23)
Prophecies Pertaining to Christ's Coming (9:1-14:21)

# Devotions in Zechariah

## Horse-Riders, Horns, and Craftsmen
Zechariah 1

Like the prophets Jeremiah (Jer. 1:1) and Ezekiel (Ezek. 1:3), Zechariah was also a priest (v. 1; Neh. 12:1-4, 17) who began his prophetic ministry as a young man (2:4). He was the son of Berechiah, the son of Iddo, the head of a priestly clan exiled in Babylon where Zechariah was born (Ezra 8:17). Zechariah returned to Jerusalem with the first group of Jews under Zerubbabel's leadership (Ezra 5:1, 6:14).

### Overview
Zechariah's first oracle was delivered in the eighth month of the second year of Darius (v. 1), October/November 520 B.C. This was about two months after Haggai's first message (see Haggai 1 discussion for more information on the historical situation). It suffices here to merely list the major events associated with Zechariah's prophetic ministry:

August 29, 520 B.C. – Haggai's first message
September 21, 520 B.C. – Temple building resumed
October 17, 520 B.C. – Haggai's second message
October – November 520 B.C. – Zechariah's ministry begins
December 18, 520 B.C. – Haggai's third and fourth messages
February 15, 519 B.C. – Zechariah's eight visions
December 7, 518 B.C. – The delegation to Bethel
March 12, 515 B.C. – Temple dedicated
Sometime later – Zechariah's final prophetic messages (chps. 9-14)

The first six chapters of the book contain an initial call to repentance (1:1-6) and the descriptions of eight visions (1:7-6:15). This is followed by four messages relating to the prophet's response to

371

Bethel's delegation for counsel (7:1-8:23). The book closes with two messages revealing the future rejection and later enthronement of the Jewish King and Messiah (9:1-14:21).

## A Call to Repentance (vv. 2-6)

The Lord had been angry with His people because of their idolatrous ways and willful ignorance of His Law. This included their disregard of honoring the Sabbath Years in which the land was to have rest from agricultural work (2 Kgs. 21:14-15). Jehovah had used the Babylonians to chasten His people, whom after seventy years, He had returned to Judah as promised through the prophet Jeremiah (Jer. 25:11).

The Jews had been tasked with rebuilding Jehovah's temple, but intense opposition stopped construction after the foundation was finished in 535 B.C. After fifteen years of no activity, the Lord used first Haggai and then Zechariah to inspire their countrymen to begin the temple rebuilding effort again.

Like Haggai, Zechariah's prophetic ministry began with a call to repentance (vv. 2-6). God was angry with them because of their complacency on a matter that was greatly important to Him. Haggai had already told them that God was withholding His blessing from the land because of their disobedience. Although the Jews had begun working again on the temple a few weeks earlier, the heart issues within the nation were not yet resolved. This is the focus of the young prophet's first message:

> *Therefore say to them, "Thus says the Lord of hosts: 'Return to Me,' says the Lord of hosts, 'and I will return to you,' says the Lord of hosts. 'Do not be like your fathers, to whom the former prophets preached, saying, "Thus says the Lord of hosts: 'Turn now from your evil ways and your evil deeds.'"' But they did not hear nor heed Me,"* says the Lord (vv. 3-4).

Zechariah exhorts his countrymen not to be like their forefathers who rebelled against God's word, and rejected His messengers. He then follows with two questions in verse 5 reminding his audience that life was brief and the opportunity for repentance was also fleeting, as indicated by the often transitory ministries of the prophets. His point was that now was the time to forsake evil and to return to the Lord. In summary, F. D. Lindsey suggests that Zechariah warned the Jews not to disobey (v. 4), delay (v. 5), or doubt (v. 6).[146] Such exhortation is good for God's people to consider in all ages as His Word and His character are immutable. In short, *the Lord of Hosts* blesses the obedient and punishes the wayward.

The Jews responded well to Zechariah's challenge: *"Just as the Lord of hosts determined to do to us, according to our ways and according to our deeds, so He has dealt with us"* (v. 6). Recognizing that all divine chastening is just, is deserved, and is an indication of God's providential care is a mark of true repentance – a changed heart.

## The First Vision – Horse and Riders (vv. 7-17)

Zechariah saw a series of eight visions in one night *"on the twenty-fourth day of the eleventh month, which is the month Shebat, in the second year of Darius"* (v. 7). The Gregorian Calendar dates this as February 15, 519 B.C. The visions were interpreted by an angel to assist Zechariah's understanding of their meanings. The visions pertain to Israel's future and span the time from the rebuilding of the temple to the time the Jewish nation will be fully restored and blessed during the Kingdom Age.

The first vision includes a description of what Zechariah saw, an explanation by the angel, and then intercession by the Angel of the Lord. The young prophet saw a man mounted on a red horse standing among the myrtle trees in a ravine, while other riders on red, sorrel, or white horses were approaching the waiting rider (v. 7).

Zechariah is perplexed as to who these men were, so he asks the interpreting angel, who indicates that an explanation will be given (v. 8). The enlightenment then comes from the rider on the red horse: *"These are the ones whom the Lord has sent to walk to and fro throughout the earth"* (v. 10). The returning riders then address the rider on the red horse as the Angel of the Lord and provide Him their report: *"We have walked to and fro throughout the earth, and behold, all the earth is resting quietly"* (v. 11).

This dialogue is both similar and different from the one the Lord has with Satan in the opening chapter of Job: *"And the Lord said to Satan, 'From where do you come?' So Satan answered the Lord and said, 'From going to and fro on the earth, and from walking back and forth on it'"* (Job 1:7). Both Satan and these riders were involved with monitoring earthly affairs, but they differed in that the riders are in submission to the Lord and provide their reports willingly without being asked. Satan's activities were apart from God's approval and thus for evil, while the riders' activities were for good. This observation suggests that the riders in the vision are good angels.

Based on the biblical symbolism of horses and the context of the narrative, F. B. Hole also believes the Angel of the Lord is talking with angelic riders:

> As a symbol, a horse is generally used to indicate strength and power, but in this first vision nothing is said to show just what form of strength is meant, though we gather not earthly kingdoms, such as Persia or Greece, since the horses walk on tours of inspection through the earth. When, however, we read Zechariah 6, we again find horses mentioned, and they are described as, *"the four spirits of the heavens;"* that is, they are angelic in character. This, we believe, they are here, and their report is that though God's city and people were still in distress at the end of the seventy years, the nations under the Persian empire were having a very quiet and restful time.[147]

The One mounted on the red horse is the One in authority and is identified in verse 11 as the Angel of the Lord. The Angel of the Lord is a pre-incarnate manifestation of the Son of God, and is usually in human form (e.g., 3:2-4). There are over two dozen such appearances in the Old Testament. This title is unique and should not be confused with the phrase "an angel of the Lord," which may refer to the manifestation of one of many holy angels.

Contextual observation confirms that appearances of "the Angel of the Lord" were *theophanies*. The Messenger (Angel) of the Lord either clearly identifies Himself as God (Gen. 31:11-13; Ex. 3:2-6) or receives worship (Judg. 6:18-20). Similarly, in the New Testament, the Son of God is called the Word (John 1:1; 1 Jn. 1:1); the Son became a man to bring the ultimate message of God to humanity. The Lord Jesus was a living message sojourning on the earth; He was both the message and the messenger of God.

The other angels in the vision, having completed their reconnaissance missions of the earth, submitted their report to the Angel of the Lord that all is at peace. His response was to immediately petition Jehovah (speaking of God the Father) on Israel's behalf: *"O Lord of hosts, how long will You not have mercy on Jerusalem and on the cities of Judah, against which You were angry these seventy years?"* (v. 12). This is an unusual role for the Angel of the Lord in the

Old Testament, who normally represents God to the people, rather than representing the people to God. No doubt the intercessory work of Christ as a Great High Priest on behalf of His people is in view (Heb. 4:14-16).

The answer to His supplication was *"good and comforting words"* by God in heaven to the interpreting angel, who then relayed God's three-part response for Zechariah to record:

> *"I am zealous for Jerusalem and for Zion with great zeal. I am exceedingly angry with the nations at ease; for I was a little angry, and they helped -- but with evil intent."* ... *"I am returning to Jerusalem with mercy; My house shall be built in it."*... *"And a surveyor's line shall be stretched out over Jerusalem."* ... *"My cities shall again spread out through prosperity; the Lord will again comfort Zion, And will again choose Jerusalem"* (vv. 14-17).

What is the explanation of this vision? With the fall of the Babylonian Empire and the rise of the Persian Empire, God has brought peace to the region. God's anger over Israel's idolatry had been appeased. Now the Jews would be permitted to rebuild the temple without hostility from their surrounding pagan nations. The myrtle tree was a lowly evergreen tree with fragrant white flowers and likely represents Israel in the vision.[148] The weak, returning remnant could not be construed to be a stately cedar or upright palm tree. At this moment, the Jewish nation was merely a lowly tree that had been granted a peaceful environment to complete the task of erecting Jehovah's temple. This era of worldwide peace also typifies the complete rest the world will realize during Christ's coming rule from Jerusalem.

Through the interpreting angel, the Lord conveyed that He loved Israel (vv. 13-14), that His wrath will be poured out on the nations (v. 15), and that His immense blessing upon Israel was coming (vv. 16-17). In contrast, the Gentile nations are proud and self-sufficient and have no regard for God's chosen people. Though they glared on the Jews with indifference and scorn, Jehovah was always watching and directing the affairs of men to accomplish His promises and purposes concerning His people. By their ill-treatment of Israel, Gentile powers pour for themselves a fuller cup of iniquity to be recompensed with intense, holy wrath in the day of vindication.

## The Second Vision – Horns and Craftsmen (vv. 18-21)

Zechariah then sees four horns followed by four craftsmen (vv. 18, 20). He asked the interpreting angel what the horns represented and the craftsmen what they were preparing to do (vv. 19, 21). Horns are used throughout Scripture to symbolize power or an authority (such as a king; Dan. 7:7-8, 20-25; Rev. 17:12). When metaphorically applied, the number four is used to indicate something that pertains to the earth or has an influence within earthly order. For example, there are four seasons, four directions, four divisions of a day, four types of soil, and four realms in which all creatures dwell. It is no wonder then that the New Testament contains four, and only four, gospel accounts which reveal Messiah from four different perspectives and to four unique earthly audiences.

How does the number four relate to the meaning of this vision? The four horns represented four earthly powers (Gentile kingdoms) that would be permitted to scatter the Jewish people. But for each horn a craftsman came into view. The four craftsmen were sent by God to confront and destroy the original four powers that had conquered and displaced God's people.

While this understanding is widely accepted, identifying who the four horns and four craftsmen actually represent is more difficult. The actions of the horns are described as completed, while the work of the craftsmen is spoken of as yet future. Some have suggested that the four horns are the previous nations that ruled over Israel: Egypt, Assyria, Babylon, and Persia. But not all these nations ruled over a dispersed Israel. Additionally, Zechariah's visions are prophetic in nature, not historical. Furthermore, these four nations cannot be both the horns and the craftsmen, as Greece defeated the Persians (the fourth horn) almost two centuries after Zechariah's prophecies. In other words, even this historical view has a futuristic aspect to its interpretation.

Since this chapter commences with the rebuilding of Jerusalem and the temple after the Jews returned from Babylon under Persian rule and chapter 2 speaks of the coming Kingdom Age, it is reasonable to assume that the application of this vision falls in-between these events. That would mean that Zechariah's second vision pertains to God's work to conclude "the time of Gentiles."

The prophecy conveys God's viewpoint in a comprehensive way. In Zechariah's day, the first horn, the Babylonian Empire, had just been removed by Persia, the first craftsman or carpenter. Later, Greece would overcome Persia, and afterwards Rome would rule over Greece. The Lord Jesus will overcome the revived Roman Empire at His second advent and will end all Jewish oppression by Gentile nations forever. Hence, for every horn, God has a craftsman to ensure the welfare of His people.

Though this vision clearly relates to Israel, C. A. Coates expounds the wonderful implications of this message for saints down through the ages:

> It is extremely encouraging to see that there has always been a counteracting power at work. The four craftsmen, or carpenters, have been present all the time, exercising a power and skill which was really greater than the power of the horns, for it was directly the power and wisdom of God. Craftsmen, or carpenters, are persons who carry on constructive work, and I believe that in Zechariah's vision they set forth those agencies by which God has carried on His spiritual work, which has always tended to build up His saints on their most holy faith so that they have been strengthened to stand, notwithstanding the presence and activity of scattering powers. Every faithful saint down through the ages has been an overcomer, and the fact that there have been overcomers shows that constructive work has been going on all the time.[149]

The four craftsmen then represent God's controlling activity over His people through the final four empires to rule humanity. Plainly, God uses instruments of judgment (kingdoms) as He sees fit to deliver His people from their enemies and to lead them on into holy sanctification.

## Meditation

> God has wisely kept us in the dark concerning future events and reserved for Himself the knowledge of them, that He may train us up in a dependence upon Himself and a continued readiness for every event.

> — Matthew Henry

# The Apple of His Eye
Zechariah 2

The chapter commences with these words, *"Then I raised my eyes and looked, and behold."* This indicates the start of a new vision within the same prophetic series of that one night.

## The Third Vision – The Surveyor (vv. 1-5)

The third vision occurs from an observation point in Jerusalem. Zechariah notices a surveyor and asks him what he is doing (v. 1). The surveyor, speaking directly to the prophet, says he is measuring Jerusalem with his line (v. 2). The interpreting angel leaves Zechariah to speak with another angel who apparently was with the surveyor (v. 3). This second angel then tells the interpreting angel to run back and explain the vision, which relates to the future of Jerusalem:

> *"Jerusalem shall be inhabited as towns without walls, because of the multitude of men and livestock in it. For I," says the Lord, "will be a wall of fire all around her, and I will be the glory in her midst"* (vv. 4-5).

Although the identity of the surveyor is not given, there are good reasons to assume that He is the Angel of the Lord. First, the Angel of the Lord is present in the first and fourth visions. Second, He promises to bless and prosper Jerusalem again and only God can unequivocally accomplish that feat (vv. 5, 8), for we know that, in a future day, Jerusalem will have God's glory within and His protection without. The city will need no walls, for the Lord will be its impenetrable defense – like a wall of fire! Furthermore, God's blessing will be so abundant that the city will overflow its boundaries. In other words, walls could not contain Jerusalem's future expansion.

## Future Joy, Awe, and Blessing in Jerusalem (vv. 6-13)

The vision indicates that the Lord will bless Jerusalem in the future with wonderful expansion and with His protection. Jerusalem will need no walls during the Millennium Kingdom and God promises it will never be destroyed again. The prophet Jeremiah offers a similar promise, which clearly relates to the second advent of Christ:

*Behold, the days are coming, says the Lord, that the city shall be built for the Lord from the Tower of Hananel to the Corner Gate. The surveyor's line shall again extend straight forward over the hill Gareb; then it shall turn toward Goath. And the whole valley of the dead bodies and of the ashes, and all the fields as far as the Brook Kidron, to the corner of the Horse Gate toward the east, shall be holy to the Lord. It shall not be plucked up or thrown down anymore forever* (Jer. 31:38-40).

The blessings foretold for Jerusalem are remarkable: The city will be protected and inhabited forever. The Lord will dwell there with His people and His glory shall be seen by all throughout the city and in the land. In a vision, Ezekiel saw the glory of the Lord return to the Millennial Temple in Jerusalem (Ezek. 43:2-5). Divine vindication will be unleashed upon nations that despoiled Israel. Many Gentiles shall also become the Lord's people and dwell with Him in Jerusalem. All the earth shall be in awe of the Lord and praise Him.

Given the Lord's great plans for Jerusalem, those exiled Jews still living in Babylon should return to Jerusalem – their chastening for idolatry was over (v. 7). This command to return would also have an application later at Christ's second advent when He will gather the Jewish people scattered by persecution back to Zion throughout the world (Ezek. 39:28-29).

The Lord tenderly refers to His covenant people as *"the apple of His eye"* and warns that any nation which despoils the Jews will reap His vengeance through the coming Messiah (v. 8). This reckoning occurs when the One honoring the Angel of the Lord sends Him to judge the nations, that is, shortly *"after glory"* (v. 8), which refers to the glorious second coming of Christ to the earth.

Theologically speaking, God has adopted Israel for Himself through a covenant and therefore views the nation as a firstborn son (Ex. 4:22; Rom. 9:4). This adoption was not an adoption of individuals, as it is with believers in the Church Age (Rom. 8:15-16), but of a nation.

Through His covenant with Abraham, Israel had been singled out from among the nations as a special object of God's favor: *"For I am a Father to Israel, and Ephraim is My firstborn"* (Jer. 31:9). Zechariah forewarns future nations of God's wrath if they should choose to invade Israel, for the nation is *"the apple of His eye"* (v. 8). When the Lord Jesus Christ returns to the earth, He will vindicate Himself and the nation of Israel. Then the entire planet will fully understand who He is and that God the Father sent Him.

Jehovah prompted Moses, Jeremiah, and Zechariah to express His deep devotion to His covenant people by invoking the term *the apple of God's eye*:

> *He found him in a desert land and in the wasteland, a howling wilderness; He encircled him, He instructed him, He kept him as the apple of His eye* (Deut. 32:10).

> *After Jeremiah announces that God has put Israel away as an adulterous wife he pleads: "Their heart cried unto the Lord, O wall of the daughter of Zion, let tears run down like a river day and night: give thyself no rest; let not the apple of thine eye cease"* (Lam. 2:18; KJV).

> *For thus says the Lord of hosts: "He sent Me after glory, to the nations which plunder you; for he who touches you touches the apple of His eye"* (v. 8).

This Hebrew idiom is derived from three different Hebrew words. In Deuteronomy 32:10, *'iyshown* literally means "the little man of the eye" (or more specifically the *'iysh* or "man" reflected in the pupil of the eye). The root word in Lamentations 2:18, *'ayin,* literally and figuratively refers to "an eye." Finally, in Zechariah 2:8, *babah* is used to speak of the "gate of the eye" (referring again to the pupil). These words relate to the minute reflection that an onlooker sees when gazing directly into another's eye. This Hebrew idiom is surprisingly close to the Latin version, *pupilla*, which means a little doll. The pupil is round, dark, and in the center of the eye, and thus reflects an image of what is directly in front of it.

Remarkably, this ancient idiom is an expression of endearment still commonly used today. The Oxford English Dictionary states that the phrase refers to "something or someone that one cherishes above all others."[150] The pupil, or aperture, through which light passes to the retina, is the tenderest part of the eye. Because sight is the most valued of our five senses, we treasure our eyes and diligently guard them from harm. The eye is an incredible organ, to which even the slightest injury is most acutely felt and may cause loss of function. It is also an organ that is not easily repaired through surgery once damaged. For these and other reasons, our eyes are dear to us! When Jehovah invokes the term *the apple of God's eye* in Scripture, He is exclusively speaking of the Jewish people whom He greatly cherishes. Beware nations of the earth! Those who mistreat the people that God has promised to honor, bless, and love forever will not stand against His vindicating fury.

Corrie Ten Boom's father, Casper, realized this truth. Adolph Hitler hated the Jews and was intent upon exterminating them; over six million Jews were murdered during World War II. But in the early days of World War II, the Ten Boom family hid Jews in their home and assisted them to escape Nazi-occupied Holland. Eventually, the Ten Boom family was arrested and imprisoned for their compassionate ministry to the Jewish people. Most of the family died in labor camps, but Corrie survived. She later wrote of her family's experience, explaining why her father had compassion for the Jewish people:

> Once the occupation of Holland was underway and the Jews began to suffer persecution, Casper, although quite old by then, devoted himself to the rescue effort. He even attempted to get his own yellow Star of David to wear, so he could identify with the Jews in their time of trouble. Although Corrie kept him from doing so, he compensated by taking off his hat to every Jew he would meet.[151] He surprised Corrie by his comment when he saw the soldiers packing Jews into the back of a truck: "Those poor people," he lamented. Corrie thought he meant the Jews, but then he continued, "I pity the poor Germans, Corrie. They have touched the apple of God's eye."[152]

Consequently, the Nazi movement was defeated, and the German people suffered much during and after Hitler's leadership. Jehovah still loves, and will always love, His covenant people. The Jewish people are the apple of God's eye. Any nation who persecutes them will inevitably reap God's fury (v. 8; Jer. 2:3)!

"In that day" (v. 11) is speaking of the Day of the Lord and refers to the Lord Jesus Christ's return to vindicate His people and Himself. He will then establish Jerusalem as His holy habitation again (v. 12). He will then receive His promised inheritance and establish the throne of David forever.

Consequently, the daughter of Zion, who had previously hung her harp on the willow while weeping by the rivers of Babylon, was now called on to sing and rejoice. Indeed, in a coming day, all flesh on earth will reap the goodness of Christ's presence and be in joyful awe of Him (vv. 10, 13). Those Gentiles rejecting the Antichrist and showing favor to the Jews during the Tribulation Period will also be received by the Lord and will become His people (v. 11)!

## Meditation

> When the author walks on the stage, the play is over. God is going to invade, all right – something so beautiful to some of us and so terrible to others that none of us will have any choice left, for this time it will be God without disguise. It will be too late then to choose your side.
>
> — C. S. Lewis

# The Serving Branch
Zechariah 3

Zechariah's fourth vision (recorded in this chapter) and his fifth vision (found in the next chapter) occur in the courtyard of the temple. The first and second visions occurred in a ravine or valley near Jerusalem (perhaps the Kidron), and the third vision from a high observation point within the city. The first two visions addressed Israel's deliverance from Gentile oppression and captivity, while the third vision foretold her future blessing and expansion during the Kingdom Age. The fourth vision addresses Israel's inward cleansing from sin and then the restoration of her priestly office and activities.

## The Fourth Vision – The Defiled Priest
Ezra supplies a roster of the Jews who were willing to take advantage of Cyrus' offer to return from Babylon to Jerusalem in 537/536 B.C. He begins by listing the key civil and religious leaders. The appointed governor of the province of Judah, Zerubbabel, is listed first and Jeshua (or Joshua; v. 1) the High Priest is next (Ezra 2:1-2).

The fourth vision commences with Joshua the High Priest in filthy attire standing before the Angel of the Lord and Satan standing on Joshua's right side opposing him (vv. 1, 3). The prophet did not see some erring and disreputable man clothed in putrid garments, but rather as one who represented those who served God in a place of high privilege. Israel's high priests once wore unsullied robes as required by the Law, but Joshua, now attired in filthy garments, illustrates the widespread moral corruption of the Jewish nation, which necessitated their Babylonian captivity.

In Eastern thinking, a man suspected of crime was considered guilty until cleared. In the case before us, both God and the adversary knew that Joshua (representing the Jewish nation) was guilty – as conveyed by the filthy garments. Commenting on the scene, William Kelly notes the devil's intentions:

383

It was to be expected that Satan should be there taking advantage of the guilt and the confessed condition of the representative high priest as a reason why God should cast Jerusalem back into fiery trouble again. Why should He pluck such a brand as that out of the fire?[153]

As previously mentioned, the Angel of the Lord is the second person of the Godhead. He, speaking on behalf of His Father in heaven, says, *"The Lord rebuke you, Satan! The Lord who has chosen Jerusalem rebuke you! Is this not a brand plucked from the fire?"* (v. 2). David reminds us that naturally speaking, *"certainly every man at his best state is but vapor"* (Ps. 39:5). So if the high priest, who represented Israel to God, needed cleansing, they all did.

## Christ's Advocacy

The Lord then commanded those standing near to *"take away the filthy garments from him."* Then He said to Joshua, *"See, I have removed your iniquity from you, and I will clothe you with rich robes"* (v. 4). Zechariah promptly chimes in: *"let them put a clean turban on his head"* (v. 5). The change in speaker is intriguing in verse 5 (i.e., from "He said" to "I said"). Edward Dennett suggests that such immediate intercession by Zechariah is strong evidence of a heart that is in communion with God:

> It would seem as if the prophet had been so brought into communion with the mind of God by the vision which he beheld that he is used to become its expression. He had heard the divine word, *"I will clothe thee* [Joshua] *with change of raiment,"* and entering into what had thus been promised, he intercedes, as it were, that it might at once be done. In this lies the principle of all prevailing intercession – the soul entering into the thoughts of God and turning them into prayer.[154]

In contrast to Zechariah's intercession for Joshua is Satan's belligerent resistance. This pictures the devil's attempts to keep the Jews from offering sacrifices to God in Jerusalem on the basis of past offenses against God. In this vision, Joshua the high priest (and also his companions mentioned later) symbolize the Jewish nation as a whole being acquitted of past wickedness and failures and then being established again in holiness before the Lord (v. 8). This is shown by the exchange of defiled priestly garments for proper holy attire. C. A. Coates explains what the change in garments symbolizes:

> Those that stand before God know that everything connected with man as in the flesh is defiling, for God has had to remove it from before His eye in the death of His Son. Man as in the flesh can have no place before God or in His holy service. Christ having died for all is the proof that all were dead, and we cannot bring before God in His service that which He accounts dead. Philosophy and vain deceit and doing our own will in humility are "filthy garments," because, however commendable in the estimation of men, they are not Christ. Paul's great service was to announce Christ, *"to the end that we may present every man perfect in Christ Jesus"* (Col. 1:28). How many things have come into the professed service of God which are "not after Christ"! They are all "filthy garments" which disqualify for holy service. The human mind, as such, is essentially unholy, for it cannot rise above the measure of man, and man is unholy as having departed from God. So we have all to stand in the presence of God's great intervention in Christ, and to see how God has provided for His own pleasure in us by investing us with Christ in the character of "festival-robes."[155]

Joshua's pure garments would permit him, as Israel's high priest, to stand in God's presence and continue to have access there as a ministering holy priest. But, God could righteously exchange Joshua's filthy garments for holy ones only by a work of grace through the coming Messiah (v. 9). Satan's accusations were legitimate against Israel, but as these offenses would be righteously judged at Calvary and forgiven in grace, the devil's claims against Israel were silenced.

Indeed, like Joshua, we all are guilty. The devil's claims against us are often true, but every indictment is voided by Christ's work of propitiation accomplished at Calvary. The Lord Jesus points to the marks in His own body to silence every claim of guilt against His own. Indeed, sin grieves the Lord, but it has no judicial sting for the saved believer who is positionally standing with Christ in righteousness.

> I hear the accuser roar of ills that I have done;
> I know them well, and thousands more, Jehovah findeth none.
>
> — S. W. Gandy

As born again believers, we, like Israel, are brands plucked from the fire and yet we are dressed in clean garments reflecting the righteousness of Christ! Without Christ we are nothing, nor can we do anything to please God – we also need continual divine cleansing (1 Jn. 1:9). Praise the Lord – in Christ, the devil no longer has any claims on us!

The opening verses of this chapter present us a lovely picture of God's just forgiveness of past sins through the advocacy of the Angel of the Lord (i.e., the Messenger or the Word of God). One of the present ministries of Christ in heaven is to be our legal representative or advocate before the Father (1 Jn. 2:1). This is a special comfort for all believers, especially knowing that Satan slanders us before God's throne day and night (Rev. 12:10).

Although the English word "advocate" is so translated only once from the Greek New Testament, the same Greek word *parakletos* is often rendered "comforter," as in the references to the Holy Spirit in the Gospel of John. The role of an advocate or a comforter is to plead the case of another person in a court of law – to be a legal intercessor. As pertaining to Christ, *Thayer's Greek Dictionary* defines the meaning of *parakletos* as "Christ's pleading for pardon of our sins before the Father." When does Christ plead our case? Is it when we acknowledge and confess our sins? No, 1 John 2:1 affirms that Christ's advocacy occurs *if* we sin, not *when* we confess our sins, even though we certainly should confess them. In other words, Christ is our Advocate at all times, not just when the believer confesses failure.

It is our Advocate's presence in heaven and not His plea per se, that provides every believer with assurance of his or her positional standing before God. S. Emery further explains the Lord's ministry of advocacy for believers when they do sin:

> His valid ministry, therefore, on our behalf, is not on the basis of an effective, verbal and persuasive pleading before the Father, but on the basis of a perfect satisfaction for all our sins ever before the Father's face. He is our propitiation of undiminishing value. ... His very presence before the Father is the plea. Continuance in the family of God is never in question, but forgiveness of our sins, and cleansing from all unrighteousness, is experienced only when we make confession (1 Jn. 1:9).[156]

James Gunn further explains why the Lord Jesus can righteously plead for every child of God to be judicially acquitted for the sins he or she commits.

> Christ is not a mere suppliant petitioner. He pleads for us on the grounds of justice, of righteousness, of obedience to the law, and endurance of its full penalty for us, on which He grounds His claim for our acquittal. The sense therefore is, "in that He is righteous."[157]

When a believer sins, Satan may abruptly call God's attention to the despicable deed. However, Christ being at the right hand of His Father (Heb. 1:3) is able to promptly proclaim that the penalty for the unrighteous act, though offensive to God, has already been paid at Calvary. In this way, all heavenly hosts, powers, and principalities will see that God is righteous and that He has justly accounted for every wrong the believer commits. God hates sin, but because He judged Christ for it, He can extend to the repentant sinner a full pardon and family status as His adopted child (Rom. 8:15). Though the believer does not need to worry about God's judicial wrath, he or she should pursue holy living to stay in fellowship with God and to avoid provoking His chastening hand. Our souls have been liberated through the work of Christ to serve God out of love, not out of the fear of judgment, for the judgment of our sins has been accomplished and true love does not fear (1 Jn. 4:18).

Understanding that our accuser constantly levies charges against us and that our faithful Advocate continually defends us should prompt the believer to keep short accounts with God. As soon as one is conscious of sin, the sin should be confessed to God as wrong, and all reveling in it should cease. Like Joshua (v. 7), believer-priests in the Church Age have a responsibility to continue in holiness and submission to enjoy the privileges of fellowshipping, serving, and worshiping the Lord.

In summary, this vision has a twofold application. Verses 1-7 contain a near-term relevance, while verses 8-10 relate to a distant fulfillment. The immediate aspect of the vision was to inform the Jewish nation that their chastening was over, that they were now restored to God in purity and that they were once again able to offer service and worship to God. Yet, what is received in grace is not without responsibility. Joshua had to walk with God and keep His commandments to enjoy the blessings and privileges of his priesthood.

The future portion of Zechariah's vision centers in the coming Jewish Messiah, the All-knowing Stone (i.e., the stone with seven eyes), who is the Serving Branch of God (v. 8). The Lord Jesus has His eye on all His people and is ready to lavish them with selfless and abounding grace. He will suddenly appear to remove wickedness from the land and to bless Israel immensely in a coming day (v. 9). In that blessed era, *"Everyone will invite his neighbor under his vine and under his fig tree"* (v. 10). All the inhabitants of the earth will then be in awe of Christ's righteous character and His immense capacity to bless and to uphold justice.

## The Serving Branch

When the Branch of the Lord appears, the redeemed will be established at His side. The devastation caused by sin will be reversed. Originally, man was created to rule over the earth in such a way to represent the image and likeness of God (Gen. 1:26; Heb. 2:6-8). When man sinned, God could not have an imperfect head ruling over a perfect creation, so God cursed the earth and made it a fitting habitation for a condemned race to suffer in their sin. Yet, in a coming day, the Branch of the Lord will completely repair the damage that resulted from sin and then everyone on the earth and creation itself will rejoice!

In the Old Testament, God speaks prophetically of His Son being a Branch in four ways, which align with the unique vantage points of Christ in the four Gospels:

> *"Behold, the days are coming," says the Lord, "that I will raise to David **a Branch of righteousness; a King** shall reign and prosper, and execute judgment and righteousness in the earth"* (Jer. 23:5; also see Isa. 11:1).

> *Hear, O Joshua, the high priest, you and your companions who sit before you, for they are a wondrous sign; for behold, I am bringing forth **My Servant the Branch** (3:8).*

> *Then speak to him, saying, "Thus says the Lord of hosts, saying: 'Behold, **the Man whose name is the Branch!** From His place He shall branch out, and He shall build the temple of the Lord'"* (6:12).

*In that day **the Branch of the Lord** shall be beautiful and glorious; and the fruit of the earth shall be excellent and appealing for those of Israel who have escaped* (Isa. 4:2).

These four divine "Branch" titles of the Lord perfectly align with the four Gospel presentations of Christ:

*Unto David a Branch ... a King* – Gospel of Matthew
*My Servant, the Branch* – Gospel of Mark
*The Man ... the Branch* – Gospel of Luke
*The Branch of the Lord* – Gospel of John

F. B. Hole summarizes the wonderful allusions to Christ's character and work as expressed by each of these Old Testaments prophets when speaking of "the Branch":

Twice in Jeremiah do we get the Lord Jesus alluded to as the Branch, or Sprout (Jer. 23:5, 33:15), but there what is emphasized is righteousness. It is the character He displays rather than the Source from whence He springs. Again in Zechariah the expression occurs twice (Zech. 3:8, 6:12). There the emphasis lies on the fact that though He springs forth from Jehovah, He is to take the place of the Servant, and enter into Manhood to serve. Reading the five occurrences in the fuller light of the New Testament, we see how full these early predictions were as to our blessed Lord. The one in Isaiah 4:2 is the first and deepest of them all.[158]

Zechariah relays Jehovah's promises to send forth His Servant the Branch (v. 8). This Branch expression represents the Gospel of Mark's perspective of Christ being the lowly Servant of Jehovah who exhausts Himself on the behalf of others.

The Holy Spirit inspired Mark to wonderfully convey to us this lowly serving aspect of Christ's ministry. Twelve of Mark's sixteen chapters begin with the word "and," and the far majority of the verses in Mark begin with conjunctions and adverbs such as "and," "now," and "then." For example, Mark 1 contains 45 verses, and 35 of them begin with "And...." More specifically, many verses in Mark begin "And Jesus..." or "And He...." Mark is careful to present a serving Savior to his audience: And Jesus was doing this, and Jesus was doing that.

But he doesn't stop there. In order for the reader to gain a higher sense of the Lord's exhausting ministry, he adds further descriptions to the verbs describing the Lord's service, employing words such as "forthwith," and "immediately." This is accomplished by repeatedly applying two Greek adverbs: *eutheos* meaning "directly," and *euthus* meaning "at once." These adverbs occur forty-six times in Mark, but only thirty-six times total in Matthew, Luke, and John. Keep in mind that Mark is the shortest of the Gospel accounts. The frequency of usage in Mark is unmistakably distinctive!

Those of the Lord's servants who are involved in various "full-time" ministries understand, in a measure, exhaustion. (Many elders and other saints know this all too well also.) Can you imagine the level of exhaustion that the Lord Jesus continually suffered in His non-stop ministry? Day in and day out, at any time of day or night, people were coming to him with their problems and ailments. Those rejecting His message confronted Him continuously. No wonder He fell asleep in the stern of a boat and did not wake up when the boat was being tossed to and fro in a violent storm. Add to this His fervent prayer life. Even though His life was marked by a constant state of physical exhaustion, He still arose early, often while it was yet dark, to spend time conversing with His Father.

Mark presents to us not just a serving Savior, but One who incessantly, steadily and promptly served others. The Lord Jesus poured His life out to satisfy the needs of others – this is what Zechariah is referring to by the expression *My Servant the Branch.* The time is coming when humanity will see the Servant Branch return to establish peace and bliss on the earth, and He will do it in just one day!

## Meditation

Where is Thy reign of peace,
And purity, and love?
When shall all hatred cease,
As in the realms above?

When comes the promised time
That war shall be no more –
Oppression, lust, and crime,
Shall flee Thy face before?

Men scorn Thy sacred Name,
And wolves devour Thy fold;
By many deeds of shame
We learn that love grows cold.

Thy Kingdom come, O God,
Thy rule, O Christ, begin;
Break with Thine iron rod
The tyrannies of sin.

— Lewis Hensley

# But by My Spirit
Zechariah 4

## The Fifth Vision – Two Olive Trees and One Lampstand

Apparently, the prophet was permitted to doze for a few minutes between the fourth and fifth visions, as the interpreting angel had to awaken him (v. 1). Given all the bizarre imagery he had seen, it was a real mercy of the Lord that Zechariah could have slept at all.

Once he was attentive, the angel asked Zechariah, *"What do you see?"* (v. 2). Zechariah said he saw two olive trees supplying oil through two receptacles and two pipes to a bowl reservoir sitting above a golden lampstand (vv. 3, 12). The seven burning lamps received a constant oil supply from this bowl through seven tubes (one for each lamp). The pipes and bowl, as depicted in the illustration below, were made of gold[159] (v. 12).

Zechariah asked the angel what the apparatus represented. After learning that the prophet had no clue as to what he was looking at, the angel explained the vision (vv. 4-5). The gold lampstand represented the pure and faithful testimony of God to be displayed by Israel to the nations. The Jewish nation was located at the crossroads of three continents – an ideal location to proclaim the glory of Jehovah. Zechariah's lampstand resembles the one in the tabernacle and later in Solomon's temple (Ex. 25:31-40; 1 Kgs. 7:49); the difference was that human priests did not need to replenish Zechariah's lampstand with oil. The seven lamps signify God's perfect vision and oversight in rebuilding the temple, and indeed, over all affairs on the earth (v. 10).

The number seven is preeminent in this vision. Seven is God's number, and represents perfection, completeness and holiness. For example, the Stone with seven eyes in the fourth vision represented Christ's omniscience – perfect sight. In this vision, the seven flames of the Lampstand show God's pure testimony of truth; its light is divine in origin because it is sourced by the pure oil – the Holy Spirit. In Scripture, the Holy Spirit is generally depicted as an active fluid, such as blowing wind (John 3), seven flames of fire (Rev. 4), rushing water from a rock (John 7), or, as witnessed in this chapter, flowing olive oil. The Holy Spirit, in these types, is not visibly doing the Father's will, but rather He enables and accomplishes the task at hand in a powerful and invisible fashion.

Zechariah asked what the olive trees represented, and the angel informed him that they symbolized Zerubbabel, Israel's governor, and Joshua, Israel's high priest, who were to lead their countrymen to complete God's House (vv. 7, 11-12, 14). The olive oil flowing from the trees to the bowl through gold pipes and to the lamps reflects the enabling power of the Holy Spirit to accomplish the construction task. Speaking of the oil, the Lord told Zechariah: *"Not by might nor by power, but by My Spirit"* (v. 6). Human wisdom, strength, and military might can never accomplish what only God's Spirit can! Hence, the bowl and conduits likely refer to the many means by which the Holy Spirit accomplishes the will of God (vv. 2-3).

In the prophet's vision, the great mountain signified the difficulties ahead, and the plain, their removal (v. 7). By God's grace, Zerubbabel would finish building the temple, as symbolized by the expression *"he shall bring forth the capstone"* (v. 7). The outcome of this stupendous achievement would be a tremendous testimony of Jehovah's glory in Jerusalem, for Jehovah was *"jealous for Jerusalem"* (1:14).

The Lord explains to His prophet that He would silence Zerubbabel's critics by completing the temple (vv. 8-9). Once the Jews' enemies witnessed its completion, they would know that Zechariah was His prophet and that the Jews were blessed by God.

## The Day of Small Things

Through Zechariah, the Lord then rebukes those who despise the day of small things:

> *For who has despised the day of small things? For these seven rejoice to see the plumb line in the hand of Zerubbabel. They are the eyes of the Lord, which scan to and fro throughout the whole earth* (v. 10).

Who is the Lord speaking of, as those who despised the day of small things? It may refer to the older generation of Jews who belittled the new temple as being insignificant, or perhaps to Jewish opponents in general. However, given the previous verses, it seems more likely that God is speaking in general to the returning remnant under Zerubbabel's leadership. Fifteen years earlier the work had stopped because the Jews were evaluating things with their own eyes instead of from God's viewpoint. Attaching smallness to those things that God greatly values leads to failure!

However, Jehovah's sovereign purposes will be accomplished despite doubters and opposition, so the Jews were not to think God was not doing something great in their midst. Zechariah refers to a portion of the prophet Hanani's message to King Asa: *"For the eyes of the Lord run to and fro throughout the whole earth, to show Himself strong on behalf of those whose heart is loyal to Him"* (2 Chron. 16:9). Both prophets rebuke those who thought too little of Jehovah's word, wisdom, and His warranting of their devotion. C. A. Coates suggests that verse 10 has a profound application for believers today:

Those who despise "the day of small things" show that they have never seen things as Zechariah saw them. They have no idea of the greatness of what is before the mind of God, and which He would bring before the minds of His people in a remnant time. Indeed, it is clear that they do not see things as the "eyes of Jehovah" see them, for we read, *"Yea, they shall rejoice, even those seven, and shall see the plummet in the hand of Zerubbabel these are the eyes of Jehovah, which run to and fro in the whole earth"* (v. 10). "The eyes of Jehovah" rejoice when they see the plummet in the hand of any builder today. Such a one has the thought of building according to the truth, of having things to correspond with the divine mind. We should bring everything to the test of the plummet. This will lead to the rejection of much that is commendable, and even imposing in the eyes of men, but there will be something which will cause the eyes of Jehovah to rejoice.[160]

When men say "not possible," God often does the impossible that He might be known. Human weakness provides a wonderful opportunity for God to add honor to His own name. Great things occur from God's point of view when small people faithfully do seemingly small things for God. Whether it is a boy taking down a giant with a stone and sling or a lad's lunch multiplied to feed thousands of hungry people, God specializes in using what is weak and unfitting to do the incredible.

The Lord Jesus reminded Paul of this truth after he had prayed three times to have the thorn in his flesh removed: *"My grace is sufficient for you, for My strength is made perfect in weakness."* Paul's response is praiseworthy, *"Therefore most gladly I will rather boast in my infirmities, that the power of Christ may rest upon me"* (2 Cor. 12:9). When little men think God small, an infinite God goes big! Paul would gladly remain weak so that the power of Christ would be more obvious in him. In this sense, the day of small things is but the beginning of greater things where God is concerned.

Indeed, the Jews returning from Babylon were weak and greatly outnumbered – how could they possibly accomplish anything for God? However, Ezra informs us that, after reading Darius' decision to uphold Cyrus' decree, all the opponents of the temple building effort *"diligently did according to what King Darius had sent"* (Ezra 6:13). The temple was then completed swiftly and it became an enduring rebuke to those who *"despised the day of small things."* Let us be careful not to ascribe smallness to what God deems important, nor to think God's greatness can somehow be limited by our smallness – *the eyes of the Lord* see things differently than we do!

## Enablement and Rejoicing

Besides enabling the completion of the work, God's Spirit would also infuse the Jews with joy. Zechariah predicted that there would be much rejoicing in Israel when the temple was dedicated to the Lord. Ezra records the festive celebration that followed a few years later:

*And they kept the Feast of Unleavened Bread seven days with joy; for
the Lord made them joyful, and turned the heart of the king of Assyria
toward them, to strengthen their hands in the work of the house of
God, the God of Israel* (Ezra 6:22).

Though the opposition had momentarily caused the Jews to stop
building the temple, God would divinely empower Jeshua and
Zerubbabel, who started the project, to also complete the task (vv. 11-
14). Zechariah mentions Zerubbabel specifically as holding the
plumbline in his hand (v. 10) – he would lead the building effort.

The final verse alludes to the two offices of king (pictured in
Zerubbabel) and priest (typified by Jeshua), which Messiah will hold in
a future day when He rules all nations: *"These are the two anointed
ones, who stand beside the Lord of the whole earth"* (v. 14). No
opposition could foil God's plan for building His temple, including the
one in which Messiah will be worshiped during the Kingdom Age.
Likewise, no power exists that can hinder the Lord Jesus Christ from
ruling over His inheritance.

We saw in the last chapter that Satan was directly opposing
Jeshua's efforts, but the Lord enabled His work to continue by
cleansing His priest and rebuking Satan: *"The Lord rebuke you, Satan!
The Lord who has chosen Jerusalem rebuke you! Is this not a brand
plucked from the fire?"* (3:2). When it is the Lord who opens a door of
ministry, the enemy cannot prevail: *"I have set before you an open
door, and no man can shut it; for you have a little strength"* (Rev. 3:8).
Ministry empowered by the Holy Spirit will bring glory to God and
will accomplish the purposes of God. Jeshua and Zerubbabel, having
neither personal ambition nor secret agendas, were empowered by the
Holy Spirit to inspire the people to rebuild the temple.

Zerubbabel and Jeshua were God's visible holy implements for
accomplishing the task at hand, but they needed to know that they
could do nothing for God without the enabling of the Holy Spirit, and
neither can we. The bowl above the lampstand containing the flowing
olive oil is wonderful picture of the believer in the Church Age being
filled with the Spirit to serve Christ (Eph. 5:18). Speaking to His
disciples the night prior to His crucifixion, the Lord Jesus said of the
Spirit, *"He abides with you, and shall be in you"* (John 14:17). The
Holy Spirit was with them then because the Lord was there, but in a
coming day (i.e., at Pentecost) the Holy Spirit would dwell in them.

Like Zerubbabel and Jeshua, if we want God to accomplish incredible feats through us, we must be determined to be clean and available vessels. Such servants will be filled by the Holy Spirit to accomplish God's sovereign purposes.

Paul told Timothy that when believers make the choice to flee ungodliness, they become vessels of honor available for God's sovereign use (2 Tim. 2:20). According to God's foreknowledge of both our failures and our obedience, He has preordained us to specific works to accomplish (Eph. 2:10). This is why Peter exhorts Christians to *"make your election sure,"* and Paul instructs us to *"walk in the works that God has foreordained."* We must truly lose our life to gain the vitality God desires for our spiritual life in Him (Luke 9:24). It is only by the empowerment of the Holy Spirit that our testimony can shine forth Christ! What the Holy Spirit accomplishes in us pleases God and results in joy; all else is born of corruption, for it is tainted by carnal motives and pride.

## Meditation

Until self-effacing men return again to spiritual leadership, we may expect a progressive deterioration in the quality of popular Christianity year after year till we reach the point where the grieved Holy Spirit withdraws – like the Shekinah from the Temple.

— A. W. Tozer

A holy life will produce the deepest impression. Lighthouses blow no horns; they only shine.

— D. L. Moody

# A Flying Scroll and a Soaring Basket
Zechariah 5

The prophet records two more visions in this chapter. First, he saw a flying scroll written on both sides, and then a woman sealed in a basket that was being carried back to Babylon by two winged-women.

## The Sixth Vision – The Flying Scroll

As the prophet turns away from the scene of the two olive trees and the gold lampstand, he sees a flying scroll (v. 1). The interpreting angel asks Zechariah to describe what he sees. He says: *"I see a flying scroll. Its length is twenty cubits and its width ten cubits"* (v. 2). The angel then explains the meaning of the vision:

> *This is the curse that goes out over the face of the whole earth: "Every thief shall be expelled," according to this side of the scroll; and, "Every perjurer shall be expelled," according to that side of it* (v. 3).

The flying scroll that Zechariah saw was 30 feet by 15 feet and was not rolled up. It was written on both sides so it could be easily read. H. A. Ironside explains that Zechariah's scroll represents the two stones on which the Ten Commandments were written, also on both sides (Ex. 32:15):

> Closely observing, he saw that it was written on both sides with curses and judgments. On the one side was God's word against those who wronged their neighbor, in accordance with the second table of the law (first mentioned, for man can best appreciate the wickedness of sin against his fellow); on the other side, the doom pronounced on those guilty of impiety, according to the first table. That law, in itself "holy, and just, and good," becomes their condemnation, for *"as many as are of the works of the law are under the curse: for it is written, Cursed is every one that continues not in all things which are*

*written in the book of the law to do them"* (Gal. 3:10). The Jew makes his boast in that law; yet it speaks only for his condemnation.[161]

Hence, there was no secret about what God expected of His covenant people – He had clearly expressed and recorded His Law for them to obey. The scroll was the same size as the holy place of the tabernacle itself and later, the portico of Solomon's temple. The holy place of the tabernacle, which a priest was permitted to enter twice daily, was as near to God's presence as man could venture on a regular basis. Hence, these dimensions are intentional and convey the idea of God's righteous presence among His people.

Furthermore, we are told that the One who pronounces the curse will also execute the punishment of those violating His Law:

*"I will send out the curse," says the Lord of hosts; "it shall enter the house of the thief and the house of the one who swears falsely by My name. It shall remain in the midst of his house and consume it, with its timber and stones"* (v. 4).

A thief and a perjurer may be able to deceive men and escape civil justice, but how does anyone escape the eye of an all-knowing, all-seeing, all-present God? Through the prophet Jeremiah, God reminds His wayward people that they cannot hide from His scrutiny: *"'Can anyone hide himself in secret places, so I shall not see him?' says the Lord; 'Do I not fill heaven and earth?' says the Lord"* (Jer. 23:24). Edward Dennett explains Zechariah's curse upon those thinking they could escape divine justice:

Thus in the cases before us the thief and the perjurer might flatter themselves that their iniquity was unknown, that they had succeeded in covering up from it all human eyes; and they might even be mixing with their neighbors without a known stain on their character. They might have gone further and said, *"The Lord shall not see, neither shall the God of Jacob regard it."* But *"He that planted the ear, shall He not hear? He that formed the eye, shall He not see?"* (Ps. 94:7, 9). Sooner or later all such are here warned that their false security will surely be disturbed, and that God's swift curse will enter their houses for their destruction. It does not follow, we apprehend, that the judgment here spoken of will of necessity be public or sudden. The language is peculiar – the curse enters, remains in their houses, and the houses are consumed.[162]

The main point of the vision is that the Law (as represented in the Scroll) decrees what God expects of His people and that He will punish with curses those who ignore it (v. 4). Lying is a sin against man and false swearing against God. Indeed, these behaviors will be prevalent during the Tribulation Period, just before Christ returns to judge the wicked and establish His Kingdom.

Swearing involves tying God's name to our statements in an attempt to validate what we say – to heighten the credibility of our words. The believer should not engage in such practices, for to do so would certainly bring low the name of God. Listen to James' warning for this sin: *"But above all things, my brethren, swear not, neither by heaven, neither by the earth, neither by any other oath: but let your yea be yea; and your nay, nay; lest ye fall into condemnation"* (Jas. 5:12). Demeaning the name of the Lord by swearing falsely is a terrible thing. As we are forgetful creatures and are rarely perfect in our speech, it behooves us to refrain from swearing oaths which we will most assuredly fall short of keeping. Certainly, the rash vows of Jephthah (Judg. 11:29-40) and Herod (Acts 12:20-23) serve as historical examples of the heavy price to be paid when one foolishly swears to God to do something.

An individual may be put into a position, such as in a court of law, where they are placed under oath. These situations are rare, but are sometimes are unavoidable. Perjury is a form of blasphemy, so if you are put "under oath," be diligent not to defame the Lord's name. *"And you shall not swear by My name falsely, nor shall you profane the name of your God: I am the Lord"* (Lev. 19:12). Swearing falsely has its consequences, for God does not forget (v. 4).

The believer should always do his or her best to convey meaningful and accurate speech and to refrain from idle talk. *"Let no corrupt word proceed out of your mouth, but what is good for necessary edification, that it may impart grace to the hearers"* (Eph. 4:29). Solomon wisely concluded regarding our speech, *"Do not be rash with your mouth, and let not your heart utter anything hastily before God. For God is in heaven, and you on earth; therefore let your words be few"* (Eccl. 5:2). May all our profane speech be replaced with praise!

A man's life is always more forcible than his speech. When men take stock of him, they reckon his deeds as dollars and his words as pennies. If his life and doctrine disagree, the mass of onlookers accept his practice and reject his preaching.

— Charles Spurgeon

## The Seventh Vision – The Woman in the Basket

Directly after the scroll vision, apparently while Zechariah is still looking upward, the angel calls his attention to a basket flying through the air (vv. 5-6). The angel then presented Zechariah with more information concerning the basket:

> *"This is their resemblance throughout the earth: Here is a lead disc lifted up, and this is a woman sitting inside the basket;" then he said, "This is Wickedness!" And he thrust her down into the basket, and threw the lead cover over its mouth. Then I raised my eyes and looked, and there were two women, coming with the wind in their wings; for they had wings like the wings of a stork, and they lifted up the basket between earth and heaven* (vv. 6-9).

In this vision, an ephah (a dry measure used in common trade) and a woman (symbolizing the influences of systemized idolatry) are combined to illustrate the reason for Israel's captivity: prosperous business rooted in paganism. The woman representing this wickedness is being restrained within the basket by a heavy lid and is being carried back to Babylon by two winged-women. The ephah, a basket holding about six gallons (similar to a bushel today), was enlarged in the vision to encompass the woman. Interestingly, both the scroll and the basket in this chapter are exaggerated to accommodate God's intended message.

At the time of God's chastening, Israel was wicked and thoroughly tainted by heathen practices. In God's original plan, woman was created to be Adam's helper and companion; however, she led Adam to disobey God in Eden. Likewise, as seen throughout Israel's history, foreign women often enticed Jewish men to depart from the Lord and to embrace false gods (e.g. Num. 25:6-8). So although women are no more inherently wicked than men, a woman is used to picture the influence of evil in this vision. For this reason, elsewhere we see systems of evil being assigned to expressions such as *"the daughter of Zion"* and *"the daughter of Babylon"* (2:7; Jer. 6:2).

The Lord Jesus employs a similar imagery in the fourth of His seven kingdom parables recorded in Matthew 13: A woman introduced leaven into good meal to corrupt the food of God's people (Matt. 13:33). However, God is quite capable of limiting the influence of wickedness among His people as shown by the heavy lead cover over the basket.

In keeping with the feminine type, the two winged-women may refer to demonic forces who desire to protect paganism and maintain its center of worship in Babylon. It is noted that when good angels appear in human form in Scripture, they are always masculine in appearance. Thus, it does not seem likely that these flying-women represented holy angels, but rather demonic forces, writes E. B. Pusey.

> It may be that there may be no symbol herein, but that he names women because it was a woman who was so carried; yet their wings were the wings of an unclean bird, strong, powerful, borne by a force not their own; with their will, since they flew; beyond their will, since the wind was in their wings; rapidly, inexorably, irresistibly, they flew and bore the Ephah between heaven and earth. No earthly power could reach or rescue it. God would not. It may be that evil spirits are symbolized, as being like to this personified human wickedness.[163]

Regardless of who or what these flying women represent, God was ensuring that pagan worship in Israel was returning to its Babylonian origin (Gen. 10). The entire system of idolatrous evil was to be deported back to its own base, which meant God had to lead His people to Babylon as captives. H. A. Ironside suggests that the basket does not picture corrupt business practices per se, but rather the *full measure* of justice needed to correct the idolatrous Jewish nation:

> The basket is the recognized symbol of measurement, telling us that God shall weigh and measure Judah's sin, and the sin of the whole house of Israel, with unerring accuracy. When their iniquity has come to the full, in wondrous grace He will separate the wickedness from the preserved remnant, dealing with it in connection with the place of its origin, the land of Shinar.[164]

In Babylon, a Jewish remnant would be refined, and when Jehovah called them back home, after seventy years of exile, they would leave their idols in Babylon forever. In short, the meaning of the vision is that paganism originated in Babylon and God was removing it from Israel and sending it back to Babylon. This understanding also aligns with Ezekiel's statement (Ezek. 5:9): When the Jews departed from Babylon to return to their homeland, their idols remained in that land from which they originated. Hence, God would not need to punish them for that offense again.

During the Tribulation Period, the vast majority of humanity will embrace false religion and follow the Antichrist in rebellion against God. Babylon, the fountainhead of all anti-God religion, is thus referred to as *"the Mother of Harlots"* by John. He says that on her forehead is written her name: "MYSTERY, BABYLON THE GREAT, THE MOTHER OF HARLOTS AND OF THE ABOMINATIONS OF THE EARTH" (Rev. 17:5). Throughout human history she has oppressed and slaughtered those faithful to God. Figuratively she is *"drunk with the blood of the saints and with the blood of the Martyrs of Jesus"* (Rev. 17:6). This anti-God movement, which Paul refers to as "the mystery of iniquity" (2 Thess. 2:7), will have its climax during the Tribulation Period.

One day the Lord Jesus will return to remove everything that is evil from the earth – Babylon, including its earth-controlling economic system, will be destroyed in an instant (Rev. 18:10)! Then from heaven we will hear these words, *"Rejoice over her, O heaven, and you holy apostles and prophets, for God has avenged you on her!"* (Rev. 18:20). Then all of Israel and the nations will gather at Jerusalem to worship the Lord during the Kingdom Age. Afterwards, the New Jerusalem will hover over a new earth and all the redeemed shall live joyfully with God in the perfection of paradise and divine bliss forever (Rev. 21-22).

This vision shows us that though God does not endorse evil, He does allow its influence to accomplish His sovereign purposes pertaining to His people.

## Meditation

Jerusalem, my happy home,
name ever dear to me,
when shall my labors have an end,
thy joys when shall I see?

When shall these eyes thy heaven-built walls
and pearly gates behold,

thy bulwarks with salvation strong,
and streets of shining gold?

Apostles, martyrs, prophets, there
around my Savior stand;
and all I love in Christ below
will join the glorious band.

O Christ, do thou my soul prepare
for that bright home of love;
that I may see thee and adore,
with all thy saints above.

— F. B. P.

# Four Chariots and a Crown
Zechariah 6

## The Eighth Vision – Two Bronze Mountains and Four Chariots (vv. 1-8)

Zechariah now describes his final nighttime vision. He sees four chariots coming out from between two bronze mountains (v. 1). The two chariots, pulled by the black and white horses, journeyed northward, while the chariot with dappled horses turned southward (vv. 2-6). The remaining chariot was pulled by red horses and was free to patrol in undesignated areas (v. 7).

The use of metaphor in this final vision is extensive, but thankfully God maintains consistent symbolic usage throughout Scripture so we can ascertain the vision's meaning. Bronze is an amalgamation of copper and tin that requires extreme heat to create; it therefore speaks of intense divine judgment (e.g., Rev. 1:15). Mountains in Scripture may refer to literal mountains, or when metaphorically applied may speak of difficulties (as in chapter 3), or kingdoms (v. 1, Dan. 2:44-45; Micah 4:1; Rev. 17:9). The latter is more frequently inferred.

The two mountains in Zechariah's final vision may be two literal mountains standing together, or they may have a metaphoric meaning. God's judgment of Gentile nations is implied by the bronze, but the mountains could represent God's kingdom overall, or perhaps where the Messiah will rule from (i.e., Mounts Zion and Olivet). Since there is a definite article in the Hebrew text (literally, "the two mountains" instead of just "two mountains"), the latter option is more likely. If this assessment is correct, then the final vision takes us back to where we started in the first vision, Jerusalem. The chariots then originated in the Kidron Valley, and represent all God's wrathful actions to punish the nations for wickedness while rescuing and protecting Jerusalem.

As explained in chapter 4, the number four symbolizes earthly order throughout Scripture. The four chariots then speak of God's patrols, or His agencies (i.e., the four Spirits), or His overall control in putting down Gentile rule as He rules over the earth. Specifically, north represents Babylon, and south, Egypt.

The colors of the four horses are similar to those described in Revelation 6, where their meanings can be deduced from the context of the passage: red – war, black – death, white – righteousness and victory, and dappled – pestilence and famine.

The speaker changes from the interpreting angel to the Lord Himself in verse 7-8:

> *"Go, walk to and fro throughout the earth." So they walked to and fro throughout the earth. And He called to me, and spoke to me, saying, "See, those who go toward the north country have given rest to My Spirit in the north country."*

Babylon to the north has always plagued God's people with wickedness and alluring pagan practices. God's heart was refreshed knowing that Babylon would never again negatively influence Israel. In summary, the vision predicts that God will destroy Israel's enemies and rule over the nations from Jerusalem. In chapters 9 through 14, Zechariah will explain the specifics of how God accomplishes this. It suffices here to note that this event will occur at Christ's second advent when He establishes His millennial kingdom on earth.

## Joshua Crowned as High Priest (vv. 9-15)

Zechariah was then commanded by the Lord to collect gold and silver from three Jewish men (Heldai, Tobijah, and Jedaiah) who had returned from exile and were visiting the home of Josiah the son of Zephaniah (vv. 9-10). He was to use the precious metals collected to fashion an elaborate crown for Joshua the High Priest (v. 11). After Zechariah completed this task, he was to place the crown on Joshua's head and to convey the following message:

> *Behold, the Man whose name is the BRANCH! From His place He shall branch out, and He shall build the temple of the Lord; yes, He shall build the temple of the Lord. He shall bear the glory, and shall sit and rule on His throne; so He shall be a priest on His throne, and the counsel of peace shall be between them both* (vv. 12-13).

After delivering this message, the prophet was to remove the crown from the priest's head and place it in the temple for safekeeping. This mysterious activity no doubt resulted in many questions for the people. For example, Why was Joshua, the priest, crowned and not Zerubbabel, who was Israel's governor? The answer to this question is that Zerubbabel was from the tribe of Judah and a descendant of David, and the next king to be crowned with those credentials would be the Messiah. If Zerubbabel had been crowned, some might have thought that he was the Messiah, but if one from the tribe of Levi was crowned, then there would be no confusion.

Joshua was briefly crowned and then the crown was removed and placed in the temple as a memorial to the fact that Messiah and His kingdom were coming (v. 14). The crown in the temple would then serve a continual warning to the Jews to remain obedient if they wanted God's future blessing (v. 15).

Hence, this vision confirms that, in a coming day, Christ, the One who earlier *from His place branched out,* will be the final Priest and King to rule over Israel from Jerusalem. During the Kingdom Age, Christ *"shall build the temple of the Lord ... and sit and rule on His throne"* (v. 13). F. B. Hole explains that the counsel of peace established by the coming Messiah will perfectly and cooperatively establish both priestly and kingly offices over Israel:

> When at last in Zion the kingly crown rests upon His head, He will not relinquish His priestly service, but "be a Priest upon His throne." The two things, which so often among men have been in opposition, will be united harmoniously in Him. How often have kingly authority and priestly grace clashed amongst sinful men? They will not do so when this prophecy is fulfilled; for, "the counsel of peace shall be between them both."[165]

This same typological picture was first presented in Genesis 14, where Mechizedek, the honorable priest and king of Jerusalem, whose birth and death are not recorded, represented the coming Messiah of endless days. C. A. Coates explains what Zechariah implied by the prediction, *"from His place He shall branch out"* in verse 10:

> The word, *"he shall grow up from his own place"* [KJV], shows how perfectly He accepted everything that was appointed for Him by the will of God, and how there was the development in Him from infancy to manhood of an obedience which was always perfect, but disclosed itself more and more fully at every step. That wondrous life is,

indeed, an eternal study for the hearts of all the redeemed. I do not think it is too much to say that we may learn how He will fill every place of glory by seeing how He filled His own place in lowly incarnation.[166]

The reason that Christ's offices of Priest and King will be entirely unified during the Millennial Kingdom is because, the Lord Jesus – the Man who is God's Branch – first established a covenant of peace between holy Jehovah and condemned sinners. H. A. Ironside writes:

> This new covenant will rest, not on an agreement entered into by man and God, but it will be established forever on the ground of "the counsel of peace" made between Jehovah of hosts and the Man whose name is "The Branch." He, the Man of God's purpose, settled every question as to sin when He died upon the tree; and now, *"having made peace through the blood of His cross,"* He is the agent through whom the reconciliation of all things in heaven and earth will be effected (Col. 1:20).[167]

There is a day coming in which *"the man whose name is the Branch,"* the Lord Jesus, who sealed the New Covenant of peace with His own blood, will reign from His temple in Jerusalem over all the earth. As mentioned in chapter 3, the branch in this chapter parallels Luke's gospel presentation of the holy humanity of Christ. In this chapter we see that the selfless, sinless Branch is destined to be exalted among all nations and peoples on the earth. Praise the Lord!

## Meditation

Our Lord is now rejected,
And by the world disowned,
By the many still neglected,
And by the few enthroned,
But soon He'll come in glory,
The hour is drawing nigh,
For the crowning day is coming by and by.

Let all that look for, hasten
The coming joyful day,
By earnest consecration,
To walk the narrow way,

By gathering in the lost ones,
For whom our Lord did die,
For the crowning day that's coming by and by.

— Daniel Whittle

# Vain Fasting
Zechariah 7

In this chapter, we pass from the realm of cryptic apocalyptic visions into direct and discernable prophetic statements. A delegation of Jews from Bethel visited the temple (which was still under construction) on the fourth day of the ninth month in the fourth year of Darius (v. 1). Their arrival would be about twenty-two months after Zechariah's eightfold night vision was received. The Bethel delegation inquired of the priests and prophets as to whether they should continue their mournful fast in the fifth month as they had done for years (vv. 2-3). Their question resulted in four separate messages by Zechariah as recorded in chapters 7 and 8.

## The First Message (vv. 4-7)

Although at this time they asked about only one specific fast we later learn that for over seventy years the Jews had been observing four different self-initiated fasts (8:18). Since the Babylonian exile was over, the visiting Bethelites were wondering if they should continue recognizing the fasts associated with their captivity.

On the tenth month they mourned the siege of Jerusalem (2 Kgs. 25:1).
On the fourth month they commemorated the fall of Jerusalem (2 Kgs. 25:3).
On the fifth month they remembered Jerusalem's destruction (2 Kgs. 25:8-10).
On the seventh month they mourned the murder of godly Gedaliah (2 Kgs. 25:25).

The Lord answered the men from Bethel through his prophet:

*Then came the word of the Lord of hosts unto me, saying, Speak unto all the people of the land, and to the priests, saying, When ye fasted*

410

*and mourned in the fifth and seventh month, even those seventy years, did ye at all fast unto Me, even to Me? And when ye did eat, and when ye did drink, did not ye eat for yourselves, and drink for yourselves? Should ye not hear the words which the Lord hath cried by the former prophets.... Execute true judgment, and show mercy and compassions every man to his brother* (vv. 4-9).

God bluntly informed the Jews that their self-concocted feasts were **their** feasts, not His; they were fasting and celebrating unto themselves. This meant that their motive and attitudes for what they were doing were flawed. Edward Dennett suggests that Zechariah's response poses a sound principle for those in the Church Age to consider also:

Instead of wondering whether they had not mourned sufficiently over their national disasters, significant of Jehovah's anger against His people, they should have gone back and enquired into the causes of their sorrows, and they would then have learned that their rebellion against God had procured for them their adversities; and, furthermore, they should have examined themselves as to whether in their fastings they had judged and humbled themselves before God, and whether they were now accepting for themselves the admonitions, the warnings, and the directions of His word. And surely, there is a loud voice in all this instruction for the people of God at the present moment. In our sorrows, our weaknesses, and our chastisements under the Lord's hand, are we also not too often content with meetings for confession and humiliation, while we forget to enquire into the causes of our failures, and to ascertain what departures from the word of God may have brought us into our low condition? Let us be warned by the case before us, and at the same time learn that, however sincerely even we may humble ourselves before God on account of past sins, there can be no restoration of blessing until we have gone down to the roots of our failure, and tested all by the word of God. The slightest departure from God's order, if known and allowed, is sufficient to grieve the Spirit of God, and to hinder blessing.[168]

Rather than self-imposed fasts, the Jews in Zechariah's day should have been concerned about honoring the Lord through obedience to His revealed Word. God was not in their fasts, because they were founded in the traditions of men. As the prophets had previously warned, the

Lord desired true spiritual revival in His people, not their humanized rituals and check-the-box religion.

## The Second Message (vv. 8-14)

In the second message, Zechariah reminds his countrymen why severe judgment had fallen on the Jewish nation (v. 8). God expected His people to practice justice, mercy, and compassion, but instead they abused the defenseless, the fatherless, and the poor (vv. 9-10). Their selfish and cruel behavior proved the futility of their religiosity.

The forefathers of those speaking to Zechariah had stony hearts that did not beat for God; hence, they were stubbornly rebellious against His word (vv. 11-12). Because they would not listen to His word or to the warnings of His prophets, God in turn did not heed their prayers (v. 13). The only solution to regain His people's proper attention and reverence was for the Lord to respond severely:

> *I scattered them with a whirlwind among all the nations which they had not known. Thus the land became desolate after them, so that no one passed through or returned; for they made the pleasant land desolate* (v. 14).

God would use the Babylonians to invade Israel, to destroy Jerusalem, to lay waste to the land, and to exile His people. God's solution purged the Jews of their idolatry and He was now starting over with them and in the land of their inheritance.

## Avoid Vain Fasting

The spiritual problem addressed by Zechariah in chapters 7 and 8 was also addressed by Isaiah two centuries earlier: God's covenant people were engaged in religiosity in which He had no part (Isa. 58:2-5). They were engaged in mindless religious sacrifices, feasts, and vows, as an outward means to somehow leverage God to bless them. The Jews in Isaiah's day even wondered if God was noticing how much they were fasting, and afflicting their souls through self-abasing religious activities. But it was obvious that their fasting was not motivated by genuine contrition because they showed no concern for the welfare of others. They were striving with each other, employers were exploiting their employees, and many were seeking their own pleasure instead of supplying the needs of others. Because their motives for their humble religious expressions were corrupt, their prayers would not be heard and their worship would be rejected. They did not yearn to know God or to obey Him; hence there was no inward reality of faith in what they were doing – God was unimpressed.

This sorrowful affliction infests much of the Church today – religious people, ignorant of who God is and what He says, are trying to impress Him through good deeds, instead of exhibiting a devotion settled in truth. Paul describes these as *"having a form of godliness but denying its power."* He then exhorts true believers, *"from such people turn away"* (2 Tim. 3:5). Believers should not be rubbing religious shoulders with those who are doing what God detests.

Believers will not value what we do not understand, nor will we sacrifice for what we do not appreciate. The entire focus of discipleship is summed up in "being," not "doing." The Lord Jesus did not say to His followers, "you cannot *become* My disciples…;" He stressed "you cannot *be* My disciples …." Discipleship is a lifelong pursuit of Christ; it is not something you suddenly arrive at one morning. A true disciple of Christ is compelled to learn of Christ (Matt. 11:29) and to be like Christ (Matt. 10:25). Before we can contemplate honoring the Lord, we must first know Him and what He desires of us.

Why did the Jews in Isaiah's time and Zechariah's time think that fasting would somehow prompt God's favor, when He had required them to corporately fast only one day per year? The Law did not require the Jews to *"afflict their souls,"* except on the Day of Atonement (Lev. 16:31). Because of this unique distinction, the Jews in New Testament times commonly referred to the Day of Atonement as *"the fast"* (Acts 27:9), and sometimes simply as "that Day" or "the Day" (Lev. 16:30). Because of its significance, it would be a day of rest (as a Sabbath day), a day of fasting and of serious reflection and repentance before the Lord.

As *"afflicting your souls"* (Lev. 23:27) is a vague term, the rabbinical writings set forth how the Jews were to observe the Day of Atonement. These call for a twenty-five-hour fast (from food and fluids), and a cessation of work, bathing, and marital relationships. The Day of Atonement was to be a day devoted to prayer and confession and there was no other day like it on the Jewish calendar.

Clearly, "the afflicting of the soul" in Isaiah's day (Isa. 58:5) was just religious fluff, void of the inner reflection and repentance prompted by "the Day of Atonement." God's commanded fast was to cause His people to pause and consider whether or not they were obeying His Law. So the Lord pointed out the futility of their present fasting. H. A. Ironside writes:

> Israel fasted "for strife and debate," but in His fasts God called on the Jews to recognize the importance of self-judgment. The fasts gave them opportunity to come before Him, to meditate on His dealings with them, to meditate on their own failures and sins, to confess them, and then to demonstrate the compassion of God by giving practical assistance to those who were needy. In other words, what God had in mind was not simply that they should deny themselves a little food, but that they should be constantly living lives of self-denial, dividing what God gave them with others, and sharing with the poor.[169]

The Jews in Isaiah's day and Zechariah's day are not the only ones adopting wrong attitudes concerning fasting. Believers in the Church Age would do well to heed his rebuke also. The Lord told His disciples:

> *When you fast, do not be like the hypocrites, with a sad countenance. For they disfigure their faces that they may appear to men to be fasting. Assuredly, I say to you, they have their reward. But you, when you fast, anoint your head and wash your face, so that you do not appear to men to be fasting, but to your Father who is in the secret place; and your Father who sees in secret will reward you openly* (Matt. 6:16-18).

First, notice that the Lord said, *"when you fast,"* to affirm that fasting should be a normal part of the believer's life. Second, fasting is not simply debasing one's self and appearing sad for sadistic reasons, but rather is a time for intense inner reflection and focused listening. Fasting for public display is contrary to its purpose and therefore negates its benefit. Hunger pangs remind us of our dependence on the Lord and lengthy times of introspection result in mental clarity to see things as God does. Third, Isaiah reminds us that heartfelt affliction of the soul would result in just and good conduct: the oppressed would be freed, those who were hungry would be fed, and the poor would be clothed (Isa. 58:6-7). The prophet firsts asks, *"Is your fasting what God has chosen?"* And then Isaiah indicates the type of fasting that would be acceptable to God – that which emphasizes moral transformation rather than ceremonial fanfare.

The Lord Jesus declared a similar message to hypocritical and ceremonial Israel during His first advent when He quoted Hosea 6:6 (on two different occasions): *"I desired mercy and not sacrifice"* (Matt. 9:13, 12:7). Fasting should result in our greater awareness of God's will and in our moral transformation. If our fasting does not lead to changed attitudes and behavior, then it did not achieve God's intended outcome.

Lastly, let us remember that vain, especially non-commanded, religious activities do not prompt God's blessing, but humble acts of righteousness do because such actions reflect His glory to others (Isa. 58:8). The Lord wanted the Jews to be a hospitable people, especially to their destitute brethren:

> *Execute true justice; show mercy and compassion everyone to his brother. Do not oppress the widow or the fatherless, the alien or the poor. Let none of you plan evil in his heart against his brother* (vv. 9-10).

Likewise, Moses exhorted the Hebrew nation: *"You shall not oppress one another, but you shall fear your God; for I am the Lord your God"* (Lev. 25:17). Besides our care for fellow believers in need, Solomon reminds us to attend to the necessities of the poor in general: *"He who has pity on the poor lends to the Lord, and He will pay back what he has given"* (Prov. 19:17). *"He who gives to the poor will not lack, but he who hides his eyes will have many curses"* (Prov. 28:27). The Lord rewards those who attend to the needy, not those who fast but ignore the needy while seeking pleasure.

In summary, God promised to heal His people, bless their fertility, answer their prayers, and to guide and satisfy them if they ceased from neglecting and speaking evil of each other (Isa. 58:9-12). This reminds us that saints cannot gather for any profitable spiritual exercise (in any dispensation) unless they first are walking with the Lord in righteousness and faithfulness in their daily lives. On this point Matthew Henry writes:

> God's judgements upon Israel of old for their sins were written to warn Christians. The duties required are not keeping fasts and offering sacrifices, but doing justly and loving mercy, which tend to the public welfare and peace. The law of God lays restraint upon the heart. But they filled their minds with prejudices against the word of

God. Nothing is harder than the heart of a presumptuous sinner. See the fatal consequences of this to their fathers. Great sins against the Lord of hosts bring great wrath from His power, which cannot be resisted. Sin, if regarded in the heart, will certainly spoil the success of prayer. The Lord always hears the cry of the broken-hearted penitent; yet all who die impenitent and unbelieving will find no remedy or refuge from miseries which while here they despised and defied, but which they then will not be able to bear.[170]

Indeed, the Church would be wise to consider the Lord's rebuke of Israel's futile practices. As previously mentioned, God is not impressed by religious ritual, humanized religious tradition, sanctimonious form, and denominational smugness. He desires personal living that conforms to divine truth (Col. 2:20-23). Zechariah's contemporaries were engaged in Judaism, not God-honoring, faith-produced biblical religion.

## Meditation

Prayer is reaching out after the unseen; fasting is letting go of all that is seen and temporal. Fasting helps express, deepen, confirm the resolution that we are ready to sacrifice anything, even ourselves to attain what we seek for the kingdom of God.

— Andrew Murray

# The Jerusalem to Come
Zechariah 8

The two messages of the previous chapter form a call to repentance for the returned Babylonian captives. The Jews were now constructing the temple as God commanded, but there were lingering attitudes that were hindering true revival and receiving God's best. The two messages in this chapter relate to the promise of restoration blessings, which could be received through true spiritual revival then, but would ultimately culminate during the Kingdom Age.

## The Third Message (vv. 1-17)
Five times in this message we read, *"Thus says the Lord."* This message opens with God declaring that He is jealous and zealous for Jerusalem and then His promise to make it a safe and prosperous city in a coming day:

> *"I am zealous for Zion with great zeal; with great fervor I am zealous for her." Thus says the Lord: "I will return to Zion, and dwell in the midst of Jerusalem. Jerusalem shall be called the City of Truth, the Mountain of the Lord of hosts, the Holy Mountain"* (vv. 2-3).

God was zealous for the Jewish nation because of His covenant with her, which established them as His people with special privileges and responsibilities. Ezekiel and Jeremiah tell us that this relationship was much like a marriage covenant (Jer. 3; Ezek. 16). God had a legal right to the affections of His people but they were giving their affections to false gods. From God's perspective, Israel was committing spiritual adultery. He had invoked His legal right to divorce Israel and punish her, but He now sought to restore her to their covenant relationship.

While there has always been a remnant of faithful Jews through the ages (Rom. 9), this restoration will not be fully realized at the national level until the kingdom age. The prophet then describes what Jerusalem

417

will be like when the mountain, the kingdom, of the Lord of Hosts is established. Jerusalem will be fully sanctified among the nations and protected by God. The streets will be safe for senior citizens to walk on and for children to play (vv. 4-5).

Truth and righteousness will prevail everywhere and it will be a marvelous sight for all to observe, even the Lord (v. 6). The Jews will be regathered from the nations and brought back to Israel to be in God's presence (v. 7). God says that *"they shall dwell in the midst of Jerusalem. They shall be My people and I will be their God, in truth and righteousness"* (v. 8). What Jew would not be ecstatic to hear such a prophecy?

In light of this wonderful promise, the Jews were commanded: *"Let your hands be strong"* (v. 9). They were to listen to Haggai and Zechariah and to finish building the temple and not to be rebellious or to suffer as their forefathers did (v. 10). The Lord of Hosts informed the Jews that, because of their delayed obedience, they had suffered lack, but He was now willing to bless them with prosperity for their diligence in building His house (v. 11). Their fields and vineyards would receive abundant rain and be prosperous (v. 12). They would no longer be accursed among the nations but a blessing (v. 13). The Jews would be safe and blessed if they walked with Jehovah. Therefore, the prophet exhorted them again: *"Do not fear, let your hands be strong."*

Then God provided evidence that He would indeed bless them for their obedience (vv. 14-17). Just as His word had declared the punishment on their fathers, which was now past, His word now with the same authority declared a time of their blessing. The main point of this message is that their season of chastening was over and it was time to go on with the Lord who was ready to pour out His blessings on Judah.

## The Fourth Message (vv. 18-23)

In his final message to the Bethel delegation, Zechariah said that the four fasts of mourning that the Jews had instituted to remember the siege, capture and destruction of Jerusalem and the murder of Gedaliah would in the future become feasts of rejoicing (vv. 18-19).

> *The fast of the fourth month, the fast of the fifth, the fast of the seventh, and the fast of the tenth, shall be joy and gladness and*

*cheerful feasts for the house of Judah. Therefore love truth and peace* (v. 19).

This prophecy will not be fully realized until the Kingdom Age, when Jerusalem will become the religious center of the world (vv. 20-23). Every nation will come there to worship and the Jews will be greatly esteemed among the nations. The reign of truth was coming, which meant peace for Israel. F. B. Hole notes that "truth precedes peace, as cause and effect. Error produces strife just as certainly as truth produces peace."[171] Hence, in the remainder of the chapter, we find predictions of the happy state of things after the Ruler of truth establishes lasting peace to Jerusalem.

*"In those days,"* the Lord of Hosts says, *"ten men from every language of the nations shall grasp the sleeve of a Jewish man, saying, 'Let us go with you, for we have heard that God is with you'"* (v. 23). From this wonderful scene, H. A. Ironside notes the practical benefit to those not experiencing the Lord's presence from those who are:

When the saints of God are enjoying Christ, others are attracted to Him and to them. So, when Israel shall be gathered round Himself, dwelling under His shadow, and happy in His love, there will be a great stirring of heart among the spared of the nations who will not have been destroyed when the stone falls from heaven: *"Many people and strong nations shall come to seek the Lord of hosts in Jerusalem, and to pray before the Lord"* (v. 22).[172]

As the nations are not presently seeking the Lord or esteeming the Jewish people, we can safely declare that the events Zechariah is foretelling have not occurred yet. To this date, the Jews have not received all the land promised to Abraham (Gen. 15:18-21); the throne of David has not been established forever (2 Sam. 7:14-17); the Gentiles have not been subdued (Jer. 30:8; Zech. 14:16-17); and they certainly are not the esteemed people of the Earth (v. 23; Isa. 66:10-18). God is a covenant-keeping God and He will honor all that He says He will do!

God is not finished with the Jewish nation. Israel will be nationally established in prosperity; Jerusalem will be the religious center of the world; Jehovah will be worshipped by the nations; and the Gentiles will greatly esteem the Jewish people. At present, the Jewish nation is locked in spiritual blindness while Christ is building His Church. When the "fullness of the Gentiles" is complete, that is, when the last Gentile soul has been added to the Church and it has been removed from the earth, God will awaken His covenant people of old during the Tribulation Period (Rom. 11:25). This seven-year period is the final week in Daniel's prophecy (Dan. 9:27).

Christ's literal kingdom on earth is promised and is coming, but today it is on the earth in spiritual form only. Those who respond to the gospel message will be citizens of Christ's kingdom to come. During the Kingdom Age, glorified saints and spiritually revitalized Israel will live on the earth with faithful Tribulation survivors in a wonderful utopia in which the prophecies of this chapter will be fulfilled. Until that time, may our hands be strong as we labor for what we know is coming – the kingdom of the Lord Jesus Christ!

## Meditation

Blessed be God that we live in these latter times - the latter times of the reign of darkness and imposture. Great is our privilege, precious our opportunity, to cooperate with the Savior in the blessed work of enlarging and establishing His kingdom throughout the world.

— Adoniram Judson

# Faithfulness in Captivity
## Zechariah 9

The book of Zechariah is the third most quoted in the New Testament with approximately forty citations. Although the books of Psalms and Isaiah are referred to more often in the New Testament, chapter count-wise, Zechariah with fourteen chapters would be the most quoted book. This is mostly because the next six chapters are saturated with Messianic prophecies. Here are some of the more notable ones:

- The King would enter Jerusalem on a previously unridden donkey (9:9).
- Christ would be betrayed for 30 shekels of silver, but these would be returned to the temple to purchase a potter's field (11:12-13).
- Christ would be pierced (12:10).
- The Shepherd would be cut down by One who loved Him and His sheep would scatter (13:6-7).
- Christ will return to the Mount of Olives (14:4).
- Christ will be King and Priest over Israel and will rule the earth during the Kingdom Age (14:9).

The remainder of Zechariah's book describes two divinely received burdens (9:1, 12:1). In chapters 9-11, He speaks of events occurring prior to, and related to, Christ's first advent, and then in chapters 12-14, Christ's second advent and the Kingdom Age, generally speaking. Yet, each section does contain prophecies pertaining to both advents. Much of the revelation in the last six chapters correlates with the content of the eight visions recorded in chapters 1-6.

## The Judgment of Nations

Isaiah, Jeremiah, Ezekiel, and Zephaniah all pronounced judgments on specific nations surrounding Israel. Zechariah pauses briefly in verses 1-8 to do the same for nations north and west of Israel. Specifically, he pronounces judgment on Syria (the land of Hadrach and Damascus; v. 1), Phoenicia (vv. 2-4) and Philistia (vv. 5-7). The prophet's most austere language is reserved for Phoenicia and its port cities of Sidon and Tyre (v. 2). Tyre was Phoenicia's capital, its main hub for commerce but a lightning rod for divine contempt, as uttered by Jewish prophets. When God's wide-sweeping judgment finally fell on these chief cities in the region, all would be in awe of God: *"For the eyes of men and all the tribes of Israel are on the Lord"* (v. 1).

Has this prophecy been fulfilled, or are these judgments still outstanding? While it is generally agreed that most of the prophetic content of verses 1-8 was fulfilled by Alexander the Great in the fourth century B.C., these predicted judgments on Israel's enemies will have their complete fulfillment at Christ's second advent.

Jeremiah had earlier predicted that Phoenicia would be punished for assisting the Philistines in their assault against the Jews (Jer. 47:4). In 585 B.C., a year after Jerusalem fell, Nebuchadnezzar confronted Tyre (Ezek. 26:7-14). After thirteen years of siege, mainland Tyre fell and was abandoned. Most of her inhabitants sought shelter within the island fortress, whose walls went straight down into the sea and were 150 feet high on the landward side. Tyre's island defenses held because the Babylonians could not prevent the city from being resupplied from the sea.

Ezekiel then prophesied that after Tyre was punished by Nebuchadnezzar, other nations would later arrive to destroy it (Ezek. 26:12). One of these nations would be Greece, over two centuries later. Tyre rebelled against Alexander the Great who destroyed the mainland portion of the city and then built a causeway (a land bridge 200 feet wide and a half mile long) to attack the island fortress. The building materials were scavenged from the conquered mainland portion of the city. This fulfilled the first statement of Ezekiel's prophecy: *"break down your walls and destroy your pleasant houses; they will lay your stones, your timber, and your soil in the midst of the water"* (Ezek. 26:12).

Alexander was able to hammer at the walls of the city with floating rams until eventually the southern wall was breached. His forces then entered and captured the city in 332 B.C. This occurred after a seven-month siege of the city. Nearly ten thousand of Tyre's citizens perished in the onslaught (including 2,000 crucified on the beach); another 30,000 were sold into slavery.[173] Alexander then destroyed much of the city – the once famed commercial metropolis was no more. Although the island has been inhabited through the centuries, the ancient island fortress of Tyre was never fully rebuilt, just as Ezekiel predicted (Ezek. 26:14). Historical information indicates that God's Word through all these prophets against Tyre has been fulfilled first by the Babylonian invasion during the sixth century B.C. and then by Alexander the Great in the fourth century B.C.

Though Alexander did decimate Tyre, the complete destruction of that city and what she stands for will occur at Christ's second advent. H. A. Ironside notes the typological fulfillment of Tyre's future destruction:

> Tyre speaks of the world as a great commercial system where men seek to enrich themselves and their families through material pursuits. They revel in every kind of extravagance and forget about God. Such materialism pervades society today as nations reach out for commercial gain and people live on a scale of luxury unknown in previous centuries. But the time is soon coming when all the things on which men have set their hearts will be destroyed and the present world system will pass away. We may see a prediction of that day in the prophecy relating to the doom of Tyre.[174]

Zechariah simply summarizes and confirms what the other prophets have already foretold: Tyre will be completely judged because of her self-exalting pride in her riches and her fortifications.

Similarly, the Philistines would reap God's wrath for their idolatry and pride (vv. 5-7). Judgment of four chief cities of Philistia was decreed by the prophet. All would suffer sorrow, but after the coming invasion, Gaza would lose her king, Ashkelon would not be inhabited, and Ashdod would be cut off and resettled by foreigners. God would put an end to their abominations and murderous ways. Alexander the Great passed by Jerusalem several times, but never put the city to siege; he did, however, conquer Philistia and its chief cities in 332 B.C. This fulfills the twofold prophecy in verse 8: God camped about His house and protected it, while judging the pride and abominations of Philistia.

In summary, Alexander the Great passed through and circled the holy land without conquering it when he overthrew the Persian Empire. Then, Damascus fell, Sidon yielded, Tyre was destroyed, and Gaza perished under Alexander's sword. He chastened Samaria after returning from Egypt, but left Jerusalem alone throughout his fast-paced invasion of the known world.

This outcome wonderfully portrays the Kingdom Age when all of Israel's nemeses will be subdued by Israel's Messiah who rules from Jerusalem. Sitting on the throne of David, He will have God's full authority to rule the world. He will continue to camp about Jerusalem and protect it from any invaders.

## Behold Your King

In chapters 3 and 6, we investigated the four "Branch" declarations in the Old Testament, which emphasize each of the four Gospel themes, that is, the four ways that the Father wanted us to appreciate His Son. Likewise, the Old Testament contains four "behold" commands to convey the same message. One of these is in verse 9:

*Rejoice greatly, O daughter of Zion! Shout, O daughter of Jerusalem!*
***Behold, your King*** *is coming to you; He is just and having salvation, lowly and riding on a donkey, a colt, the foal of a donkey.*

The word "behold" means "to earnestly look upon with regard;" it may convey surprise or wonder. As in the "Branch" expressions, these four "behold" statements are God the Father's invitation to Jews and, indeed, to mankind to gaze upon and admire His dear Son. The other three "beholds" are as follows:

***Behold! My Servant*** *whom I uphold, My Elect One in whom My soul delights! I have put My Spirit upon Him; He will bring forth justice to the Gentiles* (Isa. 42:1).

*Thus says the Lord of hosts, saying: "**Behold, the Man** whose name is the Branch! From His place He shall branch out, and He shall build the temple of the Lord"* (6:12).

*O Zion, you who bring good tidings, get up into the high mountain; O Jerusalem, you who bring good tidings, lift up your voice with* *strength, lift it up, be not afraid; say to the cities of Judah, "**Behold your God!**"* (Isa. 40:9).

These four Messianic titles perfectly align with the four Gospel presentations of Christ:

Behold your King – Gospel of Matthew
Behold My Servant – Gospel of Mark
Behold the Man – Gospel of Luke
Behold your God – Gospel of John

Verse 9 predicts that the Jewish Messiah and king will enter Jerusalem on a colt, the foal of a donkey. Throughout Jewish history, kings typically rode donkeys during times of tranquility, but mounted horses to engage the enemy in war. The Lord Jesus illustrates this symbolism in His own ministry. During His first earthly sojourn He rode the foal of a donkey while declaring His heavenly message of peace (Matt. 21:1-10). However, at His second advent to the earth, He will be riding a white horse as He executes fierce wrath and vengeance against the wicked (Rev. 19:11-16).

Just five days before His crucifixion, the Lord Jesus Christ fulfilled Zechariah's prophecy when He descended the slope of Mount Olivet on a donkey and triumphantly entered Jerusalem, the city of the Great King (Matt. 5:35). Matthew and John specifically quote Zechariah's prophesy to show that it was being fulfilled: *"Tell the daughter of Zion, 'Behold, your King is coming to you, lowly, and sitting on a donkey, a colt, the foal of a donkey'"* (Matt. 21:5). *"Then Jesus, when He had found a young donkey, sat on it; as it is written: 'Fear not, daughter of Zion; behold, your King is coming, sitting on a donkey's colt'"* (John 12:14-15). Mark and Luke also record the event (Mark 11:2-10; Luke 19:35).

The Spirit of God moved both Matthew and John to maintain their unique vantage points of Christ in their quotation of Zechariah. Matthew omits the words *"just"* and *"having salvation"* and John, additionally, the word *"lowly."* Matthew, who presents the Messiah in His kingly authority, could not speak of Christ entering into Jerusalem in righteous justice or bestowing salvation to Israel at this juncture, because the Jewish nation had rejected Him. Matthew does say that He entered Jerusalem as the lowly One, but John omits this expression because his Gospel presents Christ in His magnificent deity. It is for this reason that neither Matthew nor John call upon the daughters of Zion to rejoice and shout at this event, for Israel had refused their divine King. Thus, Matthew says, *"tell the daughter of Zion,"* and John says, *"fear not."* There can be no true rejoicing at Messiah's entrance into Jerusalem until Israel accepts the Lord Jesus Christ as her Deliverer. In chapter 12, Zechariah informs us that Israel will gladly receive Christ as her king at His second advent (12:10).

Indeed, the Lord Jesus was born King of the Jews and in the city of David (Matt. 2:2; Luke 2:4). In response to Pilate's question about Him being the King of the Jews, the Lord Jesus confirmed that He was, but that it was not yet time to establish His kingdom on earth.

> *Jesus answered, "My kingdom is not of this world. If My kingdom were of this world, My servants would fight, so that I should not be delivered to the Jews; but now My kingdom is not from here." Pilate therefore said to Him, "Are You a king then?" Jesus answered, "You say rightly that I am a king. For this cause I was born, and for this cause I have come into the world, that I should bear witness to the truth. Everyone who is of the truth hears My voice"* (John 18:36-37).

As C. E. Hocking explains, it was the Lord's claim to Jewish kingship that motivated the harsh Roman treatment of the Lord Jesus before, during, and after his civil trial.

> Pilate's interrogation, the soldier's mockery, the title-board on His cross, and the mocking of the religious leaders were all prompted because of His link with the royal house of David and the kingly rights associated with this. He is the King of the Jews, Jesus the King of the Jews, The King of Israel, even Christ a King (Matt. 27:11, 29, 37, 42; Luke 23:2).[175]

Christ is a descendant of King David (Matt. 1:1), and thus, the rightful heir to his throne, which God has promised to establish forever (2 Sam. 7:13-16). Though the Lord has already been highly exalted in heaven, He presently sits upon His Father's throne and is waiting to return to establish His earthly kingdom (Rev. 3:21, 11:2-3). However, Paul, pondering the wonderful grace extended to him, the chief of sinners, declares the Lord Jesus Christ now: *"the King eternal, immortal, invisible, to God who alone is wise, be honor and glory forever and ever"* (1 Tim. 1:17). Amen.

While the Lord Jesus does hold the title-deed to His kingdom, He has not exercised His kingship authority as King of kings and Lord of lords. Presently, He sits on His Father's throne in Heaven awaiting the day when He will triumphantly return to earth (Rev. 3:21). After the Church Age is complete and at the end of the Tribulation Period, Christ will return to the earth to destroy the Antichrist and his armies at the battle of Armageddon. Then He will establish His throne in Jerusalem (Isa. 66:11-14; Zech. 14; Rev. 19:11-21). It is at this time that the Tribulation saints, those martyred for not bowing to the Antichrist, will proclaim of the Lord Jesus:

> *They sing the song of Moses, the servant of God, and the song of the Lamb, saying: "Great and marvelous are Your works, Lord God Almighty! Just and true are Your ways, **O King of the saints!** Who shall not fear You, O Lord, and glorify Your name? For You alone are holy. For all nations shall come and worship before You, for Your judgments have been manifested"* (Rev. 15:3-4).

Zechariah says that the returning King will cut off all instruments of war in Ephraim and Judah (v. 10). Before establishing worldwide peace, the Lord will first remove all the false confidences that His people have (e.g., their war-chariots, warhorses, and their bows). Today, Israel is technologically advanced and maintains a formidable military army. However, all these human achievements will come to nothing during the Tribulation Period when demonic foes embattle and overcome much of the Jewish nation. Then, when all seems lost, the Lord will return to Jerusalem to deliver His people. Afterwards, the Lord Jesus will rule the nations with a rod of iron, and in righteousness (Ps. 2:7-9; Rev. 19:15-16).

As Pilate mockingly declared two thousand years ago, Jesus Christ is the King of the Jews; when He returns to the earth, He will fulfill that office. He will be known in all the earth as *"the King of kings"* (Rev. 17:14), and *"the King of the saints"* (Rev. 15:3).

## The Kingdom Age

After identifying the coming King of the Jews who will reign over Israel and protect her from all oppression, the prophet highlights some of the blessings of the Kingdom Age (vv. 10-17). The Messiah will end all warring and will usher in an era of universal peace (v. 10). His appearance will give Jewish captives hope, for He will gather all Jews scattered among the nations back to Israel and restore them as His privileged people (vv. 11-12). The reference to Ephraim (i.e., the Northern Kingdom) in verses 10 and 13 affirms that all twelve tribes of the Jewish nation, not just Judah, will experience restoration. Afterwards, Christ will be seen by all as He attends to Israel as a shepherd cares for his flock.

While verse 13 has a yet future aspect, it was likely partly fulfilled when God empowered the Jews to overcome the Greek Empire during the Maccabean revolt in the second century B.C. (see Daniel 8 and 11 for specifics). Just as God has His ways in a powerful thunderstorm, He would empower Judas Maccabeus and his freedom fighters to overcome Antiochus IV Epiphanes and his Greek army (v. 14). The Jews would be ecstatically grateful to God for their deliverance (v. 15). God had kept His promise to deliver them despite overwhelming Greek forces:

*The Lord their God will save them in that day, as the flock of His people. For they shall be like the jewels of a crown lifted like a banner over His land* (v. 16).

Through His protection, the Jews will realize that they are Jehovah's special people and that He utterly delights in them. Israel will then become beautiful and a striking symbol of God's manifold grace and goodness to the nations (v. 17). Not only does God want the unregenerate to be aware of His holy and awesome presence, but He also wants them to admire the rich trophies that He has fashioned in grace, that is, His saints! The Lord Jesus is not just the King of the Jews; He is the King of all the redeemed. This means that all saints will wonderfully reflect His glory forever.

## Meditation

King of saints, to whom the number
Of Thy starry host is known,
Many a name, by man forgotten,
Lives forever round Thy throne;
Lights, which earth-born mists have darkened,

There are shining full and clear,
Princes in the court of Heaven,
Nameless, unremembered here.

None can tell us; all is written
In the Lamb's great book of life,
All the faith, and prayer, and patience,
All the toiling, and the strife;
There are told Thy hidden treasures;
Number us, O Lord, with them,
When Thou makest up the jewels
Of Thy living diadem.

— John Ellerton

# "I Will Bring Them Back"
Zechariah 10

In the last half of the previous chapter, Zechariah began revealing the accomplishments of the coming Jewish Messiah to usher in the Kingdom Age. First, He will establish peace on the earth (9:10). Second, He will deliver Israel from all her enemies because of God's Covenant (9:11-12, 9:16-17). In this chapter we learn that the Messiah will judge all the false shepherds and prophets that led His people astray (vv. 1-5). He will gather His people from among the nations and will empower them to be victorious over their oppressors (vv. 6-12). All Jews in the Kingdom Age will believe on Jesus Christ and will be indwelt by the Holy Spirit.

## The False Shepherds Destroyed
The prophecy in verses 2-3 is replete with metaphor:

> *For the idols speak delusion; the diviners envision lies, and tell false dreams; they comfort in vain. Therefore the people wend their way like sheep; they are in trouble because there is no shepherd. My anger is kindled against the shepherds, and I will punish the goatherds. For the Lord of hosts will visit His flock, the house of Judah, and will make them as His royal horse in the battle.*

To better understand Zechariah's meaning, it behooves us to first identify individuals and groups of people within the prophecy.

First, **the shepherds** are false prophets and diviners who assumed credit for God's blessings and vainly led the people away from the Lord (v. 2). Godly King Josiah had *"put away those who consulted mediums and spiritists, the household gods and idols, all the abominations that were seen in the land of Judah"* (2 Kgs. 23:24), but they did not stay away! These false shepherds may include foreigners who successfully intruded into the Jewish hierarchy, but most likely they are wayward Jewish leaders, priests, and prophets (Isa. 14:9).

Second, **the goatherds** are false professors (i.e., unrepentant people) who shall be punished because they cursed and persecuted the Jews (v. 3). The shepherds of verse 2, then, are a part of the goatherds in verse 3 – they are the chief goats per se. This is consistent with the Lord's teaching about the Judgment of Nations which occurs directly after the Battle of Armageddon (Matt. 25:31-41). The ungodly goats will be separated from the faithful sheep and then massacred; only the sheep will be permitted to enter Christ's Kingdom.

Third, **the flock** are those Jews revived and restored to Jehovah during the Kingdom age (v. 3; Micah 5:4). Under the Messiah's leadership they will prosper against their enemies and wander no more among the nations.

Fourth, the Messiah is referred to as **the Cornerstone, the Nail**, the **Battle Bow**, and **the Ruler** of all men (v. 4).

Having identified the key individuals of this prophecy, next let us consider its meaning. The prophet begins by stating that it is Jehovah who showers Israel with rain and blessings, not the false prophets (v. 1). The diviners spoke false dreams and lies to deceive God's people and lead them away from the truth and thus from communion with their true Shepherd – Jehovah (v. 2). Therefore, God promised to destroy these deceivers at Christ's second coming. Not only will Christ judge those who followed the Antichrist, but He will enable the purified Jewish remnant to overcome his forces. Empowered by the Holy Spirit and under Christ's leadership, they will be like a mighty warhorse in battle (v. 3).

As previously stated, Christ is identified by four metaphors in verse 4. He is spoken of as the Cornerstone (see Isa. 28:16; 1 Pet. 2:5-8). He was previously a Rock of Stumbling to the Jews, but then became the Cornerstone for the Church – His spiritual temple of redeemed souls. The Cornerstone aligns the construction of a building and Christ's moral excellence is a pattern for all in His Temple to follow. Isaiah says that it is God alone who sets the cornerstone and foundation of salvation and all who trust in Him will not be ashamed of doing so: *"Behold, I lay in Zion a stone for a foundation, a tried stone, a precious cornerstone, a sure foundation; whoever believes will not act hastily"* (Isa. 28:16). The Cornerstone is tried, precious, and sure and therefore typifies Christ's faithfulness, proven impeccability, and fruitful ministry.

Christ is the Nail (see Isa. 22:23). The nail is an emblem of fixedness and declares Christ unmovable and fine character and disposition in accomplishing God's will (Isa. 22:23). When Messiah does return, His glorious throne shall be set in place forever.

Christ is also the Battle Bow (see Ps. 45:5). When the Lord comes to rule and reign, His enemies will be wiped out by His sharp arrows of judgment. He is God's Champion and mighty Conqueror.

Lastly, Zechariah describes Christ as the Ruler of all men. He will cause all who opposed and oppressed His people to be shamed (v. 5)!

## Israel Regathered

In Zechariah's day, many Jews once exiled in Babylon had already returned to their homeland. However, the majority of his countrymen were still spread throughout the known world at that time. The Northern Kingdom of Israel had been dispersed into slavery by the Assyrians two centuries earlier. This would all change when the Messiah returned; He would gather those from Israel and Judah back to the land promised to their patriarch Abraham (vv. 6-7; Gen. 15:18-21):

> *I will strengthen the house of Judah, and I will save the house of Joseph. I will bring them back, because I have mercy on them. They shall be as though I had not cast them aside; for I am the Lord their God, and I will hear them* (v. 6).

We learn in Ezekiel 39:28-29 that at His second advent, the Lord will bring every Jew on the planet back to the land of Israel. The process of bringing Jews back to Zion started in the early twentieth century. It will be completed when all Jews are back in the land directly after the Tribulation Period. Not just Judah, but a remnant of the entire nation will receive the Holy Spirit at Christ's second advent to complete their spiritual transformation (vv. 28-29). The following chart shows the percentage of Jews worldwide that have returned to the land of Israel in recent years. All information is derived from the *Israeli Central Bureau of Statistics*[176]:

| Year | Percent of Jews Worldwide Back in Israel |
|------|------------------------------------------|
| 1882 | 0 |
| 1900 | 1 |
| 1925 | 1 |
| 1939 | 3 |
| 1948 | 6 |
| 1955 | 13 |
| 1970 | 20 |
| 1980 | 25 |
| 1990 | 30 |
| 2000 | 37 |
| 2010 | 42 |
| 2014 | 44 |

The core Jewish population reached its peak just before WW2 at about 17 million, but was reduced to 11 million after Hitler's attempts to exterminate them. At the beginning of 2016, the core Jewish population was projected to be about 14.2 million worldwide, with 40 percent residing in the United States and 6,335,000 Jews (or about 44.6% of the world population) living in Israel. It is noted that Israel has the highest birth rate (an average of three children per woman) of any developed country in the world.

The land of Palestine once again became a Jewish state in May 1948, a situation that was immediately and violently challenged by surrounding Arab countries. The land belonging to the Jewish state was further expanded after their victory in the Six-Day War of 1967. Zechariah's prophecy predicting a Jewish regathering to the land of Israel agrees with other Old Testament prophets (Isa. 11:12; Jer. 3:18-20; Ezek. 39:28-29). Clearly, these prophecies have not been fulfilled to date. The houses of Judah and Israel have not yet fully returned to the land, nor have they come together to worship the Messiah.     But Bible prophecy is in motion; Israel has become a nation again, though God's covenant people have not yet been fully regathered to the land promised them in Scripture.

God will not forget His people or His covenant with them; rather, He will have compassion on them (v. 7). When it is time to regather all Jews to Israel, He will whistle like a shepherd signaling his flock (v. 8). Then the Jews will be strengthened and blessed and they will rejoice in the Lord with great gladness. Through divine chastening God had sown His people in faraway lands such as Assyria and Egypt (v. 9). However, He promised to bring them all home in the Kingdom Age; even the far borders of Gilead and Lebanon would be within Israel's border during the Kingdom Age (v. 10).

Clearly, both Joseph and Judah will be regathered to the land of Israel and Christ will reign over the twelve tribes of the Jewish nation again. Sadly, many Bible interpreters, ignorant of dispensational truth, have spiritualized the pure meaning of Zechariah's prophecies and concluded them already fulfilled. However, as William Kelly observes, God will make good use of Judah and Ephraim in the Day of the Lord:

> He will fight not merely *for* them, but in and by them. It is a great mistake to suppose that all will be accomplished by Jehovah single-handed. There is a judgment which He will execute on His appearing from heaven, in which the Jews can have no part whatever, namely, the destruction of the beast and the false prophet, with the flower of the rank and power of the revived Roman Empire. Thus the Western powers will be completely crushed by the Lord coming in judgment from heaven.[177]

When God moves to regather His people, no nation or circumstance will hinder His efforts. Just as He opened the Red Sea to bring the Israelites from Egypt to Canaan, He will overcome every obstacle to have all of His covenant people with Him in Israel (v. 11). The prophecy closes in verse 6 by repeating God's promise to strengthen His people to overcome their enemies and to enter into His victorious rest: *"'So I will strengthen them in the Lord, and they shall walk up and down in His name,' says the Lord"* (v. 12). Once God pours out the Holy Spirit on the faithful remnant of the Jewish nation, she will always be with the Lord and will honor Him through complete obedience. Then the Jewish nation will fulfill God's original intention for her existence – she will be a beacon of light reflecting the greatness of her God to all nations.

## Meditation

> Almighty God, Thy lofty throne
> Has justice for its cornerstone,

434

And shining bright before Thy face
Are truth and love and boundless grace.

All glory unto God we yield,
Jehovah is our Help and Shield;
All praise and honor will we bring
To Israel's Holy One, our King.

— The Psalter

# The True Shepherd Rejected
## Zechariah 11

With the commencement of this chapter, the long prophetic strain abruptly ends and the prophet returns us to the situation of his day. The bliss of the coming Kingdom Age is momentarily displaced by this dismal explanation of why the Jewish people have suffered so much heartache through the centuries – their disobedience and misplaced devotion. Their rejection of God's Son and their Messiah was the chief example.

Verses 1-3 describe the devastation to Israel's forests and foliage by a Gentile invasion occurring after Christ's rejection. Fire (speaking of judgment) would devour the cedars of Lebanon, the oaks of Bashan, and the lush thickets of the Jordan. Shepherds would then mourn the loss of pasturelands. Lions will roar because their thickets were destroyed. It is generally understood that these poetic expressions relate to the wide devastation caused by the Romans in Israel in 70 A.D., when much of Jerusalem, including the temple, was destroyed.

In the remainder of the chapter the prophet will contrast the excellence of God's True Shepherd, who was rejected (vv. 4-14), with Israel's wicked shepherds who were misleading the nation (vv. 15-17).

## The Rejected Shepherd

Having foretold the consequences to the land of Israel, after Christ's rejection, the prophet begins at verse 4 to deliver a message from the rejected Shepherd to His rebellious people:

*Thus says the Lord my God, "Feed the flock for slaughter, whose owners slaughter them and feel no guilt; those who sell them say, 'Blessed be the Lord, for I am rich'; and their shepherds do not pity them. For I will no longer pity the inhabitants of the land," says the Lord. "But indeed I will give everyone into his neighbor's hand and into the hand of his king. They shall attack the land, and I will not deliver them from their hand"* (vv. 4-6).

Christ is the One now speaking through Zechariah. He affirms that His Father has given Him charge to *"feed the flock for slaughter."* Indeed, God's True Shepherd faithfully fed and watered the flock of Israel during His first advent. However, God, foreknowing the nation's rejection of His Shepherd, had predetermined their later slaughter by foreign buyers, probably speaking of Roman legions conquering Jerusalem (v. 5). The owners selling the nation into slaughter were probably the corrupt priests and Jewish leaders such as Herod, who were in league with the Roman Empire for financial gain and public status. These heartless buyers would profit from God's sheep and God would do nothing to interfere with the onslaught (v. 6).

The flock marked for slaughter included *"the poor of the flock"* (v. 7), which represented those few Jews who had believed in God's true Shepherd – Christ. C. A. Coates explains:

> But He discriminated between the flock of Slaughter and those whom He speaks of as *"the poor of the flock,"* though, indeed, all were involved in the judgment which was imminent upon the nation. But *"the poor of the flock"* are distinguished in verse 11 as those *"that gave heed to me."* They represented the godly remnant, who had owned the state of the nation by submitting to John's baptism, and who, as repentant, gave heed to the true Shepherd, though He was rejected by those who were in the place of shepherds. As to those shepherds He says, *"My soul was vexed with them, and their soul also loathed Me"* (v. 8).[178]

Zechariah, prophetically impersonating the rejected Shepherd, picks up two staffs to demonstrate God's dealings with the flock marked for slaughter:

> *I took for myself two staffs: the one I called Beauty, and the other I called Bonds; and I fed the flock. I dismissed the three shepherds in one month. My soul loathed them, and their soul also abhorred me. Then I said, "I will not feed you. Let what is dying die, and what is perishing perish. Let those that are left eat each other's flesh." And I took my staff, Beauty, and cut it in two, that I might break the covenant which I had made with all the peoples. So it was broken on that day. Thus the poor of the flock, who were watching me, knew that it was the word of the Lord* (vv. 7-11).

437

The two staffs were "Favor" or "Beauty" and "Union" or "Bands." The prophet, representing the Lord Jesus, fed the flock during His first earthly sojourn. He also dismissed three shepherds within a short amount of time. These neglectful shepherds are not specifically identified, but apparently they were those who had been trusted with the spiritual care of Israel, but were disavowed by Christ. J. J. Stubbs suggests that the three shepherds dismissed (or "cut off"; KJV) are identified in Matthew 22 as the Pharisees, the Herodians, and the Sadducees:

> In Matthew 22 the Lord has to deal with three religious heads of the people. The three shepherds are the Pharisees, Herodians, and the Sadducees. ... the Lord as the true Shepherd dealing with three groups of leaders of the people and authoritatively, by His teaching, cutting them off. The words "cut off" do not mean to destroy or put to death, but rather to disavow (M. F. Unger). In Matthew 22 the Lord is seen disowning and renouncing the teaching of the three false shepherds. The "one month" may refer to the period of time just before the leaders of the nation crucified the Lord Jesus, which resulted in sealing the doom of the nation.[179]

Zechariah was to then break the first staff, *Beauty*, to symbolize that God was dissolving His temporary covenant with the nations that had protected Israel's national interests (vv. 8-11). These nations had served His purposes in refining the Jewish nation and bringing them into a position to receive God's favor and blessing again. Spiritually speaking, Israel was dying when God's Shepherd came to feed them, but He was rejected. So the prophet's word, *"let what is dying die, and what is perishing perish"* pertains to the aftermath of Christ's rejection and was fulfilled when Rome conquered Jerusalem in 70 A.D.

A messianic prophecy is then inserted between the breaking of the first and second staffs to ensure that the meaning of both acts is associated with the rejection of God's Shepherd by the Jewish nation:

> *Then I said to them, "If it is agreeable to you, give me my wages; and if not, refrain." So they weighed out for my wages thirty pieces of silver. And the Lord said to me, "Throw it to the potter" – that princely price they set on me. So I took the thirty pieces of silver and threw them into the house of the Lord for the potter* (vv. 12-13).

The chief priests decided that it was worth thirty pieces of silver to get rid of Jesus, and Judas agreed that it was a fair price! But according to the prophecy, not only would the Jewish Messiah be betrayed for thirty pieces of silver, but also this money would be returned to the temple and be used to buy a potter's field. Matthew confirms that Judas and the Pharisees fulfilled every detail of this prophecy (Matt. 27:3-10). Judas felt remorse for betraying the Lord and returned the silver to the temple just before hanging himself. Judas' act was not one of repentance; otherwise he would have gone to the cross seeking forgiveness instead of conversing with Israel's false shepherds at the temple.

The Pharisees could not return blood money to the temple treasury, so they used the silver to purchase a potter's field – a location to bury the unidentifiable dead. J. J. Stubbs suggests that by buying the potter's field, the Pharisees provided a perpetuating memorial of their evil actions:

> The thirty pieces of silver were thrown down in the temple, the very place where Judas cast them. They are said to be cast to the potter, because it is to him they were appointed by the Lord ultimately to go. God, whose secret operations and sovereign power extend over all men, had so arranged this matter that Judas threw down the money in the temple to bring it before the face of God as blood-money and to call down the judgment of God on the nation. The high priest, by purchasing the potter's field for this money, which received the name of "The field of blood, unto this day" (Matt. 27:8), thus perpetuated the memorial of their sin against their Messiah. So the statement of Zechariah that he took the thirty pieces of silver and "cast them to the potter in the house of the Lord" was in this way literally fulfilled. Messiah in the person of Zechariah says, "I took, I threw." Matthew says, "They took, they gave them" (see Matt. 27:6-7). The reason for this is that the act of Judas and the Jews together was the Lord's appointment (Matt. 27:10; Acts 2:23).[180]

The phrase *"a princely price they set on me"* reveals how deeply the Lord felt this scornful denunciation by His own people – those whom He came to deliver. David foretells the Lord's anguish over His betrayal and desertion:

*Reproach has broken my heart, and I am full of heaviness; I looked for someone to take pity, but there was none; and for comforters, but I found none. They also gave me gall for my food, and for my thirst they gave me vinegar to drink* (Ps. 69:20-21).

Judas' betrayal indicated just how much he valued the Lord, who had abandoned the supreme glory of Heaven to be the incarnate man born of a virgin, to live in a sin-cursed world, to endure the contradiction of sinners for thirty-three-plus years, to endlessly serve those in need to the point of exhaustion, to lay down His life and to be cursed of God to save others from Hell that they might enjoy the abundant life of God. What an insult for Judas, who had been with the Lord for more than three years, to value Christ for a mere thirty pieces of silver.

> Thirty pieces of silver
> For the Lord of life they gave;
> Thirty pieces of silver –
> Only the price of a slave!
> But this was the priestly value,
> Of the Holy One of God;
> They weighed it out in the temple,
> The price of the Savior's blood.

> — William Blane

Dear believer, what value do you place on the Lord Jesus? Is He worthy of lifelong devotion and consecration? Is He worthy of all that you can give Him during your earthly sojourn? The Lord answers these questions for us:

*If anyone desires to come after Me, let him deny himself, and take up his cross daily, and follow Me. For whoever desires to save his life will lose it, but whoever loses his life for My sake will save it. For what profit is it to a man if he gains the whole world, and is himself destroyed or lost?* (Luke 9:23-25).

Having identified the True Shepherd and foretelling His rejection, the prophet breaks the second staff "Union" or "Bands" (v. 14). This meant that breaking the staff "Union" was connected with the rejection of Christ at His first advent. God will remove national solidarity between Judah and Israel and cause disharmony among His people.

This discord would lead to Israel's collapse in 70 A.D. and to further dispersion of the Jews among the nations.

Historically speaking, other than an occasional truce, a long span of enmity existed between the ten northern tribes and the southern Kingdom after Rehoboam's succession until the Northern Kingdom was dispersed by Assyria. The Southern Kingdom included Judah and the small tribe of Benjamin. The tribe of Simeon was absorbed into the tribe of Judah during the time of the Judges.

In the last chapter (10:6-12), Zechariah foretold what Isaiah and Ezekiel had previously predicted: In a coming day, Messiah would ensure that there would be no animosity among His covenant people (Isa. 11:13; Ezek. 37:15-22). Indeed, as Edward Dennett explains, the future unification of all Jews will occur during the Kingdom Age when the Jewish nation receives the Lord Jesus Christ as their Messiah:

> When therefore Messiah returns and establishes His kingdom this [reunification] promise will be fulfilled, and it would have been fulfilled when He first came had He been received by His people. Having been rejected, as we have seen, the reunion of Judah and Ephraim was necessarily, like the gathering of the nations, postponed; and this was set forth in our passage by the cutting asunder of the staff Bands.[181]

However, disunity in Israel was not the worst outcome of rejecting God's true Shepherd; Zechariah states that the Jews will then accept a foolish shepherd (i.e., the Antichrist; vv. 14-17). He will have no concern for the Jews, only for his own needs. Instead of protecting the sheep of Israel, he will slaughter them. His arm (i.e., his strength) and his eye (i.e., his intelligence) will be cut off when the True Shepherd returns at the end of the Tribulation Period.

## Woe to the Worthless Shepherd

Regrettably, much of Israel's history has been marked by the tragic consequences of following ungodly shepherds, instead of God's leaders. Having refused Christ at His first advent, the unregenerate Jewish nation will embrace the Antichrist just before Christ's second advent. Because of their rejection of His Shepherd, God will permit the foolish shepherd to afflict the Jews with immense suffering (v. 15). The Antichrist will not care for God's covenant people; in fact, he loathes them and will seek to exterminate them during the last half of the

Tribulation Period (v. 16, 13:8-9). Yet, at His triumphal return to the earth, Christ will vindicate His name and destroy the worthless shepherd (i.e., the Antichrist who had claimed to be the Jewish Messiah; Dan. 9:27; 2 Thess. 2:4-7).

> *Woe to the worthless shepherd, who leaves the flock! A sword shall be against his arm and against his right eye; his arm shall completely wither, and his right eye shall be totally blinded* (v. 17).

John foretold this moment of vindication with explicit detail:

> *Now I saw heaven opened, and behold, a white horse. And He who sat on him was called Faithful and True, and in righteousness He judges and makes war. His eyes were like a flame of fire, and on His head were many crowns. He had a name written that no one knew except Himself. He was clothed with a robe dipped in blood, and His name is called The Word of God. And the armies in heaven, clothed in fine linen, white and clean, followed Him on white horses. Now out of His mouth goes a sharp sword, that with it He should strike the nations. And He Himself will rule them with a rod of iron. He Himself treads the winepress of the fierceness and wrath of Almighty God. And He has on His robe and on His thigh a name written: KING OF KINGS AND LORD OF LORDS* (Rev. 19:11-16).

> *And I saw the beast, the kings of the earth, and their armies, gathered together to make war against Him who sat on the horse and against His army. Then the beast was captured, and with him the false prophet who worked signs in his presence, by which he deceived those who received the mark of the beast and those who worshiped his image. These two were cast alive into the lake of fire burning with brimstone. And the rest were killed with the sword which proceeded from the mouth of Him who sat on the horse. And all the birds were filled with their flesh* (Rev. 19:19-21).

When the Lord Jesus Christ returns to Israel, He will protect His people and will quickly vanquish the Antichrist and his armies amassed against Israel (which is discussed in chapter 14). The Antichrist will be the worthless shepherd that will cause many Jews to ignore or resist God's Word. Unlike Israel's negligent shepherds through the centuries and the Antichrist, during the time of Jacob's Trouble, the Lord will marvelously feed, protect, heal, console, and lead His sheep in Israel during the Kingdom Age. The Lord promises: *"I will feed My flock, and I will make them lie down"* (Ezek. 34:15). Although the Great Shepherd presently cares for the Church, there is a day coming in which the Chief Shepherd will rule on the throne of David and will care for His covenant people of old also! Then, all those who know Him will agree with David: *"The Lord is my shepherd; I shall not want"* (Ps. 23:1).

## Meditation

The King of love my Shepherd is,
whose goodness faileth never.
I nothing lack if I am His,
and He is mine forever.

Where streams of living water flow,
my ransomed soul He leadeth;
and where the verdant pastures grow,
with food celestial feedeth.

And so through all the length of days,
Thy goodness faileth never;
Good Shepherd, may I sing Thy praise
within Thy house forever.

— H. W. Baker

# Jerusalem Attacked and Delivered
## Zechariah 12

Having introduced the Antichrist at the close of the last chapter, Zechariah is mainly occupied in the final three chapters of his book with the events of the last days. He addresses the invasion of Israel, the siege and attack of Jerusalem, and then Christ's sudden appearance to deliver the Jewish nation and to establish His kingdom.

Israel has suffered centuries of spiritual blindness and consequences for rejecting and crucifying God's True Shepherd. The culmination of this solemn era is now highlighted by the prophet. Twenty times in these three chapters Zechariah speaks of "that day" or "the day" to address events associated with Christ's earthly return. For God to keep His promises to Abraham and to David, two key events must yet occur: First, Israel must be delivered from her Gentiles enemies forever and receive her land inheritance. Second, Israel must receive the Holy Spirit and experience spiritual revival, which results in the veneration of Jesus Christ.

Zechariah begins by expressing the burden of the Almighty Creator for Jerusalem in respect to the coming Day of the Lord:

> *Thus says the Lord, who stretches out the heavens, lays the foundation of the earth, and forms the spirit of man within him: "Behold, I will make Jerusalem a cup of drunkenness to all the surrounding peoples, when they lay siege against Judah and Jerusalem. And it shall happen in that day that I will make Jerusalem a very heavy stone for all peoples; all who would heave it away will surely be cut in pieces, though all nations of the earth are gathered against it"* (vv. 1-3).

The prophetic scene commences with the Gentile armies besieging Jerusalem during the time of Jacob's Trouble. The Lord will intervene so as to make Jerusalem *"a cup of drunkenness"* and *"a very heavy stone"* to Gentile armies (vv. 2-3). In other words, the Jews located in

Jerusalem will repel the invading nations, will send them reeling, and will ultimately crush them like a bug under a rock.

The Lord will strike their horses with terror and blindness and their riders with madness (v. 4). The remaining Jews will realize that it is the Lord's doing (v. 5). The prophet likens this victorious Jewish uprising to a firepan in the woodpile or a fiery torch in the sheaves (v. 6). No invading army will be able to stand against Israel.

God will protect Jerusalem like a shield, and He will empower each Jew with the Holy Spirit – the divine Enabler (v. 7, Joel 2:27-29; Ezek. 36:24-26). With the Lord leading them, Judah will then rise up and conquer their enemies. Even the most feeble Jews will have divine power and angelic-like resolve to victoriously confront their oppressors (v. 8). Indeed, those in Judah will fight like David's mighty men of old. The Lord promises: *"It shall be in that day that I will seek to destroy all the nations that come against Jerusalem"* (v. 9). This insurgence will reassert honor to the house of David.

Furthermore, as the Lord Jesus descends from heaven to defend His covenant people at Armageddon, the Holy Spirit will open their eyes to realize that He is their Messiah. Zechariah foretells this specific event:

> *And I will pour on the house of David and on the inhabitants of Jerusalem the Spirit of grace and supplication; then they will look on Me whom they pierced. Yes, they will mourn for Him as one mourns for his only son, and grieve for Him as one grieves for a firstborn. In that day there shall be a great mourning in Jerusalem, like the mourning at Hadad Rimmon in the plain of Megiddo* (vv. 10-11).

Both Jewish leaders and the common people will receive the Holy Spirit. Their immediate response will be repentance with intense mourning. This Jewish remnant will immediately understand that long ago their forefathers crucified their Messiah and Deliverer and that their actions have resulted in terrible consequences for the Jewish nation for centuries. Such repentance and understanding could never be accomplished under the Law, but it could be through the New Covenant which will be accepted by the entire nation at Christ's Second Advent. In chapter 8, we saw that truth precedes peace, and in this chapter we learn that repentance must precede blessing.

The grief of the Spirit-filled remnant will be intense. They will feel like a family that has suffered the death of their only son (v. 10). To have no heir to continue the family name was considered a curse in the

Jewish culture. The intensity of emotions will be similar to how the nation felt when Judah's last mighty and godly king, Josiah, was killed by Pharaoh Neco in battle in 609 B.C. *"at Hadad Rimmon in the plain of Megiddo"* (v. 11). At this location Israel lost their last great king, but it will also be here where Israel receives her final and greatest King, the King of kings – the Lord Jesus Christ!

The sorrow of the remnant will be so intense at Christ's return that five times in this chapter it is said the wives will mourn apart from their husbands. J. J. Stubbs suggests an important personal application for us to consider from this text:

> This is not a reference to the Jewish custom of wives living in a separate part of the house, or that they had to worship separately. It points rather to the fact, as C. L. Feinberg says, that "the mourning will be so intense as to transcend even the closest ties of earth, those between husband and wife." Such retirement and seclusion are always very needful for the deepening of personal piety and true humility. When there is contrition for sin and personal desire to be right with God, it is good when the husband and wife in the family get privately before God. Husbands and wives should share many things in life and do things together for the Lord. Spiritual exercise should never be one-sided and left to one partner alone in marriage, but in the matter of our own souls being in the right condition and in developing personal devotion to the Lord, there need to be times when the husband and wife get separately alone with God.[182]

Undeniably, the need to be in fellowship with the Lord Jesus transcends the privileges, responsibility, and affections of all earthly relationships. In fact, our interaction with family can never be what it should be unless we are in happy fellowship with Christ, for in Him alone can we behave towards those we love as recipients of divine grace. Through repentance and experiencing Christ, the Jewish nation will receive the best that God can bestow on them through the Holy Spirit.

When Christ returns, the spiritual blindness of the Jewish nation will come to an end. By mentioning the house of David (the line of kings), the house of Nathan (likely the prophet who confronted David), and Shimei (the grandson of Levi the priest), Zechariah was confirming that all Jewish nobility, priests, and prophets would receive Jesus Christ. Every surviving Jewish family at the end of the Tribulation

Period will trust in the Lord Jesus as their Messiah and receive the Holy Spirit (vv. 12-13).

In this spiritually fruitful state, the Jews will be known as the olive tree which provides a testimony of God's goodness to the entire world (Hos. 14:6; Rom. 11:17-24). Although we see that individual Jews in the Old Testament were filled by the Holy Spirit in order to speak for the Lord or to serve Him effectively (e.g., Ex. 35:30-35; 1 Sam. 10:10), the nation as a whole has never been indwelt by the Spirit of God (Zech. 4:4-7). This will not happen until Christ's second coming to the earth (Isa. 59:21). Afterwards the Lord will gather all surviving Jews from among the Gentiles back to Israel where they will have God's protection.

God is a covenant-keeping God and His marvelous plan for the Jewish nation is still unfolding and will be completed according to His sovereign plan. Presently, the kingdom of God is on earth in its spiritual form only, but soon the King shall return and His literal, earthly, political kingdom shall be established forever! Israel will not live for Christ until the Kingdom Age, but the Church has the incredible opportunity to live for Him now through the power of the Holy Spirit.

## Meditation

I place no value on anything I have or may possess, except in relation to the kingdom of God. If anything will advance the interests of the kingdom, it shall be given away or kept, only as by giving or keeping it I shall most promote the glory of Him to whom I owe all my hopes in time or eternity.

— David Livingstone

# Faithfulness in Captivity
Zechariah 13

## A Fountain Against Sin

Zechariah continues his prophecies pertaining to the Day of the Lord in relationship to the nation of Israel. When true repentance occurs, a divine fountain is opened to cleanse away sin and uncleanness: *"In that day a fountain shall be opened for the house of David and for the inhabitants of Jerusalem, for sin and for uncleanness"* (v. 1). Besides receiving spiritual understanding as to who Christ is (the subject of this chapter), the pouring out of the Holy Spirit also provides cleansing for the nation.

But by what means can God justly cleanse away all Israel's sin and guilt in the Day of the Lord? The entire Old Testament Scripture teaches the principle that such cleansing requires blood atonement from an innocent victim. The New Testament confirms what the Old Testament typified – ultimate cleansing of sin and its consequences is accomplished only by the blood of Christ. When Israel trusts Christ at His second advent, His sacrifice becomes effectual for the nation, which is immediately regenerated by the Holy Spirit.

So whether before Mount Sinai, after the Israelites had worshiped the golden calf, or outside Eden for Adam and Eve after they ate of the forbidden tree, God seeks to restore lost fellowship with man through blood atonement. By shedding and applying the blood of an innocent animal, the covering of sin was accomplished. Atonement provided only a temporary covering for sin; ultimately, all sin would be put away by Christ's shed blood. Jewish sacrifices and the sprinkling of the blood of bulls and goats could never take away sin (Heb. 10:4), or clear the conscience of guilt (Heb. 9:14). The Jewish sacrifices were commanded only to bring sin into remembrance and to picture the ultimate means by which sin would be put away and the conscience purged from guilt (i.e., by Christ's blood).

## Jews Against False Prophets

In that day, two ills that have plagued Israel throughout much of their history will be done away with, namely idolatry and false prophets (vv. 2-3). The disdain for false prophets will be so great that even parents of these deceivers will demand that they be put to death (vv. 4-5). When the false prophets see Christ in all His glory, they abandon their prophet's attire to try to escape judgment (v. 6). Additionally, they will explain that the scars in their bodies were not caused by ritual pagan cuttings, but were the result of farming accidents or severe discipline received from parents or friends (that, my friends, is quite a beating).

Some have suggested that verse 6 is speaking of Christ and His wounds received at Calvary. However, the context of the previous verses ensures that Christ is not the object of discussion, for He would never say, *"I am no prophet."* Rather, verses 2-6 speak of the Lord's future coming when all those who engaged in false prophesying will be ashamed and will lie about their previous occupation. Zechariah does not endorse their lying, but rather shows the extent guilty people will go to remove all suspicion against them. Yet, they will not escape God's judgment.

## God's Sword Against His Shepherd

Verse 7 is one of the most sobering verses in the Bible:

> *"Awake, O sword, against My Shepherd, against the Man who is My Companion," says the Lord of hosts. "Strike the Shepherd, and the sheep will be scattered; then I will turn My hand against the little ones."*

It seems appropriate that God would smite the false shepherds of Israel with holy vindication, but why would He strike His Good Shepherd? The answer is so that we might know that God the Father was in direct control of the death of His Son (His fellow – His nearest and dearest of kin, so to speak; Lev. 6:2, 18:20).

Also speaking of this incredible truth, Isaiah says: *"Yet it pleased the Lord to bruise Him; He has put Him to grief. When You make His soul an offering for sin, He shall see His seed, He shall prolong His days, and the pleasure of the Lord shall prosper in His hand"* (Isa. 53:10). Isaiah explains that God the Father would bruise His own Son and cause Him to suffer deep grief as an *asham* (a sin offering; Jer. 51:5) for His people. This is why Christ, while nailed to the cross and veiled in darkness, cried out: *"Eli, Eli, lama sabachthani?"* that is, *"My God, My God, why have You forsaken Me?"* (Matt. 27:46). Through His acceptable sin sacrifice, God would be able to extend the offer of forgiveness to Israel and to all of humanity. Those who respond in faith will be eternally redeemed by the blood of Christ. Thus, a spiritual race of redeemed people, after His own kind, would be brought into being as His seed.

However, Isaiah also says that God will prolong His Servant's days and will prosper Him: *"He shall see the labor of His soul, and be satisfied. By His knowledge My righteous Servant shall justify many, for He shall bear their iniquities"* (Isa. 53:11). This would be possible only through His resurrection after His death and burial. The cross was not His end, but a new beginning for us to be able to love and honor Him. Christ would come forth from the grave a mighty Victor over death, Satan, and all principalities and powers (Eph. 1:19-21). The exalted Christ will then establish the will of God universally. He will establish a kingdom on earth that will honor God in every way. Then *"the pleasure of the Lord shall prosper in His hand."*

In the latter portion of verse 10, Zechariah further predicts that when Christ is crucified, His disciples would be scattered and they would suffer persecution on His behalf. This fulfillment is recorded in the book of Acts. Church history records that all Christ's disciples were martyred for their faith, except John, who suffered terrible brutality from the Romans and then lived out his latter days in exile on the penal island of Patmos.

## The Antichrist Against Israel

Turning from the suffering Savior in verse 7, Zechariah leaps ahead in time to convey some of the dreadful details as to how the nation of Israel will suffer during the Tribulation Period. This suffering will occur just before their spiritual conversion:

> *"And it shall come to pass in all the land," says the Lord, "That two-thirds in it shall be cut off and die,*
> *but one-third shall be left in it: I will bring the one-third through the fire, will refine them as silver is refined, and test them as gold is tested. They will call on My name, and I will answer them. I will say,*

*'This is My people'; and each one will say, 'The Lord is my God'"* (vv. 8-9).

Ezekiel tells us that at the beginning of the Tribulation Period, the Jews will have already taken back their land through war before the Tribulation Period commences (Ezek. 38:8). Daniel informs us that this seven-year period, the time of Jacob's Trouble, commences when Israel signs a peace treaty with the Antichrist (Dan. 9:27). The Jewish people will enjoy a short season of false peace in the first half of the Tribulation Period just before suffering a terrible holocaust. Before the Tribulation Period is over, two-thirds of the Jews in the world will be slaughtered (vv. 8-9). Only a small Jewish remnant will survive the refining fire of the Tribulation Period and be restored to God as His chosen people. There will be numerous other judgments upon the earth that will also result in much death and misery. In all, as much as eighty percent of the world's population will perish during this time of great agony.

The peace covenant will initially allow the Jews to dwell safely in unprotected villages in the land of Israel (Ezek. 38:11). This phenomenon has not occurred in over 2,500 years and, at this present time, it is hard to imagine how the Jewish nation could ever be at peace with all their Arab neighbors and especially with radical Islamist factions intent on annihilating them. Yet, the Antichrist will accomplish this seemingly impossible feat through promoting a one-world, anti-God religion.

The prophet Jeremiah wrote of this future time: *"Alas! For that day is great, so that none is like it; and it is the time of Jacob's trouble, but he shall be saved out of it"* (Jer. 30:7). When the abomination of desolation occurs at the midpoint of the Tribulation Period, there will also be war in Heaven. The archangel Michael, along with his angels, will war against the devil and his fallen angels in order to constrain evil to the earth (v. 1; Rev. 12:7-10). Satan, knowing that his time is short, will be enraged and will seek to exterminate the Jewish people (Rev. 12:12-15). However, the Lord will preserve from harm a remnant of His covenant people (Rev. 12:16-17).

During the Tribulation, there will be 144,000 Jews who are actively testifying of Jehovah (Rev. 7:4-8) and there will also be angels heralding the gospel message as they fly over the earth (Rev. 14:6-12). The devil knows that salvation is possible only while an individual is alive to choose Christ: *"And as it is appointed for men to die once, but after this the judgment"* (Heb. 9:27). Accordingly, he will attempt to exterminate all those who honor Jehovah and those who might hear and trust the kingdom gospel message. Satan will spare only those willing to take the mark of the beast and worship him. The Lord Jesus spoke of the horrific holocaust during this time:

> For then there will be great tribulation, such as has not been since the beginning of the world until this time, no, nor ever shall be. And unless those days were shortened, no flesh would be saved; but for the elect's sake those days will be shortened (Matt. 24:21-22).

If the Lord tarried longer than the appointed time to return to the earth, there would be no flesh left on the planet. As Zechariah has stated, in just over three years the Antichrist will slaughter two-thirds of all Jews worldwide (vv. 7-8). Thankfully, Zechariah does not conclude this prophecy with this dismal statistic. After acknowledging the horrific events of the Tribulation Period, he then affirms what will be accomplished for Israel afterwards. The Lord Jesus Christ will descend at the end of the Tribulation Period to protect and deliver His covenant people and to establish His Kingdom.

## God for Israel and Israel for God

Jewish survivors, the remaining third of the nation, will be refined through the fiery trial in such a way that they will wholeheartedly acknowledge Jesus Christ as their Lord, Savior, and King. This will mean that Jehovah God will finally be restored to His covenant people of old. Then every Jew will say, *"The Lord is my God"* (v. 9). C. A. Coates describes the refining process of the Jewish nation which will bring the remnant to the realization that Jesus Christ is Lord of all:

> The remnant in Israel will learn that in the smiting and cutting off of the Messiah there was an end of all hopes according to the flesh. They will see that neither promises nor covenants could be of avail to those under death. They will learn, under God's solemn dealings with them, that they are under death, but they will learn it in a deeper way when they see that Christ has been smitten on their account. They will see that every blessing must come to them on the ground of His death and resurrection. They will bless themselves in Him, and they will enter into life eternal in the day spoken of in Zechariah 14, when living

waters go out from Jerusalem as the city of the great King. But they will not reach this apart from the refining process which is described in the last verse of chapter 13.[183]

After centuries of separation, the Jewish people will finally celebrate the Lord's rule and joyfully praise Him. This will fulfill God's yearning for the Jewish nation as poetically expressed in Psalm 100: *"Know that the Lord, He is God; it is He who has made us, and not we ourselves; we are His people and the sheep of His pasture"* (Ps. 100:3). It was not enough for the Jews to merely know they were God's sheep; their Creator wanted them to understand that He Himself knew they were His sheep. He loved them and longed to care for them and He wanted them to rest in His love. All this will happen in the Kingdom Age when God's Smitten Shepherd becomes Israel's Shepherd too.

## Meditation

I saw a young sister, just before this service; and I said to her, "When did you find the Lord?" She replied, "It was when I was very ill." Yes, it is often so; God makes us ill in body that we may have time to think of Him, and turn to Him....What would become of some people if they were always in good health, or if they were always prospering? But tribulation is the black dog that goes after the stray sheep, and barks them back to the Good Shepherd. I thank God that there are such things as the visitations of correction and of holy discipline, to preserve our spirit, and bring us to Christ.

— Charles Spurgeon

# Faithfulness in Captivity
Zechariah 14

A century and a half previous to Zechariah's ministry, Ezekiel described the glory of God leaving the temple shortly before the Babylonians destroyed it (Ezek. 10). However, he later explained that God's glory will return to the Mount of Olives (just to the east of Jerusalem) in a future day and God will again dwell with His people (Ezek. 43:1-3). Zechariah closes his book by describing this future event, the second advent of Christ, in vivid detail.

This entire chapter relates to the Day of the Lord, which is yet future (v. 1). William Kelly reviews the history of Jerusalem since the time of Zechariah's writing to show that nothing like this prophecy (e.g., half of Jerusalem being conquered by a huge multi-nation army) has ever occurred to date:

> Let it be observed that siege is laid by the Assyrian [the Antichrist] with all the nations who own him as leader against Jerusalem, and that the siege is partially successful, for half the city is taken. Nothing like this has ever been since Zechariah's day: still less does anything in history resemble what follows, as we shall see presently. It was not so when Ptolemy Soter took the city about B.C. 320, nor when Antiochus the Great took it in B.C. 203, nor again in B.C. 199, when Scopus the Egyptian general took it once more, nor the following year when it yielded to Antiochus, nor even when it was pillaged in B.C. 170 by Antiochus Epiphanes, nor two years later under the frightful efforts of his army under Apollonius to destroy the city and the people, nor after that when his emissary Athenaeus profaned the sanctuary, and set up heathenism, with the utmost scorn to the law, which was followed by the exploits of the Maccabees, the issue being under Simon that the foreigner was expelled in B.C. 142, and Acra demolished, as is commonly known. Under John Hyrcanus, the Syrian king Antiochus Sidetes was obliged to abandon the siege. Passing over internal or family disputes which have no possible resemblance, and the intervention of Aretas, it is impossible to

identify with the prophecy Pompey's capture of the temple in B.C. 63, nor Crassus' plunder of the city in B.C. 54, nor the Parthian surprise in B.C. 40. Herod's siege was more similar perhaps, but essentially distinct, as we shall see by and by. Neither its final destruction by Titus nor the move of Bar-Cochba under Hadrian calls for lengthened remarks, as they are obviously different. **Nothing since bears the smallest likeness to the prophecy.**[184]

## The Mount of Olives

God's departing glory in Ezekiel's day signaled Jerusalem's doom. A similar scene occurred six centuries later on the Mount of Olives when the Lord Jesus gloriously ascended into Heaven (Acts 1:9-12). Jehovah permitted the Jews several years to repent and receive His Son, their Messiah, whom they had crucified, but they would not, and in 70 A.D. the temple and portions of Jerusalem were destroyed.

Foreknowing this catastrophe, God sent two angels to convey a message of hope to the Jewish nation, as the disciples observed the Lord ascending into heaven: *"This same Jesus, who was taken up from you into heaven, will so come in like manner as you saw Him go into heaven"* (Acts 1:11). The prophet Zechariah informs us in this chapter that the Lord Jesus will return to the Mount of Olives for the battle of Armageddon at the end of the Tribulation Period. Zechariah writes:

> *For I will gather all the nations to battle against Jerusalem; the city shall be taken ... Then the Lord will go forth and fight against those nations, as He fights in the day of battle. And in that day His feet will stand on the Mount of Olives, which faces Jerusalem on the east. And the Mount of Olives shall be split in two, from east to west, making a very large valley; half of the mountain shall move toward the north and half of it toward the south. ... And in that day it shall be that living waters shall flow from Jerusalem, half of them toward the eastern sea and half of them toward the western sea; in both summer and winter it shall occur* (vv. 2-8).

The nations will have gathered against Jerusalem under the authority of the Antichrist. The city will be conquered and half of its inhabitants will be enslaved when Christ suddenly appears, descends upon, and splits the Mount of Olives (vv. 1-4). The initial attack by Israel's enemies on Jerusalem will be successful. Feeling confident of total victory, these barbaric invaders pause to plunder homes, to rape

Jewish women, and to enslave survivors. However, just when Jerusalem seems doomed, the Lord will return to the Mount of Olives and will intervene to save the city, and also empower the Jews to overcome their enemies.

Given the prominence of the Mount of Olives in relationship to Jerusalem, everyone in the vicinity will be able to see the Lord's magnificent return and to witness what happens afterwards. E. B. Pusey describes the local geography for us:

> The Mount of Olives is the central eminence of a line of hills, of rather more than a mile in length, overhanging the city, from which it is separated only by the narrow bed of the valley of the brook Kedron. It rises 187 feet above Mount Zion, 295 feet above Mount Moriah, 443 feet above Gethsemane, and lies between the city and the wilderness toward the Dead Sea: around its northern side wound the road to Bethany and the Jordan.[185]

In the book of Revelation, John identifies five separate earthquakes during the Tribulation Period. Three of these are said to be "great" earthquakes, but the last one associated with the final bowl judgment is the mother of all earthquakes – mountains around the earth fall and islands vanish. This means that the world's geography will be quite different after the Tribulation Period. This great earthquake may occur when the Lord arrives at the Mount of Olives.

Zechariah records that Jerusalem is suddenly elevated at this time, while the vast highlands to the south become a flat plain:

> *All the land shall be turned into a plain from Geba to Rimmon south of Jerusalem. Jerusalem shall be raised up and inhabited in her place from Benjamin's Gate to the place of the First Gate and the Corner Gate, and from the Tower of Hananel to the king's winepresses* (v. 10).

Geba and Rimmon are mentioned, as these mark the northern and southern boundaries of the Southern Kingdom of Judah. Jerusalem's spiritual and literal elevation during the Kingdom Age is a direct fulfillment of Isaiah's prediction: *"Now it shall come to pass in the latter days that the mountain of the Lord's house shall be established on the top of the mountains, and shall be exalted above the hills; and all nations shall flow to it"* (Isa. 2:2). Jerusalem will be the pinnacle of divine glory and a beacon of grace to all nations during the Kingdom Age.

Notice that the prophet goes so far as to provide the exact details as to how much of the city will be impacted by this topographic change. Benjamin's Gate was on the northeast wall (Neh. 8:16; Jer. 37:13) as was the Tower of Hananel (Neh. 3:1). Benjamin's Gate may also be Ephraim's Gate or the Sheep Gate. The First Gate probably refers to the Old Gate which was located on the northern portion of the west wall and was the main entrance into the city from the north. We read that Jehoash, King of Israel, broke down the wall of Jerusalem between the gate of Ephraim to the Corner Gate about 600 feet (2 Kgs. 14:13). This breach of the northern wall probably remained open until the time of Uzziah (2 Chron. 26:9). This information confirms that Zechariah's first four references cover the full extent of the city's northern boundary from east to west. The king's winepresses and gardens were south of the city (Neh. 3:15), completing the description of the impacted area.

Furthermore, Zechariah states that when Christ returns to the earth, He will cleave the Mount of Olives in two (i.e., what is remaining of it) and will create a valley running east and west (vv. 4, 8). Two rivers will then originate from the mount; one will flow west to the Mediterranean Sea and the other east to the Dead Sea.

These events all happen prior to the Kingdom Age, and before the millennial temple complex that Ezekiel describes has been erected. The source of all life is Christ (John 1:1-4). When He steps on the Mount of Olives, refreshing rivers of life appear. Later, when He is on His throne in the temple, living water will also flow freely from the temple to replenish and heal the earth. It is this author's opinion that the flow of water from Ezekiel's future temple went eastward before it turned south and connected with the dual flowing rivers described by Zechariah (Ezek. 47:1-12; see also Joel 3:18). This seems reasonable, since both Ezekiel and Zechariah describe easterly flowing rivers that terminated in the Dead Sea, which then becomes abundant with life.

## The Battle of Armageddon

In Revelation chapter 1, John describes the Lord Jesus returning to the earth in glory and wrath. With symbolic language John says that the Lord has a sharp, two-edged sword protruding out of His mouth (Rev. 1:16). Zechariah explains what that portrayal means in his account of the Battle of Armageddon. Either as Christ is descending to the Mount of Olives or shortly after arriving, He will obliterate the Gentile armies amassed in the Megiddo Valley with a plague:

> *And this shall be the plague with which the Lord will strike all the people who fought against Jerusalem: Their flesh shall dissolve while they stand on their feet, their eyes shall dissolve in their sockets, and their tongues shall dissolve in their mouths* (v. 12). *... Such also shall be the plague on the horse and the mule, on the camel and the donkey, and on all the cattle that will be in those camps. So shall this plague be* (v. 15).

This plague will wipe out the largest army ever gathered for battle – their purpose is to eradicate the Jewish people and to conquer Israel. John provides the number of those soldiers assembled in the Jezreel Valley for the battle – 200,000,000 (Rev. 9:16). He then explains that the entire valley will become a giant winepress, for when Christ destroys this great army, their blood will freely flow out of its basin for 182 miles (Rev. 14:19-20). The voluminous amount of bodily fluids that results when 200,000,000 soldiers and their beasts instantly dissolve will then gush out of the Megiddo Valley.

When Christ arrives at the Mount of Olives, Jerusalem will be taken by the Antichrist. The Lord Jesus will rid that city of its invaders, by pouring out the Holy Spirit upon surviving Jews to empower them to overcome their enemies (v. 14). The Lord's appearance and the sudden reversal in the tide of the battle for Jerusalem will strike terror in Israel's attackers (v. 13). Horror and fright will seize those nations besieging Jerusalem. The Midianites fell into such a tumult when attacked by Gideon and his three hundred men (Judg. 7), as did the Ammonites, the Moabites, and the Edomites who advanced against Judah during Jehoshaphat's reign (2 Chron. 20).

By Jewish super-soldiers (i.e., Spirit-filled Jews), the medium of panic, and a flesh-dissolving plague, Jerusalem and all Israel will be rescued and the Antichrist and his armies will be destroyed.

## The Judgment of Nations

After the Antichrist and his invading armies are destroyed, Christ will gather the nations to be judged (Matt. 13:47-50, 25:31-46). All those who followed the Antichrist and persecuted the Jews will be killed (Rev. 19:20-21). Those who did not take his mark will be allowed to enter Christ's kingdom on earth. This will conclude *"the time of the Gentiles"* (Rom. 11:25; Rev. 11:1-2).

Besides the removal of all rebels from the earth, the wealth of the nations will flow into Israel.

> *Judah also will fight at Jerusalem. And the wealth of all the surrounding nations shall be gathered together: Gold, silver, and apparel in great abundance* (v. 14).

So not only will Jerusalem be safely inhabited after the Judgment of Nations (v. 11), but also the nations will gladly donate their gold, silver, and apparel to support the worship of the Lord in Jerusalem. After all the goats are removed from the earth, the sheep will inherit the earth with all curses levied in Eden for sin removed (Matt. 25:32-33; Rom. 8:20-21). In this blessed Utopia, the Lord Jesus Christ will establish His kingdom, receive the honor He deserves, and He shall rule the nations: *"And the Lord shall be King over all the earth. In that day it shall be – The Lord is one, 'And His name one'"* (v. 9). In that day, Jesus Christ will be acknowledged as Lord of lords and King of kings by all who dwell on the earth (Rev. 17:14, 19:16).

## No Replacement Theology

It is quite obvious to even a casual reader that the events described in this chapter have never occurred. For example, the Mount of Olives is still intact, Jerusalem is not the religious capital of the world, and the nations do not worship the Jewish Messiah there. The context of the passage is plainly future and Jewish in nature. Thus it cannot be referring to the Church.

Throughout his entire book, Zechariah distinctly references the Jews as the people of Judah (21 times), the Jewish nation of Israel (five times), and those living in the literal city of Jerusalem (41 times). He speaks of the Jewish people in the second person ("you") while referring to non-Jews as "they." Zechariah also describes them as those who orchestrated the crucifixion of their Messiah and who, at His Second Advent, will mourn that they did so (12:10). Only seriously flawed hermeneutics could spiritualize all these references and fail to see the Jewish flavor of this book.

The Jews referred to in the book of Zechariah are the same Jews as in the rest of the Old Testament. They are not the Church. The Israel that Zechariah refers to is the Jewish nation whose capital is Jerusalem. If God has no plan for the nation of Israel, why does He still refer to them as "the apple of His eye" at the very moment He will return to avenge them among the nations, exalt them as His esteemed people, and take up residence among them again?

## The Kingdom Age, Not the Eternal State

There are several clear distinctions between the Kingdom Age and the Eternal State, which those holding an amillennial viewpoint ignore. For example, the seas and oceans we know today will still be present during the Kingdom Age (v. 8; Isa. 11:9; Ezek. 47:18), but there will be no seas in the new earth (Rev. 21:1). Furthermore, Israel is not in the land specified and the millennial tribal allotments have not yet been delegated (47:13-23). Likewise, geographic locations on earth today will exist in the Millennial Kingdom (vv. 16-21; Joel 3:18) but obviously will not in the new earth. The new heaven and earth will not be created until after the Kingdom Age is concluded, Satan's last rebellion on earth is quelled (Rev. 20:7-10), and the planet we live upon is destroyed (Rev. 20:11).

Zechariah tells us that Jerusalem will be the worship center of the earth during the millennium (vv. 16-21). The Jews will again keep the Feast of Tabernacles, which from its conception pictured the future blessings of the Kingdom Age and the full communion God's people would enjoy with Jehovah (v. 16).

All nations will also come to Jerusalem to see the glory of God and to participate in this festive celebration (Isa. 2:1-4; 60:14; 66:10-18) and those who do not will be severely punished with drought (vv. 17-19). Zechariah closes his book by previewing the joyful scene in Jerusalem during the Kingdom Age:

> In that day *"HOLINESS TO THE LORD"* shall be engraved on the bells of the horses. The pots in the Lord's house shall be like the bowls before the altar. Yes, every pot in Jerusalem and Judah shall be holiness to the Lord of hosts. Everyone who sacrifices shall come and take them and cook in them. In that day there shall no longer be a Canaanite in the house of the Lord of hosts (vv. 20-21).

Under the Levitical Law, there had been clean things and unclean, holy and unholy, but now all such distinctions shall be abolished, inasmuch as all the redeemed will be holy and separated unto the Lord. No longer will men have a distinction between what is sacred and what is secular, for they will have learned that anything worth doing should be done for the glory of God!

Accordingly, no pagan or secularized religious practices will be permitted during the Kingdom Age. These closing words from Zechariah might strike us as unusual, but recall what influence menaced the returning remnant in his day – intermarriages with heathen! For example, just a few years after Zechariah wrote these words, a Gentile man who had married a wife from a notable Jewish family was given quarters in the new temple, that is, until Nehemiah found out about it (Neh. 13). Fraternizing with children of the devil has always negatively affected the spirituality of God's people, says F. B. Hole:

> This thing [intermingling with pagans] which had been so great a snare to the Jewish nation would be gone forever. And as we close our meditations on this prophet, let us not forget that a similar tendency has ever been a great snare amongst Christians. What was it that underlay all the disorders that marred the church at Corinth? It comes clearly to light in Paul's second letter to them, when in 2 Corinthians 6 … he put his finger upon the real trouble: it was their "unequal" yoking with unbelievers. All through the church's history this has been one main source of trouble and dishonor. It is so today, we have sadly to confess.[186]

However, no fake spirituality or humanized religion will be tolerated in Christ's kingdom – all will be holiness to the Lord! The Lord Jesus is the Lord Almighty, the Holy One of Israel, and He will establish holiness throughout the earth and all will honor Him. Christ will triumphantly reign over Israel and the nations in glorious righteousness!

## Meditation

Zion's mount His royal seat,
And no power His throne shall move;
Ages gather at His feet,
Son of God's eternal love.

*Door of Hope*

All the world His Name shall fear,
All the world from shore to shore;
Every isle His voice shall hear,
And the heathen rage no more.

Hail, hail, King of Zion!
Hail, Lord of lords, and King of kings!
Reign forever, King of Zion;
Reign, blessed King, forevermore.

— Fanny Crosby

# Malachi

# Overview of Malachi

## The Author

Malachi's name means "my messenger." Just a few decades after being reestablished in the land, the Jewish nation had become spiritually despondent. Malachi, Jehovah's messenger, was sent to reason with them. We know nothing else of his family or where he resided.

## Date

Malachi is likely the last Old Testament prophet to speak on God's behalf to Israel. As a governor (not a king) oversaw the affairs of Israel, we know that the date of this oracle must be after the Babylonian exile. Furthermore, because the temple is in operation again, Malachi's messages would have been several years after Haggai's and Zechariah's ministries (520 to 515 B.C.).

The specific Jewish offenses rebuked by Malachi were also apparent during Nehemiah's second trip to Jerusalem (approximately 430 to 425 B.C.; Neh. 13). Nehemiah first traveled from Babylon to Jerusalem in 445 B.C. and, after thirteen years in Jerusalem, journeyed back to Babylon to serve in the king's court. After hearing of spiritual declension in Jerusalem, Nehemiah again received permission to travel to Jerusalem to confront his wayward countrymen. It seems likely that Malachi's ministry dovetailed with this second visit of Nehemiah or occurred shortly afterwards. Therefore, it is reasonable to conclude that the book was penned between 425 and 420 B.C. However, since Ezra confronted issues of intermarriage and temple neglect when he returned to Jerusalem from Babylon in 458 B.C., an earlier date for the book of 470 to 460 B.C. is also possible.

## Theme

Malachi is God's messenger, who will identify six specific charges against complacent Israel. In four brief chapters he will ask and answer twenty-five questions before resting God's case against his countrymen. Malachi confronts religious vanity, divorce coupled with marriages to foreigners, corruption in the priesthood, and the neglect and abuse of their fellow-man, especially the helpless.

Regrettably, no Jewish revival occurred as a result of Malachi's ministry. Jehovah responded with four centuries of silence. But then, *"when the fullness of the time had come, God sent forth His Son, born of a woman, born under the law, to redeem those who were under the law"* (Gal. 4:4-5). After Malachi, God's next message and Messenger to His covenant people would be His own Son – their Messiah, whom they would reject and crucify.

The book of Malachi contrasts the fading twilight after a long day, speaking of the Old Covenant (2 Cor. 3:6-18), with the brilliant dawning of grace found in the Sun of Righteousness (4:2). In this oracle, the last of the ancient prophets bridges the gap between the two Testaments of the Bible, the first of which only condemned, and the second of which bestowed hope in better things to come.

## Outline

Israel Doubts God's Love (1:1-5)
Israel Despises God's Name (1:6-2:9)
Sins Against Other Jews (2:10-17)
The Coming Forerunner (3:1-5)
The Faithful Remnant and the Stingy Religious Majority (3:6-18)
Elijah to Come Again before Christ's Return (4:1-6)

# Devotions in Malachi

## Polluted Devotion
### Malachi 1

The book commences with these words, *"The burden of the word of the Lord to Israel by Malachi"* (v. 1). Although Malachi was burdened by God's message for his countrymen, the opening verse also hints of consolation – God's message was "to Israel" and not "against Israel." This meant, as explained in chapter 3, that the Jewish nation could still return to the Lord and experience spiritual revival.

Three post-captivity revivals had occurred among the Jews prior to their declension now being challenged by Malachi. The first spiritual awakening occurred during the days of Zerubbabel, at which time the temple was rebuilt. Two more revivals occurred during the ministry of Ezra the scribe. The first one occurred after Ezra publicly prostrated himself on the ground in front of the temple while praying and weeping aloud. The final revival, about thirteen years later, was associated with Nehemiah's arrival to rebuild the wall around Jerusalem. Now, a couple of decades later, Israel desperately needed to be revived again. But alas, no such awakening resulted from Malachi's delivered burden, and consequently four centuries of divine silence followed.

### Israel Beloved

The narrative indicates that the priests, who should have been drawing the people towards the Lord, were themselves insensitive to the things of God. Since the priests were not being God's messengers, the Lord burdened a prophet to speak for Him. His name was Malachi, and his name means "My messenger."

Though the Jews had recently finished reconstructing the temple and the wall around Jerusalem, their hearts had drifted away from Jehovah. Despite their waning affections for Him, the prophet conveys Jehovah's love for His people:

*"I have loved you," says the Lord. "Yet you say, 'In what way have You loved us?' Was not Esau Jacob's brother?" Says the Lord. "Yet Jacob I have loved; but Esau I have hated, and laid waste his mountains and his heritage for the jackals of the wilderness"* (vv. 2-3).

For over a thousand years God had continually demonstrated His faithfulness to a stiffed-necked people who had repeatedly violated their covenant relationship with Him. Jehovah's love for His people had never diminished. It would have been appropriate for Israel to respond to God's love by obeying His commandments and by unwavering devotion. However, Israel's history was marred by spiritual infidelity and rebellion. True, the Jewish nation had experienced three major revivals during the previous century, but now they had become spiritually despondent again. They offered to God merely what they did not want or appreciate. Their worship for Jehovah was again marked by heartless rote and mindless doings.

In this carnal state, Israel had the audacity to challenge the validity of God's word, and worse, to cast doubt on His covenant faithfulness to them. Since returning from Babylon over a century earlier, Jehovah had yet to fulfill His covenant with Abraham to alleviate all Gentile oppression and rule. The Jews had forgotten that when man chooses to sin, it is God who chooses the consequences of that sin. Consequently, in God's timetable, the Kingdom Age was still very far off. The prophet will explain later that only a remnant of the Jewish nation was righteous at that time, and that, in general, God's people needed reviving (3:16-18).

The Lord answers Israel's challenge to His claim of unfailing love by reminding them of two things. First, He had chosen them (in Jacob) over all other people to be His own. Isaac was the promised son of Abraham, in whom God would uphold His covenant. But Isaac had two sons. Although both sons would receive what God promised to Isaac: *"the dew of heaven, of the fatness of the earth, and plenty of grain and wine"* (Gen. 27:28, 39), only one son could receive covenantal favor. In sovereign wisdom, and against human custom, Jehovah chose the younger son Jacob over the older son Esau (even before their births) to bless with covenantal love. This did not mean that emotionally God loved Esau any less than Jacob, but in His election (for he had to choose one of the two sons) He chose Jacob to fulfill His promise to Abraham.

The second defense of Jehovah's love for Israel is expressed in the statement: "*Jacob I have loved; but Esau I have hated.*" Not only was sovereign privilege affirmed in the choice of Jacob, but there also was an ongoing reality of that choice that Israel could rejoice in. The verbs "loved" and "hated" are in the perfect tense, meaning that the reality of God's initial choice also brought continuing privilege and responsibility for Jacob's descendants. H. A. Ironside explains that God's election did not condemn Esau (and his seed) to remain out of His love any more than Gentiles were condemned for not being the chosen of God:

> It is His dealings with Jacob and Esau after long centuries had shown what they really were that are referred to. The phrase, "Jacob have I loved, but Esau have I hated," is quoted triumphantly by the apostle in Rom. 9:13 to prove the wisdom of God's choice made before the children were born, when He said, "The elder shall serve the younger." Carefully observe, there is no hyper-Calvinistic question here of reprobation for hell and predestination for heaven. It is Jehovah's inalienable right to dispose of His creatures as He wills, that the apostle is contending for; and He manifests with holy joy that He wills to show mercy to those who deserved only wrath. Jacob and Esau are cited as illustrations. Before either was born, God chose Jacob to be superior to Esau, nationally. The elder was to serve the younger, and thus own the superiority of God's choice.[187]

God's love for Israel had been expressed by the choice of Jacob. This also meant that the future Messiah and Savior would come through Jacob and not through Esau. This choice did not exclude Esau and his seed from receiving God's favor if they sought the Lord through repentance and obedience. William Kelly puts the matter this way:

> If God *"despises not any"* (Job 36:5), we may be perfectly sure He hates not any. Such an idea could not enter a mind which was nurtured in the word of God, apart from the reasonings of men. I say not this because of the smallest affinity with what is commonly called Arminianism; for I have just as little affinity with Calvinism. I believe the one to be as derogatory to God's glory as the other, though in very different ways – the one by exalting man most unduly, and the other by prescribing for God, and consequently not saying the thing that is right of Him.[188]

The point is that, because of God's choice, Edom had not received the same level of blessing and protection that Israel had. God, foreknowing Edom's stubborn pagan disposition, did not choose Esau, but neither were Esau's descendants isolated from opportunity to seek the Lord if they desired to. However, this did not occur; therefore the Lord promised that Edom would become a wasteland – a habitation fit only for jackals (v. 4).

## Edom's Destruction

Malachi is among a number of Old Testament prophets who foretold Edom's destruction. Almost three centuries earlier, the prophet Joel predicted Edom's desolation and explained why: *"Edom a desolate wilderness, because of violence against the people of Judah, for they have shed innocent blood in their land"* (Joel 3:19). Then, nearly a century after Joel, Isaiah offered Edom an opportunity to repent under the chastening hand of God through the Assyrians, but they would not (Isa. 21:11-12).      Jumping ahead to the sixth century, Ezekiel tells us why God was angry with the Edomites; they had assumed Israel was a nation no different than any other. This conclusion challenged the importance of God's Word and His special relationship with the Jewish people (Ezek. 25:8). Furthermore, Edom's sin was great because they had actually assisted Nebuchadnezzar in defeating Judah (Ezek. 25:12). Edom had sided with Babylon in the defeat of Egypt in 605 B.C., but in 593 B.C. they agreed to be part of an alliance, which included Judah and other nations, to rebel against Nebuchadnezzar (Jer. 27:1-7). However, when Babylon came against Jerusalem in 588 B.C., double-crossing Edom switched sides again and assisted Babylon in brutally conquering the Jewish nation (Jer. 49:7-22). Ezekiel said that Edom's actions were motivated by hate and revenge (Ezek. 25:12).

Jeremiah posed a logical statement for the Edomites to consider: If the Lord was determined to cause the surrounding nations, who had no fraternal ties with the Jews, to drink from His cup of wrath, how much more judgment did the Edomites deserve for oppressing and betraying their own distant kin (Jer. 49:12)? Jeremiah specifically explains why God's wrath would be poured out on them: *"'Your fierceness has deceived you, the pride of your heart, O you who dwell in the clefts of the rock, who hold the height of the hill! Though you make your nest as high as the eagle, I will bring you down from there,' says the Lord"*

(Jer. 49:16). Edom's pride had summoned God's judgment; they were high on themselves, but God would bring them low.

So, in the fifth century, the Lord affirms His judgment against Edom through Malachi:

> *They may build, but I will throw down; they shall be called the Territory of Wickedness, and the people against whom the Lord will have indignation forever. Your eyes shall see, and you shall say, "The Lord is magnified beyond the border of Israel"* (vv. 4-5).

Unlike their prophecies to Moab and Ammon, the prophets did not promise Edom a future inheritance or restoration to their land. No matter what advancements they strove for as a nation, God was against them for their wickedness; they would not prosper.

History records that in the years following the Babylonian invasion, the Nabateans drove the Edomites westward from their land into southern Judah. The descendants of the Edomites became known as the Idumeans. According to Josephus, the Idumeans became subject to John Hyrcanus I, a Maccabean, in 125 B.C. and were forced to accept Judaism; at that juncture, the Edomites ceased to be a distinct people.[189] Today, there are still remnants of the Moabites and Ammonites living in their respective regions; this cannot be said of the Edomites.

The Edomites will not have an inheritance or a place in Christ's coming kingdom. In fact, they will no longer exist. Therefore, Israel should consider Edom's demise and rejoice in God's love shown to them through His eternal covenant. Israel's God has shown Himself strong and faithful beyond Israel's border! The *"Territory of Wickedness"* (Edom) would be destroyed in God's wrath, but "the holy land" (Zech. 2:12), speaking of Israel, will continue under God's hand of blessing.

## Polluted Sacrifices

In his first message, Nehemiah confirmed Jehovah's steadfast love for and faithfulness to Israel to hopefully provoke their endearment of Him (1:1-5). In his second of six oracles, he will address how Israel has dishonored God's Name and why the priests deserved God's discipline (1:6-2:9). In his rebuke, Malachi offers Israel a fourfold spiritual reality-check: The reality of their profession (v. 6), the reality of their gifts (vv. 7-8), the reality of their service (vv. 9-11), and the reality of their attitude (vv. 12-14). May we have the courage to honestly examine ourselves in each of these facets of spirituality also.

The Jews were offering polluted sacrifices, instead of giving their best to the Lord. Their sacrifices were an abomination to Jehovah because they reflected the low esteem His people had for Him and His covenant. Interestingly, the prophet begins his rebuke by invoking a rare title for Jehovah – *the one Father*, which Malachi applies again in the next chapter:

> *If then I am* **the Father***, where is My honor? And if I am a Master, where is My reverence? Says the Lord of hosts* (v. 6).

> *Have we not all* **one Father***? Has not one God created us?* (2:10).

Most of the New Testament names for God are found in one form or another in the Old Testament, but one significant name – "Father" – is not, at least not in the same familiarity. A few passages express the Fatherly *position* of God, but not the relational intimacy of sonship: *"A Father of the fatherless, a judge [a defender] of the widows, is God in His holy habitation"* (Ps. 68:5). Old Testament saints did not refer in a familiar sense to God as "Father." This is a strictly New Testament dynamic made possible through the gospel of Jesus Christ.

On resurrection day, while speaking to Mary Magdalene, the Lord said, *"I ascend unto My Father, and your Father; and to My God, and your God"* (John 20:17). In the Old Testament we read of the "children of Israel" and the "people of God," but it is not until the New Testament that the intimate term "children of God" is found. Jehovah told Moses at Mount Sinai that the nation of Israel was like a son to Him (Ex. 4:22). He also decreed later when Israel was at Sinai that children should honor their parents (Ex. 20:12).

Accordingly, the title "Father" employed by Malachi is not meant to convey God's tenderness towards His wayward children, but rather to rebuke their lack of respect and obedience towards Him: *"A son honors his father, and a servant his master. If then I am the Father, where is My honor?"* (v. 6). It was appropriate for servants to respect the status of their masters. Likewise, fathers were respected within their clans and families, but the Father of them all was scorned and insulted by their lip-service to His covenant and their superficial religiosity. The

Jews did not truly fear Jehovah's name; otherwise they would revere Him with obedience and respect.

The priests, who were responsible for teaching the people God's commandments and prompting their devotion toward Him, had utterly failed in their primary duty. Rather than rendering sincere service to God, they had shown disdain for His name by their insensitivity to sin, by lackadaisically performing priestly duties, and by false piety (v. 6).

Malachi then puts these lethargic and ignorant priests in a defensive role by questioning God, *"In what way have we despised Your name?"* (v. 6). Malachi then answers their fictitious question: *"You offer defiled food on My altar"* (v. 7). By accepting blind, sick, and lame animals from the people and then offering them to God on His altar (v. 8), the priests had broken Levitical Law and had offended the Lord (Lev. 22:18-25). From God's perspective, the priests had corrupted His table. *"The table of the Lord"* was His provision of food for the serving priests and God wanted to provide the best for those representing Him (Lev. 24:5-9).

To prove how insulting to God such behavior was, Malachi tells the priests to offer such inferior animals to their governor and see if he would be pleased with them (v. 8). This inferred that the governor would not be pleased, but rather affronted. How much more then should the Creator of all things be outraged by such offensive behavior. Malachi then wishes that someone would shut the doors of the temple to prevent the priests from kindling a fire on God's altar. In other words, it would be better to offer no sacrifices to God than to offer what was offensive to Him (vv. 9-10).

Malachi's rebuke of lethargic devotion towards the Lord is applicable for today. Although we are not under the edicts of the Law, we also offend the Lord by giving Him the "leftovers" of our time and resources in the Church Age. If we displace the meetings of the church with secular activities we teach our children what measly value the things of God have for us (Heb. 10:25). If we give meagerly to the Lord's work, we show God how much we truly value His Son and what He accomplished at Calvary. If we neglect honoring the Lord's name in our speech and behavior through the week, why should He receive our praise and prayers on Sunday with any more legitimacy than He did of the Jewish nation in Malachi's day? Twice the prophet inquires of God's people, *"Is it not evil"* to do such things?

## The Lord's Table

When ordering the Levitical priesthood and sacrifices, God wonderfully provided for the needs of His priests, mainly through the peace offerings. God, the priests, and the common people all partook of this freewill offering, which symbolized the fellowship that God longs to enjoy with His people (Ex. 24:9-11). While atoning blood was being applied to the altar to sanctify it, the priest also appropriated the offering by eating it. This repeats the same idea of Exodus 12 where the blood of a victim (the Passover lamb) was applied to sanctify the one who ate the victim's flesh. The themes of blood atonement, substitutional death, and sanctification to God are all interconnected in Scripture and, ultimately, have their typological climax and fulfillment at Calvary. This is why the Lord Jesus instituted the Lord's Supper – He did not want believers to forget Him, nor the work that He accomplished to secure their salvation.

Accordingly, by offering substandard sacrifices, the Jews were tainting all that God was representing to them about the future work of Christ on their behalf. This weighty violation demanded God's chastening judgment instead of His blessing. Malachi informs his foolish and naive countrymen that their sacrificing behavior was provoking Jehovah to move against them; they had defiled the Lord's Table (vv. 8, 13-14).

The Bronze Altar would be God's Table to supply His priests' needs, but the priests had to eat what was provided by the Lord before Him in the tabernacle. The New Testament equivalent of this privileged place of communion and blessing with the Lord is referred to as the "Lord's Table" (1 Cor. 10:16-22). The Lord's Table is an expression that is used in both the Old and New Testaments to convey the concept of divine provision and fellowship (Ps. 23:5, 78:19; Mal. 1:7, 12; 1 Cor. 9:13, 10:18). Both the Levitical priests under the old covenant of the Law (Lev. 6:16, 26, 7:6, 31-32) and believer priests under the new covenant of grace (1 Cor. 10:20-21) have been invited to abide at the Lord's Table.

The peace offering symbolizes God's fellowship with man through Christ; it was the only offering of which God, the offering priest, and the offerer all received a portion. As the believer's fellowship with God, provision from God, and ability to bless God are all figuratively demonstrated within the peace offering, there is much application for the Church to consider.

The story of King David's kindness to Mephibosheth, the crippled son of Jonathan (2 Sam. 9:13), is a fitting allegory of the Lord's Table. Normally, a new king would exterminate all remaining heirs of the previous dynasty in order to prevent a potential takeover. However, King David, because of his love for Jonathan and the covenant he had made with him (1 Sam. 18:3), set a place at his table for Mephibosheth for the remainder of his life. Mephibosheth never had to worry about where his next meal would come from, and he could enjoy daily fellowship with the king. Similarly, though once the enemies of God, believers in Christ now have the opportunity to enjoy fellowship with Him and with other believers at His table and to receive daily wherewithal to serve Him.

Often the biblical term "the Lord's Table" (which speaks of a spiritual table where believers receive blessings and enjoy fellowship in Christ – see 1 Corinthians 10) is confused with the biblical term "the Lord's Supper" (which refers to the remembrance meeting of the local church – see 1 Corinthians 11). Consequently, most of Christendom refers to the Lord's Supper with the non-scriptural term "the communion service." There is *communion with Christ* at the Lord's Table, but more specifically, there is a *remembrance of Christ* at every Lord's Supper – the value of His death is proclaimed afresh. The Lord's Table is spiritual and is set by Him, whereas the table at the Lord's Supper is physical and is set by us; at the former we receive provisions from the Lord, but at the latter we worship and remember Him.

To summarize, the Lord's Table speaks of the sum total of the spiritual blessings we have in Christ, while the Lord's Supper refers to the remembrance meeting of the Church. In the sense that the souls of believers are refreshed through Spirit-led worship, the Lord's Table probably includes the Lord's Supper, but the distinct terminology and significance of each should not be lost. It is a great privilege to remember and refresh the Savior during the Lord's Supper, and it is a blessing to the heart of every believer to commune with and receive from the Savior at His Table.

Paul therefore exhorts the believers at Corinth not to remove themselves from the Lord's Table to partake of the world's resources; to do so is to fellowship with demons:

> *I do not want you to have fellowship with demons. You cannot drink*
> *the cup of the Lord and the cup of demons; you cannot partake of the*
> *Lord's table and of the table of demons. Or do we provoke the Lord to*
> *jealousy? Are we stronger than He?* (1 Cor. 10:20-22).

May each believer realize the importance of eating at the Lord's
Table and, accordingly, choose to abide with Him there. Failure to do
so will provoke the Lord's jealousy and His chastening hand. Why
would a believer ever want to sever his or her communion with the
Lord? It is a great privilege and honor to sup at His Table!

In this sense, Gentile believers in the Church Age can worship and
serve the Lord effectively wherever they are located. This seems to be a
partial fulfillment of Malachi's prediction in verse 11: *"For from the*
*rising of the sun, even to its going down, My name shall be great*
*among the Gentiles."* However, the complete fulfillment of this
prophecy will obviously be in the Kingdom Age, when all Gentiles
everywhere will come to Jerusalem to worship the Lord (Isa. 11:3-4,
62:7).

## God Deserves the Best

Returning to the present state of things, the prophet explains that
the priests had committed two offenses against Jehovah. First, they had
profaned His Table by offering to Him stolen, lame, and sick animals
(v. 13). Because of their negligence, God bemoans, *"The table of the*
*Lord is defiled; and its fruit, its food, is contemptible"* (v. 12). Second,
the priests held God's provision for them at His table in contempt,
*"'Oh, what a weariness!' and you sneer at it"* (v. 13). Offering to God
what He demanded had become burdensome and they now loathed the
offerings. Although they knew what the Law demanded, they did not
feel obliged to obey it – their awe of God and reverence for His ways
had been supplanted by smug religious rote. Hamilton Smith suggests
that the same disposition for the things of God can occur today also:

Profession without practice, and service without devotedness, will
lead to weariness in the things of the Lord, and what people are weary
of they will end by despising. ... Alas, can we not see in our day this
same weariness in the things of the Lord? Are there not many who
were once active in the service of the Lord, but who have now grown
weary? Possibly their practice fell below their preaching, then the
preaching was continued when the devotedness was gone, and now at

last they have grown weary. The hands hang down and the knees are feeble; the hands never lifted up in supplication, the knees never bent in prayer. They have grown weary – weary of prayer, weary of reading the Bible, weary of remembering the Lord, weary of preaching the gospel, and weary of hearing it, weary of the Lord's things, and weary of the Lord's people. And what we weary of we despise; little wonder, then, that they end by puffing at the Lord's things and the Lord's people. How deeply important to have Christ ever before us, the true motive for all service — to "consider Him," the Leader and Completer of faith, "that endured such contradiction of sinners against Himself, *lest ye be wearied and faint in your minds.*"[190]

The prophet then turns from their weariness of service and offering putrid things to the Lord to the subject of free-will vows. Vows were not mandatory, but it was offensive to God for someone to utter a vow and repay it with what was unfit (v. 14). No one would offer a king such compensation because of fear of his retribution; yet, God's people had no remorse in offering what was inferior to the Lord of Hosts, their Great King, whose name should be revered among the nations.

The Jews were to dedicate their best to God, not what was deemed unclean or unwanted. The same is true today; God desires believers to be daily consecrated to Him in holiness – to be acceptable living sacrifices.

*I beseech you therefore, brethren, by the mercies of God, that you present your bodies a living sacrifice, holy, acceptable to God, which is your reasonable service. And do not be conformed to this world, but be transformed by the renewing of your mind, that you may prove what is that good and acceptable and perfect will of God* (Rom. 12:1-2).

These verses summarize the New Testament equivalent to a dedication ceremony, which is to recur day after day – it is not a onetime event. We must keep ourselves clean from worldliness (Jas. 4:4), from humanism (Col. 2:8), from unlawful lusting (Gal. 5:16-17), and from the deeds of the flesh (Col. 3:5). A holy life is essential for dedicated service and is only possible when we are in communion with the Lord and partaking from His table. Matthew Henry exhorts believers in the Church Age not to repeat the mindless and heartless sacrifices of the Jews in Malachi's day:

If we worship God ignorantly, and without understanding, we bring the blind for sacrifice; if we do it carelessly, if we are cold, dull, and dead in it, we bring the sick; if we rest in the bodily exercise, and do not make heart-work of it, we bring the lame; and if we suffer vain thoughts and distractions to lodge within us, we bring the torn. And is not this evil? Is it not a great affront to God, and a great wrong and injury to our own souls? In order to the acceptance of our actions with God, it is not enough to do that which, for the matter of it, is good; but we must do it from a right principle, in a right manner, and for a right end.[191]

The Law affirmed that it was both appropriate and expected that the Jews would, in thankful adoration, offer back to the Lord the best things they had received from Him. Malachi warned the Jews that offering anything less than their best to God was an insult to Him, not an act of worship! God gave us His best, His only Son, the Lord Jesus Christ; may we endeavor to give Him our best too!

## Meditation

Give of your best to the Master;
Give Him first place in your heart;
Give Him first place in your service;
Consecrate every part.

Give, and to you will be given;
God His beloved Son gave;
Gratefully seeking to serve Him,
Give Him the best that you have.

— Howard B. Grose

# Corrupt Priests and Treacherous Husbands
## Malachi 2

Having validated God's charge against His priests in the previous chapter, the prophet now admonishes them to honor the Lord or be cursed by God:

> *"And now, O priests, this commandment is for you. If you will not hear, and if you will not take it to heart, to give glory to My name," says the Lord of hosts, "I will send a curse upon you, and I will curse your blessings. Yes, I have cursed them already, because you do not take it to heart"* (vv. 1-2).

Under God's covenant with Israel, curses were promised for disobedience (Deut. 27:15-26, 28:15-68). Through their blatant defiance, the priests had shown no appreciation for Jehovah's name nor had they attached proper significance to the place He had determined to set His name. God would not tolerate this transgression any longer; He was ready to invoke the judicial consequences of the Law if they did not immediately repent.

Though the Church is not under the Law, believers today are also responsible to honor God's name by obedient conduct and to respect where He chooses to set His name. The name to be honored today is the Lord Jesus Christ – He is the head of the Church. And as P. Harding explains, those who gather in His name (speaking of the local church) have a vital obligation to honor Him through their collective testimony:

> To be gathered to the name of the Lord Jesus Christ surely means that He is the center of attraction, that His Lordship is owned and that His word is paramount. It means … finding sufficiency in Him. His name is the sum of all that He is and involves His claims as absolute Lord. All must be in keeping with the loveliness, majesty, dignity, and holiness of His name. His name is all important and of necessity excludes all other names. It is the believers' privilege to exalt His name. Each local assembly has a responsibility to bear a faithful and

479

harmonious testimony to all the truth of God in the locality, by complete obedience to His word and thus bring glory to His name. Those so gathered need to hear, take heed and honor God by obedience. The word of God is not given merely to increase head knowledge but to affect the heart and govern the life. One learns from these verses the important lesson that obedience from the heart brings glory to God.[192]

Regrettably, the hearts of the Jewish priests were far from the Lord, so they did not feel the weight of disgracing the Lord's name as keenly as Malachi did. The prophet then warns them that their continued disobedience and devotionless rituals would result in hardships for their descendants also (v. 3). The prophet's intense rhetoric indicates that their polluted sacrifices were a serious offense against the Lord.

Under the Law, the dung of an animal to be sacrificed was to be burned outside the camp with the remainder of the animal not burnt on the Bronze Altar (Ex. 29:14). The priests had brought sickly and maimed sacrifices to His altar, but the Lord had utterly rejected them, and was, so to speak, throwing what was putrid to Him back in their faces. The lingering stench of dung on their faces would remind them of how disgusted He was over their vain and rank practices.

Under Levitical Law contact with dung would make the priests unclean, and unable to serve the Lord in the temple. God's stern warning was for the purpose of purifying a corrupt priesthood, so that He could continue honoring His covenant with faithful Levi (v. 4).

Having thoroughly rebuked the offensive behavior of the priests, Malachi reviews the historical ramifications of God's covenant with Levi (Num. 18:7-21, 19-21), which was also affirmed with Levi's grandson Phinehas (Num. 25:10-13). The purpose of this was to acknowledge what God expected of His priests (vv. 5-9). Levi revered God (v. 5), his conduct was upright and he rightly instructed the people to turn from sin to the Lord (v. 6). Levi's descendants were to lead the people in truth towards God; they were God's chosen messengers for this task (v. 7). Hamilton Smith summarizes the reasoning for mentioning Levi at this juncture and also the godly pattern established by the priests at Sinai:

The prophet presents a beautiful picture of the priesthood as established by God in the beginning. We can only get a true estimate of our condition in the end of a dispensation by comparing it with the condition at the beginning. Thus only shall we learn the extent of our departure from what is according to the mind of God. In the beginning the priest was marked by (1) life, (2) peace, (3) the fear of the Lord, (4) the law of truth in his mouth, (5) iniquity not found in his lips, (6) a walk with God in peace and equity, and (7) blessing to others – turning them from iniquity and instructing them in knowledge. Such is the mind of the Lord for the one who is "the messenger of the Lord of hosts" in this dark world (vv. 5-7).[193]

Sadly, the priesthood in Malachi's day had failed miserably to keep this charge and they caused the people to stumble over the Law (v. 8). Instead of maintaining lawful edicts, the priests had shown partiality and they compromised doing what God expected of them. The Lord was now poised to severely judge them for their transgressions (v. 9). It is with this sobering threat that Malachi concludes his second message to Judah.

## God's People Should Be Faithful

The prophet's third message focuses on how God's covenant people should behave. He will show that they were negligent in their relationship to the Lord (vv. 8-9), to others (v. 10), to the world (vv. 11-12), in family relationships (vv. 13-15), and in their attitude towards divine correction (v. 16). Malachi begins this message by posing three questions to reveal Judah's unfaithfulness to Jehovah and each other:

*Have we not all one Father? Has not one God created us? Why do we deal treacherously with one another by profaning the covenant of the fathers?* (v. 10).

The answer to the first two questions was obviously affirmative, but the third question was designed to prompt self-reflection and a reasonable decision. It is not reasonable to deal treacherously with the Creator, the Father of our nation, by transgressing our covenant with Him. For example, some men in Judah were marrying foreign women (v. 11). One hundred and fourteen such unions near or at this time are noted in Ezra 10. Jews were forbidden to marry foreigners (Ex. 34:11-16; Deut. 7:3-4) for two obvious reasons. First, these mixed marriages often caused Jewish husbands to embrace the gods that their wives worshiped. Second, it meant that the children of these marriages would learn the tongue of their mother instead of the Hebrew language. In consequence, these children would not be able to understand God's Law nor to live for Him (Neh. 13:23-31).

The prophet states that these Jewish husbands were following in the steps of the Northern Kingdom's overt paganism which God judged through the Assyrians. Permitting any hint of idolatry in their homes, while at the same time publicly observing the Levitical feasts and sacrifices, was treachery from God's point of view (see Jer. 3:1-11). Malachi promised that judgment was coming and offenders would be "cut off" (v. 12). This meant that either the man would die or that he would have no descendants in the commonwealth of Israel.

Regrettably, some Jewish men had divorced their Jewish wives just so they could marry foreign women (vv. 14-15). The practice of abandoning their wives to gratify fleeting passions was detestable in God's sight. The prophet states the consequence of such behavior in verse 13: God would not accept the offerings of these guilty husbands, no matter how much they wept before the Lord at His altar. They had wounded their wives emotionally, violated His Law, and produced corrupt seed (pagan children). Their children were to be set apart to Him, not to false deities!

Malachi's harsh rebuke of Jewish men divorcing their wives for carnal reasons demonstrates God's anger over unbiblical divorce (vv. 11-14). Plainly, *"God hates divorce"* and loathes the pain and violence it causes. The prophet likens such divorces to a covering garment, in that the terrible consequences of this sin are apparent for all to see (v. 16). The Lord promised to judge those Jewish men for their shameful behavior. As shown in Ezra 10, the right course of action was to put away all foreign wives and their children from among them and marry only Jewish wives. God did not want a corrupted people, but a pure and holy nation to honor Him. Hence, the prophet warns these Jewish men, *"Therefore take heed to your spirit, that you do not deal treacherously"* (v. 16).

The Lord Jesus clarified to His Jewish audience that divorce was only permitted (but not demanded) for infidelity (Matt. 19:5-6). Under the Law, the punishment for adultery was death, meaning that the innocent party could remarry after the judicial death of his or her unfaithful spouse. Rather, than legitimate divorce for unfaithfulness, the Jewish men were frivolously putting away their wives in order to legally justify their sensual appetites. Such lewd behavior was an affront to God's moral character, to His design for marriage, and to His Law to maintain His people's purity.

The prophet closes his third message by rejecting judicial relativity. No matter how much the Jews had perverted proper justice and negated God's Laws, God had not changed and He would faithfully execute justice on all offenders without partiality (v. 17)!

## Marital Companionship

God has a wonderful plan for marriage and family life, which, as Malachi tells us, necessitates a husband not forsaking the companion and wife of his youth:

> *The Lord has been witness between you and the wife of your youth, with whom you have dealt treacherously; yet she is your **companion** and your wife by covenant (v. 14).*

As originally instituted, God's aspiration for marriage was for a man and woman to enjoy intimate companionship (Gen. 2:18-20). By entering into a marriage covenant, a man and a woman become companions for life in God's best plan. Since the marriage covenant initiates blessed camaraderie between a man and a woman as husband and wife, we pause to examine the biblical meaning of marital companionship by evaluating the two Hebrew words used in the Old Testament to speak of the marriage partner or companion.

First, the Hebrew word Malachi employs for "companion" in verse 14 is *chabereth*, which means "a consort or wife." Its root word *chaber* means "to be associated with or united to" or "to be knit together." Hence, one aspect of companionship is a sense of duty and a commitment to stay knitted together. It is interesting that the modern Hebrew word for marriage, *kiddushin*, means "sanctification" (being set apart). The marriage bond "sets apart" a husband and wife to fulfill a lifetime covenant of intimate and committed companionship before God. A marriage must be based on a forged commitment of both parties to stay together no matter what. Not only is the mindset of staying together a necessity for a marriage to thrive, but it is one of the greatest gifts to pass along to your children.

Second, Solomon rebukes an adulterous wife in Proverbs 2:17, *"Who forsakes the **companion** of her youth, and forgets the covenant of her God."* The Hebrew word for "companion," *alluwph*, means "to be familiar and intimate, with a foremost friend." Besides commitment, another key aspect of the marriage covenant is intimacy, a deep desire to disclose and to be familiar with one another. If your spouse is not your best earthly friend (i.e., behind the Lord), you are missing God's design for marriage.

Biblical companionship, therefore, consists of an unwavering duty of *commitment* and open disclosure that promotes *intimacy*. When will a marriage relationship be most satisfying? When total commitment leads to open disclosure. Full disclosure promotes exuberant passion being shared between a husband and wife. Jehovah's passion for Israel – His wife through covenant – is poetically described in Ezekiel 16:8:

> *"When I passed by you again and looked upon you, indeed your time was the time of love; so I spread My wing over you and covered your nakedness. Yes, I swore an oath to you and entered into a covenant with you, and you became Mine," says the Lord God.*

The Hebrew word for "love" in this verse is *dowd*, meaning "to boil" (i.e. figuratively: "to love" and, by implication, "a lover"). This word is rendered "love" seven times in the Old Testament and always confers the sense of a boiling pot of fervent passion between a man and a woman (not necessarily sexually). Romantic fervency in marriage develops out of commitment and intimacy.

## A Godly Seed

Though the primary design for marriage is companionship, God also desires godly children through the marriage union of a man and a woman (v. 15). God does not desire merely morally-sound children; rather *"He seeks godly offspring."* God longs for spiritually-minded people in the world and He knows this training begins in the home (2 Cor. 12:14; Eph. 6:1-4). Parents have a God-given responsibility to train up their children for the One who gave them. C. H. Mackintosh explains why lackadaisical parenting produces unruly children:

> God has put into the parents' hand the reins of government and the rod of authority; but if parents through indolence [apathy] suffer the reins to drop from their hands, and if through false tenderness or moral weakness, the rod of authority is not applied, need we marvel if the children grow up in utter lawlessness? How could it be otherwise? Children are, as a rule, very much what we make them. If they are

made to be obedient, they will be so, and if they are allowed to have their own way, the result will be accordingly.[194]

As children are permitted to dabble in a God-hating system of thinking, a proportionate lack of appetite for spiritual things will be observed. Just as it would be natural for a toddler to choose to eat an ice cream cone instead of a serving of broccoli, it would be the propensity of the flesh to desire the onions, garlic, and leeks of Egypt rather than God's food for the spiritual man – bland manna. Just as the flesh cannot please God, no provision made for the flesh can please Him either, because such things strengthen the flesh and weaken the spiritual man (Rom. 6:11-12).

Christian parents cannot enjoy communion with God while at the same time allowing their children to be drawn into secular philosophies and to be controlled by the world's pleasures. Satan, with striking subtlety, is carrying away many young people into the darkness of a "teen culture" while those stronger in the faith calmly watch and do nothing. Let us be mindful of Satan's devices before he devours the next generation!

In summary, the Lord was ready to severely judge His people because husbands were dishonoring Him! They were breaking their marriage covenants with Him and with their Jewish wives because carnal appetites were drawing them away from God's best for the family and for themselves. Broken marriages lead to a collapsed home life. Shattered homes become the restless abodes for broken-hearted children. The companionship of one man and one woman for life is God's primary purpose for marriage. His secondary purpose is His desire for marriage to produce godly seed – not just children, but godly children from godly parents.

Let us remember that a Christian family is not a household of Christians, but a Christian household. It is more than Christ dwelling within the hearts of family members; it is a family that is pursuing the heart of God. If the Bible is not at the center of family life and all home affairs, that home cannot be called a true Christian home. The vital focus and objective of every Christian household is the glory of God! The Jews in Malachi's day had lost this important focus and were severely punished. May we both rely on the Lord and learn from their failures, and thus avoid the consequences of unbiblical marital life and family life. *"Unless the Lord builds the house, they labor in vain who build it"* (Ps. 127:1).

## Meditation

The greatest benefits God has conferred on human life, fatherhood, motherhood, childhood, and home become the greatest curse if Jesus Christ is not the head.

— Oswald Chambers

# The Door of Repentance
## Malachi 3

## The First Advent of Christ

The prophet begins his fourth of six messages by delivering a messianic prophecy pertaining to Christ's first advent:

*"Behold, I send My messenger, and he will prepare the way before Me. And the Lord, whom you seek, will suddenly come to His temple, even the Messenger of the covenant, in whom you delight. Behold, He is coming," says the Lord of hosts* (v. 1).

Malachi foretold that Christ would have a forerunner (a messenger) to prepare the people for His coming. Interestingly, Malachi's name means "My Messenger," which is probably why he was chosen to reveal this prophecy. Isaiah also predicts this forerunner (Isa. 40:3-5), and all four Gospels record that John the baptizer, the son of Zechariah and Elizabeth, was the fulfillment of their prophecies (Matt. 3:3; 11:10-14; Mark 1:2-3; Luke 3:4-5, 7:27; John 1:23). The Lord Jesus also affirms that John was the direct fulfillment of this prophecy (Matt. 11:7-10). In fact, John began his ministry by declaring that he was the foretold forerunner of Christ:

*In those days John the Baptist came preaching in the wilderness of Judea, and saying, "Repent, for the kingdom of heaven is at hand!" For this is he who was spoken of by the prophet Isaiah, saying: "The voice of one crying in the wilderness: 'Prepare the way of the Lord; make His paths straight'"* (Matt 3:1-3).

In the latter portion of verse 1, Malachi speaks of a second Messenger who will come after the first messenger has arrived. This is speaking of Jesus Christ, who is the eternal Word of God (John 1:1-3). In Himself, He was God's message to the Jewish nation and He appeared after John did.

The prophet further prophesied that God's Messenger, Christ, would make a sudden appearance in the temple during the ministry of His forerunner, a matter that John (the apostle) validates in his gospel account (John 2:13-15). John the baptizer was imprisoned and beheaded shortly after Christ drove the merchants and money changers from the temple with a whip. Both the temple and Christ's forerunner have come and gone, meaning that this prophecy has already been fulfilled by Jesus Christ – and that no other supposed Jewish messiah can do so.

## The Second Advent of Christ

Malachi then leaps forward in time to speak of what the Messiah will ultimately accomplish in the earth by posing two questions: *"But who can endure the day of His coming? And who can stand when He appears?"* (v. 2). During His first advent, the Lord came to seek and save the lost (Luke 19:10), but during His second coming He will avenge Himself of all His enemies, punish wickedness on the earth, and refine and restore the nation of Israel to Himself. Clearly the prophet's questions pertain to His second visitation.

Many of the Old Testament narratives which detail God's dealings for His covenant people also provide a prophetic blueprint for how He will accomplish their final spiritual conversion. It took the Babylonian exile and the destruction of the temple and Jerusalem to purge the Jews of idolatry in Jeremiah's day. Likewise, during the Time of Jacob's Trouble, God will use immense suffering to open the eyes of the Jewish nation to the unsearchable riches of the Lord Jesus Christ. Through the Refiner's fire (vv. 3-4), they will no longer be reprobate silver (Jer. 6:30), but will become purified silver which reflects the Refiner's own features. Then the Jewish people will be washed clean by the divine "Launderers' soap" (v. 2) and be established with Him and blessed by Him forever!

In the day of Christ's coming, justice will be swiftly executed against sorcerers, adulterers, perjurers, and exploiters of wages, widows, and orphans (v. 5). These transgressors did not fear the Lord previously, but they will when He wreaks fiery vengeance on all the wicked and oppressors of the helpless.

# Try to Out Give God

But how is it possible that all past and present wickedness throughout the entire world could be righteously judged by God? The answer to this question is the same reason that the covenant of Jacob will be upheld for all time: *"For I am the Lord, I do not change; therefore you are not consumed, O sons of Jacob"* (v. 6). God does not change. He knows all things – therefore He will not forget or overlook any offenses against Himself. With this in mind, Malachi delivers his fifth message which assures Israel that they can reliably hope in God, if they choose to obey Him.

God is Spirit (John 4:24), eternal (Gen. 21:33; Heb. 9:14), immutable (Num. 23:19; Mal. 3:6) and self-existing – the very meaning of His name, *Yahweh* (Ex. 3:13-15). Therefore, He does not forget what offends Him (i.e., what has not been blotted out by the blood of Christ) and He does not neglect His previous promises. This is why Jacob is not consumed, though they provoked the eternal God to anger many times through the centuries (v. 7).

Regardless of past offenses, the Lord's arms were wide open to those who humbly repented of their sins and returned to Him. To those He promised: *"Return to Me, and I will return to you"* (v. 7). Regrettably, the Jews had drifted so far from the Lord that they did not even realize just how far their hearts were from Him. So Malachi states what they were thinking, *"In what way shall we return?"* They clearly had lost the Lord's presence, and yet did not miss Him.

Historically speaking, Israel's tendency, as in Malachi's day, was to give first place to their own things, and then give any surplus to God. Their selfish actions showed that the Lord was not preeminent in their lives. The Lord Jesus tied both aspects of devotion and sacrifice together as a spiritual reality check for His disciples:

*If anyone comes to Me and does not hate his father and mother, wife and children, brothers and sisters, yes, and his own life also, he cannot be My disciple* (Luke 14:26-27).

*Whoever of you does not forsake all that he has cannot be My disciple* (Luke 14:33).

Matthew and John further explain Luke's emphasis. Matthew clarifies that a disciple must not love anyone (including family members) more than the Lord (Matt. 10:37), which means, as John states, Christ must remain the believer's first love (Rev. 2:4). When a believer has this type of affinity to the Lord Jesus, he or she will enjoy the abundant life of Christ, which offers the best enjoyment of all other natural relationships as well (John 10:10). Esteeming others or things above the Lord always results in spiritual despondency. It can be no other way, spiritually speaking; Christ must have first place in our thoughts and affections.

Given Malachi's rebuke of his tightfisted countrymen, F. B. Hole asks a probing question for believers to consider today:

> And what is the practice in Christendom today, and even among true Christians? We fear that a very similar charge could be maintained against all too many of us. Small wonder, then, if we see but small result from the work in which we do engage.[195]

If the Jews under the Law earned such a stern reprimand for stinginess, how much greater accountability do believers living under grace have to the Lord for the same sin?

To introduce the means by which Israel could return to the Lord, the prophet answers the implied question *"In what way shall we return?"* as if it had been genuinely asked:

> *"Will a man rob God? Yet you have robbed Me! But you say, 'In what way have we robbed You?' In tithes and offerings. You are cursed with a curse, for you have robbed Me, even this whole nation. Bring all the tithes into the storehouse, that there may be food in My house, and try Me now in this,"* Says the Lord of hosts, *"If I will not open for you the windows of heaven and pour out for you such blessing that there will not be room enough to receive it"* (vv. 8-10).

Those Jews who wanted God's blessing had to cease from robbing the Lord through hoarding tithes and offerings, which were God's under their covenantal agreement (Lev. 27:30-32; Num. 18:21-32). William MacDonald summarizes what the Law demanded of them:

> Under the Mosaic Law, the Israelites were required to give a tenth of all produce and livestock to the Lord (or they could redeem it with money and add a fifth part). The tithes were in addition to numerous

offerings, and were an acknowledgement that everything belonged to God and that He was the Giver of all possessions.[196]

If they continued robbing the Lord, then He would smite them with drought or pestilence which would rob them of the agricultural blessings that He desired to confer on them (v. 11). However, if they brought their tithes and offerings to the temple, as the Law required, then they would be blessed in such a way that even the nations would take notice (v. 12).

Malachi's warning to the Jews reminds us that miserliness towards the Lord is a spiritual problem, not a financial one. The prophet told the Jews to test the Lord – see if they could out give Him (v. 10). He then implied that God would open the windows of heaven and shower upon the obedient His overflowing goodness. The Lord always provides resources for His children to worship Him – that is, if we have willing hearts to honor Him with what He has graciously given us.

## Fear God and Be Blessed

In contrast with the rich blessings promised Israel for obedience, Malachi's final message charged the Jews with speaking harsh words against the Lord (v. 13). Again the prophet portrays the wayward nation as being ignorant of or insensitive to their sin by inquiring, *"What have we spoken against You?"* (v. 13). Malachi then answers the question he posed on their behalf.

First, the Jews were justifying their disobedience because they saw no benefit in pursuing righteousness through Law-keeping when the wicked seem to prosper and go unpunished (vv. 14-15). The Jews in Malachi's day would have benefitted from reading what an elderly David wrote in Psalm 37:

> *Do not fret because of evildoers, nor be envious of the workers of iniquity. For they shall soon be cut down like the grass, and wither as the green herb. Trust in the Lord, and do good; dwell in the land, and feed on His faithfulness* (Ps. 37:1-3).

Sometimes it seems as though the wicked are flourishing in life and prevailing over God's people. But David encourages the righteous to trust in the Lord, and not to envy or fret over evildoers; their doom is guaranteed. It is easy to get tunnel vision and miss the big picture during times of injustice, but God will judge every evil; nobody is going to escape His justice. Therefore, God's people should permit God to do what only He can – righteously judge the wicked – while they do what they are supposed to do – be faithful to His commandments.

This sort of reasoning (i.e., that disobedience is justified because there is nothing to be gained by obedience) is nothing more than an excuse to do what carnal flesh wants to do, rather than submitting to the Lord. However, God will not be mocked. He has *"a book of remembrance"* in which the names of *"those who fear the Lord and who meditate on His name"* are recorded (v. 16). Indeed this must be one of the books opened at the Great White Throne judgment of the wicked at the end of the Kingdom Age (Rev. 20:11-15). It must be a ledger of the redeemed souls, similar to The Lamb's Book of Life. And John tells us that *"anyone not found written in the Book of Life was cast into the lake of fire"* (Rev. 20:15).

God does not forget who are His and who deserves His condemnation! In fact, on judgment day, God, speaking of those written in His book of remembrance, says, *"'They shall be Mine,' says the Lord of hosts, 'on the day that I make them My jewels. And I will spare them as a man spares his own son who serves him'"* (v. 17). The point is that obedience demonstrates faith (Jas. 2:17) and true faith will be rewarded. Each believer will be a unique, gleaming jewel of grace for His supreme crown of majesty.

Although the door of repentance was open for the Jewish nation, Malachi's barrage of question-answer indictments shows us that the majority of Israelites had no hope of recovery. Hamilton Smith summarizes this observation:

> The Jews at this time were morally insensible and spiritually blind. Satisfied with a correct position and the outward performance of religious observances, they were utterly insensible to their low condition, and spiritually blind to all that the Lord was for them. If God reminds them of His love, they say, "*Wherein* hast Thou loved us?" (Mal. 1:2). If He rebukes them for despising His name, they say, "*Wherein* have we despised it?" (Mal. 1:6). If He reproaches them with offering polluted bread, they say, "*Wherein* have we polluted Thee?" (Mal. 1:7). If they are accused of having wearied the Lord, they say, "*Wherein* have we wearied Him?" (Mal. 2:17). If God charges them with robbery, they say, "*Wherein* have we robbed Thee?" (Mal. 3:8). If He says, "Your words have been stout against

Me," they say, "*What* have we spoken so much against Thee?" (Mal. 3:13). If He beseeches them to return to Him, they say, "*Wherein* shall we return?" (Mal. 3:7).[197]

Unfortunately, the majority would not enter Malachi's door of repentance to be spared by God, their Father. (This somber reality is pictured in the parable of the Lost Son in Luke 15 when the older son refused to enter the same door of repentance that the younger son had passed through to be restored to his father.) Yet, for those who would, verse 17 is a source of comfort and cheer. These tried and tested individuals valued God's fellowship as a Father above all else. In pondering the implications of verse 17, H. A. Ironside offers this practical counsel for enjoying God's presence continually:

> Occupation with the evil can only weaken the hand and distress the spirit. But occupation with Him who sits in peace above all the mists of earth will strengthen and cheer, and prove the only real power for practical holiness and victory over all the might of the enemy.[198]

On judgment day, Israel will observe that there is a vast distinction between the wicked and the righteous (v. 18)! Thankfully, through God's Word and His indwelling Spirit, believers in the Church Age can know the difference and choose to live victoriously for God now!

## Meditation

> Hell is God's great compliment to the reality of human freedom and the dignity of human choice.
>
> — G. K. Chesterton

> Those who go to heaven ride on a pass and enter into blessings that they never earned, but all who go to hell pay their own way.
>
> — John R. Rice

# The Sun of Righteousness
## Malachi 4

Malachi concluded the previous chapter by foretelling a coming *day* in which everyone will know who the righteous and the wicked are and who served the Lord and who did not (3:18). In this chapter, the prophet continues to speak of the Day of the Lord, but also offers a promise of hope for Israel.

## The Day of the Lord

The Lord's coming will be marked by intense and swift judgment of the proud; they will be completely uprooted and destroyed to ensure that only the righteous enter Christ's kingdom (v. 1). The intensity of this judgment is likened to a rapidly moving fire that swiftly incinerates wheat or oat stubble (i.e., the unwanted portion of an already harvested crop).

The New Testament is careful to show a consistent separation of the righteous and the wicked for judgment at Christ's second advent. The Lord Jesus said that He will first gather the good grain unto Himself and then what is not desired, such as tares, will be gathered by angels and burned (Matt. 13:24-32, 36-43). In the same series of Kingdom Parables, the Lord said that His dragnet will scoop up all the nations and He will separate the good from the bad caught in the net, with the good entering His Kingdom and the bad destined for fire (Matt. 13:47-50). Likewise, John spoke of two harvests at Christ's second coming: the first sickle gathers the grain (believers) and the second, the ripe clusters of grapes (the wicked) to be smashed in God's winepress of wrath (Rev. 14:14-20). Not one wicked person will escape God's wrath, nor will one righteous person be excluded from communion with Christ in paradise.

This contrast is further expanded in verses 2 and 3, when the Sun of Righteousness suddenly appears to provide rays of healing and blessing to those fearing God's name (i.e., the righteous; v. 2), but intense heat to the wicked (v. 3). The finality of this judgment is obvious, for the righteous will trampled upon the ashes of the wicked (i.e., the remains of their bodies). This outcome answers the cynical inquiry in chapter 3 as to what advantage the righteous have over the wicked who seem to prosper regardless of their evil doings. The prophet has now shown that this is a limited viewpoint, for the wicked will die at Christ's coming and will be judged by God forever in the Lake of Fire (Rev. 19:20, 20:10).

It is debated whether *the Sun of Righteousness* symbolizes the Lord's sudden appearance or is a metaphorical representation of Himself personally; this author favors the latter view. In the closing passage of Scripture, Christ likens Himself to *"the bright and morning star"* (Rev. 22:16). Focusing on Christ, instead of the spiritual darkness that we are living in, inspires hope for the glorious day which is to come. For this reason John writes, *"For the testimony of Jesus is the spirit of prophecy"* (Rev. 19:10). Bible prophecy is centered in the person of Jesus Christ, the Bright and Morning Star.

Scripture describes predawn events of His coming in order to encourage those who are watching and waiting for Him. The Lord is going to return to Jerusalem with mercy and comfort. He will reestablish His covenant people of old in the land He set aside for them and He will remain with them and they will worship Him in His temple! *The Sun of Righteousnes* is Israel's hope, not the Church's, though we will certainly rejoice with Israel when the Lord vindicates His name on earth. As *the Day of the Lord* approaches, dark times will precede the curtain call of the Church Age (2 Thess. 2:3), yet believers have the hope of their *Bright and Morning Star* or *the Day of Christ* (Rev. 22:16). He shall come for His beloved bride just moments before the dawning of the Day of the Lord, and then the *Sun of Righteousness* (v. 2) shall rise in His full fury and flood the earth with His glory!

## Remember the Law

Having foretold the outcome of Christ's glorious coming, Malachi implores his countrymen:

> *Remember the Law of Moses, My servant, which I commanded him in Horeb for all Israel, with the statutes and judgments* (v. 4).

The One speaking through Malachi was the same "I AM" who gave Moses the Law on Mount Horeb and who worked many spectacular signs and wonders during Israel's exodus from Egypt and their forty-year wilderness experience that followed. By mentioning that Moses was a proven servant of the Lord, the prophet was exhorting his countrymen to follow Moses example of faithfulness. Through obedience, Moses received from the Lord high accolades, God's blessing, and a place in Christ's future kingdom – and so could they.

## Elijah Is Coming

The prophet concludes his oracle by promising that Elijah would come before the Day of the Lord transpired (v. 5). William Kelly notes the positive, twofold effect for the Jewish nation by mentioning both Moses and Elijah by name:

> First is the remembrance of the Law of Moses. They look back, and this is the test to judge their whole course from first to last. Second, they will look forward: *"Behold I send you Elijah the prophet."* Thus, though about Israel, it shows us the two ways of judging aright the present – in the light of the past, and in that of the future. It always therefore requires faith to judge according to God. Hence Malachi brings in morally the giver of the Law and the restorer of the Law, the two great pillars of the Jewish nation, heralding the way before Jehovah who alone can bestow and sustain the blessing.[199]

Elijah's ministry would *"turn the hearts of the fathers to the children, and the hearts of the children to their fathers"* (v. 6). This meant that Elijah's ministry would result in repentance and revival of the Jewish nation which would unite everyone under Christ's rule. To not experience spiritual reviving through Christ meant that Israel was still under the curse of the Law. The only way for the Jewish nation to escape the dreadful Day of the Lord is to receive their Messiah, and thankfully a remnant will experience the abundant life of salvation that He alone offers.

F. B. Hole summarizes how Malachi's references to God's messenger (3:1) and to Elijah (4:5) tie together:

> At His first advent the messenger sent in advance was clearly John the Baptist, who prepared the way of the Lord, and came in the spirit and power of Elijah, though not the Elijah of which Malachi 4:5

speaks, for he is to come before the great and dreadful day of the Lord in judgment. John came after the fashion of Elijah, but before the coming of the Messiah in grace, who is the Master, identified here with Jehovah.[200]

Clearly, John the baptizer was not Elijah in person (John 1:21-23), but he was God's messenger (3:1) who came in the spirit of Elijah's ministry to call the nation to repentance, hence preparing the way of the Lord. An angel confirmed that this would be the focus of John's ministry even before he was born (Luke 1:17). Then, years later, the Lord Jesus affirmed John's Elijah-like ministry:

*For all the prophets and the law prophesied until John. And if you are willing to receive it, he is Elijah who is to come. He who has ears to hear, let him hear!* (Matt. 11:13-15).

As in the days of Elijah, Israel did not receive John's message of repentance either (Matt. 17:12-13). So while John fulfilled the prophecy in the execution of an Elijah-type ministry, it was not successful; therefore Elijah must yet come in such a way that results in national revival of the Jewish nation (v. 6). Since that will not occur until the Tribulation Period, many believe that Elijah, who did not previously experience death, but must (Heb. 9:27), will be one of the two witnesses for Christ in Revelation 11 (perhaps Enoch will be the other for the same reason). These two men, whoever they are, will preach repentance, will withstand the Antichrist, and will perform great wonders (Rev. 11:1-13).

Whether this will be Elijah himself (as possibly indicated in Matt. 17:11), or another who comes like John in the spirit of Elijah's ministry, is debated. However, the prophecy predicts that Israel will not come to Christ without a supernaturally empowered ministry like Elijah's to call them to repentance. It is with this promise of Christ's coming to judge the wicked, to reward the righteous, and to restore the nation of Israel to Himself that the Old Testament closes. God is not finished with the Jewish nation. Their hope is in Christ and He is coming in power and in glory. May the Sun of Righteousness rise soon!

# Epilogue

The Old Testament is the history of man, specifically Israel, under the Law. So it is appropriate that the final word is "curse." The purpose of the Law was twofold. First, the Law was to show sin; the Law could not save anyone because no one could keep it (Rom. 3:20). Second, it was to point the guilty sinner to God's sole solution – a Savior (Gal. 3:24).

Thankfully, the New Testament completes what the Old Covenant could not. The New Testament is the account of God's grace coming to man through Christ, hence its final statement to believers is, *"The grace of our Lord Jesus Christ be with you all"* (Rev. 22:21). How joyful and fruitful we should be to be living for God in the age of grace and how much happier we shall be when Christ rules the world in righteousness during the Kingdom Age!

Seeing God's many promises to Israel and the many signs of Christ's coming, the Church (which shall be removed from the earth before the Day of the Lord) would do well to consider Malachi's challenge to the Jewish nation to trust and obey the Lord. We close our study of the Old Testament with a call for revival by H. A. Ironside:

> The hour is late. The Judge is at the door. The coming of the Lord draws nigh. Lowliness and self-judgment become us all. May we have grace given to discern the signs of the times, and to bow our hearts to His Word.[201]

## Meditation

In hope we lift our wishful, longing eyes,
Waiting to see the Morning Star arise;
How bright, how gladsome will His advent be,
Before the Sun shines forth in majesty!

How will our eyes to see His face delight,
Whose love has cheered us through the darksome night!
How will our ears drink in His well-known voice,
Whose faintest whispers make our soul rejoice!

— James G. Deck

# Endnotes

1    E. B. Pusey, *Barnes Notes – Minor Prophets* (Baker Book House, Grand Rapids, MI; reprinted 1851), Hos. 1:2

2    William Kelly, *Hosea*, STEM Publishing, Hos. 1:
http://stempublishing.com/authors/kelly/1Oldtest/hosea.html

3    E. B. Pusey, op. cit., Hos. 1:2

4    H. A. Ironside, *Notes on the Minor Prophets* (Shiloh Christian Library, no date); p. 8

5    R. B. Chisholm Jr. & Dallas Theological Seminary, *The Bible Knowledge Commentary: An Exposition of the Scriptures* (Victor Books, Wheaton, IL; 1983-1985), p. 1379

6    J. M. Flanigan, *What the Bible Teaches – Hosea* (John Ritchie LTD, Kilmarnock, Scotland; 2015), Hos. 1:2-3

7    W. J. Hocking, *Ruth*, STEM Publishing (intro.):
http://stempublishing.com/authors/WJ_Hocking/WJH_Ruth0.html

8    C. A. Coates, *C. A. Coates Commentary – Hosea* (Kingston Bible Trust, West Sussex, UK), chp. 1

9    E. B. Pusey, op. cit., Hos. 2:5

10    C. A. Coates, op. cit., chp. 2

11    E. B. Pusey, op. cit., Hos. 3:1

12    H. A. Ironside, op. cit., p. 10

13    E. B. Pusey, op. cit., Hos. 4:1

14    C. A. Coates, op. cit., chp. 4

15    H. A. Ironside, op. cit., p. 38

16    William Kelly, op. cit., Hos. 4

17    E. B. Pusey, op. cit., Hos. 5:1

18    E. B. Pusey, op. cit., Hos. 5:15

19    William Kelly, op. cit., Hos. 6

20    R. B. Chisholm Jr., op. cit., p. 1395

21    E. B. Pusey, op. cit., Hos. 7:6

22    H. A. Ironside, op. cit., p. 64

23    J. M. Flanigan, op. cit., Hos. 8:8

24    J. M. Flanigan, op. cit., Hos. 10:9

25    William MacDonald, *Believer's Bible Commentary* (Thomas Nelson Publishers, Nashville: 1989); Hos. 11:1

26    C. H. Mackintosh, *Genesis to Deuteronomy* (Loizeaux Brothers, Inc., Neptune, NJ; 1972), p. 122.

27    C. A. Coates, op. cit., chp. 12

28    J. M. Flanigan, op. cit., Hos. 12:13

29  R. B. Chisholm Jr., op. cit., p. 1406

30  H. A. Ironside, op. cit., p. 108

31  D. Gilliland, *What the Bible Teaches – Joel* (John Ritchie LTD, Kilmarnock, Scotland; 2015), Joel Introduction

32  William MacDonald, op. cit., Joel 1:1-4

33  R. B. Chisholm Jr., op. cit., p. 1414

34  H. A. Ironside, op. cit., p. 119

35  D. Gilliland, op. cit., Joel 2

36  E. B. Pusey, op. cit., Joel 2:14

37  William Kelly, *Joel*, STEM Publishing, Joel 2: http://stempublishing.com/authors/kelly/1Oldtest/joel.html

38  J. N. Darby, *Synopsis of the Books of the Bible Vol. II – Ezra-Malachi* (Stow Hill Bible and Tract Depot, Kingston on the Thames; 1949), p. 367

39  David Jeremiah, *What in the World Is Going On?* (Thomas Nelson, Nashville, TN; 2008), p. 194

40  D. Gilliland, op. cit., Joel 3

41  Y. Yadin, "Hazor, the Rediscovery of a Great Citadel of the Bible" (Random House, New York, NY; 1975). I. Finkelstein, "Hazor and the North in the Iron Age: A Low Chronology Perspective," Bulletin of the American Schools of Oriental Research 314 (1999) 55–70. Both are cited in Austin et al., "Amos's Earthquake," p. 658

42  Franz & Frost, *"Amos's Earthquake: An Extraordinary Middle East Seismic Event of 750 B.C."* International Geology Review [pp. 657-671]: http://cof.quantumfuturegroup.org/sources/734 [last accessed March 31, 2017]

43  E. B. Pusey, op. cit., Amos 1:3

44  D. R. Sunukjian & Dallas Theological Seminary, *The Bible Knowledge Commentary: An Exposition of the Scriptures* (Victor Books, Wheaton, IL; 1983-1985), p. 1430

45  E. B. Pusey, op. cit., Amos 2:12

46  E. B. Pusey, op. cit., Amos 3:3

47  William MacDonald, *Believer's Bible Commentary* (Thomas Nelson Publishers, Nashville, TN; 1989), p. 852

48  William Kelly, *Hosea*, STEM Publishing, Amos 6: http://stempublishing.com/authors/kelly/1Oldtest/amos.html

49  Rabbi Davis, *An Exposition on Pertinent Passages of Amos* (Beth Elohim Messianic Synagogue): Website: http://www.rabdavis.org/an-exposition-on-pertinent-passages-of-amos/ [last accessed March 30, 2017]

50  D. R. Sunukjian, op. cit., pp. 1441-1442

51  D. R. Sunukjian, op. cit., p. 1443

52  H. A. Ironside, op. cit., p. 169

53  H. A. Ironside, op. cit., pp. 143-144

54  D. R. Sunukjian, op. cit., p. 1447

55  E. B. Pusey, op. cit., Amos 8:8

56  NASA, *Five Millennium Catalog of Solar Eclipses* (800 BCE to 701 BCE)

https://eclipse.gsfc.nasa.gov/SEcat5/SE-0799--0700.html [last accessed March 31, 2017]

[57] Note: The NASA model data is based on the Julian calendar, and therefore one additional year is added to reflect the Gregorian Calendar, which does not have a 0 B.C. (e.g., 1 B.C. to 1 A.D.).

[58] Helaine Smith, *Encyclopedia of the History of Science, Technology, and Medicine in Non-Western Cultures* (Kluwer Academic Publishers, Dordrecht, Netherlands; 1997), p. 275

[59] J. Hay, *What the Bible Teaches – Joel* (John Ritchie LTD, Kilmarnock, Scotland; 2015), Amos 8

[60] Matthew Henry, *Matthew Henry's Concise Commentary on the Whole Bible* (e-Sword, electronic version); Amos 9:1

[61] William Kelly, op. cit., Amos 9:1

[62] William Kelly, *Obadiah*, STEM Publishing, Obadiah: http://stempublishing.com/authors/kelly/1Oldtest/obadiah.html

[63] W. L. Baker & Dallas Theological Seminary, *The Bible Knowledge Commentary: An Exposition of the Scriptures* (Victor Books, Wheaton, IL; 1983-1985), pp. 1458-1459

[64] Matthew Henry, *Matthew Henry's Concise Commentary on the Whole Bible* (e-Sword, electronic version); Obadiah

[65] H. A. Ironside, op. cit., p. 201

[66] W. W. Fereday, *Jonah*, STEM Publishing, In the Fish's Belly: http://stempublishing.com/authors/fereday/JONAH.html

[67] G. C. Willis, *Lessons From Jonah the Prophet*, STEM Publishing http://stempublishing.com/authors/GC_Willis/GCW_Jonah.html

[68] Warren Wiersbe, *Wiersbe's Expository Outlines on the Old Testament* (Victor Books, Wheaton, IL; 1993), Jonah 1:1

[69] H. A. Ironside, op. cit., p. 207

[70] Christian Evidence Ministries: Oceanography [Online] http://www.christianevidences.org/oceanography [last accessed June 21, 2016]

[71] NOAA's National Marine Fisheries: The Kid's Times: The Spear Whale (Vol. 2 Issue) www.nmfs.noaa.gov/pr/pdfs/education/kids_times_whale_sperm.pdf [last accessed April 7, 2017]

[72] Donald J. Wiseman, *Jonah's Nineveh* (The Tyndale Biblical Archaeology Lecture, 1977), Tyndale Bulletin #30, p. 37 http://www.tyndalehouse.com/TynBul/Library/TynBull_1979_30_02_Wiseman_ JonahsNineveh.pdf [last accessed April 8, 2017]

[73] W. L. Baker, op. cit., p. 1468

[74] International Standard Bible http://www.internationalstandardbible.com/N/nineveh.html [last accessed April 8, 2017]

[75] Donald J. Wiseman, op. cit., p. 50

[76] H. Clay Trumbull, "Jonah in Nineveh" (*Journal of Biblical Literature*, Vol. 2, No.1; 1892), p. 56

[77] J. G. Bellett, *Jonah*, STEM Publishing, Jonah 4: http://stempublishing.com/authors/bellett/MINORP05.html

[78] J. N. Darby, op. cit., p. 387

[79] W. W. Fereday, op. cit., *The Compassionate Creator*

[80] Oswald Chambers, *My Utmost for His Highest* – Jan. 17th

[81] E. B. Pusey, op. cit., Micah 1:8

[82] James B. Pritchard, *Ancient Near Eastern Texts*, 2nd ed. (Princeton University Press, Princeton, NJ; 1955), p. 287

[83] J. A. Martin & Dallas Theological Seminary, *The Bible Knowledge Commentary: An Exposition of the Scriptures* (Victor Books, Wheaton, IL; 1983-1985), p. 1479

[84] H. A. Ironside, op. cit., p. 225

[85] A. W. Tozer, *Knowledge of the Holy* (Send the Light Trust; 1976), Chp. 1

[86] J. M. Flanigan, *What the Bible Teaches – Hosea* (John Ritchie LTD, Kilmarnock, Scotland; 2015), Micah 2:6-11

[87] H. A. Ironside, op. cit., p. 227

[88] E. B. Pusey, op. cit., Micah 2:9

[89] C. A. Coates, op. cit., Micah 4

[90] J. M. Flanigan, op. cit., Micah 4:5-7

[91] E. B. Pusey, op. cit., Micah 5:2

[92] Warren Henderson, *The Bible: Myth or Divine Truth?* (Warren A. Henderson, Pomona, KS; 2008), p. 38

[93] J. N. Darby, op. cit., p. 392

[94] William MacDonald, op. cit., p. 1135

[95] William Kelly, *Micah*, STEM Publishing, Micah: http://stempublishing.com/authors/kelly/1Oldtest/micah.html

[96] H. A. Ironside, *Daniel the Prophet*, op. cit., p. 159

[97] William MacDonald, op. cit., p. 1136

[98] P. Harding, *What the Bible Teaches – Hosea* (John Ritchie LTD, Kilmarnock, Scotland; 2015), Nahum 1:2-8

[99] William Kelly, Nahum, STEM Publishing, Nahum: http://stempublishing.com/authors/kelly/1Oldtest/nahum.html

[100] Ctesias preserved in Diodorus Siculus, *Bibliotheca Historia* (Book 2, 24:1-28:1)

[101] Elliot Johnson & Dallas Theological Seminary, *The Bible Knowledge Commentary: An Exposition of the Scriptures* (Victor Books, Wheaton, IL; 1983-1985), p. 1493

[102] Carleton L. Brownson, *Xenophon in Seven Volumes* (Harvard University Press, Cambridge, MA; 1922), Book 3, Chp. 4

[103] http://www.history-book.net/maps/niniveh_01.jpg [last accessed on May 20, 2017]

[104] Diodorus Siculus, *Bibliotheca Historia* (Book 2, 26:9, 27.1-28.7)

[105] Ibid.

[106] Daniel D. Luckenbill, *Ancient Records of Assyria and Babylonia*, 2 Vol., (*Histories and Mysteries of Man* by University of Chicago Press, Chicago; 1927), 2:420, par. 1178

[107] Gordon Franz, *Nahum, Nineveh and Those Nasty Assyrians* (Associates for Biblical Research; May 28, 2009) http://www.biblearchaeology.org/post/2009/05/28/Nahum2c-Nineveh-and-Those-Nasty-Assyrians.aspx [last accessed May 18, 2017]

[108] E. B. Pusey, op. cit., Nahum 3:1

[109] Donald J. Wiseman, *Jonah's Nineveh* (The Tyndale Biblical Archaeology Lecture, 1977), Tyndale Bulletin #30, p. 37 http://www.tyndalehouse.com/TynBul/Library/TynBull_1979_30_02_Wiseman_JonahsNineveh.pdf [last accessed April 8, 2017]

[110] P. Harding, op. cit., Nahum 3:15

[111] James Catron, *Old Testament Poetry and Prophecy* (Emmaus Bible College, Dubuque, IA; 1993), p. 57

[112] J. N. Darby, op. cit., p. 401

[113] A. J. Broomhall, *Hudson Taylor and China's Open Century, Book Six: Assault on the Nine* (Hodder and Stoughton and Overseas Missionary Fellowship, London; 1988), p 107

[114] Hamilton Smith, *Habakkuk*, STEM Publishing, Hab. 1: http://stempublishing.com/authors/smith/HABAKKUK.html

[115] H. A. Ironside, op. cit., p. 278

[116] H. L. Rossier, *The Prophet Habakkuk*, STEM Publishing, Hab. 2: http://stempublishing.com/authors/rossier/Habakkuk.html

[117] P. Harding, op. cit., Hab. 2:1

[118] William Kelly, *Habakkuk*, STEM Publishing, Hab. 1: http://stempublishing.com/authors/kelly/1Oldtest/habakkuk.html

[119] H. A. Ironside, op. cit., p. 287

[120] J. Ronald Blue & Dallas Theological Seminary, *The Bible Knowledge Commentary: An Exposition of the Scriptures* (Victor Books, Wheaton, IL; 1983-1985), p. 1517

[121] Hamilton Smith, op. cit., Hab. 2

[122] H. A. Ironside, op. cit., p. 296

[123] C. I. Scofield, *The Scofield Study Bible* (NKJV) (Oxford University Press, New York, NY; 2002), p. 1255

[124] P. Harding, op. cit., Hab. 3:19

[125] C. I. Scofield, op. cit., p. 1256

[126] P. Harding, op. cit., Zeph. 1:4

[127] Charles L. Feinberg, *The Minor Prophets* (Moody Press, Chicago, IL; 1990), chp. 12

[128] Matthew Henry, MHCC derived from *Matthew Henry Commentary Vol. 2* (MacDonald Pub. Co., McLean, VA), p. 188

[129] Charles L. Feinberg, op. cit.

130 C. A. Coates, op. cit., Zeph. 3
131 William Kelly, *Zephaniah*, STEM Publishing, Zeph. 3:
http://stempublishing.com/authors/kelly/1Oldtest/zephania.html
132 P. Harding, op. cit., Zeph. 3:20
133 Hamilton Smith, *Haggai*, STEM Publishing, Hag. 1:
http://stempublishing.com/authors/smith/Haggai.html
134 J. N. Darby, *Haggai*, STEM Publishing, Hag. 2:
http://stempublishing.com/authors/darby/New8_95/38Haggai_2.html
135 William Kelly, *Haggai*, STEM Publishing, Hag. 2:
http://stempublishing.com/authors/kelly/1Oldtest/haggai.html
136 C. A. Coates, op. cit., Hag. 1
137 H. A. Ironside, *Notes on the Book of Ezra* (Shiloh Christian Library, no date), p. 24
138 Edward Dennett, *Haggai*, STEM Publishing, Hag. 2:
http://stempublishing.com/authors/dennett/haggaied.html
139 C. A. Coates, op. cit., Hag. 2
140 Jeremy Hughes, *Secrets of the Times* (Sheffield Academic Press, Sheffield; 1990), p. 229
141 Sir Robert Anderson, *The Coming Prince*: Chapter 5 – The Prophetic Year
http://www.WhatSaithTheScripture.com
142 Ibid., Preface to the Tenth Edition [last accessed March 28, 2017]
143 F. D. Lindsey & Dallas Theological Seminary, *The Bible Knowledge Commentary: An Exposition of the Scriptures* (Victor Books, Wheaton, IL; 1983-1985), p. 1544
144 P. Harding, op. cit., Hag. 2:20-23
145 H. A. Ironside, op. cit., pp. 339-340
146 F. D. Lindsey, op. cit., p. 1550
147 F. B. Hole, *Zechariah*, STEM Publishing, Zech. 1:
http://stempublishing.com/authors/hole/Zion/Zechariah.html
148 J. J. Stubbs, *What the Bible Teaches – Zechariah* (John Ritchie LTD, Kilmarnock, Scotland; 2015), Zech. 1:7
149 C. A. Coates, op. cit., Zech. 1
150 *Oxford English Dictionary* (Oxford University Press, NY); 1989
151 Corrie ten Boom, *Father ten Boom: God's Man* (Old Tappan, NJ: Fleming H. Revell, 1978), p. 67
152 Corrie ten Boom, with John and Elizabeth Sherrill, *The Hiding Place*, 25th Anniversary Ed. (Chosen Books, 1997; orig. Old Tappan, NJ: Fleming H. Revell, 1971), p. 68
153 William Kelly, *Zechariah*, STEM Publishing, Zech. 3:
http://stempublishing.com/authors/kelly/1Oldtest/zecharia.html
154 Edward Dennett, *Haggai*, STEM Publishing, Zech. 3:
http://stempublishing.com/authors/dennett/Zecharia.html
155 C. A. Coates, op. cit., Zech. 3
156 S. Emery, *Treasury of Bible Doctrine* (Precious Seed Magazine, UK: 1977), p. 210

157 James Gunn, *Christ the Fullness of the Godhead* (Loizeaux Brothers, Neptune, NJ: 1982), p. 167

158 F. B. Hole, *Isaiah*, STEM Publishing, Isa. 4: http://stempublishing.com/authors/hole/Art/ISAIAH.htm

159 http://www.advertisingbydesign.com/TheWord/articles/two-witnesses.html [last accessed August 12, 2017]

160 C. A. Coates, op. cit., Zech. 4

161 H. A. Ironside, op. cit., p. 366

162 Edward Dennett, op. cit., Zech. 5

163 E. B. Pusey, op. cit., Zech. 5:9

164 H. A. Ironside, op. cit., p. 368

165 F. B. Hole, op. cit., Zech. 6

166 C. A. Coates, op. cit., Zech. 6

167 H. A. Ironside, op. cit., p. 375

168 Edward Dennett, op. cit., Zech. 7

169 H. A. Ironside, *Isaiah* – Revised Edition (Loizeaux, Neptune, NJ; 2000), p. 247

170 Matthew Henry, *Matthew Henry's Concise Commentary on the Whole Bible* (e-Sword, electronic version); Zech. 7

171 F. B. Hole, op. cit., Zech. 8

172 H. A. Ironside, op. cit., p. 389

173 Quintus Curtius Rufus, *History of Alexander the Great of Macedonia*; Section 4.4.10-21

174 H. A. Ironside, *Isaiah* – Revised Edition, op. cit., p. 108

175 C. E. Hockings, *Treasury of Bible Doctrine – The Names and Titles of Christ* (Precious Seed Magazine, UK: 1977), p. 104

176 Jewish Virtual Library – Vital Statistic: Population of Israel [last accessed March 28, 2017]: http://www.jewishvirtuallibrary.org/jsource/Society_&_Culture /Population_of_Israel.html

177 William Kelly, op. cit., Zech. 10

178 C. A. Coates, op. cit., Zech. 11

179 J. J. Stubbs, op. cit., Zech. 11:8

180 J. J. Stubbs, op. cit., Zech. 11:13

181 Edward Dennett, op. cit., Zech. 11

182 J. J. Stubbs, op. cit., Zech. 12:11

183 C. A. Coates, op. cit., Zech. 13

184 William Kelly, op. cit., Zech. 14

185 E. B. Pusey, op. cit., Zech. 14:4

186 F. B. Hole, op. cit., Zech. 14

187 H. A. Ironside, op. cit., pp. 437-438

188 William Kelly, *Malachi*, STEM Publishing, Mal. 1: http://stempublishing.com/authors/kelly/1Oldtest/malachi.html

189 Josephus, *Antiquities* 13.9.1; 15:4

190 Hamilton Smith, *Malachi*, STEM Publishing, Mal. 1: http://stempublishing.com/authors/smith/Malachi.html

[191] Matthew Henry, *Matthew Henry's Concise Commentary on the Whole Bible* (e-Sword, electronic version); Mal. 1

[192] P. Harding, op. cit., Mal. 2:2

[193] Hamilton Smith, op. cit. Mal. 2

[194] C. H. Mackintosh, *The Mackintosh Treasury* (Gute Botschaft, Dillenburg, Germany; reprinted by Loizeaux Brothers, Inc., Neptune, NJ; 1972), p. 500

[195] F. B. Hole, *Malachi*, STEM Publishing, Mal. 3: http://stempublishing.com/authors/hole/Zion/Malachi.html

[196] William MacDonald, op. cit., p. 1176

[197] Hamilton Smith, op. cit. Mal. 3

[198] H. A. Ironside, op. cit., p. 456

[199] William Kelly, op. cit., Mal. 4

[200] F. B. Hole, op. cit., Mal. 3

[201] H. A. Ironside, op. cit., p. 450

www.ingramcontent.com/pod-product-compliance
Lightning Source LLC
Chambersburg PA
CBHW060233100426
42742CB00011B/1518

* 9 781939 770455 *